THE DEATH OF DEATH
IN THE DEATH OF CHRIST

THE DEATH OF DEATH
IN THE
DEATH OF CHRIST

JOHN OWEN D.D.

with an
Introductory Essay by
J. I. Packer, M.A., D.Phil.

THE BANNER OF TRUTH TRUST

THE BANNER OF TRUTH TRUST
3 Murrayfield Road, Edinburgh EH12 6EL, UK
P.O. Box 621, Carlisle, PA 17013, USA

*

From Volume 10 of the *Works of John Owen*, 1852
(reprinted, Edinburgh: Banner of Truth, 1967).
First Banner of Truth reprint of
The Death of Death, 1959
Reprinted 1963
Reprinted 1983
Reprinted 1985
Reprinted 1989
Reprinted 1995
Reprinted 1999
Reprinted 2002
Reprinted 2007

ISBN-10: 0 85151 382 4
ISBN-13: 978 0 85151 382 9

*

Printed in the U.S.A. by
Versa Press, Inc.,
East Peoria, IL

CONTENTS

CONTENTS

BOOK III.

BOOK IV.

INTRODUCTORY ESSAY.

I.

The Death of Death in the Death of Christ is a polemical work, designed to show, among other things, that the doctrine of universal redemption is unscriptural and destructive of the gospel. There are many, therefore, to whom it is not likely to be of interest. Those who see no need for doctrinal exactness and have no time for theological debates which show up divisions between so-called Evangelicals may well regret its reappearance. Some may find the very sound of Owen's thesis so shocking that they will refuse to read his book at all; so passionate a thing is prejudice, and so proud are we of our theological shibboleths. But it is hoped that this reprint will find itself readers of a different spirit. There are signs today of a new upsurge of interest in the theology of the Bible: a new readiness to test traditions, to search the Scriptures and to think through the faith. It is to those who share this readiness that Owen's treatise is offered, in the belief that it will help us in one of the most urgent tasks facing Evangelical Christendom today—the recovery of the gospel.

This last remark may cause some raising of eyebrows, but it seems to be warranted by the facts.

There is no doubt that Evangelicalism today is in a state of perplexity and unsettlement. In such matters as the practice of evangelism, the teaching of holiness, the building up of local church life, the pastor's dealing with souls and the exercise of discipline, there is evidence of widespread dissatisfaction with things as they are and of equally widespread uncertainty as to the road ahead. This is a complex phenomenon, to which many factors have contributed; but, if we go to the root of the matter, we shall find that these perplexities are all ultimately due to our having lost our grip on the biblical gospel. Without realising it, we have during the past century bartered that gospel for a substitute product which, though it looks similar enough in points of detail, is as a whole a decidedly different thing. Hence our troubles; for the substitute product does not answer the ends for which the authentic gospel has in past days proved itself so mighty. The new gospel conspicuously fails to produce deep reverence, deep repentance, deep humility, a spirit of worship, a concern for the church. Why? We would suggest that the reason lies in its own character and content. It fails to make men God-centred in their thoughts and God-fearing in their hearts because this is not primarily what it is trying to do. One way of stating the difference between it and the old gospel is to say that it is too exclusively concerned to be "helpful" to man—to bring peace, comfort, happiness, satisfaction—and too little concerned to glorify God. The old gospel was "helpful," too—more so, indeed, than is the new—but (so to speak) incidentally, for its first concern was always to give glory to God. It was always and essentially a proclamation of Divine sovereignty in mercy and judgment, a summons to bow down and worship the mighty Lord on whom man depends for all good, both in nature and in grace. Its centre of reference was unambiguously God. But in the new gospel the centre of reference is man. This is just to say that the old gospel was *religious* in a way that the new gospel is not. Whereas the chief aim of the old was to teach men to worship God, the concern of the new seems limited to making them feel better. The subject of the old gospel was God and His ways with men; the subject of the new is man and the help God gives him. There is a world of difference. The whole perspective and emphasis of gospel preaching has changed.

From this change of interest has sprung a change of content, for the new gospel has in effect reformulated the biblical message in the supposed interests of "helpfulness." Accordingly, the themes of man's natural inability to believe, of God's free election being the ultimate cause of salvation, and of Christ dying specifically for His sheep, are not preached. These doctrines, it would be said, are not "helpful"; they would drive sinners to despair, by suggesting to them that it is not in their own power to be saved through Christ. (The possibility that such despair might be salutary is not considered; it is taken for granted that it cannot be, because it is so shattering to our self-esteem.) However this may be (and we shall say more about it later), the result of these omissions is that part of the biblical gospel is now preached as if it were the whole of that gospel; and a half-truth masquerading as the whole truth becomes a complete untruth. Thus, we appeal to men as if they all had the ability to receive Christ at any time; we speak of His redeeming work as if He had done no more by dying than make it possible for us to save ourselves by believing; we speak of God's love as if it were no more than a general willingness to receive any who will turn and trust; and we depict the Father and the Son, not as sovereignly active in drawing sinners to themselves, but as waiting in quiet impotence "at the door of our hearts" for us to let them in. It is undeniable that this is how we preach; perhaps this is what we really believe. But it needs to be said with emphasis that this set of twisted half-truths is something other than the biblical gospel. The Bible is against us when we preach in this way; and the fact that such preaching has become almost standard practice among us only shows how urgent it is that we should review this matter. To recover the old, authentic, biblical gospel, and to bring our preaching and practice back into line with it, is perhaps our most pressing present need. And it is at this point that Owen's treatise on redemption can give us help.

II.

" But wait a minute," says someone, " it's all very well to talk like this about the gospel; but surely what Owen is doing is defending limited atonement—one of the five points of Calvinism? When you speak of recovering the gospel, don't you mean that you just want us all to become Calvinists?"

These questions are worth considering, for they will no doubt occur to many. At the same time, however, they are questions that reflect a great deal of prejudice and ignorance. " Defending limited atonement "—as if this was all that a Reformed theologian expounding the heart of the gospel could ever really want to do! " You just want us all to become Calvinists "—as if Reformed theologians had no interest beyond recruiting for their party, and as if becoming a Calvinist was the last stage of theological depravity, and had nothing to do with the gospel at all   Before we answer these questions directly, we must try to remove the prejudices which underlie them by making clear what Calvinism really is; and therefore we would ask the reader to take note of the following facts, historical and theological, about Calvinism in general and the " five points " in particular.

First, it should be observed that the " five points of Calvinism," so-called, are simply the Calvinistic answer to a five-point manifesto (the Remonstrance) put out by certain " Belgic semi-Pelagians[1] " in the early seventeenth century. The theology which it contained (known to history as Arminianism) stemmed from two philosophical principles: first, that divine sovereignty is not compatible with human freedom, nor therefore with human responsibility; second, that ability limits obligation. (The charge of semi-Pelagianism was thus fully justified.) From these principles, the Arminians drew two deductions: first, that since the Bible regards faith as a free and responsible human act, it cannot be caused by God, but is exercised independently of Him; second, that since the Bible regards faith as obligatory on the part of all who hear the gospel, ability to believe must be universal. Hence, they maintained, Scripture must be interpreted as teaching the following positions: (1.) Man is never so completely corrupted by sin that he cannot savingly believe the gospel when it is put before him, nor (2.) is he ever so completely controlled by God that he cannot reject it. (3.) God's election of those who shall be saved is prompted by His foreseeing that they will

[1] Owen, *Works* (ed. Goold), x. 6.

of their own accord believe. (4.) Christ's death did not ensure the salvation of anyone, for it did not secure the gift of faith to anyone (there is no such gift); what it did was rather to create a possibility of salvation for everyone if they believe. (5.) It rests with believers to keep themselves in a state of grace by keeping up their faith; those who fail here fall away and are lost. Thus, Arminianism made man's salvation depend ultimately on man himself, saving faith being viewed throughout as man's own work and, because his own, not God's in him.

The Synod of Dort was convened in 1618 to pronounce on this theology, and the " five points of Calvinism " represent its counter-affirmations. They stem from a very different principle—the biblical principle that " salvation is of the Lord " ;[1] and they may be summarized thus: (1.) Fallen man in his natural state lacks all power to believe the gospel, just as he lacks all power to believe the law, despite all external inducements that may be extended to him. (2.) God's election is a free, sovereign, unconditional choice of sinners, as sinners, to be redeemed by Christ, given faith and brought to glory. (3.) The redeeming work of Christ had as its end and goal the salvation of the elect. (4.) The work of the Holy Spirit in bringing men to faith never fails to achieve its object. (5.) Believers are kept in faith and grace by the unconquerable power of God till they come to glory. These five points are conveniently denoted by the mnemonic TULIP: Total depravity, Unconditional election, Limited atonement, Irresistible grace, Preservation of the saints.

Now, here are two coherent interpretations of the biblical gospel, which stand in evident opposition to each other. The difference between them is not primarily one of emphasis, but of content. One proclaims a God who saves; the other speaks of a God Who enables man to save himself. One view presents the three great acts of the Holy Trinity for the recovering of lost mankind—election by the Father, redemption by the Son, calling by the Spirit—as directed towards the same persons, and as securing their salvation infallibly. The other view gives each act a different reference (the objects of redemption being all mankind, of calling, those who hear the gospel, and of election, those hearers who respond), and denies that any man's salvation is secured by any of them. The two theologies thus conceive the plan of salvation in quite different terms. One makes salvation depend on the work of God, the other on a work of man; one regards faith as part of God's gift of salvation, the other as man's own contribution to salvation; one gives all the glory of saving believers to God, the other divides the praise between God, Who, so to speak, built the machinery of salvation, and man, who by believing operated it. Plainly, these differences are important, and the permanent value of the " five points," as a summary of

[1] Jon. ii. 9.

Calvinism, is that they make clear the points at which, and the extent to which, these two conceptions are at variance.

However. it would not be correct simply to equate Calvinism with the " five points." Five points of our own will make this clear.

In the first place, Calvinism is something much broader than the " five points " indicate. Calvinism is a whole world-view, stemming from a clear vision of God as the whole world's Maker and King. Calvinism is the consistent endeavour to acknowledge the Creator as the Lord, working all things after the counsel of His will. Calvinism is a theocentric way of thinking about all life under the direction and control of God's own Word. Calvinism, in other words, is the theology of the Bible viewed from the perspective of the Bible—the God-centred outlook which sees the Creator as the source, and means, and end, of everything that is, both in nature and in grace. Calvinism is thus theism (belief in God as the ground of all things), religion (dependence on God as the giver of all things), and evangelicalism (trust in God through Christ for all things), all in their purest and most highly developed form. And Calvinism is a unified philosophy of history which sees the whole diversity of processes and events that take place in God's world as no more, and no less, than the outworking of His great preordained plan for His creatures and His church. The five points assert no more than that God is sovereign in saving the individual, but Calvinism, as such, is concerned with the much broader assertion that He is sovereign everywhere.

Then, in the second place, the " five points " present Calvinistic soteriology in a negative and polemical form, whereas Calvinism in itself is essentially expository, pastoral and constructive. It can define its position in terms of Scripture without any reference to Arminianism, and it does not need to be forever fighting real or imaginary Arminians in order to keep itself alive. Calvinism has no interest in negatives, as such; when Calvinists fight, they fight for positive Evangelical values. The negative cast of the " five points " is misleading chiefly with regard to the third (limited atonement, or particular redemption), which is often read with stress on the adjective and taken as indicating that Calvinists have a special interest in confining the limits of divine mercy. But in fact the purpose of this phraseology, as we shall see, is to safeguard the central affirmation of the gospel—that Christ is a Redeemer who really does redeem. Similarly, the denials of an election that is conditional and of grace that is resistible, are intended to safeguard the positive truth that it is God Who saves. The real negations are those of Arminianism, which denies that election, redemption and calling are saving acts of God. Calvinism negates these negations in order to assert the positive content of the gospel, for the positive purpose of strengthening faith and building up the church.

Thirdly, the very act of setting out Calvinistic soteriology in the form of five distinct points (a number due, as we saw, merely to the fact that there were five Arminian points for the Synod of Dort to answer) tends to obscure the organic character of Calvinistic thought on this subject. For the five points, though separately stated, are really inseparable. They hang together; you cannot reject one without rejecting them all, at least in the sense in which the Synod meant them. For to Calvinism there is really only *one* point to be made in the field of soteriology: the point that *God saves sinners*. *God*—the Triune Jehovah, Father, Son and Spirit; three Persons working together in sovereign wisdom, power and love to achieve the salvation of a chosen people, the Father electing, the Son fulfilling the Father's will by redeeming, the Spirit executing the purpose of Father and Son by renewing. *Saves*—does everything, first to last, that is involved in bringing man from death in sin to life in glory: plans, achieves and communicates redemption, calls and keeps, justifies, sanctifies, glorifies. *Sinners*—men as God finds them, guilty, vile, helpless, powerless, unable to lift a finger to do God's will or better their spiritual lot. *God saves sinners*—and the force of this confession may not be weakened by disrupting the unity of the work of the Trinity, or by dividing the achievement of salvation between God and man and making the decisive part man's own, or by soft-pedalling the sinner's inability so as to allow him to share the praise of his salvation with his Saviour. This is the one point of Calvinistic soteriology which the " five points " are concerned to establish and Arminianism in all its forms to deny: namely, that sinners do not save themselves in any sense at all, but that salvation, first and last, whole and entire, past, present and future, is of the Lord, to whom be glory for ever; amen.

This leads to our fourth remark, which is this: the five-point formula obscures the depth of the difference between Calvinistic and Arminian soteriology. There seems no doubt that it seriously misleads many here. In the formula, the stress falls on the adjectives, and this naturally gives the impression that in regard to the three great saving acts of God the debate concerns the adjectives merely—that both sides agree as to what election, redemption, and the gift of internal grace are, and differ only as to the position of man in relation to them: whether the first is conditional upon faith being foreseen or not; whether the second intends the salvation of every man or not; whether the third always proves invincible or not. But this is a complete misconception. The change of adjective in each case involves changing the meaning of the noun. An election that is conditional, a redemption that is universal, an internal grace that is resistible, is not the same kind of election, redemption, internal grace, as Calvinism asserts. The real issue concerns, not the appropriateness of adjectives, but the definition of nouns. Both sides saw this clearly when the controversy first began, and it is important that we should see it too, for otherwise we cannot discuss the Calvinist-Arminian debate to any purpose at all. It is worth setting out the different definitions side by side.

(i.) God's act of election was defined by the Arminians as a resolve to receive to sonship and glory a duly qualified class of people—believers in Christ.[1] This becomes a resolve to receive individual persons only in virtue of God's foreseeing the contingent fact that they will of their own accord believe. There is nothing in the decree of election to ensure that the class of believers will ever have any members; God does not determine to make any man believe. But Calvinists define election as a choice of particular undeserving persons to be saved from sin and brought to glory, and to that end to be redeemed by the death of Christ and given faith by the Spirit's effectual calling. Where the Arminian says: " I owe my election to my faith," the Calvinist says: " I owe my faith to my election." Clearly, these two concepts of election are very far apart.

(ii.) Christ's work of redemption was defined by the Arminians as the removing of an obstacle (the unsatisfied claims of justice) which stood in the way of God's offering pardon to sinners, as He desired to do, on condition that they believe. Redemption, according to Arminianism, secured for God a right to make this offer, but did not of itself ensure that anyone would ever accept it; for faith, being a work of man's own, is not a gift that comes to him from Calvary. Christ's death created an opportunity for the exercise of saving faith, but that is all it did. Calvinists, however, define redemption as Christ's actual substitutionary endurance of the penalty of sin in the place of certain specified sinners, through which God was reconciled to them, their liability to punishment was for ever destroyed, and a title to eternal life was secured for them. In consequence of this, they now have in God's sight a right to the gift of faith, as the means of entry into the enjoyment of their inheritance. Calvary, in other words, not merely made possible the salvation of those for whom Christ died; it ensured that they would be brought to faith and their salvation made actual. The Cross *saves*. Where the Arminian will only say: " I could not have gained my salvation without Calvary," the Calvinist will say: " Christ gained my salvation for me at Calvary." The former makes the Cross the *sine qua non* of salvation, the latter sees it as the actual procuring cause of salvation, and traces the source of every spiritual blessing, faith included, back to the great transaction between God and His Son carried through on Calvary's hill. Clearly, these two concepts of redemption are quite at variance.

(iii.) The Spirit's gift of internal grace was defined by the

[1] Plus any others who, though they had not heard the gospel, lived up to the light they had—though this point need not concern us here.

Arminians as " moral suasion," the bare bestowal of an understanding of God's truth. This, they granted—indeed, insisted—does not of itself ensure that anyone will ever make the response of faith. But Calvinists define this gift as not merely an enlightening, but also a regenerating work of God in men, " taking away their heart of stone, and giving unto them a heart of flesh; renewing their wills, and by His almighty power determining them to that which is good; and effectually drawing them to Jesus Christ; yet so as they come most freely, *being made willing by his grace.*"[1] Grace proves irresistible just because it destroys the disposition to resist. Where the Arminian, therefore, will be content to say: " I decided for Christ," " I made up my mind to be a Christian," the Calvinist will wish to speak of his conversion in more theological fashion, to make plain whose work it really was:

> " Long my imprisoned spirit lay
> Fast bound in sin and nature's night:
> Thine eye diffused a quickening ray;
> I woke; the dungeon flamed with light;
>
> *My chains fell off: my heart was free:*
> I rose, went forth, and followed thee."[2]

Clearly, these two notions of internal grace are sharply opposed to each other.

Now, the Calvinist contends that the Arminian idea of election, redemption and calling as acts of God which do not save cuts at the very heart of their biblical meaning; that to say in the Arminian sense that God elects believers, and Christ died for all men, and the Spirit quickens those who receive the word, is really to say that in the biblical sense God elects nobody, and Christ died for nobody, and the Spirit quickens nobody. The matter at issue in this controversy, therefore, is the meaning to be given to these biblical terms, and to some others which are also soteriologically significant, such as the love of God, the covenant of grace, and the verb " save " itself, with its synonyms. Arminians gloss them all in terms of the principle that salvation does not directly depend on any decree or act of God, but on man's independent activity in believing. Calvinists maintain that this principle is itself unscriptural and irreligious, and that such glossing demonstrably perverts the sense of Scripture and undermines the gospel at every point where it is practised. This, and nothing less than this, is what the Arminian controversy is about.

There is a fifth way in which the five-point formula is deficient. Its very form (a series of denials of Arminian assertions) lends colour

---

[1] *Westminster Confession*, x. 1.

[2] Granted, it was Charles Wesley who wrote this; but it is one of the many passages in his hymns which make one ask, with " Rabbi " Duncan, " Where's your Arminianism now, friend?"

to the impression that Calvinism is a modification of Arminianism; that Arminianism has a certain primacy in order of nature, and developed Calvinism is an offshoot from it. Even when one shows this to be false as a matter of history, the suspicion remains in many minds that it is a true account of the relation of the two views themselves. For it is widely supposed that Arminianism (which, as we now see, corresponds pretty closely to the new gospel of our own day) is the result of reading the Scriptures in a " natural," unbiased, unsophisticated way. and that Calvinism is an unnatural growth, the product less of the texts themselves than of unhallowed logic working on the texts, wresting their plain sense and upsetting their balance by forcing them into a systematic framework which they do not themselves provide. Whatever may have been true of individual Calvinists, as a generalisation about Calvinism nothing could be further from the truth than this. Certainly, Arminianism is " natural " in one sense, in that it represents a characteristic perversion of biblical teaching by the fallen mind of man, who even in salvation cannot bear to renounce the delusion of being master of his fate and captain of his soul. This perversion appeared before in the Pelagianism and semi-Pelagianism of the Patristic period and the later Scholasticism, and has recurred since the seventeenth century both in Roman theology and, among Protestants, in various types of rationalistic liberalism and modern Evangelical teaching; and no doubt it will always be with us. As long as the fallen human mind is what it is, the Arminian way of thinking will continue to be a natural type of mistake. But it is not natural in any other sense. In fact, it is Calvinism that understands the Scriptures in their natural, one would have thought, inescapable meaning; Calvinism that keeps to what they actually say; Calvinism that insists on taking seriously the biblical assertions that God saves, and that He saves those whom He has chosen to save, and that He saves them by grace without works, so that no man may boast, and that Christ is given to them as a perfect Saviour, and that their whole salvation flows to them from the Cross, and that the work of redeeming them was finished on the Cross. It is Calvinism that gives due honour to the Cross. When the Calvinist sings:

> " There is a green hill far away,
>   Without a city wall,
>   Where the dear Lord was crucified,
>   *Who died to save us all;*
>
> " *He died that we might be forgiven,*
>   *He died to make us good;*
>   *That we might go at last to Heaven,*
>   *Saved by His precious blood.*"

he means it. He will not gloss the italicised statements by saying that God's saving purpose in the death of His Son was a mere

ineffectual wish, depending for its fulfilment on man's willingness
to believe, so that for all God could do Christ might have died and
none been saved at all. He insists that the Bible sees the Cross as
revealing God's power to save, not His impotence. Christ did not
win a hypothetical salvation for hypothetical believers, a mere
possibility of salvation for any who might possibly believe, but a real
salvation for His own chosen people. His precious blood really
does " save us all "; the intended effects of His self-offering do in
fact follow, just because the Cross was what it was. Its saving
power does not depend on faith being added to it; its saving power
is such that faith flows from it. The Cross secured the full salvation
of all for whom Christ died. " God forbid," therefore, " that I
should glory, save in the cross of our Lord Jesus Christ."[1]

Now the real nature of Calvinistic soteriology becomes plain. It
is no artificial oddity, nor a product of over-bold logic. Its central
confession, that *God saves sinners*, that *Christ redeemed us by His
blood*, is the witness both of the Bible and of the believing heart.
The Calvinist is the Christian who confesses before men in his
theology just what he believes in his heart before God when he prays.
He thinks and speaks at all times of the sovereign grace of God in
the way that every Christian does when he pleads for the souls of
others, or when he obeys the impulse of worship which rises unbidden
within him, prompting him to deny himself all praise and to give
all the glory of his salvation to his Saviour. Calvinism is the
natural theology written on the heart of the new man in Christ,
whereas Arminianism is an intellectual sin of infirmity, natural only
in the sense in which all such sins are natural, even to the regenerate.
Calvinistic thinking is the Christian being himself on the intellectual
level; Arminian thinking is the Christian failing to be himself
through the weakness of the flesh. Calvinism is what the Christian
church has always held and taught when its mind has not been
distracted by controversy and false traditions from attending to
what Scripture actually says; that is the significance of the Patristic
testimonies to the teaching of the " five points," which can be quoted
in abundance. (Owen appends a few on redemption; a much larger
collection may be seen in John Gill's *The Cause of God and Truth*.)
So that really it is most misleading to call this soteriology " Calvinism " at all, for it is not a peculiarity of John Calvin and the divines
of Dort, but a part of the revealed truth of God and the catholic
Christian faith. " Calvinism " is one of the " odious names " by
which down the centuries prejudice has been raised against it. But
the thing itself is just the biblical gospel.[2]

[1] Gal. vi. 14.
[2] C. H. Spurgeon was thus abundantly right when he declared: " I have my own
private opinion that there is no such thing as preaching Christ and Him crucified,
unless we preach what is nowadays called Calvinism. It is a nickname to call it
Calvinism; Calvinism is the gospel, and nothing else. I do not believe we can

In the light of these facts, we can now give a direct answer to the questions with which we began.

" Surely all that Owen is doing is defending limited atonement?" Not really. He is doing much more than that. Strictly speaking, the aim of Owen's book is not defensive at all, but constructive. It is a biblical and theological enquiry; its purpose is simply to make clear what Scripture actually teaches about the central subject of the gospel—the achievement of the Saviour. As its title proclaims, it is " a treatise of the redemption and reconciliation that is in the blood of Christ: with the merit thereof, and the satisfaction wrought thereby." The question which Owen, like the Dort divines before him, is really concerned to answer is just this: what is the gospel? All agree that it is a proclamation of Christ as Redeemer, but there is a dispute as to the nature and extent of His redeeming work: well, what saith the Scripture? what aim and accomplishment does the Bible assign to the work of Christ? This is what Owen is concerned to elucidate. It is true that he tackles the subject in a directly controversial way, and shapes his book as a polemic against the " spreading persuasion . . . of *a general ransom*, to be paid by Christ for all; that he dies to redeem *all and every one*.[1] But his work is a systematic expository treatise, not a mere episodic wrangle. Owen treats the controversy as providing the occasion for a full display of the relevant biblical teaching in its own proper order and connection. As in Hooker's *Laws of Ecclesiastical Polity*, the polemics themselves are incidental and of secondary interest; their chief value lies in the way that the author uses them to further his own design and carry forward his own argument.

That argument is essentially very simple. Owen sees that the question which has occasioned his writing—the extent of the atonement—involves the further question of its nature, since if it was offered to save some who will finally perish, then it cannot have been a transaction securing the actual salvation of all for whom it was designed. But, says Owen, this is precisely the kind of transaction that the Bible says it was. The first two books of his treatise are a massive demonstration of the fact that according to Scripture the Redeemer's death actually saves His people, as it was meant to do. The third book consists of a series of sixteen arguments against the hypothesis of universal redemption, all aimed to show, on the one hand, that Scripture speaks of Christ's redeeming work as

[1] P. (47) *inf.*

preach the gospel . . . unless we preach the sovereignty of God in His dispensation of grace; nor unless we exalt the electing, unchangeable, eternal, immutable, conquering love of Jehovah; nor do I think we can preach the gospel unless we base it upon the special and particular redemption of His elect and chosen people which Christ wrought out upon the Cross; nor can I comprehend a gospel which lets saints fall away after they are called." ("Spurgeon's Autobiography," Vol. I, Ch. XVI, p. 172.)

effective, which precludes its having been intended for any who perish, and, on the other, that if its intended extent had been universal, then *either* all will be saved (which Scripture denies, and the advocates of the " general ransom " do not affirm), *or else* the Father and the Son have failed to do what they set out to do— " which to assert," says Owen, " seems to us blasphemously injurious to the wisdom, power and perfection of God, as likewise derogatory to the worth and value of the death of Christ."[1]

Owen's arguments ring a series of changes on this dilemma. Finally, in the fourth book, Owen shows with great cogency that the three classes of texts alleged to prove that Christ died for persons who will not be saved (those saying that He died for " the world," for " all," and those thought to envisage the perishing of those for whom He died), cannot on sound principles of exegesis be held to teach any such thing; and, further, that the theological inferences by which universal redemption is supposed to be established are really quite fallacious. The true evangelical evaluation of the claim that Christ died for every man, even those who perish, comes through at point after point in Owen's book. So far from magnifying the love and grace of God, this claim dishonours both it and Him, for it reduces God's love to an impotent wish and turns the whole economy of " saving " grace, so-called (" saving " is really a misnomer on this view), into a monumental divine failure. Also, so far from magnifying the merit and worth of Christ's death, it cheapens it, for it makes Christ die in vain. Lastly, so far from affording faith additional encouragement, it destroys the Scriptural ground of assurance altogether, for it denies that the knowledge that Christ died for me (or did or does anything else for me) is a sufficient ground for inferring my eternal salvation; my salvation, on this view, depends not on what Christ did for me, but on what I subsequently do for myself. Thus this view takes from God's love and Christ's redemption the glory that Scripture gives them, and introduces the anti-scriptural principle of self-salvation at the point where the Bible explicitly says: " not of works, lest any man should boast."[2] You cannot have it both ways: an atonement of universal extent is a depreciated atonement. It has lost its saving power; it leaves us to save ourselves. The doctrine of the general ransom must accordingly be rejected, as Owen rejects it, as a grievous mistake. By contrast, however, the doctrine which Owen sets out, as he himself shows, is both biblical and God-honouring. It exalts Christ, for it teaches Christians to glory in His Cross alone, and to draw their hope and assurance only from the death and intercession of their Saviour. It is, in other words, genuinely Evangelical. It is, indeed, the gospel of God and the catholic faith.

It is safe to say that no comparable exposition of the work of

[1] *Ibid.* [2] Eph. ii. 9.

redemption as planned and executed by the Triune Jehovah has ever been done since Owen published his. None has been needed. Discussing this work, Andrew Thomson notes how Owen "makes you feel when he has reached the end of his subject, that he has also exhausted it."[1] That is demonstrably the case here. His interpretation of the texts is sure; his power of theological construction is superb; nothing that needs discussing is omitted, and (so far as the writer can discover) no arguments for or against his position have been used since his day which he has not himself noted and dealt with. One searches his book in vain for the leaps and flights of logic by which Reformed theologians are supposed to establish their positions; all that one finds is solid, painstaking exegesis and a careful following through of biblical ways of thinking. Owen's work is a constructive, broad-based biblical analysis of the heart of the gospel, and must be taken seriously as such. It may not be written off as a piece of special pleading for a traditional shibboleth, for nobody has a right to dismiss the doctrine of the limitedness of atonement as a monstrosity of Calvinistic logic until he has refuted Owen's proof that it is part of the uniform biblical presentation of redemption, clearly taught in plain text after plain text. And nobody has done that yet.

" You talked about recovering the gospel," said our questioner; " don't you mean that you just want us all to become Calvinists?"

This question presumably concerns, not the word, but the thing. Whether we call ourselves Calvinists hardly matters; what matters is that we should understand the gospel biblically. But that, we think, does in fact mean understanding it as historic Calvinism does. The alternative is to misunderstand and distort it. We said earlier that modern Evangelicalism, by and large, has ceased to preach the gospel in the old way, and we frankly admit that the new gospel, insofar as it deviates from the old, seems to us a distortion of the biblical message. And we can now see what has gone wrong. Our theological currency has been debased. Our minds have been conditioned to think of the Cross as a redemption which does less than redeem, and of Christ as a Saviour who does less than save, and of God's love as a weak affection which cannot keep anyone from hell without help, and of faith as the human help which God needs for this purpose. As a result, we are no longer free either to believe the biblical gospel or to preach it. We cannot believe it, because our thoughts are caught in the toils of synergism. We are haunted by the Arminian idea that if faith and unbelief are to be responsible acts, they must be independent acts; hence we are not free to believe that we are saved entirely by divine grace through a

[1] " Life of John Owen," p. 38 (*Works*, ed. Goold, 1).

faith which is itself God's gift and flows to us from Calvary. Instead, we involve ourselves in a bewildering kind of double-think about salvation, telling ourselves one moment that it all depends on God and next moment that it all depends on us. The resultant mental muddle deprives God of much of the glory that we should give Him as author and finisher of salvation, and ourselves of much of the comfort we might draw from knowing that God is for us.

And when we come to preach the gospel, our false preconceptions make us say just the opposite of what we intend. We want (rightly) to proclaim Christ as Saviour; yet we end up saying that Christ, having made salvation possible, has left us to become our own saviours. It comes about in this way. We want to magnify the saving grace of God and the saving power of Christ. So we declare that God's redeeming love extends to every man, and that Christ has died to save every man, and we proclaim that the glory of divine mercy is to be measured by these facts. And then, in order to avoid universalism, we have to depreciate all that we were previously extolling, and to explain that, after all, nothing that God and Christ have done can save us unless we add something to it; the decisive factor which actually saves us is our own believing. What we say comes to this—that Christ saves us with our help; and what that means, when one thinks it out, is this—that we save ourselves with Christ's help. This is a hollow anticlimax. But if we start by affirming that God has a saving love for all, and Christ died a saving death for all, and yet balk at becoming universalists, there is nothing else that we can say. And let us be clear on what we have done when we have put the matter in this fashion. We have not exalted grace and the Cross; we have cheapened them. We have limited the atonement far more drastically than Calvinism does, for whereas Calvinism asserts that Christ's death, as such, saves all whom it was meant to save, we have denied that Christ's death, as such, is sufficient to save any of them.[1] We have flattered impenitent sinners by assuring them that it is in their power to

---

[1] Compare this, from C. H. Spurgeon: " We are often told that we limit the atonement of Christ, because we say that Christ has not made a satisfaction for all men, or all men would be saved. Now, our reply to this is, that, on the other hand, our opponents limit it: we do not. The Arminians say, Christ died for all men. Ask them what they mean by it. Did Christ die so as to secure the salvation of all men? They say, " No, certainly not." We ask them the next question— Did Christ die so as to secure the salvation of any man in particular? They answer " No." They are obliged to admit this, if they are consistent. They say " No. Christ has died that any man may be saved if "—and then follow certain conditions of salvation. Now, who is it that limits the death of Christ? Why, you. You say that Christ did not die so as infallibly to secure the salvation of anybody. We beg your pardon, when you say we limit Christ's death; we say, " No, my dear sir, it is you that do it." We say Christ so died that he infallibly secured the salvation of a multitude that no man can number, who through Christ's death not only may be saved, but are saved, must be saved and cannot by any possibility run the hazard of being anything but saved. You are welcome to your atonement; you may keep it. We will never renounce ours for the sake of it."

repent and believe, though God cannot make them do it. Perhaps we have also trivialised faith and repentance in order to make this assurance plausible ("it's very simple—just open your heart to the Lord. . . ."). Certainly, we have effectively denied God's sovereignty, and undermined the basic conviction of religion—that man is always in God's hands. In truth, we have lost a great deal. And it is, perhaps, no wonder that our preaching begets so little reverence and humility, and that our professed converts are so self-confident and so deficient in self-knowledge, and in the good works which Scripture regards as the fruit of true repentance.

It is from degenerate faith and preaching of this kind that Owen's book could set us free. If we listen to him, he will teach us both how to believe the Scripture gospel and how to preach it. For the first: he will lead us to bow down before a sovereign Saviour Who really saves, and to praise Him for a redeeming death which made it certain that all for whom He died will come to glory. It cannot be over-emphasised that we have not seen the full meaning of the Cross till we have seen it as the divines of Dort display it—as the centre of the gospel, flanked on the one hand by total inability and unconditional election, and on the other by irresistible grace and final preservation. For the full meaning of the Cross only appears when the atonement is defined in terms of these four truths. Christ died to save a certain company of helpless sinners upon whom God had set His free saving love. Christ's death ensured the calling and keeping—the present and final salvation—of all whose sins He bore. That is what Calvary meant, and means. The Cross *saved*; the Cross *saves*. This is the heart of true Evangelical faith; as Cowper sang—

> "Dear dying Lamb, *Thy precious blood*
> *Shall never lose its power,*
> *Till all the ransomed church of God*
> *Be saved to sin no more.*"

This is the triumphant conviction which underlay the old gospel, as it does the whole New Testament. And this is what Owen will teach us unequivocally to believe.

Then, secondly, Owen could set us free, if we would hear him, to preach the biblical gospel. This assertion may sound paradoxical, for it is often imagined that those who will not preach that Christ died to save every man are left with no gospel at all. On the contrary, however, what they are left with is just the gospel of the New Testament. What does it mean to preach "the gospel of the grace of God"? Owen only touches on this briefly and incidentally,[1] but his comments are full of light. Preaching the gospel, he tells us, is not a matter of telling the congregation that God has set His love on each of them and Christ has died to save each of them, for

[1] See pp. (199-204, 292-8) *inf.*

these assertions, biblically understood, would imply that they will all infallibly be saved, and this cannot be known to be true. The knowledge of being the object of God's eternal love and Christ's redeeming death belongs to the individual's assurance,[1] which in the nature of the case cannot precede faith's saving exercise; it is to be inferred from the fact that one has believed, not proposed as a reason why one should believe. According to Scripture, preaching the gospel is entirely a matter of proclaiming to men, as truth from God which all are bound to believe and act on, the following four facts:

(1.) that all men are sinners, and cannot do anything to save themselves;

(2.) that Jesus Christ, God's Son, is a perfect Saviour for sinners, even the worst;

(3.) that the Father and the Son have promised that all who know themselves to be sinners and put faith in Christ as Saviour shall be received into favour, and none cast out (which promise is " a certain infallible truth, grounded upon the superabundant sufficiency of the oblation of Christ in itself, for whomsoever (few or more) it be intended "[2]);

(4.) that God has made repentance and faith a duty, requiring of every man who hears the gospel " a serious full recumbency and rolling of the soul upon Christ in the promise of the gospel, as an all-sufficient Saviour, able to deliver and save to the utmost them that come to God by him; ready, able and willing, through the preciousness of his blood and sufficiency of his ransom, to save every soul that shall freely give up themselves unto him for that end."[3]

The preacher's task, in other words, is to *display Christ*: to explain man's need of Him, His sufficiency to save, and His offer of Himself in the promises as Saviour to all who truly turn to Him; and to show as fully and plainly as he can how these truths apply to the congregation before him. It is not for him to say, nor for his hearers to ask, for whom Christ died in particular. " There is none called on by the gospel once to enquire after the purpose and intention of God concerning the particular object of the death of Christ, every one being fully assured that his death shall be profitable to them that believe in him and obey him." After saving faith has been exercised, " it lies on a believer to assure his soul, according as he find the fruit of the death of Christ in him and towards him, of the

---

[1] " What, I pray, is it according to Scripture, for a man to be assured that Christ died for him in particular? Is it not the very highest improvement of faith? doth it not include a sense of the spiritual love of God shed abroad in our hearts? Is it not the top of the apostle's consolation, Rom. viii. 34, and the bottom of all his joyful assurance, Gal. ii. 20?" (p. 297 *inf.*).

[2] P. (203) *inf.*   [3] P. (295f) *inf.*

good-will and eternal love of God to him in sending his Son to die for him in particular ";[1] but not before. The task to which the gospel calls him is simply to exercise faith, which he is both warranted and obliged to do by God's command and promise.

Some comments on this conception of what preaching the gospel means are in order.

First, we should observe that the old gospel of Owen contains no less full and free an offer of salvation than its modern counterpart. It presents ample grounds of faith (the sufficiency of Christ, and the promise of God), and cogent motives to faith (the sinner's need, and the Creator's command, which is also the Redeemer's invitation). The new gospel gains nothing here by asserting universal redemption. The old gospel, certainly, has no room for the cheap sentimentalising which turns God's free mercy to sinners into a constitutional soft-heartedness on His part which we can take for granted; nor will it countenance the degrading presentation of Christ as the baffled Saviour, balked in what He hoped to do by human unbelief; nor will it indulge in maudlin appeals to the unconverted to let Christ save them out of pity for His disappointment.   The pitiable Saviour and the pathetic God of modern pulpits are unknown to the old gospel. The old gospel tells men that they need God, but not that God needs them (a modern falsehood); it does not exhort them to pity Christ, but announces that Christ has pitied them, though pity was the last thing they deserved.   It never loses sight of the Divine majesty and sovereign power of the Christ whom it proclaims, but rejects flatly all representations of Him which would obscure His free omnipotence.   Does this mean, however, that the preacher of the old gospel is inhibited or confined in offering Christ to men and inviting them to receive Him?   Not at all.   In actual fact, just because he recognises that Divine mercy is sovereign and free, he is in a position to make far more of the offer of Christ in his preaching than is the expositor of the new gospel; for this offer is itself a far more wonderful thing on his principles than it can ever be in the eyes of those who regard love to all sinners as a necessity of God's nature, and therefore a matter of course.   To think that the holy Creator, who never needed man for His happiness and might justly have banished our fallen race for ever without mercy, should actually have chosen to redeem some of them! and that His own Son was willing to undergo death and descend into hell to save them! and that now from His throne He should speak to ungodly men as He does in the words of the gospel, urging upon them the command to repent and believe in the form of a compassionate invitation to pity themselves and choose life!   These thoughts are the focal points round which the preaching of the old gospel revolves.   It is all wonderful, just because none of it can be taken for granted.   But

[1] *Loc. cit.*

perhaps the most wonderful thing of all—the holiest spot in all the holy ground of gospel truth—is the free invitation which " the Lord Christ " (as Owen loves to call Him) issues repeatedly to guilty sinners to come to Him and find rest for their souls. It is the glory of these invitations that it is an omnipotent King who gives them, just as it is a chief part of the glory of the enthroned Christ that He condescends still to utter them. And it is the glory of the gospel ministry that the preacher goes to men as Christ's ambassador, charged to deliver the King's invitation personally to every sinner present and to summon them all to turn and live. Owen himself enlarges on this in a passage addressed to the unconverted.

" Consider the infinite condescension and love of Christ, in his invitations and calls of you to come unto him for life, deliverance, mercy, grace, peace and eternal salvation. Multitudes of these invitations and calls are recorded in the Scripture, and they are all of them filled up with those blessed encouragements which divine wisdom knows to be suited unto lost, convinced sinners. . . . In the declaration and preaching of them, Jesus Christ yet stands before sinners, calling, inviting, encouraging them to come unto him.

" This is somewhat of the word which he now speaks unto you: Why will ye die? why will ye perish? why will ye not have compassion on your own souls? Can your hearts endure, or can your hands be strong, in the day of wrath that is approaching? . . . Look unto me, and be saved; come unto me, and I will ease you of all sins, sorrows, fears, burdens, and give rest unto your souls. Come, I entreat you; lay aside all procrastinations, all delays; put me off no more; eternity lies at the door . . . do not so hate me as that you will rather perish than accept of deliverance by me.

" These and the like things doth the Lord Christ continually declare, proclaim, plead and urge upon the souls of sinners. . . . He doth it in the preaching of the word, as if he were present with you, stood amongst you, and spake personally to every one of you. . . . He hath appointed the ministers of the gospel to appear before you, and to deal with you in his stead, avowing as his own the invitations which are given you in his name, 2 Cor. v. 19, 20."[1]

These invitations are *universal*; Christ addresses them to sinners, as such, and every man, as he believes God to be true, is bound to treat them as God's words to him personally and to accept the universal assurance which accompanies them, that all who come to Christ will be received. Again, these invitations are *real*; Christ genuinely offers Himself to all who hear the gospel, and is in truth a perfect Saviour to all who trust Him. The question of the extent of the atonement does not arise in evangelistic preaching; the message to be delivered is simply this—that Christ Jesus, the sovereign Lord, who died for sinners, now invites sinners freely to

[1] *Works*, I. 422.

Himself. God commands all to repent and believe; Christ promises life and peace to all who do so. Furthermore, these invitations are *marvellously gracious*; men despise and reject them, and are never in any case worthy of them, and yet Christ still issues them. He need not, but He does. " Come unto me . . . and I will give you rest " remains His word to the world, never cancelled, always to be preached. He whose death has ensured the salvation of all His people is to be proclaimed everywhere as a perfect Saviour, and all men invited and urged to believe on Him, whoever they are, whatever they have been. Upon these three insights the evangelism of the old gospel is based.

It is a very ill-informed supposition that evangelistic preaching which proceeds on these principles must be anaemic and half-hearted by comparison with what Arminians can do. Those who study the printed sermons of worthy expositors of the old gospel, such as Bunyan (whose preaching Owen himself much admired), or Whitefield, or Spurgeon, will find that in fact they hold forth the Saviour and summon sinners to Him with a fulness, warmth, intensity and moving force unmatched in Protestant pulpit literature. And it will be found on analysis that the very thing which gave their preaching its unique power to overwhelm their audiences with broken-hearted joy at the riches of God's grace—and still gives it that power, let it be said, even with hard-boiled modern readers— was their insistence on the fact that grace is *free*. They knew that the dimensions of Divine love are not half understood till one realises that God need not have chosen to save nor given his Son to die; nor need Christ have taken upon him vicarious damnation to redeem men, nor need He invite sinners indiscriminately to Himself as He does; but that all God's gracious dealings spring entirely from His own free purpose. Knowing this, they stressed it, and it is this stress that sets their evangelistic preaching in a class by itself. Other Evangelicals, possessed of a more superficial and less adequate theology of grace, have laid the main emphasis in their gospel preaching on the sinner's need of forgiveness, or peace, or power, and of the way to get them by " deciding for Christ." It is not to be denied that their preaching has done good (for God will use His truth, even when imperfectly held and mixed with error), although this type of evangelism is always open to the criticism of being too man-centred and pietistic; but it has been left (necessarily) to Calvinists and those who, like the Wesleys, fall into Calvinistic ways of thought as soon as they begin a sermon to the unconverted, to preach the gospel in a way which highlights above everything else the free love, willing condescension, patient long-suffering and infinite kindness of the Lord Jesus Christ. And, without doubt, this is the most Scriptural and edifying way to preach it; for gospel invitations to sinners never honour God and exalt Christ more, nor

are more powerful to awaken and confirm faith, than when full
weight is laid on the free omnipotence of the mercy from which
they flow. It looks, indeed, as if the preachers of the old gospel
are the only people whose position allows them to do justice to the
revelation of Divine goodness in the free offer of Christ to sinners.

Then, in the second place, the old gospel safeguards values which
the new gospel loses. We saw before that the new gospel, by
asserting universal redemption and a universal Divine saving
purpose, compels itself to cheapen grace and the Cross by denying
that the Father and the Son are sovereign in salvation; for it assures
us that, after God and Christ have done all that they can, or will,
it depends finally on each man's own choice whether God's purpose to
save him is realised or not. This position has two unhappy results.
The first is that it compels us to misunderstand the significance of
the gracious invitations of Christ in the gospel of which we have
been speaking; for we now have to read them, not as expressions of
the tender patience of a mighty sovereign, but as the pathetic
pleadings of impotent desire; and so the enthroned Lord is suddenly
metamorphosed into a weak, futile figure tapping forlornly at the
door of the human heart, which He is powerless to open. This is
a shameful dishonour to the Christ of the New Testament. The
second implication is equally serious: for this view in effect denies
our dependence on God when it comes to vital decisions, takes us
out of His hand, tells us that we are, after all, what sin taught us to
think we were—masters of our fate, captain of our souls—and so
undermines the very foundation of man's religious relationship with
his Maker. It can hardly be wondered at that the converts of the
new gospel are so often both irreverent and irreligious, for such is the
natural tendency of this teaching. The old gospel, however, speaks
very differently and has a very different tendency. On the one
hand, in expounding man's need of Christ, it stresses something
which the new gospel effectively ignores—that sinners cannot obey
the gospel, any more than the law, without renewal of heart. On
the other hand, in declaring Christ's power to save, it proclaims
Him as the author and chief agent of conversion, coming by His
Spirit as the gospel goes forth to renew men's hearts and draw them
to Himself. Accordingly, in applying the message, the old gospel,
while stressing that faith is man's duty, stresses also that faith is
not in man's power, but that God must give what He commands.
It announces, not merely that men *must* come to Christ for salvation,
but also that they *cannot* come unless Christ Himself draws them.
Thus it labours to overthrow self-confidence, to convince sinners
that their salvation is altogether out of their hands, and to shut them
up to a self-despairing dependence on the glorious grace of a sovereign
Saviour, not only for their righteousness but for their faith too.

It is not likely, therefore, that a preacher of the old gospel will be happy to express the application of it in the form of a demand to "decide for Christ," as the current phrase is. For, on the one hand, this phrase carries the wrong associations. It suggests voting a person into office—an act in which the candidate plays no part beyond offering himself for election, and everything then being settled by the voter's independent choice. But we do not vote God's Son into office as our Saviour, nor does He remain passive while preachers campaign on His behalf, whipping up support for His cause. We ought not to think of evangelism as a kind of electioneering. And then, on the other hand, this phrase obscures the very thing that is essential in repentance and faith—the denying of self in a personal approach to Christ. It is not at all obvious that deciding *for* Christ is the same as coming *to* Him and resting *on* Him and turning *from* sin and self-effort; it sounds like something much less, and is accordingly calculated to instil defective notions of what the gospel really requires of sinners. It is not a very apt phrase from any point of view.

To the question: what must I do to be saved? the old gospel replies: believe on the Lord Jesus Christ. To the further question: what does it mean to believe on the Lord Jesus Christ? its reply is: it means knowing oneself to be a sinner, and Christ to have died for sinners; abandoning all self-righteousness and self-confidence, and casting oneself wholly upon Him for pardon and peace; and exchanging one's natural enmity and rebellion against God for a spirit of grateful submission to the will of Christ through the renewing of one's heart by the Holy Ghost. And to the further question still: how am I to go about believing on Christ and repenting, if I have no natural ability to do these things? it answers: look to Christ, speak to Christ, cry to Christ, just as you are; confess your sin, your impenitence, your unbelief, and cast yourself on His mercy; ask Him to give you a new heart, working in you true repentance and firm faith; ask Him to take away your evil heart of unbelief and to write His law within you, that you may never henceforth stray from Him. Turn to Him and trust Him as best you can, and pray for grace to turn and trust more thoroughly; use the means of grace expectantly, looking to Christ to draw near to you as you seek to draw near to Him; watch, pray, read and hear God's Word, worship and commune with God's people, and so continue till you know in yourself beyond doubt that you are indeed a changed being, a penitent believer, and the new heart which you desired has been put within you. The emphasis in this advice is on the need to call upon Christ directly, as the very first step.

> " Let not conscience make you linger,
> Nor of fitness fondly dream;
> All the fitness He requireth
> Is to feel your need of Him "—

so do not postpone action till you think you are better, but honestly confess your badness and give yourself up here and now to the Christ who alone can make you better; and wait on Him till His light rises in your soul, as Scripture promises that it shall do. Anything less than this direct dealing with Christ is disobedience of the gospel. Such is the exercise of spirit to which the old evangel summons its hearers. " I believe—help thou mine unbelief ": this must become their cry.

And the old gospel is proclaimed in the sure confidence that the Christ of whom it testifies, the Christ who is the real speaker when the Scriptural invitations to trust Him are expounded and applied, is not passively waiting for man's decision as the word goes forth, but is omnipotently active, working with and through the word to bring His people to faith in Himself. The preaching of the new gospel is often described as the task of " bringing men to Christ "— as if only men move, while Christ stands still. But the task of preaching the old gospel could more properly be described as bringing Christ to men, for those who preach it know that as they do their work of setting Christ before men's eyes, the mighty Saviour whom they proclaim is busy doing His work through their words, visiting sinners with salvation, awakening them to faith, drawing them in mercy to Himself.

It is this older gospel which Owen will teach us to preach: the gospel of the sovereign grace of God in Christ as the author and finisher of faith and salvation. It is the only gospel which can be preached on Owen's principles, but those who have tasted its sweetness will not in any case be found looking for another. In the matter of believing and preaching the gospel, as in other things, Jeremiah's words still have their application: " Thus saith the Lord, Stand ye in the ways, and see, and ask for the old paths, where is the good way, and walk therein, and ye shall find rest for your souls."[1] To find ourselves debarred, as Owen would debar us, from taking up with the fashionable modern substitute gospel may not, after all, be a bad thing, either for us, or for the Church.

More might be said, but to go further would be to exceed the limits of an introductory essay. The foregoing remarks are made simply to show how important it is at the present time that we should attend most carefully to Owen's analysis of what the Bible says about the saving work of Christ.

III.

It only remains to add a few remarks about this treatise itself. It was Owen's second major work, and his first masterpiece. (Its

[1] Jer. vi. 16.

predecessor, *A Display of Arminianism*, published in 1642, when Owen was twenty-six, was a competent piece of prentice-work, rather of the nature of a research thesis.)

The Death of Death is a solid book, made up of detailed exposition and close argument, and requires hard study, as Owen fully realised; a cursory glance will not yield much. (" READER. . . . If thou art, as many in this pretending age, *a sign or title gazer*, and comest into books as Cato into the theatre, to go out again—thou has had thy entertainment; farewell!"[1]) Owen felt, however, that he had a right to ask for hard study, for his book was a product of hard work (" a more than seven-years' serious inquiry . . . into the mind of God about these things, with a serious perusal of all which I could attain that the wit of man, in former or latter days, hath published in opposition to the truth "[2]), and he was sure in his own mind that a certain finality attached to what he had written. (" Altogether hopeless of success I am not; but fully resolved that I shall not live to see a solid answer given unto it."[3]) Time has justified his optimism.[4]

Something should be said about his opponents. He is writing against three variations on the theme of universal redemption: that of classical Arminianism, noted earlier; that of the theological faculty at Saumur (the position known as Amyraldism, after its leading exponent); and that of Thomas More, a lay theologian of East Anglia. The second of these views originated with a Scots professor at Saumur, John Cameron; it was taken up and developed by two of his pupils, Amyraut (Amyraldus) and Testard, and became the occasion of a prolonged controversy in which Amyraut, Daillé and Blondel were opposed by Rivet, Spanheim and Des Marets (Maresius). The Saumur position won some support among Reformed divines in Britain, being held in modified form by (among others) Bishops Usher and Davenant, and Richard Baxter. None of these, however, had advocated it in print at the time when Owen wrote.[5]

---

[1] Opening words, " To the Reader."   [2] P. (37) *inf.*   [3] P. (44) *inf.*

[4] Owen indicates more than once that for a complete statement of the case against universal redemption he would need to write a further book, dealing with " the other part of this controversy, concerning the cause of sending Christ " (pp. 133, 283 *inf.*). Its main thesis, apparently, would have been that " the fountain and cause of God's sending Christ, is his eternal love to his elect, and to them alone " (p. 119 *inf.*), and it would have contained " a more large explication of God's purpose of election and reprobation, showing how the death of Christ was a means set apart and appointed for the saving of his elect, and not at all undergone or suffered for those which, in his eternal counsel, he did determine should perish for their sins " (p. 133). It looks, therefore, as if it would have included the " clearing of our doctrine of reprobation, and of the administration of God's providence towards the reprobates, and over all their actions," which Owen promised in the epistle prefixed to *A Display of Arminianism* (*Works*, x. 9), but never wrote. However, we can understand his concluding that it was really needless to slaughter the same adversary twice.

[5] Davenant's *Duae Dissertationes*, one of which defends universal redemption

Goold's summary of the Saumur position may be quoted. "Admitting that, by the purpose of God, and through the death of Christ, the elect are infallibly secured in the enjoyment of salvation, they contended for an antecedent decree, by which God is free to give salvation to all men through Christ, on the *condition* that they believe on him. Hence their system was termed *hypothetic(al) universalism*. The vital difference between it and the strict Arminian theory lies in the absolute security asserted in the former for the spiritual recovery of the elect. They agree, however, in attributing some kind of universality to the atonement, and in maintaining that, on a certain *condition*, within the reach of fulfilment by all men . . . all men have access to the benefits of Christ's death." From this, Goold continues, " the readers of Owen will understand . . . why he dwells with peculiar keenness and reiteration of statement upon a refutation of the conditional system. . . . It was plausible; it had many learned men for its advocates; it had obtained currency in the foreign churches; and it seems to have been embraced by More."[1]

More is described by Thomas Edwards as " a great Sectary, that did much hurt in Lincolnshire, Norfolk, and Cambridgeshire; who was famous also in Boston, (King's) Lynn, and even in Holland, and was followed from place to place by many."[2] Baxter's description is kinder: " a Weaver of *Wisbitch* and *Lyn*, of excellent Parts."[3] (More's doctrine of redemption, of course, was substantially Baxter's own.) Owen, however, has a poor view of his abilities, and makes no secret of the fact. More's book, *The Universality of God's Free Grace in Christ to Mankind*, appeared in 1646 (not, as Goold says, 1643), and must have exercised a considerable influence, for within three years it had evoked four weighty works which were in whole or part polemics against it:

A Refutation . . . of Thomas More, by Thomas Whitfield, 1646; *Vindiciae Redemptionis*, by John Stalham, 1647; *The Universalist Examined and Convicted*, by Obadiah Howe, 1648; and Owen's own book, published in the same year.

More's exposition seems to be of little intrinsic importance; Owen, however, selects it as the fullest statement of the case for universal redemption that had yet appeared in English and uses it unmercifully as a chopping-block. The modern reader, however,

---

[1] " Prefatory Note " in *Works*, x. 140.   [2] *Gangraena*, 11. 86.
[3] *Reliquiae Baxterianae*, i. 50.

---

on Amyraldean lines, came out posthumously in 1650. Owen was not impressed and wrote of it: " I undertake to demonstrate that the main foundation of his whole dissertation about the death of Christ, with many inferences from thence, are neither found in, nor founded on the word; but that the several parts therein are mutually conflicting and destructive of each other " (*Works*, x. 433 (1650).

Baxter wrote a formal disputation defending universal redemption but never printed it; it was published after his death, however, in 1694.

will probably find it convenient to skip the sections devoted to refuting More (I. viii., the closing pages of II. iii. and IV. vi.) on his first passage through Owen's treatise.

Finally, a word about the style of this work. There is no denying that Owen is heavy and hard to read. This is not so much due to obscure arrangement as to two other factors. The first is his lumbering literary gait. "Owen travels through it (his subject) with the elephant's grace and solid step, if sometimes also with his ungainly motion," says Thomson.[1] That puts it kindly. Much of Owen's prose reads like a roughly-dashed-off translation of a piece of thinking done in Ciceronian Latin. It has, no doubt, a certain clumsy dignity; so has Stonehenge; but it is trying to the reader to have to go over sentences two or three times to see their meaning, and this necessity makes it much harder to follow an argument. The present writer, however, has found that the hard places in Owen usually come out as soon as one reads them aloud. The second obscuring factor is Owen's austerity as an expositor. He has a lordly disdain for broad introductions which ease the mind gently into a subject, and for comprehensive summaries which gather up scattered points into a small space. He obviously carries the whole of his design in his head, and expects his readers to do the same. Nor are his chapter divisions reliable pointers to the structure of his discourse, for though a change of subject is usually marked by a chapter division, Owen often starts a new chapter where there is no break in the thought at all. Nor is he concerned about literary proportions; the space given to a topic is determined by its intrinsic complexity rather than its relative importance, and the reader is left to work out what is basic and what is secondary by noting how things link together. The reader will probably find it helpful to use a pencil and paper in his study of the book and jot down the progress of the exposition; and it is hoped that the subjoined Analysis will also be of service in helping him keep his bearings.

We would conclude by repeating that the reward to be reaped from studying Owen is worth all the labour involved, and by making the following observations for the student's guidance. (1.) It is important to start with the epistle " To the Reader," for there Owen indicates in short compass what he is trying to do, and why. (2.) It is important to read the treatise as a whole, in the order in which it stands, and not to jump into parts III. and IV. before mastering the contents of Parts I. and II., where the biblical foundations of Owen's whole position are laid. (3.) It is hardly possible to grasp the strength and cogency of this massive statement on a first reading. The work must be read and re-read to be appreciated.

J. I. PACKER.

---

[1] *Loc. cit.*

ANALYSIS

Books I.-II. contain a survey of the biblical account of redemption through the death of Christ, arranged with a view to determining its intended and accomplished end. I. i., ii., are introductory; I.iii.-II. v. form a single exposition and defence of biblical teaching on this subject.

1. *Introduction to the treatise* (I. i.).

> Scripture describes the end intended and accomplished by the Father and the Son through the Son's death as the full salvation (actual reconciliation, justification, sanctification, adoption and glorification) of the Church.
>
> The view that Christ's death was a " general ransom " for all implies *either* that the Father and the Son have failed in their saving purpose, *or* that all will be saved, *or* that the purpose of Christ's death was not to save any particular persons absolutely.
>
> Since this third alternative, which the advocates of a " general ransom " embrace, is dishonouring to Christ and harmful to faith, Owen will oppose it.

2. *Preliminary definitions: " end " and " means " analysed and related* (I. ii.).

3. *The biblical doctrine of redemption stated and defended* (I. iii.-II. v.).

> (i) *The agent of it: the Triune God* (I. iii.-v.).
>
> > The Father (1) sent His Son into the world, by (*a*) appointing Him to His Mediatorial work; (*b*) giving Him all gifts and graces needed for His work; (*c*) entering into covenant with Him about His work;
> > (2) laid on Him the punishment of sin. (I. iii.).
> > The Son (1) took flesh;
> > (2) offered Himself;
> > (3) intercedes. (I. iv).
> > The Spirit concurred with Christ in His incarnation, oblation and intercession. (I. v).
>
> (ii) *The means of it: the oblation and intercession of Christ* (I. vi.-viii.).
>
> > Note (*a*) both acts have the same *end* (bringing many sons to glory);
> > (*b*) both acts respect the same *persons;*
> > (*c*) *the second rests on the first,* securing the communication to these persons of what the first procured for them. (I. vi).
> > —Proof of this assertion:
> > > *a.* From the uniform conjunction of these two acts in Scripture.
> > > *b.* From their both being acts of the same priestly office.

   c. From the nature of Christ's intercession.

   d. From the identity of what the oblation procured and the intercession bestows.

   e. From Christ's own conjunction of the two acts in Jn. xvii.

   f. From the result of denying this conjunction—the destruction of all assurance drawn from the fact of Christ's death for one. (I. vii).

  —Answer to More's arguments against this conjunction:

   a. As to Christ being a double Mediator, both general and special, alleged from 1 Tim. ii. 5, iv. 10; Heb. ix. 15.

   b. As to Christ interceding for unbelieving sinners as well as believing saints, alleged from Is. liii. 12; Lk. xxiii. 34; Jn. xvii. 21-23; Mt. v. 14-16; Jn. i. 9.

   c. As to Christ being a priest for all in respect of one end, and for some only in respect of all ends, alleged from Heb. ii. 9, ix. 14, 15, 26; Jn. i. 29; 1 Jn. ii. 2; Mt. xxvi. 28. (I. viii).

(iii) *The end of it: the glory of God, through the saving of the elect* (II. i.-v.).

 1. *Statement of the true view:*

  the ultimate, supreme end of Christ's death was to bring glory to God;

  the immediate, subordinate end of it was to bring us to God (which includes the bestowing of both grace and glory, faith and salvation). (*II.* 1).

 2. *Rejection of alternative views:*

  the end of Christ's death was not (*a*) His own good (His exaltation), nor (*b*) His Father's good (the securing for God of a desired liberty to pardon human sin); for

   (1) the assumption, " God could not pardon sin unless ... ," is unproveable;

   (2) this view makes the cause of sending Christ a general wish rather than a specific will to save;

   (3) it makes Christ free by His death, not His people, but His Father;

   (4) such an end is compatible with none being saved at all; also, this view involves reducing the covenant of grace to a conditional promise of saving believers which Christ's death procured, whereas Scripture depicts it as an unconditional promise to save sinners, of which Christ's death and the gift of obedient faith form a chief part. (II. ii).

 3. *Proof of the true view,* from three classes of Scriptures:

   (1) those showing that God's intention in Christ's death was actually to save some;

   (2) those showing that the effect of Christ's death was actually to save some;

   (3) those identifying the persons for whom Christ died as God's elect.

  —More's objections to Owen's exegesis of this latter class of texts answered. (II. iii).

4. *Disproof of the alternative view* (that of the Arminians, the Amyral-
deans, and More), which gives the *impetration* of salvation a
wider scope than its *application*:

    (a) *Definition of* " *impetration* " *and* " *application*."

        NB. 1. The distinction between them has no place in the
saving will of Christ, only in the order of His saving
acts;

          2. Though there are conditions involved in God's
method of bestowing salvation, there are none in
His will to bestow it;

          3. Not all the blessings obtained for us by Christ are
bestowed conditionally (e.g., faith);

          4. Both impetration and application in this case have
in view the same persons. Scripture asserts this
by conjoining them, and the alternative is incredible.

    (b) *Statement of their relation, and of the plan of salvation, as
understood by Owen's opponents.* These all deny that
Christ's death procures faith, but differ as to whether faith
is God's gift or man's independent contribution.

    (c) *Statement of their relation as understood by Owen:* God in love
sent His Son to secure redemption for the elect in order that
He might apply it to them, and so bring them to God, for
the praise of God's glory.

        NB. 1. God sent his Son *out of love to the elect only.*

          2. Christ's death was *of infinite worth*, sufficient to
redeem an infinite number.

          3. Christ's death was intended by God *to compass the
actual salvation of the elect.*

          4. Christ's death secured *a complete salvation.* (II. iv).

    (d) *Refutation of the idea of a conditional purchase of salvation.*
(II. v).

Book III. contains sixteen arguments against the " general ransom "
idea. All except the third have a directly exegetical basis, and aim
to show that this idea is inconsistent with the biblical witness to
Christ's work. Between them, they deal with every significant
category and concept which the Bible employs to define that work.

Arg. 1. From the fact that the new covenant, which Christ's death ratified,
is not made with all men.

    2. From the fact that the gospel, which reveals faith in Christ to be the
only way of salvation, is not published to all men. (III. i).

    3. From the dilemmas involved in asserting that the divine intention
in Christ's death was to redeem every man.

    4. From the fact that Christ is said to die for one of the two classes
(elect and reprobate) into which God divided men, and not for the
other.

    5. From the fact that Scripture nowhere asserts that Christ died for
all men, as such. (III. ii).

    6. From the fact that Christ died as sponsor (surety) for those for whom
He died.

    7. From the fact that Christ is a Mediator, and as such a priest, for
those for whom He died. (III. iii).

8. From the fact that Christ's death cleanses and sanctifies those for whom He died, whereas not all men are cleansed and sanctified.
9. From the fact that faith (which is necessary to salvation) was procured by the death of Christ, whereas not all men have faith.
10. From the fact that the deliverance of Israel from Egypt is a type of Christ's saving work. (III. iv).

(The next five arguments form a group on their own. They have a common form, and are all taken from the biblical terms in which Christ's work is described.)

11 (i). From the fact that Christ's death wrought *redemption* (deliverance by payment). (III. v).
12 (ii). From the fact that Christ's death effected *reconciliation* between God and men. (III. vi.)
13 (iii). From the fact that Christ's death made *satisfaction* for sins. (III. vii-ix.)
14 (iv). From the fact that Christ's death *merited* salvation for men.
15 (v). From the fact that Christ *died for* men. (III. x).
16. From particular texts: Gen. iii. 15; Mt. vii. 33, xi. 25; Jn. x. 11 ff.; Rom. viii. 32-34; Eph. i. 7; 2 Cor. v. 21; Jn. xvii. 9; Eph. v. 25. (III. xi.)

Book IV. contains a refutation of all the exegetical and theological arguments for universal redemption that Owen has met, and a full study of all texts alleged to teach it. The discussion of arguments from specific biblical statements occupies chapters i.-vi.; chapter vii. deals with more general theological arguments.

A. *Refutation of exegetical arguments for universal redemption* (i.-vi.).

(a) *The three classes of disputed texts:*

those describing the intended and accomplished end of Christ's death in general and indefinite terms;

those seeming to suggest its ineffectiveness for some for whom Christ died;

those making general offers of Christ, and promises of salvation through Him, to all who will believe, including some who in the event do not.

(b) *Biblical principles accounting for these modes of speech:*

1. *Christ's blood is of infinite worth*, sufficient to save all. This fact is the ground of the universal preaching of the gospel, and of the general promise that all who believe will be saved.
2. *The barrier between Jew and Gentile is broken down, and the restriction of grace ended, under the new covenant.* Many of the general expressions in Scripture intend only to stress this fact.
3. *Man's duty and God's purpose are distinct things:* so that God's command in the gospel, that all should repent and believe, cannot be held to imply His intention that all should do so.
4. *The Jews supposed that salvation was restrained to themselves.* Phrases like " the world," " all men," " all nations," " every creature," are often used emphatically to contradict this mistake.
5. *General terms like " world " and " all " are complex and equivocal in meaning*, and must be interpreted where they occur in the light of the context.
6. *Scripture speaks sometimes according to the appearance and human*

estimate of things, and may ascribe to the members of a professing Christian community things that are peculiar to God's children when some of them are really hypocrites, and reprobate.

7. *Judgments of charity, which it is our duty (as it was the apostles') to make about the spiritual state of persons professing faith, may not be true.*

8. *The offers and promises of the gospel are intended to teach the infallible connection that there is between faith and salvation; not the divine intention that all should repent and believe.*

9. *The mixed distribution of elect and reprobate throughout the world and the church makes it necessary that the gospel promises should be unrestricted in form, and should be preached to many whom God does not intend to save.*

10. *The faith which the gospel requires involves a number of acts in a specific order:* first, believing that we cannot save ourselves, but that God has provided a Saviour, Jesus Christ; then, resting on Christ for salvation, according to the gospel invitation and promise; finally, inferring from the fact that God has enabled us to do this that Christ died for us individually. (IV. i.)

(c) *Exegesis of the disputed texts:*

1. Those containing the word " *world* ": Jn. iii. 16 (IV. ii.); 1 Jn. ii. 1-2; Jn. vi. 51; 2 Cor. v. 19; Jn. i. 9, 29, iii. 17, iv. 42, 1 Jn. iv. 14. (IV. iii.)

2. Those containing the word " *all* ": 1 Tim. ii. 4-6; 2 Pet. iii. 9; Heb. ii. 9; 2 Cor. v. 14-15; 1 Cor. xv. 22; Rom. v. 18. (IV. iv.)

3. Those apparently envisaging the perishing of those for whom Christ died: Rom. xiv. 15; 1 Cor. viii. 11; 2 Pet. ii. 1; Heb. x. 29. (IV. v.)

(d) *Discussion of the arguments of Thomas More* (a detailed reply to the twentieth chapter of More's book). (IV. vi.)

Answer to arg. 1, from the necessity of taking Scripture in its plain sense;

2, from the unlimitedness of Scripture phrases;

3, from the exalting of Christ to be Lord and Judge of all mankind;

4, from the preaching of salvation through Christ to the world;

5, from the confession of Christ as Lord that all must make;

6, from various Scripture assertions concerning

i. God's saving love for the world (1 Jn. iv. 14; Jn. i. 4, 7; 1 Tim. i. 15, etc.);

ii. Christ's purpose to save the world;

iii. An alleged universal call to repentance;

iv. The guilt of unbelief (Jn. xvi. 7-11, etc.);

v. God's alleged desire that none should perish (Ezek. xviii. 23, 32, etc.);

vi. The universal reference of Christ's death;

vii. The privileges of believers;

viii. The parallel between Christ and Adam;

ix. The command to preach the gospel everywhere;

x. The alleged duty of praying that every individual man may be saved;

B. *Refutation of theological arguments for universal redemption* (IV. vii.).

Reply to arg. 1, from the alleged duty of every man to believe that Christ died for him (answer: there is no such duty as the Arminians assert);

2, from the alleged obstacle to faith which the doctrine of particular redemption sets up (answer: it sets up none);

3, that the doctrine of universal redemption exalts God's free grace (answer: in fact, it cheapens it);

4, that the doctrine of universal redemption exalts Christ's merit (answer: in fact, it depreciates it);

5, that the doctrine of particular redemption mars gospel consolation and assurance (answer: the doctrine of universal redemption does this, but the doctrine of particular redemption is "the true solid foundation of all durable consolation": see Rom. viii. 32-34).

TO THE RIGHT HONOURABLE

ROBERT, EARL OF WARWICK,[1] ETC.

My LORD,

IT is not for the benefit of any protection to the ensuing treatise,—let it stand or fall as it shall be found in the judgments of men; nor that I might take advantage to set forth any of that worth and honour which, being personal, have truly ennobled your lordship, and made a way for the delivering over of your family unto posterity with an eminent lustre added to the roll of your worthy progenitors,— which, if by myself desired, my unfitness to perform must needs render unacceptable in the performance; neither yet have I the least desire to attempt a farther advancement of myself into your lordship's favour, being much beneath what I have already received, and fully resolved to own no other esteem among the sons of men but what shall be accounted due (be it more or less) to the discharge of my duty to my master, Jesus Christ, whose wholly I would be;—it is not all, nor one of these, nor any such as these, the usual subjects and ends of dedications, real or pretended, that prevailed upon me unto this boldness of prefixing your honoured name to this ensuing treatise (which yet, for the matter's sake contained in it, I cannot judge unworthy of any Christian eye); but only that I might take the advantage to testify (as I do) to all the world the answering of my heart unto that obligation which your lordship was pleased to put upon me, in the undeserved, undesired favour of opening that door wherewith you are intrusted, to give me an entrance to that place for the preaching of the gospel whither I was directed by the providence of the Most High, and where I was sought by his people. In which place this I dare say, by the grace of God, that such a stock of prayers and thankfulness as your heart, which hath learned to value the least of Christ, in whomsoever it be, will not despise, is tendered to and for your lordship, even on his behalf who is less than the least of all the saints of God, and unworthy the name which yet he is bold to subscribe himself by,—Your honour's most obliged servant in the service of Jesus Christ,

JOHN OWEN.

---

1 This nobleman is represented by Neal as having been "the greatest patron of the Puritans." He was admiral of the parliamentary fleet. He seized on the ships belonging to the king, and during the whole course of the war made use of them against the royal interest. Owen had received the presentation to Coggeshall from this nobleman, whose upright and amiable character was celebrated long after his death under the designation of THE GOOD EARL OF WARWICK.—ED.

TWO ATTESTATIONS

TOUCHING THE ENSUING TREATISE.

READER,

THERE are two rotten pillars on which the fabric of late Arminianism (an egg of the old Pelagianism, which we had well hoped had been long since chilled, but is sit upon and brooded by the wanton wits of our degenerate and apostate spirits) doth principally stand.

The one is, That *God loveth all alike*, Cain as well as Abel, Judas as the rest of the apostles.

The other is, That *God giveth* (nay is bound, " ex debito," so to do) *both Christ, the great gift of his eternal love, for all alike to work out their redemption, and* " vires credendi," *power to believe in Christ to all alike to whom he gives the gospel;* whereby that redemption may effectually be applied for their salvation, if they please to make right use of that which is so put into their power.

The former destroys the *free* and *special* grace of God, by making it *universal;* the latter gives cause to man of glorying in himself rather than in God,—God concurring no farther to the salvation of a believer than a reprobate. Christ died for both alike;—God giving power of accepting Christ to both alike, men themselves determining the whole matter by their free-will; Christ making both savable, themselves make them to be saved.

This cursed doctrine of theirs crosseth the main drift of the holy Scripture; which is to abase and pull down the pride of man, to make him even to despair of himself, and to advance and set up the glory of God's free grace from the beginning to the end of man's salvation. His hand hath laid the foundation of his spiritual house; his hand shall also finish it.

The reverend and learned author of this book hath received strength from God (like another Samson) to pull down this rotten house upon the head of those Philistines who would uphold it. Read it diligently, and I doubt not but you will say with me, there is such variety of choice matter running through every vein of each discourse here handled, and carried along with such strength of sound and deep judgment, and with such life and power of a heavenly spirit, and all expressed in such pithy and pregnant words of wisdom, that you will both delight in the reading and praise God for the writer. That both he and it may be more and more profitable shall be my hearty prayers.—The unworthiest of the ministers of the gospel,

STANLEY GOWER.[1]

CHRISTIAN READER,

UNTO such alone are these directed. If all and every one in the world in this gospel-day did bear this precious name of Christian, or if the name of Christ were known to all, then were this compellation very improper, because it is distinguish-

---

[1] A Puritan divine of considerable eminence, and a member of the Westminster Assembly. He was at first minister of Brampton Bryan, Herefordshire. Latterly he was a minister at Dorchester, where he seems to have been alive about 1660.--ED.

ing. But if God distinguish men and men, choose we or refuse we, so it is, and so it will be ; there is a difference,—a difference which God and Christ doth make of mere good pleasure.

This book contends earnestly for this truth against the error of *universal redemption*. With thy leave I cannot but call it an error; unless it had been, it were, and while the world continueth it should be, found indeed that Adam and all that come of him, in a natural way of generation, are first set by Christ, the second Adam, in an estate of redeemed ones and made Christians, and then they fall, whole nations of them, and forfeit that estate also, and lose their Christendom, and thereby it is come to pass that they are become atheists, without God in the world, and heathen, Jews, and Turks, as we see they are at this day.

The author of this book I know not so much as by name; it is of the book itself that I take upon me the boldness to write these few lines. It being delivered unto me to peruse, I did read it with delight and profit:—with delight, in the keenness of argument, clearness and fulness of answers, and candour in language; —with profit, in the vindication of abused Scriptures, the opening of obscure places, and chiefly in disclosing the hid mystery of God and the Father and of Christ, in the glorious and gracious work of redemption. The like pleasure and profit this tractate promiseth to all diligent readers thereof, for the present controversy is so managed that the doctrine of faith, which we ought to believe, is with dexterity plentifully taught; yea, the glory of each person in the unity of the Godhead about the work of redemption is distinctly held forth with shining splendour, and the error of the Arminians smitten in the jaw-bone, and the broachers of it bridled with bit and curb.

When, on earth, the blood can be without the water and the Spirit,—can witness alone, or can witness there where the water and the Spirit agree not to the record; when, in heaven, the Word shall witness without the Father and the Holy Ghost,— when the Father, the Word, and the Holy Ghost shall not be one, as in *essence*, so in *willing, working, witnessing the redemption of sinners;*—then shall universal redemption of all and every sinner by Christ be found a truth, though the Father elect them not, nor the Spirit of grace neither sanctify nor seal them. The glory of God's free and severing grace, and the salvation of the elect through the redemption that is in Jesus Christ (which is external, or none at all), are the unfeigned desires and utmost aims of all that are truly Christian. In pursuit of which desire and aims, I profess myself to be for ever to serve thee.—Thine in Christ Jesus,

RICHARD BYFIELD.[1]

1 Richard Byfield was ejected by the Act of Uniformity from Long Ditton, in the county of Surrey. Besides some sermons and tracts, he was the author of a quarto volume, "The Doctrine of the Sabbath Vindicated," etc. He suffered suspension and sequestration for four years for not reading the Book of Sports. He was a member of the Westminster Assembly. During the time of Cromwell, a difference occurred between him and the patron of the parish, Sir John Evelyn, about the repairs of the church. Cromwell brought them together, succeeded in reconciling them, and, to cement the reconciliation, generously advanced £100, one-half of the sum needed for the repairs. Byfield did not know Owen, even by name, when he gave his recommendation to this work. It was then of some importance to our author that he should have the sanction of Byfield's name ; and the favour is requited when the latter owes most of his own reputation with posterity to the countenance which he gave to the young and rising theological author of his day.—ED.

TO THE READER.

READER,

IF thou intendest to go any farther, I would entreat thee to stay here a little. If thou art, as many in this pretending age, *a sign or title gazer*, and comest into books as Cato into the theatre, to go out again,—thou hast had thy entertainment; farewell! With him that resolves a serious view of the following discourse, and really desireth satisfaction from the word and Christian reason, about the great things contained therein, I desire a few words in the portal. Divers things there are of no small consideration to the business we have in hand, which I am persuaded thou canst not be unacquainted with; and therefore I will not trouble thee with a needless repetition of them.

I shall only crave thy leave to preface a little to the point in hand, and my present undertaking therein, with the result of some of my thoughts concerning the whole, after a more than seven-years' serious inquiry (bottomed, I hope, upon the strength of Christ, and guided by his Spirit) into the mind of God about these things, with a serious perusal of all which I could attain that the wit of man, in former or latter days, hath published in opposition to the truth; which I desire, according to the measure of the gift received, here to assert. Some things, then, as to the chief point in hand I would desire the reader to observe; as,—

First, That the assertion of *universal redemption*, or the general ransom, so as to make it in the least measure beneficial for the end intended, goes not *alone*. Election of free grace, as the fountain of all following dispensations, all discriminating purposes of the Almighty, depending on his own good pleasure and will, must be removed out of the way. Hence, those who would for the present (" populo ut placerent, quas fecere fabulas,") desirously retain some show of asserting the liberty of eternally distinguishing free grace, do themselves utterly raze, in respect of any fruit or profitable issue, the whole imaginary fabric of general redemption, which they had before erected. Some of these make the decree of election to be " antecedaneous to the death of Christ" (as themselves absurdly speak), or the decree of the death of Christ: then frame a twofold election;[1]—one, of some to be the sons; the other, of the rest to be servants. But this election of some to be servants the Scripture calls reprobation, and speaks of it as the issue of hatred, or a purpose of rejection, Rom. ix. 11-13. To be a servant, in opposition to children and their liberty, is as high a curse as can be expressed, Gen. ix. 25. Is this Scripture election? Besides, if Christ died to bring those he died for unto the adoption and inheritance of children, what good could possibly redound to them thereby who were predestinated before to be only servants? Others[2] make a general conditionate decree of redemption to be antecedaneous to election; which they assert to be the first discriminating purpose concerning the sons of men, and to depend on the alone good pleasure of God. That any others shall partake of the death of Christ or the fruits thereof, either unto grace or glory, but only those persons so elected, that they deny. "Cui bono" now? To what purpose serves the general ransom, but only to assert that Almighty God would have the precious blood of his dear Son poured out for innumerable souls whom he will not have to share in any drop thereof, and so, in respect of them, to be spilt in vain, or else to be shed for them only that they might be the deeper damned? This fountain, then, of free grace, this foundation of

1 T. M., Universality of Free Grace. [He refers to an author of the name of Thomas More. See page 153 of this preface.—ED.]   2 Camero, Amirald, etc.

the new covenant, this bottom of all gospel dispensations, this fruitful womb of all eternally distinguishing mercies, the purpose of God according to election, must be opposed, slighted, blasphemed, that the figment of the sons of men may not appear to be "truncus ficulnus, inutile lignum,"—an unprofitable stock; and all the thoughts of the Most High, differencing between man and man, must be made to take " occasion," say some, to be " caused," say others, by their holy, self-spiritual endeavours. " Gratum opus agricolis,"—a savoury sacrifice to the Roman Belus, a sacred orgie to the long-bewailed manes of St Pelagius.

And here, secondly, free-will, " amor et deliciæ humani generis," corrupted nature's deformed darling, the Pallas or beloved self-conception of darkened minds, finds open hearts and arms for its adulterous embraces; yea, the die being cast, and Rubicon passed over, " eo devenere fata ecclesiæ," that having opposed the free distinguishing grace of God as the sole sworn enemy thereof, it advanceth itself, or an inbred native ability in every one to embrace a portion of generally exposed mercy, under the name of free grace. " Tantane nos tenuit generis fiducia vestri?" This, this is Universalists' free grace, which in the Scripture phrase is cursed, corrupted nature. Neither can it otherwise be. A general ransom without free-will is but " phantasiæ inutile pondus,"—" a burdensome fancy;" the merit of the death of Christ being to them as an ointment in a box, that hath neither virtue nor power to act or reach out its own application unto particulars, being only set out in the gospel to the view of all, that those who will, by their own strength, lay hold on it and apply it to themselves may be healed. Hence the dear esteem and high valuation which this old idol free-will hath attained in these days, being so useful to the general ransom that it cannot live a day without it. Should it pass for true what the Scripture affirms, namely, that we are by nature " dead in trespasses and sins," etc., there would not be left of the general ransom a shred to take fire from the hearth. Like the wood of the vine, it would not yield a pin to hang a garment upon : all which you shall find fully declared in the ensuing treatise. But here, as though all the undertakings and Babylonish attempts of the old Pelagians, with their varnished offspring, the late Arminians, were slight and easy, I shall show you greater abominations than these, and farther discoveries of the imagery of the hearts of the sons of men. In pursuance of this persuasion of universal redemption, not a few have arrived (whither it naturally leads them) to deny the satisfaction and merit of Christ. Witness P—— H——, who, not being able to untie, ventured boldly to cut this Gordian knot, but so as to make both ends of the chain useless. To the question, Whether Christ died for all men or no? he answers, " That he died neither for all nor any, so as to purchase life and salvation for them." Ὦ τᾶν ποῖόν σε ἴπος φύγεν ἕρκος ὀδόντων; Shall cursed Socinianism be worded into a glorious discovery of free grace? Ask now for proofs of this assertion, as you might justly expect Achillean arguments from those who delight ἀκίνητα κινεῖν, and throw down such foundations (as shall put all the righteous in the world to a loss thereby), " Projicit ampullas et sesquipedalia verba," ὑπέρογκα ματαιότητος, great swelling words of vanity, drummy expressions, a noise from emptiness, the usual language of men who know not what they speak, nor whereof they do affirm, is all that is produced. Such contemptible products have our tympanous mountains! Poor creatures, whose souls are merchandised by the painted faces of novelty and vanity, whilst these Joabs salute you with the kisses of free grace, you see not the sword that is in their hands, whereby they smite you under the fifth rib, in the very heart-blood of faith and all Christian consolation. It seems our blessed Redeemer's deep humiliation, in bearing the chastisement of our peace and the punishment of our transgressions, being made a curse and sin, deserted under wrath and the power of death, procuring redemption and the remission of sins through the effusion of his blood, offering himself up a sacrifice to God, to make reconciliation and purchase an atonement, his pursuing this undertaking with continued intercession in the holy of holies, with all the benefits of his mediatorship, do no way procure either life and salvation or remission of sins, but only serve to declare that we are not indeed what his word affirms we are,—namely, cursed, guilty, defiled, and only not actually cast into hell. "Judas, betrayest thou the Son of man with a kiss?" See this at large confuted, lib. iii. Now, this last assertion, thoroughly fancied, hath opened a door and given an inlet to all those pretended heights and new-named glorious attainments which have metamorphosed the person and mediation of Christ into an imaginary diffused goodness and love, communicated from the Creator unto the new creation; than which familistical fables Cerdon's two principles were not more absurd; the Platonic numbers nor the Valentinian Æones,[1] flowing from the teeming wombs of Πλήρωμα, Αἰών, Τέλειος, Βυθός, Σιγή, and the rest, vented for high glorious attainments in Christian religion, near fifteen hundred years ago, were not less intelligible. Neither did the corroding of Scriptures by that Pontic vermin Marcion equalize the contempt and scorn cast upon them by these impotent impostors, exempting their whispered discoveries from their trial, and exalting their revelations above their authority. Neither do some stay here; but "his gradibus itur in cœlum," heaven itself is broke open for all. From universal redemption, through universal justification, in a general covenant, they have arrived ("haud ignota loquor") at universal salvation; neither can any forfeiture be made of the purchased inheritance.

"Quare agite, ô juvenes, tantarum in munere laudum,
Cingite fronde comas, et pocula porgite dextris,
Communemque vocate Deum, et date vina volentes."[3]

"March on, brave youths, i' th' praise of such free grace,
Surround your locks with bays; and full cups place
In your right hands: drink freely on, then call
O' th' common hope, the ransom general."

These and the like persuasions I no way dislike, because wholly new to the men of this generation; that I may add this by the way:—Every age hath its employment in the discovery of truth. We are not come to the bottom of vice or virtue. The whole world hath been employed in the practice of iniquity five thousand years and upwards, and yet "aspice hoc novum" may be set on many villanies. Behold daily new inventions! No wonder, then, if all truth be not yet discovered. Something may be revealed to them who as yet sit by. Admire not if Saul also be among the prophets, for who is their father? Is he not free in his dispensations? Are all the depths of Scripture, where the elephants may swim, just fathomed to the bottom? Let any man observe the progress of the last century in unfolding the truths of God, and he will scarce be obstinate that no more is left as yet undiscovered. Only the itching of corrupted fancies, the boldness of darkened minds and lascivious wanton wits, in venting new-created nothings, insignificant vanities, with an intermixed dash of blasphemy, is that which I desire to oppose; and that especially considering the genius (if I may so speak) of the days wherein we live; in which, what by one means, what by another, there is almost a general deflection after novelty grown amongst us. [3]"Some are credulous, some negligent, some fall into errors, some seek them." A great suspicion also every day grows upon me, which I would thank any one upon solid grounds to free me from, that pride of spirit, with an Herostratus-like design to grow big in the mouths of men, hath acted many in the conception and publication of some easily-invented false opinions. Is it not to be thought, also, that it is from the same humour possessing many, that every one of them almost strives to put on beyond his companions in framing some singular artifice? To be a follower of others, though in desperate engagements, is too mean an undertaking.

"Aude[4] aliquod brevibus Gyaris, et carcere dignum,
Si vis esse aliquis: probitas laudatur et alget."[5]

1 Iren. lib. ii., cap. 6, 7, 14, 15, etc.; Clem. Strom. iii.; Epiph. Hæres. xxxi.; Tertul. ad Valen.
2 Virg. Æn. viii. 273, et seq.
3 "Quidam creduli, quidam negligentes sunt, quibusdam mendacium obrepit, quibusdam placet."
4 "In tam occupata civitate fabulas vulgaris nequitia non invenit."—Sen. Ep. 120.
5 Juv. Sat. i. 74.

And let it be no small peccadillo, no underling opinion, friends, if in these busy times you would have it taken notice of. Of ordinary errors you may cry,—

> " Quis leget hæc ?———nemo hercule nemo,
> Vel duo, vel nemo." [1]

They must be glorious attainments, beyond the understanding of men, and above the wisdom of the word, which attract the eyes of poor deluded souls. The great shepherd of the sheep, our Lord Jesus Christ, recover his poor wanderers to his own fold! But to return thither from whence we have digressed:—

This is that fatal Helena, a useless, barren, fruitless fancy, for whose enthroning such irksome, tedious contentions have been caused to the churches of God; a mere Rome, a desolate, dirty place of cottages, until all the world be robbed and spoiled to adorn it. Suppose Christ died for all, yet if God in his free purpose hath chosen some to obtain life and salvation, passing by others, will it be profitable only to the *former*, or unto *all?* Surely the purpose of God must stand, and he will do all his pleasure. Wherefore, election either, with Huberus, by a wild contradiction, must be made universal, or the thoughts of the Most High suspended on the free-will of man. Add this borrowed feather to the general ransom, that at least it may have some colour of pompous ostentation. Yet if the free grace of God work effectually in some, not in others, can those others, passed by in its powerful operation, have any benefit by universal redemption? No more than the Egyptians had in the angel's passing over those houses whose doors were not sprinkled with blood, leaving some dead behind him. Almighty, powerful, free grace, then, must strike its sail, that free-will, like the Alexandrian ships to the Roman havens, may come in with top and top-gallant; for without it the whole territory of universal redemption will certainly be famished. But let these doctrines of God's eternal election, the free grace of conversion, perseverance, and their necessary consequents, be asserted, "movet cornicula risum, furtivis nudata coloribus;" it hath not the least appearance of profit or consolation but what it robs from the sovereignty and grace of God. But of these things more afterward.

Some flourishing pretences are usually held out by the abettors of the general ransom; which by thy patience, courteous reader, we will a little view in the entrance, to remove some prejudice that may lie in the way of truth:—

First, The glory of God, they say, is exceedingly exalted by it; his *good-will and kindness towards men abundantly manifested in this enlargement of its extent;* and his free grace, by others restrained, set out with a powerful endearment. This they say; which is, in effect, " All things will be well when God is contented with that portion of glory which is of our assigning." The princes of the earth account it their greatest wisdom to varnish over their favours, and to set out with a full mouth what they have done with half a hand; but will it be acceptable to lie for God, by extending his bounty beyond the marks and eternal bounds fixed to it in his word? Change first a hair of your own heads, or add a cubit to your own statures, before you come in with an addition of glory, not owned by him, to the Almighty. But so, for the most part, is it with corrupted nature in all such mysterious things; discovering the baseness and vileness thereof. If God be apprehended to be as large in grace as that is in offence (I mean in respect of particular offenders, for in respect of his he is larger), though it be free, and he hath proclaimed to all that he may do what he will with his own, giving no account of his matters, all shall be well,—he is gracious, merciful, etc; but if once the Scripture is conceived to hold out his sovereignty and free distinguishing grace, suited in its dispensation to his own purpose according to election, he is " immanis, truculentus, diabolo, Tiberio tetrior (horresco referens)." The learned know well where to find this language, and I will not be instrumental to propagate their blasphemies to others. " Si deus homini non placuerit, deus non erit," said Ter-

1 Pers. Sat. i. 2.

tullian of the heathen deities; and shall it be so with us? God forbid! This pride is inbred;[1] it is a part of our corruption to defend it. If we maintain, then, the glory of God, let us speak in his own language, or be for ever silent. That is glorious in him which he ascribes unto himself. Our inventions, though never so splendid in our own eyes, are unto him an abomination, a striving to pull him down from his eternal excellency, to make him altogether like unto us. God would never allow that the will of the creature should be the measure of his honour. The obedience of paradise was to have been regulated. God's prescription hath been the bottom of his acceptation of any duty ever since he had a creature to worship him. The very heathen knew that that service alone was welcome to God which himself required, and that glory owned which himself had revealed that he would appear glorious in it. Hence, as Epimenides[2] advised the Athenians in a time of danger to sacrifice Θεῷ προσήκοντι, "to him to whom it was meet and due,"—which gave occasion to the altar which Paul saw bearing the superscription of Ἀγνώστῳ Θεῷ, "To the unknown God,"—so Socrates tells us in Plato,[3] that every god will be worshipped τῷ μάλιστα αὐτῷ ἀρίσκοντι τρόπῳ, "in that way which pleaseth best his own mind;" and in Christianity, Hierome sets it down for a rule, that "honos præter mandatum est dedecus," God is dishonoured by that honour which is ascribed to him beyond his own prescription: and one wittily on the second commandment, "Non imago, non simulachrum damnatur, sed non facies tibi." Assigning to God any thing by him not assumed is a *making to ourselves*, a deifying of our own imaginations. Let all men, then, cease squaring the glory of God by their own corrupted principles and more corrupted persuasions. The word alone is to be arbitrator in the things of God; which also I hope will appear, by the following treatise, to hold out nothing in the matter in hand contrary to those natural notions of God and his goodness which in the sad ruins of innocency have been retained. On these grounds we affirm, that all that glory of God which is pretended to be asserted by the general ransom, however it may seem glorious to purblind nature, is indeed a sinful flourish, for the obscuring of that glory wherein God is delighted.

Secondly, It is strongly pretended that the worth and value of the satisfaction of Christ, by the opposite opinion limited to a few, are exceedingly magnified in this extending of them to all; when, besides what was said before unto human extending of the things of God beyond the bounds by himself fixed unto them, the merit of the death of Christ, consisting in its own internal worth and sufficiency, with that obligation which, by his obedience unto death, was put upon the justice of God for its application unto them for whom he died, is quite enervated and overthrown by it, made of no account, and such as never produced of itself absolutely the least good to any particular soul: which is so fully manifested in the following treatise, as I cannot but desire the reader's sincere consideration of it, it being a matter of no small importance.

Thirdly, A seeming smile cast upon the opinion of universal redemption by many texts of Scripture, with the ambiguity of some words, which though in themselves either figurative or indefinite, yet seem to be of a universal extent, maketh the abettors of it exceedingly rejoice. Now, concerning this I shall only desire the reader not to be startled at the multitude of places of Scripture which he may find heaped up by some of late about this business (especially by Thomas More, in his "Universality of Free Grace"), as though they proved and confirmed that for which they are produced, but rather prepare himself to admire at the confidence of men, particularly of him now named, to make such a flourish with colours and drums, having indeed no soldiers at all; for, notwithstanding all their pretences, it will appear that they hang the whole weight of their building on

1 "Natura sic apparet vitiata ut hoc majoris vitii sit non videre."—Aug.
2 Laert. in Vit. Epimen. 3 Plato de Legib., lib. vii.

three or four texts of Scripture,—namely, 1 Tim. ii. 5, 6; John iii. 16, 17; Heb. ii. 9; 1 John ii. 2, with some few others,—and the ambiguity of two or three words, which themselves cannot deny to be of exceeding various acceptations. All which are at large discussed in the ensuing treatise, no one place that hath with the least show or colour been brought forth by any of our adversaries, in their own defence, or for the opposing of the effectual redemption of the elect only, being omitted, the book of Thomas More being in all the strength thereof fully met withal and enervated.

Fourthly, Some men have, by I know not what misprision,[1] entertained a persuasion that the opinion of the Universalists serves exceedingly to set forth the love and free grace of God; yea, they make free grace, that glorious expression, to be that alone which is couched in their persuasion,—namely, that " God loves all alike, gave Christ to die for all, and is ready to save all if they will lay hold on him;"—under which notion how greedily the hook as well as the bait is swallowed by many we have daily experience, when the truth is, it is utterly destructive to the free distinguishing grace of God in all the dispensations and workings thereof. It evidently opposeth God's free grace of election, as hath been declared, and therein that very love from which God sent his Son. His free distinguishing grace, also, of effectual calling must be made by it to give place to nature's darling, free-will; yea, and the whole covenant of grace made void, by holding it out no otherwise but as a general removing of the wrath which was due to the breach of the covenant of works: for what else can be imagined (though this certainly they have not, John iii. 36) to be granted to the most of those " all" with whom they affirm this covenant to be made? Yea, notwithstanding their flourish of free grace, as themselves are forced to grant, that after all that was effected by the death of Christ, it was possible that none should be saved, so I hope I have clearly proved that if he accomplished by his death no more than they ascribe unto it, it is utterly impossible that any one should be saved. " Quid dignum tanto?"

Fifthly, The opinion of universal redemption is not a little advantaged by presenting to convinced men a seeming ready way to extricate themselves out of all their doubts and perplexities, and to give them all the comfort the death of Christ can afford before they feel any power of that death working within them, or find any efficacy of free grace drawing their hearts to the embracing of Christ in the promise, or obtaining a particular interest in him; which are tedious things to flesh and blood to attend unto and wait upon. Some boast that, by this persuasion, that hath been effected in an hour which they waited for before seven years without success. To dispel this poor empty flourish, I shall show, in the progress, that it is very ready and apt to deceive multitudes with a plausible delusion, but really undermines the very foundations of that strong unfailing consolation which God hath showed himself abundantly willing that the heirs of promise should receive.

These and the like are the general pretences wherewith the abettors of a general ransom do seek to commend themselves and opinion to the affections of credulous souls; through them making an open and easy passage into their belief, for the swallowing and digesting of that bitter potion which lurks in the bottom of their cup. Of these I thought meet to give the reader a brief view in the entrance, to take off his mind from empty generals, that he might be the better prepared to weigh all things carefully in an equal balance, when he shall come to consider those particulars afterward insisted on, wherein the great strength of our adversaries lies. It remaineth only that I give the Christian reader a brief account of my call unto, and undertaking in, this work, and so close this preface. First, then, I will assure thee it is not the least thirst in my affections to be drinking of the waters of Meribah, nor the least desire to have a share in Ishmael's portion,

1 The word is here used in the obsolete sense of "*mistake*," and has no reference to the legal offence of evasion or concealment now understood by the term.—ED.

to have my hand against others, and theirs against me, that put me upon this task. I never like myself worse than when faced with a vizard of disputing in controversies. The complexion of my soul is much more pleasant unto me in the waters of Shiloah :—

> " —— Nuper me in littore vidi,
> Cum placidum ventis staret mare." 1

What invitation there can be in itself for any one to lodge, much less abide, in this quarrelsome, scrambling territory, where, as Tertullian[2] says of Pontus, "omne quod flat Aquilo est," no wind blows but what is sharp and keen, I know not. Small pleasure in those walks which are attended with dangerous precipices and unpleasing difficulties on every side:—

> "Utque viam teneas, nulloque errore traharis ;
> Per tamen adversi gradieris cornua Tauri,
> Hæmoniosque arcus, violentique ora Leonis." 3

No quiet nor peace in these things and ways, but continual brawls and dissensions :—

> " —— Non hospes ab hospite tutus,
> Non socer a genero: fratrum quoque gratia rara est." 4

The strongest bonds of nearest relations are too commonly broken by them. Were it not for that precept, Jude 3, and the like, of "contending earnestly for the faith once delivered unto the saints," with the sounding of my bowels for the loss of poor seduced souls, I could willingly engage myself into an unchangeable resolution to fly all wordy battles and paper combats for the residue of my few and evil days.

It is not, then (that I may return), any salamandrian complexion that was the motive to this undertaking. Neither, secondly, was it any conceit of my own abilities for this work, as though I were the fittest among many to undertake it. I know that as in all things I am "less than the least of all saints," so in these I am

> —— οὔτε τρίτος οὔτε τίταρτος
> Οὔτε δυωδίκατος οὐδ' ἐν λόγῳ οὐδ' ἐν ἀριθμῷ.

Abler[5] pens have had, within these few years, the discussing and ventilating of some of these questions in our own language. Some have come to my hands, but none of weight, before I had well-nigh finished this heap of mine own, which was some twelve months since and upwards. In some of these, at least, in all of them, I had rested fully satisfied, but that I observed they had all tied up themselves to some certain parts of the controversy, especially the removing of objections, neither compassing nor methodizing the whole; whereby I discerned that the nature of the things under debate,—namely, satisfaction, reconciliation, redemption, and the like,—was left exceedingly in the dark, and the strong foundation of the whole building not so much as once discovered. It was always upon my desires that some one would undertake the main, and unfold out of the word, from the bottom, the whole dispensation of the love of God to his elect in Jesus Christ, with the conveyance of it through the promises of the gospel, being in all the fruits thereof purchased and procured by the oblation and intercession of Jesus Christ; by which it could not but be made apparent what was the great design of the blessed Trinity in this great work of redemption, with how vain an attempt and fruitless endeavour it must needs be to extend it beyond the bounds and limits assigned unto it by the principal agents therein. That arguments also might be produced for the confirmation of the truth we assert, in opposition to the error opposed, and so the weak established and dissenters convinced, was much in my wishes. The doctrine of the satisfaction of Christ, his merit, and the reconciliation wrought thereby, understood aright by few, and of late oppugned by some, being so nearly related to the point of redemption, I desired also to have seen cleared, unfolded,

---

1 Virg. Buc. Ecl. ii. 25.   2 Ad. Mar.   3 Ovid. Met. ii. 79.   4 Ovid. Met. i. 144.
5 Vindic. Redempt., by my reverend and learned brother, Mr John Stalham; Mr Rutherford, Christ Drawing Sinners.

vindicated, by some able pen. But now, after long waiting, finding none to answer my expectation, although of myself I can truly say, with him in the Comedian, " Ego me neque tam astutum esse, neque ita perspicacem id scio," that I should be fit for such an undertaking, the counsel of the poet also running much in my mind,—

" Sumite materiam vestris, qui scribitis, æquam
Viribus; et versate diu, quid ferre recusent,
Quid valeant humeri." [1]

Yet, at the last, laying aside all such thoughts, by looking up to Him who sup. plieth seed to the sower, and doth all our works for us, I suffered myself to be overcome unto the work with that of another, " Ab alio quovis hoc fieri mallem quam a me; sed a me tamen potius quam a nemine;"—" I had rather it should have been done by any than myself, of myself only rather than of none;" especially considering the industrious diligence of the opposers of truth in these days:—

" Scribimus indocti doctique,———
Ut jugulent homines, surgunt de nocte latrones;
Ut teipsum serves non expergisceris?" [2]

Add unto the former desire a consideration of the frequent conferences I had been invited unto about these things, the daily spreading of the opinions here opposed about the parts where I live, and a greater noise concerning their prevailing in other places, with the advantage they had obtained by some military abettors, with the stirring up of divers eminent and learned friends, and you have the sum of what I desire to hold forth as the cause of my undertaking this task. What the Lord hath enabled me to perform therein must be left to the judgment of others. Altogether hopeless of success I am not; but fully resolved that I shall not live to see a solid answer given unto it. If any shall undertake to vellicate and pluck some of the branches, rent from the roots and principles of the whole discourse, I shall freely give them leave to enjoy their own wisdom and imaginary conquest. If any shall seriously undertake to debate the whole cause, if I live to see it effected, I shall engage myself, by the Lord's assistance, to be their humble convert or fair antagonist. In that which is already accomplished by the good hand of the Lord, I hope the learned may find something for their contentment, and the weak for their strengthening and satisfaction; that in all some glory may redound to Him whose it is, and whose truth is here unfolded by the unworthiest labourer in his vineyard, J. O.

1 Hor. De Art. Poet., ver. 38.　　2 Hor. Epist. lib. ii. Epist. i. 117; lib. i. Epist. ii. 32.

DEATH OF DEATH IN THE DEATH OF CHRIST.

A TREATISE OF THE REDEMPTION AND RECONCILIATION THAT IS IN THE BLOOD OF CHRIST,
WITH THE MERIT THEREOF, AND SATISFACTION WROUGHT THEREBY.

BOOK I.

CHAPTER I.

In general of the end of the death of Christ, as it is in the Scripture proposed.

BY the end of the death of Christ, we mean in general, both,—first, that which his Father and himself intended *in* it; and, secondly, that which was effectually fulfilled and accomplished *by* it. Concerning either we may take a brief view of the expressions used by the Holy Ghost:—

I. For the first. Will you know the *end* wherefore, and the intention wherewith, Christ came into the world? Let us ask himself (who knew his own mind, as also all the secrets of his Father's bosom), and he will tell us that the "Son of man came to save that which was lost," Matt. xviii. 11,—to recover and save poor lost sinners; that was his intent and design, as is again asserted, Luke xix. 10. Ask also his apostles, who know his mind, and they will tell you the same. So Paul, 1 Tim. i. 15, "This is a faithful saying, and worthy of all acceptation, that Christ Jesus came into the world to save sinners." Now, if you will ask who these sinners are towards whom he hath this gracious intent and purpose, himself tells you, Matt. xx. 28, that he came to "give his life a ransom for *many;*" in other places called *us*, believers, distinguished from the world: for he "gave himself for *our* sins, that he might deliver *us* from this present evil *world*, according to the will of God and our Father," Gal. i. 4. That was the will and intention of God, that he should give himself for *us*, that we might be saved, being separated from the world. They are his *church:* Eph. v. 25-27, "He loved the church, and gave himself for it; that he might sanctify and cleanse it with the washing of water by the word, that he might present it to himself a glorious church, not having spot, or wrinkle, or any such thing; but that it should be holy and without blemish:" which last words express also the very aim and end of Christ in giving himself for any, even that they may be made *fit* for God, and brought nigh unto him;—the like whereof is also asserted, Tit. ii. 14, "He gave himself for us, that he might redeem us from all iniquity, and purify unto himself a peculiar people, zealous of good works." Thus clear, then, and apparent, is the intention and design of Christ and his Father in this great work, even what it was, and towards whom,— namely, to save us, to deliver us from the evil world, to purge and wash us, to make us holy, zealous, fruitful in good works, to render us acceptable, and to bring us unto God; for through him "we have access into the grace wherein we stand," Rom. v. 2.

II. The effect, also, and actual product of the work itself, or what is accomplished and fulfilled by the death, blood-shedding, or oblation of Jesus Christ, is no less clearly manifested, but is as fully, and very often more distinctly, expressed;—as, first, *Reconciliation* with God, by removing and slaying the enmity that was between him and us; for "when we were enemies we were reconciled to God by the death of his Son," Rom. v. 10. "God was in him reconciling the world unto himself, not imputing their trespasses unto them," 2 Cor. v. 19; yea, he hath "reconciled us to himself by Jesus Christ," verse 18. And if you would know how this reconciliation was effected, the apostle will tell you that "he abolished in his flesh the enmity, the law of commandments consisting in ordinances; for to make in himself of twain one new man, so making peace; and that he might reconcile both unto God in one body by the cross, having slain the enmity thereby," Eph. ii. 15, 16: so that "he is our peace," verse 14. Secondly, *Justification*, by taking away the guilt of sins, procuring remission and pardon of them, redeeming us from their power, with the curse and wrath due unto us for them; for "by his own blood he entered into the holy place, having obtained eternal redemption for us," Heb. ix. 12. "He redeemed us from the curse, being made a curse for us," Gal. iii. 13; "his own self bearing our sins in his own body on the tree," 1 Pet. ii. 24. We have "all sinned, and come short of the glory of God;" but are "justified freely by his grace through the redemption that is in Christ Jesus, whom God hath set forth to be a propitiation through faith in his blood, to declare his righteousness for the remission of sins," Rom. iii. 23–25: for "in him we have redemption through his blood, even the forgiveness of sins," Col. i. 14. Thirdly, *Sanctification*, by the purging away of the uncleanness and pollution of our sins, renewing in us the image of God, and supplying us with the graces of the Spirit of holiness: for "the blood of Christ, who through the eternal Spirit offered himself to God, purgeth our consciences from dead works, that we may serve the living God," Heb. ix. 14; yea, "the blood of Jesus Christ cleanseth us from all sin," 1 John i. 7. "By himself he purged our sins,"

Heb. i. 3. To "sanctify the people with his own blood, he suffered without the gate," chap. xiii. 12. "He gave himself for the church to sanctify and cleanse it, that it should be holy and without blemish," Eph. v. 25-27. Peculiarly amongst the graces of the Spirit, "it is given to us," ὑπὲρ Χριστοῦ, "for Christ's sake, to believe on him," Phil. i. 29; God "blessing us in him with all spiritual blessings in heavenly places," Eph. i. 3. Fourthly, *Adoption*, with that evangelical liberty and all those glorious privileges which appertain to the sons of God; for "God sent forth his Son, made of a woman, made under the law, to redeem them that were under the law, that we might receive the adoption of sons," Gal. iv. 4, 5. Fifthly, Neither do the effects of the death of Christ rest here; they leave us not until we are settled in heaven, in glory and immortality for ever. Our inheritance is a "purchased possession," Eph. i. 14: "And for this cause he is the mediator of the new testament, that by means of death, for the redemption of the transgressions that were under the first testament, they which are called might receive the promise of eternal inheritance," Heb. ix. 15. The sum of all is,—The death and bloodshedding of Jesus Christ hath wrought, and doth effectually procure, for all those that are concerned in it, eternal redemption, consisting in grace here and glory hereafter.

III. Thus full, clear, and evident are the expressions in the Scripture concerning the *ends* and *effects* of the death of Christ, that a man would think every one might run and read. But we must stay: among all things in Christian religion, there is scarce any thing more questioned than this, which seems to be a most fundamental principle. A spreading persuasion there is of *a general ransom* to be paid by Christ for all; that he died to redeem *all and every one*, —not only for *many*, his *church*, the *elect* of God, but for every one also of the posterity of Adam. Now, the masters of this opinion do see full well and easily, that if *that* be the *end* of the death of Christ which we have from the Scripture asserted, if those before recounted be the immediate *fruits* and *products* thereof, then one of these two things will necessarily follow:—that either, first, God and Christ failed of their end proposed, and did not accomplish that which they intended, the death of Christ being not a fitly-proportioned *means* for the attaining of that end (for any cause of failing cannot be assigned); which to assert seems to us blasphemously injurious to the wisdom, power, and perfection of God, as likewise derogatory to the worth and value of the death of Christ;—or else, that all men, all the posterity of Adam, must be saved, purged, sanctified, and glorified; which surely they will not maintain, at least the Scripture and the woful experience of millions will not allow. Wherefore, to cast a tolerable colour upon their persuasion, they must and do deny that God or his Son had any such absolute aim or end in the death or blood-shedding of Jesus Christ, or that any such thing was immediately procured and purchased by it, as we before recounted; but that God intended nothing, neither was any thing effected by Christ,—that no benefit ariseth to any immediately by his death but what is common to all and every soul, though never so cursedly unbelieving here and eternally damned hereafter, until an act of some, not procured for them by Christ, (for if it were, why have they it not all alike?) to wit, faith, do distinguish them from others. Now, this seeming to me to enervate the virtue, value, fruits and effects of the satisfaction and death of Christ,—serving, besides, for a basis and foundation to a dangerous, uncomfortable, erroneous persuasion,—I shall, by the Lord's assistance, declare what the Scripture holds out in both these things, both that assertion which is intended to be proved, and that which is brought for the proof thereof; desiring the Lord by his Spirit to lead us into all truth, to give us understanding in all things, and if any one be otherwise minded, to reveal that also unto him.

CHAPTER II.

Of the nature of an end in general, and some distinctions about it.

I. THE *end* of any thing is that which the *agent* intendeth to accomplish in and by the operation which is proper unto its nature, and which it applieth itself unto,—that which any one aimeth at, and designeth in himself to attain, as a thing good and desirable unto him in the state and condition wherein he is. So the end which Noah proposed unto himself in the building of the ark was the preservation of himself and others. According to the will of God, he made an ark to preserve himself and his family from the flood: "According to all that God commanded him, so did he," Gen. vi. 22. That which the agent doth, or whereto he applieth himself, for the compassing his proposed *end*, is called the *means;* which two do complete the whole reason of working in free *intellectual* agents, for I speak only of such as work according to choice or election. So Absalom intending a revolt from his father, to procure the crown and kingdom for himself, " he prepared him horses and chariots, and fifty men to run before him," 2 Sam. xv. 1; and farther, by fair words and glossing compliances, "he stole the hearts of the men of Israel," verse 6; then pretends a sacrifice at Hebron, where he makes a strong conspiracy, verse 12;—all which were the *means* he used for the attaining of his fore-proposed end.

II. Between both these, *end* and *means*, there is this relation, that (though in sundry kinds) they are mutually causes one of another. The end is the first, principal, *moving cause* of the whole. It is that for whose sake the whole work is. No agent applies itself to action but for an end; and were it not by that determined to some certain effect, thing, way, or manner of working, it would no more do one thing than another. The inhabitants of the old world desiring and intending unity and cohabitation, with perhaps some reserves to provide for their safety against a second storm, they cry, " Go to, let us build us a city, and a tower whose top may reach unto heaven; and let us make us a name, lest we be scattered abroad upon the face of the whole earth," Gen. xi. 4. First, They lay down their *aim* and *design*, and then let out the *means* in their apprehension conducing thereunto. And manifest, then, it is, that the whole reason and method of affairs that a wise worker or agent, according to the counsel, proposeth to himself, is taken from the *end* which he aims at; that is, in intention and contrivance, the beginning of all that order which is in working. Now, the *means* are all those things which are used for the attaining of the end proposed,—as meat for the preservation of life, sailing in a ship for him that would pass the sea, laws for the quiet continuance of human society; and they are the procuring cause of the end, in one kind or another. Their existence is for the end's sake, and the end hath its rise out of them, following them either *morally* as their desert, or *naturally* as their fruit and product. First, In a *moral* sense. When the action and the end are to be measured or considered in reference to a moral rule, or *law* prescribed to the agent, then the *means* are the deserving or meritorious cause of the end; as, if Adam had continued in his innocency, and done all things according to the law given unto him, the end procured thereby had been a blessed life to eternity; as now the end of any sinful act is death, the curse of the law. Secondly, When the means are considered only in their *natural* relation, then they are the instrumentally efficient cause of the end. So Joab intending the death of Abner, " he smote him with his spear under the fifth rib, that he died," 2 Sam. iii. 27. And when Benaiah, by the command of Solomon, fell upon Shimei, the wounds he gave him were the efficient of his death, 1 Kings ii. 46. In which regard there is no difference between the murdering of an innocent man and the executing of an offender; but as they are under a moral consideration, their ends follow their deservings, in respect of conformity to the rule, and so there is χάσμα μέγα between them.

III. The former consideration, by reason of the defect and perverseness of some agents (for otherwise these things are coincident), holds out a twofold end of things,—first, of the work, and, secondly, of the workman; of the act and the agent: for when the means assigned for the attaining of any end are not proportioned unto it, nor, fitted for it, according to that rule which the agent is to work by, then it cannot be but that he must aim at one thing and another follow, in respect of the morality of the work. So Adam is enticed into a desire to be like God; this now he makes his aim, which to effect he eats the forbidden fruit, and that contracts a guilt which he aimed not at. But when the agent acts aright, and as it should do,—when it aims at an end that is proper to it, belonging to its proper perfection and condition, and worketh by such means as are fit and suitable to the end proposed,—the end of the work and the workman are one and the same; as when Abel intended the worship of the Lord, he offered a sacrifice through faith, acceptable unto him; or as a man, desiring salvation through Christ, applieth himself to get an interest in him. Now, the sole reason of this diversity is, that secondary agents, such as men are, have an end set and appointed to their actions by Him which giveth them an external rule or law to work by, which shall always attend them in their working, whether they will or no. God only, whose will and good pleasure is the sole rule of all those works which outwardly are of him, can never deviate in his actions, nor have any end attend or follow his acts not precisely by him intended.

IV. Again; the end of every free agent is either that which he effecteth, or that for whose sake he doth effect it. When a man builds a house to let to hire, that which he effecteth is the building of a house; that which moveth him to do it is love of gain. The physician cures the patient, and is moved to it by his reward. The end which Judas aimed at in his going to the priests, bargaining with them, conducting the soldiers to the garden, kissing Christ, was the betraying of his Master; but the end for whose sake the whole undertaking was set on foot was the obtaining of the thirty pieces of silver: "What will ye give me, and I will do it?" The end which God effected by the death of Christ was the satisfaction of his justice: the end for whose sake he did it was either supreme, or his own glory; or subordinate, ours with him.

V. Moreover, the *means* are of two sorts:—First, Such as have a true goodness in themselves without reference to any farther kind; though not so considered as we use them for means. No means, as a means, is considered as good in itself, but only as conducible to a farther end; it is repugnant to the nature of means, as such, to be considered as good in themselves. Study is in itself the most noble employment of the soul; but, aiming at wisdom or knowledge, we consider it as good only inasmuch as it conduceth to that end, otherwise as " a weariness of the flesh," Eccl. xii. 12. Secondly, Such as have no good at all in any kind, as in themselves considered, but merely as conducing to that end which they are fit to attain. They receive all their goodness (which is but relative) from that whereunto they are appointed, in themselves no way desirable; as the cutting off a leg or an arm for the preservation of life, taking a bitter potion for health's sake, throwing corn and lading into the sea to prevent ship-wreck. Of which nature is the death of Christ, as we shall afterward declare.

VI. These things being thus proposed in general, our next task must be to accommodate them to the present business in hand; which we shall do in order, by laying down the *agent* working, the *means* wrought, and the *end* effected, in the great work of our redemption; for these three must be orderly considered and distinctly, that we may have a right apprehension of the whole: into the first whereof, σὺν Θεῷ, we make an entrance in [chapter third.]

CHAPTER III.

Of the agent or chief author of the work of our redemption, and of the first thing distinctly ascribed to the person of the Father.

I. THE agent in, and chief author of, this great work of our redemption is the whole blessed Trinity; for all the works which outwardly are of the Deity are undivided and belong equally to each person, their distinct manner of subsistence and order being observed. It is true, there were sundry other instrumental causes in the oblation, or rather passion of Christ, but the work cannot in any sense be ascribed unto them;—for in respect of God the Father, the issue of their endeavours was exceeding contrary to their own intentions, and in the close they did nothing but what the " hand and counsel of God had before determined should be done," Acts iv. 28; and in respect of Christ they were no way able to accomplish what they aimed at, for he himself laid down his life, and none was able to take it from him, John x. 17, 18: so that they are to be excluded from this consideration. In the several persons of the holy Trinity, the joint author of the whole work, the Scripture proposeth distinct and sundry acts or operations peculiarly assigned unto them; which, according to our weak manner of apprehension, we are to consider severally and apart; which also we shall do, beginning with them that are ascribed to the Father.

II. Two peculiar acts there are in this work of our redemption by the blood of Jesus, which may be and are properly assigned to the person of the FATHER:—First, The sending of his Son into the world for this employment. Secondly, A laying the punishment due to our sin upon him.

1. The Father loves the world, and sends his Son to die: He "sent his Son into the world that the world through him might be saved," John iii. 16, 17. He " sending his Son in the likeness of sinful flesh, and for sin, condemned sin in the flesh, that the righteousness

of the law might be fulfilled in us," Rom. viii. 3, 4. He "set him forth
to be a propitiation through faith in his blood," chap. iii. 25. For
"when the fulness of the time was come, God sent forth his Son, made
of a woman, made under the law, to redeem them that were under
the law, that we might receive the adoption of sons," Gal. iv. 4, 5. So
more than twenty times in the Gospel of John there is mention of
this sending; and our Saviour describes himself by this periphrasis,
"Him whom the Father hath sent," John x. 36; and the Father
by this, "He who sent me," chap. v. 37. So that this action of
sending is appropriate to the Father, according to his promise that
he would "send us a Saviour, a great one, to deliver us," Isa. xix. 20;
and to the profession of our Saviour, "I have not spoken in secret
from the beginning; from the time that it was, there am I: and now
the Lord God, and his Spirit, hath sent me," Isa. xlviii. 16. Hence
the Father himself is sometimes called our Saviour: 1 Tim. i. 1,
"According to the commandment Θεοῦ σωτῆρος ἡμῶν,"—"of God our
Saviour." Some copies, indeed, read it, Θεοῦ καὶ σωτῆρος ἡμῶν,—"of
God and our Saviour;" but the interposition of that particle καὶ
arose, doubtless, from a misprision that Christ alone is called Saviour.
But directly this is the same with that parallel place of Tit. i. 3,
Κατ' ἐπιταγὴν τοῦ σωτῆρος ἡμῶν Θεοῦ,—"According to the commandment of God our Saviour," where no interposition of that conjunc-
tive particle can have place; the same title being also in other places
ascribed to him, as Luke i. 47, "My spirit hath rejoiced in God my
Saviour." As also 1 Tim. iv. 10, "We trust in the living God,
who is the Saviour of all men, specially of them that believe;"
though in this last place it be not ascribed unto him with reference
to his redeeming us by Christ, but his saving and preserving all by
his providence. So also Tit. ii. 10, iii. 4; Deut. xxxii. 15; 1 Sam.
x. 19; Ps. xxiv. 5, xxv. 5; Isa. xii. 2, xl. 10, xlv. 15; Jer. xiv. 8; Micah
vii. 7; Hab. iii. 18; most of which places have reference to his sending of Christ, which is also distinguished into three several acts,
which in order we must lay down: —

(1.) An authoritative imposition of the office of Mediator, which
Christ closed withal by his voluntary susception of it, willingly undergoing the office, wherein by dispensation the Father had and exercised a kind of superiority, which the Son, though "in the form
of God," humbled himself unto, Phil. ii. 6–8. And of this there may
conceived two parts:—

[1.] The *purposed imposition of his counsel*, or his eternal counsel for the setting apart of his Son incarnate to this office, saying
unto him, "Thou art my Son; this day have I begotten thee. Ask
of me, and I shall give thee the nations for thine inheritance, and the
uttermost parts of the earth for thy possession," Ps. ii. 7, 8. He said
unto him, "Sit thou at my right hand until I make thine enemies

thy footstool;" for " the LORD sware, and will not repent, Thou art a priest for ever after the order of Melchizedek," Ps. cx. 1, 4. He appointed him to be " heir of all things," Heb. i. 2, having " ordained him to be Judge of quick and dead," Acts x. 42; for unto this he was "ordained before the foundation of the world," 1 Pet. i. 20, and "determined, *ὁρισθείς*, to be the Son of God with power," Rom. i. 4, " that he might be the first-born among many brethren," chap. viii. 29. I know that this is an act eternally established in the mind and will of God, and so not to be ranged in order with the others, which are all temporary, and had their beginning in the fulness of time, of all which this first is the spring and fountain, according to that of James, Acts xv. 18, " Known unto God are all his works from the beginning of the world;" but yet, it being no unusual form of speaking that the purpose should also be comprehended in that which holds out the accomplishment of it, aiming at truth and not exactness, we pass it thus.

[2.] The actual *inauguration* or solemn admission of Christ into his office; " committing all judgment unto the Son," John v. 22; " making him to be both Lord and Christ," Acts ii. 36; " appointing him over his whole house," Heb. iii. 1–6;—which is that "anointing of the most Holy," Dan. ix. 24; God " anointing him with the oil of gladness above his fellows," Ps. xlv. 7: for the actual setting apart of Christ to his office is said to be by unction, because all those holy things which were types of him, as the ark, the altar, etc., were set apart and consecrated by anointing, Exod. xxx. 25–28, etc. To this also belongs that public testification by innumerable angels from heaven of his nativity, declared by one of them to the shepherds. " Behold," saith he, " I bring you good tidings of great joy, which shall be unto all people; for unto you is born this day in the city of David a Saviour, which is Christ the Lord," Luke ii. 10, 11;—which message was attended by and closed with that triumphant exultation of the host of heaven, " Glory be to God on high, on earth peace, towards men good-will," verse 14: with that redoubled voice which afterward came from the excellent glory, " This is my beloved Son, in whom I am well-pleased," Matt. iii. 17, xvii. 5; 2 Pet. i. 17. If these things ought to be distinguished and placed in their own order, they may be considered in these three several acts:— First, The glorious proclamation which he made of his nativity, when he "prepared him a body," Heb. x. 5, bringing his First-begotten into the world, and saying, " Let all the angels of God worship him," chap. i. 6, sending them to proclaim the message which we before recounted. Secondly, Sending the Spirit visibly, in the form of a dove, to light upon him at the time of his baptism, Matt. iii. 16, when he was endued with a fulness thereof, for the accomplishment of the work and discharge of the office whereunto he was designed, attended with that voice whereby he owned him from heaven as his only-beloved. Thirdly, The "crowning of him with glory and honour," in his resurrection, ascension, and sitting down "on the right hand of the Majesty on high," Heb. i. 3; setting "him as his king upon his holy hill of Zion," Ps. ii. 6; when "all power was given unto him in heaven and in earth," Matt. xxviii. 18, "all things being put under his feet," Heb. ii. 7, 8; himself highly exalted, and "a name given him above every name, that at," etc., Phil. ii. 9–11. Of which it pleased him to appoint witnesses of all sorts; —angels from heaven, Luke xxiv. 4, Acts i. 10 ; the dead out of the graves, Matt. xxvii. 52; the apostles among and unto the living, Acts ii. 32; with those more than five hundred brethren, to whom he appeared at once, 1 Cor. xv. 6. Thus gloriously was he inaugurated into his office, in the several acts and degrees thereof, God saying unto him, "It is a light thing that thou shouldest be my servant to raise up the tribes of Jacob, and to restore the preserved of Israel: I will also give thee for a light to the Gentiles, that thou mayest be my salvation unto the end of the earth," Isa. xlix. 6.

Between these two acts I confess there intercedes a twofold promise of God;—one, of giving a Saviour to his people, a Mediator, according to his former purpose, as Gen. iii. 15, "The seed of the woman shall break the serpent's head;" and, "The sceptre shall not depart from Judah, nor a lawgiver from between his feet, till Shiloh come; and unto him shall the gathering of the people be," chap. xlix. 10. Which he also foresignified by many sacrifices and other types, with prophetical predictions: "Of which salvation the prophets have inquired and searched diligently, who prophesied of the grace that should come unto you; searching what or what manner of time the Spirit of Christ which was in them did signify, when it testified beforehand the sufferings of Christ, and the glory that should follow. Unto whom it was revealed, that not unto themselves, but unto us they did minister the things which are now reported unto you by them that have preached the gospel unto you with the Holy Ghost sent down from heaven; which things the angels desire to look into," 1 Pet. i. 10–12. The other is a promise of applying the benefits purchased by this Saviour so designed to them that should believe on him, to be given in fulness of time, according to the former promises; telling Abraham, that " in his seed all the families of the earth should be blessed," and justifying himself by the same faith, Gen. xii. 3, xv. 6. But these things belong rather to the application wholly, which was equal both before and after his actual mission.

(2.) The second act of the Father's sending the Son is the furnishing of him in his sending with a fulness of all gifts and graces that might any way be requisite for the office he was to undertake, the work he was to undergo, and the charge he had over the house of God. There was, indeed, in Christ a twofold fulness and perfection of all spiritual excellencies:—

First, the *natural* all-sufficient perfection of his Deity, as one with his Father in respect of his divine nature: for his glory was "the glory of the only-begotten of the Father," John i. 14. He was "in the form of God, and thought it not robbery to be equal with God," Phil. ii. 6; being the "fellow of the LORD of hosts," Zech. xiii. 7. Whence that glorious appearance, Isa. vi. 3, 4, when the seraphims cried one to another, and said, "Holy, holy, holy, is the LORD of hosts: the whole earth is full of his glory. And the posts of the door moved at the voice of him that cried, and the house was filled with smoke." And the prophet cried, "Mine eyes have seen the King, the LORD of hosts," verse 5. Even concerning this vision the apostle saith, "Isaiah saw him, and spake of his glory," John xii. 41. Of which glory ἐκένωσε, he as it were emptied himself for a season, when he was "found in the form" or condition "of a servant, humbling himself unto death," Phil. ii. 7, 8; laying aside that glory which attended his Deity, outwardly appearing to have "neither form, nor beauty, nor comeliness, that he should be desired," Isa. liii. 2. But this fulness we do not treat of, it being not communicated to him, but essentially belonging to his person, which is eternally begotten of the person of his Father.

The second fulness that was in Christ was a *communicated* fulness, which was in him by dispensation from his Father, bestowed upon him to fit him for his work and office as he was and is the "Mediator between God and men, the man Christ Jesus," 1 Tim. ii. 5; not as he is the "LORD of hosts," but as he is "Emmanuel, God with us," Matt. i. 23; as he was a "son given to us, called Wonderful, Counsellor, The mighty God, The everlasting Father, The Prince of Peace, upon whose shoulder the government was to be," Isa. ix. 6. It is a fulness of grace; not that essential which is of the nature of the Deity, but that which is habitual and infused into the humanity as personally united to the other; which, though it be not absolutely infinite, as the other is, yet it extends itself to all perfections of grace, both in respect of parts and degrees. There is no grace that is not in Christ, and every grace is in him in the highest degree: so that whatsoever the perfection of grace, either for the several kinds or respective advancements thereof, requireth, is in him habitually, by the collation of his Father for this very purpose, and for the accomplishment of the work designed; which, though (as before) it cannot properly be said to be infinite, yet it is boundless and endless. It is in him as the light in the beams of the sun, and as water in a living fountain which can never fail. He is the "candlestick" from whence the "golden pipes do empty the golden oil out of themselves," Zech. iv. 12, into all that are his; for he is "the beginning, the first-born from the

dead, in all things having the pre-eminence; for it pleased the
Father that in him should all fulness dwell," Col. i. 18, 19.   In him
he caused to be "hid all the treasures of wisdom and knowledge,"
chap. ii. 3; and "in him dwelt all the fulness of the Godhead σωματικῶς,"
substantially or personally, verse 9; that " of his fulness we might
all receive grace for grace," John i. 16, in a continual supply.   So
that, setting upon the work of redemption, he looks upon this in the
first place.   " The Spirit of the Lord GOD," saith he, " is upon me;
because the LORD hath anointed me to preach good tidings unto
the meek; he hath sent me to bind up the broken-hearted, to
proclaim liberty to the captives, and the opening of the prison to
them that are bound; to proclaim the acceptable year of the LORD,
and the day of vengeance of our God; to comfort all that mourn,"
Isa. lxi. 1, 2.   And this was the "anointing with the oil of gladness"
which he had " above his fellows," Ps. xlv. 7; " it was upon his head,
and ran down to his beard, yea, down to the skirts of his garments,"
Ps. cxxxiii. 2, that every one covered with the garment of his
righteousness might be made partaker of it.   " The Spirit of the
LORD did rest upon him, the spirit of wisdom and understanding, the
spirit of counsel and might, the spirit of knowledge and of the fear
of the LORD," Isa. xi. 2; and that not in parcels and beginnings as in
us, proportioned to our measure and degrees of sanctification, but in
a fulness, for " he received not the Spirit by measure," John iii. 34;
—that is, it was not so with him when he came to the full measure
of the stature of his age, as Eph. iv. 13; for otherwise it was manifested in him and collated on him by degrees, for he " increased in
wisdom and stature, and in favour with God and man," Luke ii. 52.
Hereunto was added " all power in heaven and earth, which was
given unto him," Matt. xxviii. 18; " power over all flesh, to give
eternal life to as many as he would," John xvii. 2.   Which we might
branch into many particulars, but so much shall suffice to set forth
the second act of God in sending his Son.

(3.) The third act of this sending is his entering into covenant
and compact with his Son concerning the work to be undertaken,
and the issue or event thereof; of which there be two parts:—

First, His promise to protect and assist him in the accomplishment
and perfect fulfilling of the whole business and dispensation about
which he was employed, or which he was to undertake.   The Father
engaged himself, that for his part, upon his Son's undertaking this
great work of redemption, he would not be wanting in any assistance
in trials, strength against oppositions, encouragement against temptations, and strong consolation in the midst of terrors, which might be
any way necessary or requisite to carry him on through all difficulties
to the end of so great an employment;—upon which he undertakes
this heavy burden, so full of misery and trouble: for the Father

before this engagement requires no less of him than that he should " become a Saviour, and be afflicted in all the affliction of his people," Isa. lxiii. 8, 9 : yea, that although he were " the fellow of the LORD of hosts," yet he should endure the " sword" that was drawn against him as the "shepherd" of the sheep, Zech. xiii. 7; " treading the wine-press alone, until he became red in his apparel," Isa. lxiii. 2, 3 : yea, to be " stricken, smitten of God, and afflicted; wounded for our trans-gressions, and bruised for our iniquities; to be bruised and put to grief; to make his soul an offering for sin, and to bear the iniquity of many," Isa. liii.; to be destitute of comfort so far as to cry, " My God, my God, why hast thou forsaken me?" Ps. xxii. 1. No wonder, then, if upon this undertaking the Lord promised to make "his mouth like a sharp sword, to hide him in the shadow of his hand, to make him a polished shaft, and to hide him in his quiver, to make him his servant in whom he would be glorified," Isa. xlix. 2, 3; that though " the kings of the earth should set themselves, and the rulers take counsel together, against him, yet he would laugh them to scorn, and set him as king upon his holy hill of Zion," Ps. ii. 2, 4, 6; though the " builders did reject him," yet he should " be-come the head of the corner," to the amazement and astonishment of all the world, Ps. cxviii. 22, 23; Matt. xxi. 42, Mark xii. 10, Luke xx. 17, Acts iv. 11, 12, 1 Pet. ii. 4; yea, he would "lay him for a foundation, a stone, a tried stone, a precious corner-stone, a sure foun-dation," Isa. xxviii. 16, that " whosoever should fall upon him should be broken, but upon whomsoever he should fall he should grind him to powder," Matt. xxi. 44. Hence arose that confidence of our Saviour in his greatest and utmost trials, being assured, by virtue of his Father's engagement in this covenant, upon a treaty with him about the redemption of man, that he would never leave him nor forsake him. " I gave," saith he, " my back to the smiters, and my cheeks to them that plucked off the hair: I hid not my face from shame and spitting," Isa. l. 6. But with what confidence, blessed Saviour, didst thou undergo all this shame and sorrow! Why, " The Lord GOD will help me; therefore shall I not be confounded: therefore have I set my face like a flint, and I know that I shall not be ashamed. He is near that justifieth me; who will contend with me? let us stand together: who is mine adversary? let him come near to me. Behold, the Lord GOD will help me; who is he that shall condemn me? lo ! they shall all wax old as a garment; the moth shall eat them up," verses 7-9. With this assurance he was brought as a " lamb to the slaughter, and as a sheep before her shearers is dumb, so he opened not his mouth," Isa. liii. 7: for " when he was reviled, he reviled not again; when he suffered, he threatened not; but committed himself to him that judgeth righteously," 1 Pet. ii. 23. So that the ground of our Saviour's confidence and assurance in this great undertaking, and a strong motive to exercise his graces received in the utmost endurings, was this engagement of his Father upon this compact of assistance and protection.

Secondly, [His promise] of success, or a good issue out of all his sufferings, and a happy accomplishment and attainment of the end of his great undertaking. Now, of all the rest this chiefly is to be considered, as directly conducing to the business proposed, which yet would not have been so clear without the former considerations; for whatsoever it was that God promised his Son should be fulfilled and attained by him, that certainly was it at which the Son aimed in the whole undertaking, and designed it as the end of the work that was committed to him, and which alone he could and did claim upon the accomplishment of his Father's will. What this was, and the promises whereby it is at large set forth, ye have Isa. xlix.: "Thou shalt be my servant," saith the Lord, " to raise up the tribes of Jacob, and to restore the preserved of Israel: I will also give thee for a light to the Gentiles, that thou mayest be my salvation to the end of the earth. Kings shall see and arise, princes also shall worship, because of the LORD that is faithful." And he will certainly accomplish this engagement: " I will preserve thee, and give thee for a covenant of the people, to establish the earth, to cause to inherit the desolate heritages; that thou mayest say to the prisoners, Go forth; to them that are in darkness, Show yourselves. They shall feed in the ways, and their pastures shall be in all high places. They shall not hunger nor thirst; neither shall the heat nor sun smite them: for he that hath mercy on them shall lead them, even by the springs of water shall he guide them. And I will make all my mountains a way, and my highways shall be exalted. Behold, these shall come from far: and, lo, these from the north and from the west; and these from the land of Sinim," verses 6–12. By all which expressions the Lord evidently and clearly engageth himself to his Son, that he should gather to himself a glorious church of believers from among Jews and Gentiles, through all the world, that should be brought unto him, and certainly fed in full pasture, and refreshed by the springs of water, all the spiritual springs of living water which flow from God in Christ for their everlasting salvation. This, then, our Saviour certainly aimed at, as being the promise upon which he undertook the work,—the gathering of the sons of God together, their bringing unto God, and passing to eternal salvation; which being well considered, it will utterly overthrow the general ransom or universal redemption, as afterward will appear. In the 53d chapter of the same prophecy, the Lord is more express and punctual in these promises to his Son, assuring him that when he "made his soul an offering for sin, he should see his seed, and prolong his days, and the pleasure of the LORD should prosper in his hand; that he should see of the travail of his soul, and be satisfied; by his knowledge he should justify many; that he should divide a portion with the great, and the spoil with the strong," verses 10–12. He was, you see, to see his seed by covenant, and to raise up a spiritual seed unto God, a faithful people, to be prolonged and preserved throughout all generations; which, how well it consists with their persuasion who in terms have affirmed " that the death of Christ might have had its full and utmost effect and yet none be saved," I cannot see, though some have boldly affirmed it and all the assertors of universal redemption do tacitly grant, when they come to the assigning of the proper ends and effects of the death of Christ. " The pleasure of the LORD," also, was to " prosper in his hand;" which what it was he declares, Heb. ii. 10, even " bringing of many sons unto glory;" for " God sent his only-begotten Son into the world that we might live through him," 1 John iv. 9; as we shall afterward more abundantly declare. But the promises of God made unto him in their agreement, and so, consequently, his own aim and intention, may be seen in nothing more manifestly than in the request that our Saviour makes upon the accomplishment of the work about which he was sent; which certainly was neither for more nor less than God had engaged himself to him for. " I have," saith he, " glorified thee on earth, I have finished the work which thou gavest me to do," John xvii. 4. And now, what doth he require after the manifestation of his eternal glory, of which for a season he had emptied himself, verse 5? Clearly a full confluence of the love of God and fruits of that love upon all his elect, in faith, sanctification, and glory. God gave them unto him, and he sanctified himself to be a sacrifice for their sake, praying for their sanctification, verses 17–19; their preservation in peace, or communion one with another, and union with God, verses 20, 21, " I pray not for these alone" (that is, his apostles), " but for them also which shall believe on me through their word; that they all may be one; as thou, Father, art in me, and I in thee, that they also may be one in us;" and lastly, their glory, verse 24, " Father, I will that they also, whom thou hast given me, be with me where I am; that they may behold my glory, which thou hast given me." All which several *postulata* are no doubt grounded upon the fore-cited promises, which by his Father were made unto him. And in this, not one word concerning all and every one, but expressly the contrary, verse 9. Let this, then, be diligently observed, that the promise of God unto his Son, and the request of the Son unto his Father, are directed to this peculiar end of bringing sons unto God. And this is the first act, consisting of these three particulars.

2. The second is of laying upon him the punishment of sins, everywhere ascribed unto the Father: " Awake, O sword, against my shepherd, against the man that is my fellow, saith the LORD of

hosts: smite the shepherd, and the sheep shall be scattered," Zech.
xiii. 7.   What here is set down imperatively, by way of command, is
in the gospel indicatively expounded: " I will smite the shepherd,
and the sheep of the flock shall be scattered abroad," Matt. xxvi. 31.
" He was stricken, smitten of God, and afflicted;" yea, " the LORD
laid upon him the iniquity of us all;" yea, "it pleased the LORD to
bruise him, and to put him to grief," Isa. liii. 4, 6, 10.   " He made
him to be sin for us, who knew no sin; that we might be made the
righteousness of God in him," 2 Cor. v. 21.   The adjunct in both
places is put for the subject, as the opposition between his being
made sin and our being made righteousness declareth.   " Him who
knew no sin,"—that is, who deserved no punishment,—" him hath
he made to be sin," or laid the punishment due to sin upon him.   Or
perhaps, in the latter place, sin may be taken for an offering or sacrifice
for the expiation of sin, ἁμαρτία answering in this place to the word
חטאת in the Old Testament, which signifieth both sin and the sacrifice
for it.   And this the Lord did; for as for Herod, Pontius Pilate, with
the Gentiles, and the people of Israel, when they were gathered together, they did nothing but " what his hand and counsel had determined before to be done," Acts iv. 27, 28.   Whence the great shak-
ings of our Saviour were in his close conflict with his Father's wrath,
and that burden which by himself he immediately imposed on him.
When there was no hand or instrument outwardly appearing to put
him to any suffering or cruciating torment, then he " began to be
sorrowful, even unto death," Matt. xxvi. 37, 38; to wit, when he was
in the garden with his three choice apostles, before the traitor or
any of his accomplices appeared, then was he "sore amazed, and very
heavy," Mark xiv. 33.   That was the time, " in the days of his flesh,
when he offered up prayers and supplications with strong crying and
tears unto him that was able to save him from death," Heb. v. 7;
which how he performed the evangelist describeth, Luke xxii. 43, 44:
" There appeared an angel unto him from heaven, strengthening
him.   But being in an agony he prayed more earnestly: and his sweat
was as it were great drops of blood falling down to the ground."
Surely it was a close and strong trial, and that immediately from his
Father, he now underwent; for how meekly and cheerfully doth he
submit, without any regret or trouble of spirit, to all the cruelty of
men and violence offered to his body, until this conflict being renewed again, he cries, " My God, my God, why hast thou forsaken
me?"   And this, by the way, will be worth our observation, that we
may know with whom our Saviour chiefly had to do, and what was
that which he underwent for sinners; which also will give some light
to the grand query concerning the persons of them for whom he
undertook all this.   His sufferings were far from consisting in mere
corporal perpessions and afflictions, with such impressions upon his

soul and spirit as were the effects and issues only of them. It was no more nor less than the curse of the law of God which he underwent for us: for he freed us from the curse " by being made a curse," Gal. iii. 13; which contained all the punishment that was due to sin, either in the severity of God's justice, or according to the exigence of that law which required obedience. That the execration of the law should be only *temporal death*, as the law was considered to be the instrument of the Jewish polity, and serving that economy or dispensation, is true; but that it should be no more, as it is the universal rule of obedience, and the bond of the covenant between God and man, is a foolish dream. Nay, but in dying for us Christ did not only aim at our good, but also directly died in our stead. The punishment due to our sin and the chastisement of our peace was upon him; which that it was the pains of hell, in their nature and being, in their weight and pressure, though not in tendence and continuance (it being impossible that he should be detained by death), who can deny and not be injurious to the justice of God, which will inevitably inflict those pains to eternity upon sinners? It is true, indeed, there is a relaxation of the law in respect of the persons suffering, God admitting of commutation; as in the old law, when in their sacrifices the life of the beast was accepted (in respect to the carnal part of the ordinances) for the life of the man. This is fully revealed, and we believe it; but for any change of the punishment, in respect of the nature of it, where is the least intimation of any alteration? We conclude, then, this second act of God, in laying the punishment on him for us, with that of the prophet, " All we like sheep have gone astray; we have turned every one to his own way; and the LORD hath laid on him the iniquity of us all," Isa. liii. 6: and add thereunto this observation, that it seems strange to me that Christ should undergo the pains of hell in their stead who lay in the pains of hell before he underwent those pains, and shall continue in them to eternity; for " their worm dieth not, neither is their fire quenched." To which I may add this dilemma to our Universalists:—God imposed his wrath due unto, and Christ underwent the pains of hell for, either all the sins of all men, or all the sins of some men, or some sins of all men.   If the last, some sins of all men, then have all men some sins to answer for, and so shall no man be saved; for if God enter into judgment with us, though it were with all mankind for one sin, no flesh should be justified in his sight: " If the LORD should mark iniquities, who should stand?" Ps. cxxx. 3.   We might all go to cast all that we have " to the moles and to the bats, to go into the clefts of the rocks, and into the tops of the ragged rocks, for fear of the LORD, and for the glory of his majesty," Isa. ii. 20, 21. If the second, that is it which we affirm, that Christ in their stead and room suffered for all the sins of all the elect in the world. If the first,

why, then, are not all freed from the punishment of all their sins?
You will say, " Because of their unbelief; they will not believe." But
this unbelief, is it a sin, or not? If not, why should they be punished
for it? If it be, then Christ underwent the punishment due to it,
or not. If so, then why must that hinder them more than their
other sins for which he died from partaking of the fruit of his death?
If he did not, then did he not die for all their sins. Let them choose
which part they will.

CHAPTER IV.

Of those things which in the work of redemption are peculiarly ascribed to the
person of the Son.

SECONDLY, The SON was an *agent* in this great work, concurring
by a voluntary susception, or willing undertaking of the office imposed on him; for when the Lord said, " Sacrifice and offering he
would not: in burnt-offerings and sacrifices for sin he had no pleasure,"
then said Christ, " Lo, I come, (in the volume of the book it is written
of me,) to do thy will, O God," Heb. x. 6, 7. All other ways being
rejected as insufficient, Christ undertaketh the task, " in whom alone
the Father was well pleased," Matt. iii. 17. Hence he professeth
that " he came not to do his own will, but the will of him that sent
him," John vi. 38; yea, that it was his meat and drink to do his
Father's will, and to finish his work, chap. iv. 34. The first words
that we find recorded of him in the Scripture are to the same purpose, " Wist ye not that I must be about my Father's business?" Luke
ii. 49. And at the close of all he saith, " I have glorified thee on the
earth; I have finished the work which thou gavest me to do," John
xvii. 4; calling it everywhere his Father's work that he did, or his
Father's will which he came to accomplish, with reference to the
imposition which we before treated of. Now, this undertaking of
the Son may be referred to three heads. The first being a common
foundation for both the others, being as it were the means in respect
of them as the end, and yet in some sort partaking of the nature of
a distinct action, with a goodness in itself in reference to the main
end proposed to all three, we shall consider it apart; and that is,—
First, His *incarnation*, as usually it is called, or his *taking of flesh*,
and pitching his tent amongst us, John i. 14. His "being made of a
woman," Gal. iv. 4, is usually called his ἐνσάρκωσις, or incarnation;
for this was " the mystery of godliness, that God should be manifested
in the flesh," 1 Tim. iii. 16, thereby assuming not any singular person, but our human nature, into personal union with himself. For,
" forasmuch as the children are partakers of flesh and blood, he also

himself likewise took part of the same; that through death he might destroy him that had the power of death, that is, the devil," Heb. ii. 14. It was the children that he considered, the "children whom the Lord gave him," verse 13. Their participation in flesh and blood moved him to partake of the same,—not because all the world, all the posterity of Adam, but because the *children* were in that condition; for their sakes he sanctified himself. Now, this emptying of the Deity, this humbling of himself, this dwelling amongst us, was the sole act of the second person, or the divine nature in the second person, the Father and the Spirit having no concurrence in it but by liking, approbation, and eternal counsel.

Secondly, His *oblation*, or "offering himself up to God for us without spot, to purge our consciences from dead works," Heb. ix. 14; "for he loved us, and washed us from our sins in his own blood," Rev. i. 5. "He loved the church, and gave himself for it, that he might sanctify and cleanse it," Eph. v. 25, 26; taking the cup of wrath at his Father's hands due to us, and drinking it off, "but not for himself," Dan. ix. 26: for, "for our sakes he sanctified himself," John xvii. 19, that is, to be an offering, an oblation for sin; for "when we were yet without strength, in due time Christ died for the ungodly," Rom. v. 6;—this being that which was typified out by all the institutions, ordinances, and sacrifices of old; which when they were to have an end, then said Christ, "Lo, I come to do thy will." Now, though the perfecting or consummating of this oblation be set out in the Scripture chiefly in respect of what Christ suffered, and not so much in respect of what he did, because it is chiefly considered as the means used by these three blessed agents for the attaining of a farther end, yet in respect of his own voluntary giving up himself to be so an oblation and a sacrifice, without which it would not have been of any value (for if the will of Christ had not been in it, it could never have purged our sins), therefore, in that regard, I refer it to his actions. He was the "Lamb of God, which taketh away the sin of the world," John i. 29; the Lamb of God, which himself had provided for a sacrifice. And how did this Lamb behave himself in it? with unwillingness and struggling? No; he opened not his mouth: "He was brought as a lamb to the slaughter, and as a sheep before her shearers is dumb, so he opened not his mouth," Isa. liii. 7. Whence he saith, "I lay down my life. No man taketh it from me, but I lay it down of myself. I have power to lay it down, and I have power to take it again," John x. 17, 18. He might have been cruciated on the part of God; but his death could not have been an oblation and offering had not his will concurred. "But he loved me," saith the apostle, "and gave himself for me," Gal. ii. 20. Now, that alone deserves the name of a gift which is from a free and a willing mind, as Christ's was when "he loved us, and gave himself for us an offering and a sacrifice to God for a sweet-smelling savour," Eph. v. 2. He does it cheerfully: "Lo, I come to do thy will, O God," Heb. x. 9; and so "his own self bare our sins in his own body on the tree," 1 Pet. ii. 24. Now, this oblation or offering of Christ I would not tie up to any one thing, action, or passion, performance, or suffering; but it compriseth the whole economy and dispensation of God manifested in the flesh and conversing among us, with all those things which he performed in the days of his flesh, when he offered up prayers and supplications, with strong cries and tears, until he had fully "by himself purged our sins, and sat down on the right hand of the Majesty on high," Heb. i. 3, "expecting till his enemies be made his footstool," chap. x. 13,—all the whole dispensation of his coming and ministering, until he had given his soul a price of redemption for many, Matt. xxvi. 28. But for his entering into the holy of holies, sprinkled with his own blood, and appearing so for us before the majesty of God, by some accounted as the continuation of his oblation, we may refer unto,—

Thirdly, His *intercession* for all and every one of those for whom he gave himself for an oblation. He did not suffer for them, and then refuse to intercede for them; he did not do the greater, and omit the less. The price of our redemption is more precious in the eyes of God and his Son than that it should, as it were, be cast away on perishing souls, without any care taken of what becomes of them afterward. Nay, this also is imposed on Christ, with a promise annexed: "Ask of me," saith the Lord, "and I will give thee the nations for thine inheritance, and the uttermost parts of the earth for thy possession," Ps. ii. 8; who accordingly tells his disciples that he had more work to do for them in heaven. "I go," saith he, "to prepare a place for you, that I may come again and receive you unto myself," John xiv. 2, 3. For as "the high priest went into the second [tabernacle] alone once every year, not without blood, which he offered for himself and the errors of the people," Heb. ix. 7; so "Christ being come an high priest of good things to come, by his own blood entered once into the holy place, having obtained eternal redemption for us," verses 11, 12. Now, what was this holy place whereinto he entered thus sprinkled with the blood of the covenant? and to what end did he enter into it? Why, "he is not entered into the holy places made with hands, which are the figures of the true; but into heaven itself, now to appear in the presence of God for us," verse 24. And what doth he there appear for? Why, to be our advocate, to plead our cause with God, for the application of the good things procured by his oblation unto all them for whom he was an offering; as the apostle tells us, "If any man sin, we have an advocate with the Father, Jesus Christ the righteous," 1 John ii. 1. Why, how comes that to pass? "He is the propitiation for our sins," verse 2. His being ἱλασμός, a propitiatory sacrifice for our sins, is the foundation of his interceding, the ground of it; and, therefore, they both belong to the same persons. Now, by the way, we know that Christ refused to pray for the world, in opposition to his elect. " I pray for them," saith he: " I pray not for the world, but for them thou hast given me," John xvii. 9. And therefore there was no foundation for such an interceding for them, because he was not ἱλασμός for them. Again; we know the Father always heareth the Son (" I knew," saith he, " that thou hearest me always," chap. xi. 42), that is, so to grant his request, according to the fore-mentioned engagement, Ps. ii. 8; and, therefore, if he should intercede for all, all should undoubtedly be saved, for " he is able to save them to the uttermost that come unto God by him, seeing he ever liveth to make intercession for them," Heb. vii. 25. Hence is that confidence of the apostle, upon that intercession of Christ, " Who shall lay any thing to the charge of God's elect? It is God that justifieth. Who is he that condemneth? It is Christ that died, yea rather, that is risen again, who is even at the right hand of God, who also maketh intercession for us," Rom. viii. 33, 34. Where, also, we cannot but observe that those for whom he died may assuredly conclude he maketh intercession for them, and that none shall lay any thing to their charge,—which breaks the neck of the general ransom; for according to that, he died for millions that have no interest in his intercession, who shall have their sins laid to their charge, and perish under them: which might be farther cleared up from the very nature of this intercession, which is not a humble, dejected supplication, which beseems not that glorious state of advancement which he is possessed of that sits at the right hand of the Majesty on high, but an authoritative presenting himself before the throne of his Father, sprinkled with his own blood, for the making out to his people all spiritual things that are procured by his oblation, saying, " Father, I will that those whom thou hast given me be with me where I am," John xvii. 24. So that for whomsoever he suffered, he appears for them in heaven with his satisfaction and merit. Here, also, we must call to mind what the Father promised his Son upon his undertaking of this employment; for there is no doubt but that for that, and that alone, doth Christ, upon the accomplishment of the whole, intercede with him about: which was in sum that he might be the captain of salvation to all that believe on him, and effectually bring many sons to glory. And hence it is, having such an high priest over the house of God, we may draw near with the full assurance of faith, for by one offering he hath perfected for ever them that are sanctified, Heb. x. 14. But of this more must be said afterward.

CHAPTER V.

The peculiar actions of the Holy Spirit in this business.

THIRDLY, IN few words we may consider the actions of that agent, who in order is the *third* in that blessed *One*, whose all is the whole, the HOLY SPIRIT, who is evidently concurring, in his own distinct operation, to all the several chief or grand parts of this work. We may refer them to three heads:—

First, The incarnation of the Son, with his plenary assistance in the course of his conversation whilst he dwelt amongst us; for his mother was found ἐν γαστρὶ ἔχουσα, "to have conceived in her womb of the Holy Ghost," Matt. i. 18. If you ask, with Mary, how that could be? the angel resolves both her and us, as far as it is lawful for us to be acquainted with these mysterious things: Luke i. 35, "The Holy Ghost shall come upon thee, and the power of the Highest shall overshadow thee: therefore also that holy thing which shall be born of thee shall be called the Son of God." It was an overshadowing power in the Spirit: so called by an allusion taken from fowls that cover their eggs, that so by their warmth young may be hatched; for by the sole power of the Spirit was this conception, who did "incubare fœtui," as in the beginning of the world. Now, in process, as this child was conceived by the power, so he was filled with the Spirit, and "waxed strong" in it, Luke i. 80; until, having received a fulness thereof, and not by any limited measure, in the gifts and graces of it, he was thoroughly furnished and fitted for his great undertaking.

Secondly, In his *oblation*, or passion (for they are both the same, with several respects,—one to what he suffered, the other to what he did with, by, and under those sufferings), how "by the Eternal Spirit he offered himself without spot to God," Heb. ix. 14: whether it be meant of the offering himself a bloody sacrifice on the cross, or his presentation of himself continually before his Father,— it is by the Eternal Spirit. The willing offering himself through that Spirit was the eternal fire under this sacrifice, which made it acceptable unto God. That which some contend, that by the eternal Spirit is here meant our Saviour's own Deity, I see no great ground for. Some Greek and Latin copies read, not, as we commonly, Πνεύματος αἰωνίου, but Πνεύματος ἁγίου, and so the doubt is quite removed: and I see no reason why he may not as well be said to offer himself through the Holy Spirit, as to be "declared to be the Son of God, according to the Spirit of holiness, by the resurrection from the dead," as Rom. i. 4; as also to be "quickened by the Spirit," 1 Pet. iii. 18. The working of the Spirit was required as well in his oblation as resurrection, in his dying as quickening.

Thirdly, In his *resurrection;* of which the apostle, Rom. viii. 11, " But if the Spirit of him that raised up Jesus from the dead dwell in you, he that raised up Christ from the dead shall also quicken your mortal bodies by his Spirit that dwelleth in you." And thus have we discovered the blessed agents and undertakers in this work, their several actions and orderly concurrence unto the whole; which, though they may be thus distinguished, yet they are not so divided but that every one must be ascribed to the whole nature, whereof each person is "in solidum" partaker. And as they begin it, so they will jointly carry along the application of it unto its ultimate issue and accomplishment; for we must "give thanks to the Father, which hath made us meet" (that is, by his Spirit) " to be partakers of the inheritance of the saints in light: who hath delivered us from the power of darkness, and hath translated us into the kingdom of his dear Son: in whom we have redemption through his blood, even the forgiveness of sins," Col. i. 12, 13.

CHAPTER VI.

The means used by the fore-recounted agents in this work.

OUR next employment, following the order of execution, not intention, will be the discovery or laying down of the *means* in this work; which are, indeed, no other but the several actions before recounted, but now to be considered under another respect,—as they are a means ordained for the obtaining of a proposed end; of which afterward. Now, because the several actions of Father and Spirit were all exercised towards Christ, and terminated in him, as God and man, he only and his performances are to be considered as the means in this work, the several concurrences of both the other persons before mentioned being presupposed as necessarily antecedent or concomitant.

The means, then, used or ordained by these agents for the end proposed is that whole *economy* or dispensation carried along to the end, from whence our Saviour Jesus Christ is called a Mediator; which may be, and are usually, as I mentioned before, distinguished into two parts:—First, his *oblation;* secondly, his *intercession.*

By his *oblation* we do not design only the particular offering of himself upon the cross an offering to his Father, as the Lamb of God without spot or blemish, when he bare our sins or carried them up with him in his own body on the tree, which was the sum and complement of his oblation and that wherein it did chiefly consist; but also his whole humiliation, or state of emptying himself, whether by yielding voluntary obedience unto the law, as being made under it, that he might be the end thereof to them that believe, Rom. x. 4, or by his subjection to the curse of the law, in the antecedent misery and suffering of life, as well as by submitting to death, the death of the cross: for no action of his as mediator is to be excluded from a concurrence to make up the whole means in this work. Neither by his *intercession* do I understand only that heavenly appearance of his in the most holy place for the applying unto us all good things purchased and procured by his oblation; but also every act of his exaltation conducing thereunto, from his resurrection to his "sitting down at the right hand of the Majesty on high, angels, and principalities, and powers, being made subject unto him." Of all which his resurrection, being the basis, as it were, and the foundation of the rest ("for if he is not risen, then is our faith in vain," 1 Cor. xv. 13, 14; and then are we "yet in our sins," verse 17; "of all men most miserable," verse 19), is especially to be considered, as that to which a great part of the effect is often ascribed; for "he was delivered for our offences, and was raised again for our justification," Rom. iv. 25;— where, and in such other places, by his resurrection the whole following dispensation and the perpetual intercession of Christ for us in heaven is intended; for "God raised up his son Jesus to bless us, in turning every one of us from our iniquities," Acts iii. 26.

Now, this whole dispensation, with especial regard to the death and blood-shedding of Christ, is the means we speak of, agreeably to what was said before of such in general; for it is not a thing in itself desirable for its own sake. The death of Christ had nothing in it (we speak of his sufferings distinguished from his obedience) that was good, but only as it conduced to a farther end, even the end proposed for the manifestation of God's glorious grace. What good was it, that Herod and Pontius Pilate, with the Gentiles and people of Israel, should, with such horrid villany and cruelty, gather themselves together against God's holy child, whom he had anointed? Acts iv. 27: or what good was it, that the Son of God should be made sin and a curse, to be bruised, afflicted, and to undergo such wrath as the whole frame of nature, as it were, trembled to behold? What good, what beauty and form is in all this, that it should be desired in itself and for itself? Doubtless none at all. It must, then, be looked upon as a means conducing to such an end; the glory and lustre thereof must quite take away all the darkness and confusion that was about the thing itself. And even so it was intended by the blessed agents in it, by "whose determinate counsel and foreknowledge he was delivered and slain," Acts ii. 23; there being done unto him "whatsoever his hand and counsel had determined," chap. iv. 28: which what it was must be afterward declared. Now, concerning the whole some things are to be observed:—

That though the *oblation* and *intercession* of Jesus Christ are distinct acts in themselves, and have distinct immediate products and issues assigned ofttimes unto them (which I should now have laid down, but that I must take up this in another place), yet they are not in any respect or regard to be divided or separated, as that the one should have any respect to any persons or any thing which the other also doth not in its kind equally respect. But there is this manifold union between them:—

First, In that they are both alike intended for the obtaining and accomplishing the same entire and complete end proposed,—to wit, the effectual bringing of many sons to glory, for the praise of God's grace; of which afterward.

Secondly, That what persons soever the one respecteth, in the good things it obtaineth, the same, all, and none else, doth the other respect, in applying the good things so obtained; for " he was delivered for our offences, and was raised again for our justification," Rom. iv. 25. That is, in brief, the object of the one is of no larger extent than the object of the other; or, for whom Christ offered himself, for all those, and only those, doth he intercede, according to his own word, " For their sake I sanctify myself" (to be an oblation), " that they also might be sanctified through the truth," John xvii. 19.

Thirdly, That the *oblation* of Christ is, as it were, the foundation of his intercession, inasmuch as by the oblation was procured every thing that, by virtue of his intercession, is bestowed; and that because the sole end why Christ procured any thing by his death was that it might be applied to them for whom it was so procured. The sum is, that the oblation and intercession of Jesus Christ are one entire means for the producing of the same effect, the very end of the oblation being that all those things which are bestowed by the intercession of Christ, and without whose application it should certainly fail of the end proposed in it, be effected accordingly; so that it cannot be affirmed that the death or offering of Christ concerned any one person or thing more, in respect of procuring any good, than his intercession doth for the collating of it: for, interceding there for all good purchased, and prevailing in all his intercessions (for the Father always hears his Son), it is evident that every one for whom Christ died must actually have applied unto him all the good things purchased by his death; which, because it is evidently destructive to the adverse cause, we must a little stay to confirm it, only telling you the main proof of it lies in our following proposal of assigning the proper end intended and effected by the death of Christ, so that the chief proof must be deferred until then. I shall now only propose those reasons which may be handled apart, not merely depending upon that.

CHAPTER VII.

Containing reasons to prove the oblation and intercession of Christ to be one entire means respecting the accomplishment of the same proposed end, and to have the same personal object.

I. OUR first reason is taken from that perpetual union which the Scripture maketh of both these, almost always joining them together, and so manifesting those things to be most inseparable which are looked upon as the distinct fruits and effects of them: " By his knowledge shall my righteous servant justify many, for he shall bear their iniquities," Isa. liii. 11. The actual justification of sinners, the immediate fruit of his *intercession*, certainly follows his bearing of their iniquities. And in the next verse they are of God so put together that surely none ought to presume to put them asunder: "He bare the sin of many" (behold his *oblation!*), " and made intercession for the transgressors;" even for those many transgressors whose sin he bears. And there is one expression in that chapter, verse 5, which makes it evident that the utmost application of all good things for which he *intercedes* is the immediate effect of his passion: " With his stripes we are healed." Our total healing is the fruit and procurement of his stripes, or the *oblation* consummated thereby. So also, Rom. iv. 25, " He was delivered for our offences, and was raised again for our justification." For whose offences he died, for their justification he rose;—and therefore, if he died for all, all must also be justified, or the Lord faileth in his aim and design, both in the death and resurrection of his Son; which though some have boldly affirmed, yet for my part I cannot but abhor the owning of so blasphemous a fancy. Rather let us close with that of the apostle, grounding the assurance of our eternal glory and freedom from all accusations upon the death of Christ, and that because his intercession also for us doth inseparably and necessarily follow it. " Who," saith he, " shall lay any thing to the charge of God's elect?" (It seems, also, that it is only they for whom Christ died.) " It is God that justifieth. Who is he that condemneth? It is Christ that died," (shall none, then, be condemned for whom Christ died? what, then, becomes of the general ransom?) " yea rather, who is risen again, who is even at the right hand of God, who also maketh intercession for us," Rom. viii. 33, 34. Here is an equal extent of the one and the other; those persons who are concerned in the one are all of them concerned in the other. That he died for *all* and intercedeth only for *some* will scarcely be squared to this text, especially considering the foundation of all this, which is (verse 32) that love of God which moved him to give up Christ to death for us all; upon which the apostle infers a kind of impossibility in not giving us all good things in him; which how it can be reconciled with their opinion who affirm that he gave his Son for millions to whom he will give neither grace nor glory, I cannot see. But we rest in that of the same apostle: " When we were yet without strength, in due time Christ died for the ungodly;" so that, "being now justified by his blood, we shall be saved from wrath through him," Rom. v. 6, 9;—the same between the oblation and intercession of Christ, with their fruits and effects, being intimated in very many other places.

II. To offer and to intercede, to sacrifice and to pray, are both acts of the same sacerdotal office, and both required in him who is a *priest;* so that if he omit either of these, he cannot be a faithful *priest* for them: if either he doth not offer for them, or not intercede for the success of his oblation on their behalf, he is wanting in the discharge of his office by him undertaken. Both these we find conjoined (as before) in Jesus Christ: 1 John ii. 1, 2, "If any man sin, we have an *advocate* with the Father, Jesus Christ the righteous: and he is the *propitiation* for our sins." He must be an *advocate* to intercede, as well as offer a propitiatory sacrifice, if he will be such a merciful *high priest* over the house of God as that the children should be encouraged to go to God by him. This the apostle exceedingly clears and evidently proves in the Epistle to the Hebrews, describing the priesthood of Christ, in the execution thereof, to consist in these two acts, of offering up himself in and by the shedding of his blood, and interceding for us to the utmost; upon the performance of both which he presseth an exhortation to draw near with confidence to the throne of grace, for he is " come an high priest of good things to come, not by the blood of goats and calves, but by his own blood he entered into the holy place, having obtained eternal redemption for us," chap. ix. 11, 12. His bloody oblation gave him entrance into the holy place not made with hands, there to accomplish the remaining part of his office, the apostle comparing his entrance into heaven for us with the entrance of the high priest into the holy place, with the blood of bulls and goats upon him, verses 12, 13 (which, doubtless, was to pray for them in whose behalf he had offered, verse 7); so presenting himself before his Father that his former oblation might have its efficacy. And hence he is said to have ἀπαράβατον ἱερωσύνην, because he continueth for ever, chap. vii. 24; so being " able to save to the uttermost them that come unto God by him, verse 25: wherefore we have "boldness to enter into the holiest by the blood of Jesus," chap. x. 19–22. So, then, it is evident that both these are acts of the same priestly office in Christ: and if he perform either of them for any, he must of necessity perform the other for them also; for he will not exercise any act or duty of his priestly function in their behalf for whom he is not a priest: and for whom he is a priest he must perform both, seeing he is faithful in the discharge of his function to the utmost in the behalf of the sinners for whom he undertakes. These two, then, oblation and intercession, must in respect of their objects be of equal extent, and can by no means be separated. And here, by the way (the thing being by this argument, in my apprehension, made so clear), I cannot but demand of those who oppose us about the death of Christ, whether they will sustain that he intercedeth for all or no;—if not, then they make him but half a priest; if they will, they must be necessitated either to defend this error, that all shall be saved, or own this blasphemy, that Christ is not heard of his Father, nor can prevail in his intercession, which yet the saints on earth are sure to do when they make their supplications according to the will of God, Rom. viii. 27, 1 John v. 14. Besides that, of our Saviour it is expressly said that the Father always heareth him, John xi. 42; and if that were true when he was yet in the *way*, in the days of his flesh, and had not finished the great work he was sent about, how much more then *now*, when, having done the will and finished the work of God, he is set down on the right hand of the Majesty on high, desiring and requesting the accomplishing of the promises that were made unto him upon his undertaking this work! of which before.

III. The *nature* of the intercession of Christ will also prove no less than what we assert, requiring an inseparable conjunction between it and its oblation: for as it is now perfected in heaven, it is not a humble dejection of himself, with cries, tears, and supplications; nay, it cannot be conceived to be *vocal*, by the way of entreaty, but merely *real*, by the presentation of himself, sprinkled with the blood of the covenant, before the throne of grace in our behalf. "For Christ," saith the apostle, "is not entered into the holy places made with hands, but into heaven itself, now to *appear* in the presence of God for us," Heb. ix. 24. His intercession there is an *appearing* for us in heaven in the presence of God, a demonstration of his sacred body, wherein for us he suffered: for (as we said before) the apostle, in the ninth to the Hebrews, compares his entrance into heaven for us unto the entrance of the high priest into the holy place, which was with the blood of bulls and goats upon him, verses 12, 13; our Saviour's being with his own blood, so presenting himself that his former oblation might have its perpetual efficacy, until the many sons given unto him are brought to glory. And herein his intercession consisteth, being nothing, as it were, but his oblation continued. He was a "Lamb slain from the foundation of the world," Rev. xiii. 8. Now, his intercession before his actual oblation in the fulness of time being nothing but a presenting of the engagement that was upon him for the work in due time to be accomplished, certainly that which follows it is nothing but a presenting of what according to that engagement is fulfilled; so that it is nothing but a continuation of his oblation in postulating, by remembrance and declaration of it, those things which by it were procured. How, then, is it possible that the one of these should be of larger compass and extent than the other? Can he be said to *offer* for them for whom he doth not *intercede*, when his *intercession* is nothing but a presenting of his oblation in the behalf of them for whom he suffered, and for the bestowing of those good things which by that were purchased.

IV. Again: if the *oblation* and death of Christ procured and obtained that every good thing should be bestowed which is actually conferred by the intervening of his *intercession*, then they have both of them the same aim, and are both means tending to one and the same end. Now, for the proof of this supposal, we must remember that which we delivered before concerning the *compact* and *agreement* that was between the Father and the Son, upon his voluntary engaging of himself unto this great work of redemption; for upon that engagement, the Lord proposed unto him as the end of his sufferings, and promised unto him as the reward of his labours, the fruit of his deservings, every thing which he afterward intercedeth for. Many particulars I before instanced in, and therefore now, to avoid repetition, will wholly omit them, referring the reader to chapter iii. for satisfaction: only, I shall demand what is the ground and foundation of our Saviour's *intercession*, understanding it to be by the way of entreaty, either virtual or formal, as it may be conceived to be either real or oral, for the obtaining of any thing. Must it not rest upon some promise made unto him? or is there any good bestowed that is not promised? Is it not apparent that the intercession of Christ doth rest on such a promise as Ps. ii. 8, "Ask of me, and I will give thee the heathen for thine inheritance," etc.? Now, upon what consideration was this promise and engagement made unto our Saviour? Was it not for his undergoing of that about which "the kings set themselves, and the rulers took counsel together against him," verse 2? which the apostles interpret of Herod and Pontius Pilate, with the people of the Jews, persecuting him to death, and doing to him "whatsoever the hand and counsel of God had before determined to be done," Acts iv. 27, 28. The intercession of Christ, then, being founded on promises made unto him, and these promises being nothing but an engagement to bestow and actually collate upon them for whom he suffered all those good things which his death and *oblation* did merit and purchase, it cannot be but that he intercedeth for all for whom he died, that his death procured all and every thing which upon his *intercession* is bestowed; and until they are bestowed, it hath not its full fruits and effects. For that which some say, namely, that the death of Christ doth procure that which is never granted, we shall see afterward whether it do not contradict Scripture, yea, and common sense.

V. Farther: what Christ hath put together let no man presume to put asunder; distinguish between them they may, but separate them they may not. Now, these things concerning which we treat (the oblation and intercession of Christ) are by himself conjoined, yea united, John xvii.; for there and then he did both offer and intercede. He did then as perfectly offer himself, in respect of his own will and intention, verse 4, as on the cross; and as perfectly intercede as now in heaven: who, then, can divide these things, or put them asunder? especially considering that the Scripture affirmeth that the one of them without the other would have been unprofitable, 1 Cor. xv. 17; for complete remission and redemption could not be obtained for us without the entering of our high priest into the most holy place, Heb. ix. 12.

VI. Lastly, A separating and dividing of the death and intercession of Christ, in respect to the objects of them, cuts off all that consolation which any soul might hope to attain by an assurance that Christ died for him. That the doctrine of the general ransom is an uncomfortable doctrine, cutting all the nerves and sinews of that strong consolation which God is so abundantly willing that we should receive, shall be afterward declared. For the present, I will only show how it trencheth upon our comfort in this particular. The main foundation of all the confidence and assurance whereof in this life we may be made partakers (which amounts to "joy unspeakable, and full of glory") ariseth from this strict connection of the *oblation* and *intercession* of Jesus Christ;—that by the one he hath procured all good things for us, and by the other he will procure them to be actually bestowed, whereby he doth never leave our sins, but follows them into every court, until they be fully pardoned and clearly expiated, Heb. ix. 26. He will never leave us until he hath saved to the uttermost them that come unto God by him. His death without his resurrection would have profited us nothing; all our faith in him had been in vain, 1 Cor. xv. 17. So that separated from it, with the intercession following, either in his own intention or in the several procurements of the one or the other, it will yield us but little consolation; but in this connection it is a sure bottom for a soul to build upon, Heb. vii. 25. "What good will it do me to be persuaded that Christ died for my sins, if, notwithstanding that, my sins may appear against me for my condemnation, where and when Christ will not appear for my justification?" If you will ask, with the apostle, "Who is he that condemneth?" "It is Christ that died," it may easily be answered, Rom. viii. 34. "Why, God by his law may condemn me, notwithstanding Christ died for me!" Yea, but saith the apostle, "He is risen again, and sitteth at the right hand of God, making intercession for us." He rests not in his death, but he will certainly make intercession for them for whom he died: and this alone gives firm

consolation. Our sins dare not appear, nor any of our accusers against
us, where he appeareth for us.   Cavilling objections against this text
shall be afterward considered; and so I hope I have sufficiently confirmed and proved what in the beginning of this chapter I did propose about the identity of the object of the oblation and intercession
of Jesus Christ.

CHAPTER VIII.

Objections against the former proposal answered.

BY what was said in the last chapter, it clearly appeareth that the
oblation and intercession of Christ are of equal compass and extent
in respect of their objects, or the persons for whom he once offered
himself and doth continually intercede, and so are to be looked on
as one joint *means* for the attaining of a certain proposed *end;* which
what it is comes next to be considered.   But because I find some objections laid by some against the former truth, I must remove them
before I proceed; which I shall do "as a man removeth dung until it
be all gone."

The sum of one of our former arguments was,—That to sacrifice and
intercede belong both to the same person, as high priest; which name
none can answer, neither hath any performed that office, until both
by him be accomplished.   Wherefore, our Saviour being the most
absolute, and, indeed, the only true high priest, in whom were really
all those perfections which in others received a weak typical representation, doth perform both these in the behalf of them for whose sakes
he was such.

I. An argument not unlike to this I find by some to be undertaken
to be answered, being in these words proposed, "The ransom and
mediation of Christ is no larger than his office of priest, prophet, and
king; but these offices pertain to his church and chosen therefore
his ransom pertains to them only."

The intention and meaning of the argument is the same with
what we proposed,—namely, that Christ offered not for them for whom
he is no priest, and he is a priest only for them for whom he doth
also intercede.   If afterward I shall have occasion to make use of
this argument, I shall, by the Lord's assistance, give more weight and
strength to it than it seems to have in their proposal, whose interest
it is to present it as slightly as possible, that they may seem fairly to
have waived it.   But the evasion, such as it is, let us look upon.

"This," saith the answerer, "is a sober objection;" which friendly
term I imagined at first he had given for this reason, because he found
it kind and easy to be satisfied.   But reading the answer and finding

that, so wide from yielding any colour or appearance of what was pretended, it only served him to vent some new, weak, false conceptions, I imagined that it must be some other kindness that caused him to give this "objection," as he calls it, so much milder an entertainment than those others, which equally gall him, which hear nothing but, "This is horrid, that blasphemy, that detestable, bominable, and false," as being, indeed, by those of his persuasion neither to be endured nor avoided. And at length I conceived that the reason of it was intimated in the first words of his pretended answer; which are, that "this objection doth not deny the death of Christ for all men, but only his ransom and mediation for all men." Now, truly, if it be so, I am not of his judgment, but so far from thinking it a "sober objection," that I cannot be persuaded that any man in his right wits would once propose it. That Christ should die for all, and yet not be a ransom for all, himself affirming that he came to "give his life a ransom for many," Matt. xx. 28, is to me a plain contradiction. The death of Christ, in the first most general notion and apprehension thereof, is a *ransom*. Nay, do not this answerer and those who are of the same persuasion with him make the ransom of as large extent as any thing in, or about, or following the death of Christ? Or have they yet some farther distinction to make, or rather division about the ends of the death of Christ? as we have had already: "For some he not only paid a ransom, but also intercedeth for them; which he doth not for all for whom he paid a ransom." Will they now go a step backward, and say that for some he not only died, but also paid a ransom for them; which he did not for all for whom he died? Who, then, were those that he thus died for? They must be some beyond all and every man; for, as they contend, for them he paid a ransom. But let us see what he says farther; in so easy a cause as this it is a shame to take advantages.

"The answer to this objection," saith he, "is easy and plain in the Scripture, for the mediation of Christ is both more general and more special;—more general, as he is the 'one mediator between God and men,' 1 Tim. ii. 5; and more special, as he is 'the mediator of the new testament, that they which are called might receive the promise of eternal inheritance,' Heb. ix. 15. According to that it is said, 'He is the Saviour of all men, specially of those that believe,' 1 Tim. iv. 10. So in all the offices of Christ, the priest, the prophet, the king, there is that which is more general, and that which is more special and peculiar."

And this is that which he calls a clear and plain answer from the Scripture, leaving the application of it unto the argument to other men's conjecture; which, as far as I can conceive, must be thus:—It is true Christ paid a ransom for none but those for whom he is a mediator and priest; but Christ is to be considered two ways:

First, As a general mediator and priest for all; secondly, As a special mediator and priest for some. Now, he pays the ransom as a general mediator. This I conceive may be some part of his meaning; for in itself the whole is in expression so barbarous and remote from common sense,—in substance such a wild, unchristian madness, as contempt would far better suit it than a reply. The truth is, for sense and expression in men who, from their manual trades, leap into the office of preaching and employment of writing, I know no reason why we should expect. Only, it can never enough be lamented that wildness, in such tattered rags, should find entertainment, whilst sober truth is shut out of doors; for what, I pray you, is the meaning of this distinction, "Christ is either a general mediator between God and man, or a special mediator of the new testament?" Was it ever heard before that Christ was any way a mediator but as he is so of the new testament? A mediator is not of one; all mediation respects an agreement of several parties; and every mediator is the mediator of a covenant. Now, if Christ be a mediator more generally than as he is so of the new covenant, of what covenant, I beseech you, was that? Of the covenant of works? Would not such an assertion overthrow the whole gospel? Would it not be derogatory to the honour of Jesus Christ that he should be the mediator of a cancelled covenant? Is it not contrary to Scripture, affirming him a "surety" (not of the first, but) "of a better testament?" Heb. vii. 22. Are not such bold assertors fitter to be catechised than to preach? But we must not let it pass thus. The man harps upon something that he hath heard from some Arminian doctor, though he hath had the ill-hap so poorly to make out his conceptions. Wherefore, being in some measure acquainted with their occasions, which they colour with those texts of Scripture which are here produced, I shall briefly remove the poor shift, that so our former argument may stand unshaken.

The poverty of the answer, as before expressed, hath been sufficiently already declared. The fruits of Christ's mediation have been distinguished by some into those that are more general and those which are more peculiar, which, in some sense, may be tolerable; but that the offices of Christ should be said to be either general or peculiar, and himself in relation to them so considered, is a gross, unshapen fancy. I answer, then, to the thing intended, that we deny any such general mediation, or function of office in general, in Christ, as should extend itself beyond his church or chosen. It was his "church" which he "redeemed with his own blood," Acts xx. 28; his "church" that "he loved and gave himself for it, that he might sanctify and cleanse it with the washing of water by the word, that he might present it to himself a glorious church," Eph. v. 25–27. They were his "sheep" he "laid down his life for," John x. 15; and "appeareth in heaven for us," Heb. ix. 24. Not one word of mediating for any other in the Scripture. Look upon his *incarnation*. It was "because the *children* were partakers of flesh and blood," chap. ii. 14; not because all the world were so. Look upon his *oblation:* " For *their sakes,*"saith he, ("those whom thou hast given me,") "do I sanctify myself," John xvii. 19; that is, to be an oblation, which was the work he had then in hand. Look upon his *resurrection:* " He was delivered for *our* offences, and was raised again for *our* justification,"Rom. iv. 25. Look upon his *ascension:* " I go," saith he, " to my Father and *your* Father, and that to prepare a place for *you,*" John xiv. 2. Look upon his *perpetuated intercession.* Is it not to " save to the uttermost *them that come unto God by him?*" Heb. vii. 25. Not one word of this general mediation for all. Nay, if you will hear himself, he denies in plain terms to mediate for all: " I pray not," saith he, " for the world, but for them which thou hast given me," John xvii. 9.

But let us see what is brought to confirm this distinction. 1 Tim. ii. 5 is quoted for the maintenance thereof: " For there is one God, and one mediator between God and men, the man Christ Jesus." What then, I pray? what will be concluded hence? Cannot Christ be a mediator between God and men, but he must be a mediator for all men? Are not the elect men? do not the children partake of flesh and blood? doth not his church consist of men? What reason is there to assert, out of an indefinite proposition, a universal conclusion? Because Christ was a mediator for men (which were true had he been so only for his apostles), shall we conclude therefore he was so for all men? " Apage nugas!"

But let us see another proof, which haply may give more strength to the uncouth distinction we oppose, and that is 1 Tim. iv. 10, " Who is the Saviour of all men, specially of those that believe." Had it been, " Who is the *Mediator* of all men, specially of them that believe," it had been more likely. But the consciences, or at least the foreheads of these men! Is there any word here spoken of Christ as mediator? Is it not the "living God" in whom we trust that is the Saviour here mentioned, as the words going before in the same verse are? And is Christ called so in respect of his mediation? That God the Father is often called Saviour I showed before, and that he is here intended, as is agreed upon by all sound interpreters, so also it is clear from the matter in hand, which is the protecting providence of God, general towards all, special and peculiar towards his church. Thus he is said to " save man and beast," Ps. xxxvi. 6, 'Ανθρώπους καὶ κτήνη σώσεις κύριε, rendering the Hebrew יְשִׁיעַ by σώσεις, " Thou shalt save or preserve." It is God, then, that is here called the " Saviour of all," by deliverance and protection in danger, of which the apostle treats, and that by his providence, which is peculiar towards believers; and what this makes for a universal mediation I know not.

Now, the very context in this place will not admit of any other interpretation; for the words render a reason why, notwithstanding all the injury and reproaches wherewith the people of God are continually assaulted, yet they should cheerfully go forward to run with joy the race that is set before them; even because as God preserveth all (for " in him we live, and move, and have our being," Acts xvii. 28; Ps. cxlv. 14–16), so that he will not suffer any to be injured and unrevenged, Gen. ix. 5, so is he especially the preserver of them that do believe; for they are as the apple of his eye, Zech. ii. 8; Deut. xxxii. 10.   So that if he should suffer them to be pressed for a season, yet let them not let go their hope and confidence, nor be weary of well-doing, but still rest on and trust in him.   This encouragement being that which the apostle was to lay down, what motive would it be hereunto to tell believers that God would have those saved who neither do nor ever will or shall believe?—that I say nothing how strange it seems that Christ should be the Saviour of them who are never saved, to whom he never gives grace to believe, for whom he denies to intercede, John xvii. 9; which yet is no small part of his mediation whereby he saves sinners.   Neither the subject, then, nor the predicate proposition, " He is the Saviour of all men," is rightly apprehended by them who would wrest it to the maintenance of *universal redemption.*   For the subject, " He," it is God the Father, and not Christ the mediator; and for the predicate, it is a *providential* preservation, and not a purchased salvation that is intimated;—that is, the providence of God protecting and governing all, but watching in an especial manner for the good of them that are his, that they be not always unjustly and cruelly traduced and reviled, with other pressures, that the apostle here rests upon; as also he shows that it was his course to do, 2 Cor. i. 9, 10: " But we had the sentence of death in ourselves, that we should not trust in ourselves, but in God which raiseth the dead: who delivered us from so great a death, and doth deliver us: in whom we trust that he will yet deliver us;" for "he is the Saviour of all men, specially of those that believe."   If any shall conceive that these words (" Because we hope in the living God, who is," etc.) do not render an account of the ground of Paul's confidence in going through with his labours and afflictions, but rather are an expression of the head and sum of that doctrine for which he was so turmoiled and afflicted, I will not much oppose it; for then, also, it includes nothing but an assertion of the true God and dependence on him, in opposition to all the idols of the Gentiles, and other vain conceits whereby they exalted themselves into the throne of the Most High.   But that Christ should be said to be a Saviour of,—1. Those who are never saved from their sins, as he saves his people, Matt. i. 21; 2. Of those who never hear one word of saving or a Saviour; 3. That he should be a Saviour in a twofold sense,—(1.) For all, (2.) For believers; 4. That to believe is the condition whereby Christ becomes a Saviour in an especial manner unto any, and that condition not procured nor purchased by him;—that this, I say, is the sense of this place, " credat Judæus Apella." To me nothing is more certain than that to whom Christ is in any sense a Saviour in the work of redemption, he saves them to the uttermost from all their sins of infidelity and disobedience, with the saving of grace here and glory hereafter.

II. Farther attempts, also, there are to give strength to this evasion, and so to invalidate our former argument, which I must also remove.

" Christ," say they,[1] " in some sort intercedeth and putteth in for transgressors, even the sons of men, yet in and of the world, that the Spirit may so still unite and bless those that believe on him, and so go forth in their confessions and conversations, and in the ministration of the gospel by his servants, that those among whom they dwell and converse might be convinced and brought to believe the report of the gospel, Isa. liii. 12; as once, Luke xxiii. 34; as himself left a pattern to us, John xvii. 21-23; that so the men of the world might be convinced, and the convinced allured to Christ and to God in him, Matt. v. 14-16; yea, so as that he doth in some measure enlighten every man that cometh into the world, John i. 9. But in a more special manner doth he intercede," etc.

Here is a twofold intercession of Christ as mediator:—1. For all sinners, that they may believe (for that is it which is intended by the many cloudy expressions wherein it is involved). 2. For believers, that they may be saved. It is the first member of the distinction which we oppose; and therefore must insist a little upon it.

First, Our author saith, " It is an interceding in *some sort*." I ask, in what sort? Is it directly, or indirectly? Is it by virtue of his blood shed for them, or otherwise? Is it with an intention and desire to obtain for them the good things interceded for, or with purpose that they shall go without them? Is it for all and every man, or only for those who live in the outward pale of the church? Is faith the thing required for them, or something else? Is that desired absolutely, or upon some condition? All which queries must be clearly answered before this general intercession can be made intelligible.

First, Whether it be directly or indirectly, and by consequence only, that this intercession after a sort is used, for that thing interceded for is represented not as the immediate issue or aim of the prayer of Christ, but as a reflex arising from a blessing obtained by others; for the prayer set down is that God would so bless believers, that those amongst whom they dwell may believe the report of the gospel. It is believers that are the direct object of this intercession, and others are only glanced at through them. The good also so desired

1 More's Universality of Grace.

for them is considered either as an accident that may come to pass, or follow the flourishing of believers, κατὰ συμβεβηκός, or as an end intended to be accomplished by it. If the first, then their good is no more intended than their evil. If the latter, why is it not effected? why is not the intention of our Saviour accomplished? Is it for want of wisdom to choose suitable and proportionable means to the end proposed? or is it for want of power to effect what he intendeth?

Secondly, Is it by virtue of his blood shed for them, or otherwise? —If it be, then Christ intercedeth for them that they may enjoy those things which for them by his oblation he did procure; for this it is to make his death and blood-shedding to be the foundation of his intercession; then it follows that Christ by his death procured faith for all, because he intercedeth that all may believe, grounding that intercession upon the merit of his death. But, first, this is more than the assertors of universal redemption will sustain; among all the ends of the death of Christ by them assigned, the effectual and infallible bestowing of faith on those for whom he died is none: secondly, if by his death he hath purchased it for all, and by intercession entreateth for it, why is it not actually bestowed on them? is not a concurrence of both these sufficient for the making out of that one spiritual blessing?—But, secondly, If it be not founded on his death and blood-shedding, then we desire that they would describe unto us this intercession of Christ, differing from his appearing for us in heaven sprinkled with his own blood.

Thirdly, Doth he intercede for them that they should believe, with an intention or desire that they should do so, or no? If not, it is but a mock intercession, and an entreaty for that which he would not have granted. If so, why is it not accomplished? why do not all believe? Yea, if he died for all, and prayed for all, that they might believe, why are not all saved? for Christ is always heard of his Father, John xi. 42.

Fourthly, Is it for all and every one in the world that Christ makes this intercession, or only for those who live within the pale of the church? If only for these latter, then this doth not prove a general intercession for all, but only one more large than that for believers; for if he leaves out any one in the world, the present hypothesis falls to the ground. If for all, how can it consist in that petition, "that the *Spirit would so lead, guide, and bless believers,* and so go forth in the ministration of the gospel by his servants, that others (that is, all and every one in the world) may be convinced and brought to believe?" How, I say, can this be spoken with any reference to those millions of souls that never see a believer, that hear no report of the gospel?

Fifthly, If his intercession be for faith, then either Christ intercedeth for it *absolutely,* that they may certainly have it, or upon *condition*, and that either on the part of God or man.—If *absolutely*, then all do actually believe; or that is not true, the Father always hears him, John xi. 42.   If upon condition *on the part of God*, it can be nothing but this, *if he will or please*.   Now, the adding of this condition may denote in our Saviour two things:—1. A nescience of what is his Father's will in the thing interceded for: which, first, cannot stand with the unity of his person as now in glory; and, secondly, cannot be, because he hath the assurance of a promise to be heard in whatever he asketh, Ps. ii. 8.   Or, 2. An advancement of his Father's will, by submission to that as the prime cause of the good to be bestowed; which may well stand with absolute intercession, by virtue whereof all must believe.—Secondly, Is it a condition *on the part of those for whom he doth intercede?*   Now, I beseech you, what condition is that? where in the Scripture assigned? where is it said that Christ doth intercede for men that they may have faith if they do such and such things?   Nay, what condition can rationally be assigned of this desire?   " Some often intimate that it is, if they suffer the Spirit to have his work upon their hearts, and obey the grace of God."   Now, what is it to obey the grace of God? Is it not to believe?   Therefore, it seems that Christ intercedeth for them that they may believe, upon condition that they do believe. Others, more cautiously, assert the good using of the means of grace that they do enjoy to be the condition upon which the benefit of this intercession doth depend.   But again,—1. What is the good using of the means of grace but submitting to them, that is, believing? and so we are as before.   2. All have not the means of grace, to use well or ill.   3. Christ prays that they may use the means of grace well, or he doth not.   If not, then how can he pray that they may believe, seeing to use well the means of grace, by yielding obedience unto them, is indeed to believe?   If he do, then he doth it absolutely, or upon condition, and so the argument is renewed again as in the entrance.   Many more reasons might be easily produced to show the madness of this assertion, but those may suffice.   Only we must look upon the proof and confirmations of it.

First, then, the words of the prophet Isaiah, chap. liii. 12, " He made intercession for the transgressors," are insisted on.—*Ans.* The transgressors here, *for whom* our Saviour is said to make intercession, are either all the transgressors for whom he suffered, as is most likely from the description we have of them, verse 6, or the transgressors only *by whom* he suffered, that acted in his sufferings, as some suppose.   If the first, then this place proves that Christ intercedes for all those for whom he suffered; which differs not from that which we contend for.   If the latter, then we may consider it as accomplished.   How he then did it, so it is here foretold that he should, which is the next place urged, namely,—

Luke xxiii. 34, "Then said Jesus, Father, forgive them; for they know not what they do."—*Ans.* The conclusion which from these words is inferred being, "Therefore there is a general intercession for all, that they may believe," I might well leave the whole argument to the silent judgment of men, without any farther opening and discovery of its invalidity and weakness; but because the ablest of that side have usually insisted much on this place for a general successless intercession, I will a little consider the inference in its dependence on these words of the gospel, and search whether it have any appearance of strength in it. To which end we must observe,—

Secondly, That this prayer is not for all men, but only for that handful of the Jews by whom he was crucified. Now, from a prayer for them to infer a prayer for all and every man that ever were, are, or shall be, is a wild deduction.

It doth not appear that he prayed for all his crucifiers neither, but only for those who did it out of ignorance, as appears by the reason annexed to his supplication: "For they know not what they do." And though, Acts iii. 17, it is said that the rulers also did it ignorantly, yet that all of them did so is not apparent; that some did is certain from that place; and so it is that some of them were converted, as afterward. Indefinite propositions must not in such things be made universal. Now, doth it follow that because Christ prayed for the pardon of their sins who crucified him out of ignorance, as some of them did, that therefore he intercedeth for all that they may believe; crucifiers who never once heard of his crucifying?

Thirdly, Christ in those words doth not so much as pray for those men that they might believe, but only that that sin of them in crucifying of him might be forgiven, not laid to their charge. Hence to conclude, therefore he intercedeth for all men that they may believe, even because he prayed that the sin of crucifying himself might be forgiven them that did it, is a strange inference.

Fourthly, There is another evident limitation in the business; for among his crucifiers he prays only for them that were present at his death, amongst whom, doubtless, many came more out of curiosity, to see and observe, as is usual in such cases, than out of malice and despite. So that whereas some urge that notwithstanding this prayer, yet the chief of the priests continued in their unbelief, it is not to the purpose, for it cannot be proved that they were present at his crucifying.

Fifthly, It cannot be affirmed with any probability that our Saviour should pray for all and every one of them, supposing some of them to be finally impenitent: for he himself *knew* full well "what was in man," John ii. 25; yea, he "knew from the beginning who they were that believed not," chap. vi. 64. Now, it is contrary to the rule which we have, 1 John v. 16, "There is a sin unto death," etc., to pray for them whom we know to be finally impenitent, and to sin unto death.

Sixthly, It seems to me that this supplication was effectual and successful, that the Son was heard in this request also, faith and forgiveness being granted to them for whom he prayed; so that this makes nothing for a general, ineffectual intercession, it being both special and effectual: for, Acts iii., of them whom Peter tells, that they "denied the Holy One, and desired a murderer," verse 14, "and killed the Prince of Life," verse 15,—of these, I say, five thousand believed: chap. iv. 4, " Many of them which heard the word believed, and the number of them was about five thousand." And if any others were among them whom our Saviour prayed for, they might be converted afterward. Neither were the rulers without the compass of the fruits of this prayer; for " a great company of the priests were obedient to the faith," chap. vi. 7. So that nothing can possibly be hence inferred for the purpose intended.

Seventhly, We may, nay we must, grant a twofold praying in our Saviour;—one, by virtue of his office as he was mediator; the other, in answer of his duty, as he was subject to the law. It is true, he who was mediator was made subject to the law; but yet those things which he did in obedience to the law as a private person were not acts of mediation, nor works of him as mediator, though of him who was mediator. Now, as he was subject to the law, our Saviour was bound to forgive offences and wrongs done unto him, and to pray for his enemies; as also he had taught us to do, whereof in this he gave us an example: Matt. v. 44, " I say unto you, Love your enemies, bless them that curse you, do good to them that hate you, and pray for them which despitefully use you, and persecute you;" which doubtless he inferreth from that law, Lev. xix. 18, " Thou shalt not avenge, nor bear any grudge against the children of thy people, but thou shalt love thy neighbour as thyself,"—quite contrary to the wicked gloss put upon it by the Pharisees. And in this sense our Saviour here, as a private person, to whom revenge was forbidden, pardon enjoined, prayer commanded, prays for his very enemies and crucifiers; which doth not at all concern his interceding for us as mediator, wherein he was always heard, and so is nothing to the purpose in hand.

Again, John xvii. 21–23 is urged to confirm this general intercession, which we have exploded; our Saviour praying that, by the unity, concord, and flourishing of his servants, the world might believe and know that God had sent him. From which words, though some make a seeming flourish, yet the thing pretended is no way confirmed; for,—

First, If Christ really intended and desired that the whole world, or all men in the world, should believe, he would also, no doubt, have prayed for more effectual means of grace to be granted unto them than only a beholding of the blessed condition of his (which yet is granted only to a small part of the world); at least for the preaching of the word to them all, that by it, as the only ordinary way, they might come to the knowledge of him. But this we do not find that ever he prayed for, or that God hath granted it; nay, he blessed his Father that so it was not, because so it seemed good in his sight, Matt. xi. 25, 26.

Secondly, Such a gloss or interpretation must not be put upon the place as should run cross to the express words of our Saviour, verse 9, "I pray not for the world;" for if he here prayed that the world should have true, holy, saving faith, he prayed for as great a blessing and privilege for the world as any he procured or interceded for for his own. Wherefore,—

Thirdly, Say some, the world is here taken for the world of the elect, the world to be saved,—God's people throughout the world. Certain it is that the world is not here taken properly *pro mundo continente*, for the world *containing*, but figuratively *pro mundo contento*, for the world *contained*, or men in the world. Neither can it be made appear that it must be taken universally, for all the men in the world, as seldom it is in the Scripture, which afterward we shall make appear; but it may be understood indefinitely, for men in the world, few or more, as the elect are in their several generations. But this exposition, though it hath great authors, I cannot absolutely adhere unto, because through this whole chapter the world is taken either for the world of reprobates, opposed to them that are given to Christ by his Father, or for the world of unbelievers (the same men under another notion), opposed to them who are committed to his Father by Christ. Wherefore I answer,—

Fourthly, That by *believing*, verse 21, and *knowing*, verse 23, is not meant believing in a strict sense, or a saving comprehension and receiving of Jesus Christ, and so becoming the sons of God,—which neither ever was, nor ever will be, fulfilled in every man in the world, nor was ever prayed for,—but a conviction and acknowledgment that the Lord Christ is not, what before they had taken him to be, a seducer and a false prophet, but indeed what he said, one that came out from God, able to protect and do good for and to his own: which kind of conviction and acknowledgment that it is often termed believing in the Scripture is more evident than that it should need to be proved; and that this is here meant the evidence of the thing is such as that it is consented unto by expositors of all sorts. Now, this is not for any good of the world, but for the vindication of his people and the exaltation of his own glory; and so proves not at all the thing in question. But of this word " world " afterward.

The following place of Matthew, chap. v. 15, 16 (containing some

instructions given by our Saviour to his apostles, so to improve the
knowledge and light which of him they had, and were farther to
receive, in the preaching of the word and holiness of life, that they
might be a means to draw men to glorify God) is certainly brought
in to make up a show of a number, as very many other places are,
the author not once considering what is to be proved by them, nor to
what end they are used; and therefore without farther inquiry may
well be laid aside, as not at all belonging to the business in hand,
nor to be dragged within many leagues of the conclusion, by all the
strength and skill of Mr More.

Neither is that other place of John, chap. i. 9, any thing more ad-
visedly or seasonably urged, though wretchedly glossed, and rendered,
" In some measure enlightening every one that comes into the world."
The Scripture says that " Christ is the true Light, that lighteth every
man that cometh into the world; " In some measure," says Mr More.
Now, I beseech you, in what measure is this? How far, unto what
degree, in what measure, is illumination from Christ? by whom or
by what means, separated from him, independent of him, is the rest
made up? who supplies the defect of Christ? I know your aim is
to hug in your illumination by the light of nature, and I know not
what common helps that you dream of, towards them who are utterly
deprived of all gospel means of grace, and that not only for the
knowledge of God as Creator, but also of him as in Christ the Redeemer: but whether the calves of your own setting up should be
thus sacrificed unto, with wresting and perverting the word of God,
and undervaluing of the grace of Christ, you will one day, I hope,
be convinced. It sufficeth us that Christ is said to enlighten every
one, because he is the only true light, and every one that is enlightened receiveth his light from him, who is the sum, the fountain
thereof. And so the general defence of this general, ineffectual intercession is vanished. But yet farther, it is particularly replied, concerning the priesthood of Christ, that,—

III. "As a priest in respect of one end, he offered sacrifice,—that
is, propitiation for all men, Heb. ii. 9, ix. 26; John i. 29; 1 John ii. 2;
—in respect of all the ends, propitiation, and sealing the new testament, and testification to the truth;—and of the uttermost end in all,
for his called and chosen ones, Heb. ix. 14, 15; Matt. xxvi. 28."
(What follows after, being repeated out of another place, hath been
already answered.)

Ans. First, These words, as here placed, have no tolerable sense in
them, neither is it an easy thing to gather the mind of the author
out of them, so far are they from being a clear answer to the argument, as was pretended. Words of Scripture, indeed, are used, but
wrested and corrupted, not only to the countenance of error, but to
bear a part in unreasonable expressions. For what, I pray, is the

meaning of these words: "He offered sacrifice in respect of one end, then of all ends, then of the uttermost end in all?" To inquire backwards:—1. What is this " uttermost end in all?" Is that "in all," in or among all the ends proposed and accomplished? or in all those for whom he offered sacrifice? or is it the uttermost end and proposal of God and Christ in his oblation? If this latter, that is the glory of God; now there is no such thing once intimated in the places of Scripture quoted, Heb. ix. 14, 15; Matt. xxvi. 28. 2. Do those places hold out the uttermost end of the death of Christ (subordinate to God's glory)? Why, in one of them it is the obtaining of redemption, and in the other the shedding of his blood for the remission of sins is expressed! Now, all this you affirm to be the first end of the death of Christ, in the first words used in this place, calling it " propitiation,"—that is, an atonement for the remission of sins; which remission of sins and redemption are for the substance one and the same, both of them the immediate fruits and first end of the death of Christ, as is apparent, Eph. i. 7; Col. i. 14. So here you have confounded the first and last end of the death of Christ, spoiling, indeed, and casting down (as you may lawfully do, for it is your own), the whole frame and building, whose foundation is this, that there be several and diverse ends of the death of Christ towards several persons, so that some of them belong unto all, and all of them only to some; which is the πρῶτον ψεῦδος of the whole book. 3. Christ's offering himself to put away sin, out of Heb. ix. 26, [you make to be] the place for the first end of the death of Christ, and his shedding of his blood for the remission of sins, from Matt. xxvi. 28, to be the last! Pray, when you write next, give us the difference between these two. 4. You say, "He offered sacrifice in respect of one end,—that is, propitiation for all men." Now, truly, if ye know the meaning of sacrifice and propitiation, this will scarce appear sense unto you upon a second view.

But, [secondly,] to leave your words and take your meaning, it seems to be this, in respect of one end that Christ proposed to himself in his sacrifice, he is a priest for all, he aimed to attain and accomplish it for them; but in respect of other ends, he is so only for his chosen and called. Now, truly, this is an easy kind of answering, which, if it will pass for good and warrantable, you may easily disappoint all your adversaries, even first by laying down their arguments, then saying your own opinion is otherwise; for the very thing that is here imposed on us for an answer is the τὸ κρινόμενον, the chief matter in debate. We absolutely deny that the several ends of the death of Christ, or the good things procured by his death, are thus distributed as is here pretended. To prove our assertion, and to give a reason of our denial of this dividing of these things in respect of their objects, we produce the argument above proposed concerning the priesthood of Christ; to which the answer given is a bare repetition of the thing in question.

But you will say divers places of Scripture are quoted for the confirmation of this answer. But these, as I told you before, are brought forth for pomp and show, nothing at all being to be found in them to the business in hand; such are Heb. ix. 26; John i. 29. For what consequence is there from an affirmation indefinite, that Christ bare or took away sin, to this, that he is a priest for all and every one in respect of propitiation? Besides, in that of John i. 29 there is a manifest allusion to the paschal lamb, by which there was a typical, ceremonial purification and cleansing of sin; which was proper only to the people of Israel, the type of the elect of God, and not of all in the world, of all sorts, reprobates and unbelievers also. Those other two places of Heb. ii. 9, 1 John ii. 2, shall be considered apart, because they seem to have some strength for the main of the cause; though apparently there is no word in them that can be wrested to give the least colour to such an uncouth distinction as that which we oppose. And thus our argument from the *equal objective extent of the oblation* and *intercession* of Jesus Christ is confirmed and vindicated, and, withal, the *means* used by the blessed Trinity for the accomplishment of the *proposed end unfolded; which end, what it was, is next to be considered.*

BOOK II.

CHAPTER I.

Some previous considerations to a more particular inquiry after the proper end and effect of the death of Christ.

THE main thing upon which the whole controversy about the death of Christ turneth, and upon which the greatest weight of the business dependeth, comes next to our consideration, being that which we have prepared the way unto by all that hath been already said. It is about the proper end of the death of Christ; which whoso can rightly constitute and make manifest may well be admitted for a day's-man and umpire in the whole contestation: for if it be the end of Christ's death which most of our adversaries assign, we will not deny but that Christ died for all and every one; and if that be the end of it which we maintain so to be, they will not extend it beyond the elect, beyond believers. This, then, must be fully cleared and solidly confirmed by them who hope for any success in their undertakings. The end of the death of Christ we asserted, in the beginning of our discourse, to be our approximation or drawing nigh unto God; that being a general expression for the whole reduction and recovery of sinners from the state of alienation, misery, and wrath, into grace, peace, and eternal communion with him. Now, there being a twofold end in things, one of the worker, the other of the work wrought, we have manifested how that, unless it be either for want of wisdom and certitude of mind in the agent, in choosing and using unsuitable means for the attaining of the end proposed, or for want of skill and power to make use of and rightly to improve well-proportioned means to the best advantage, these things are always coincident; the work effecteth what the workman intendeth. In the business in hand, the agent is the blessed Three in One, as was before declared; and the means whereby they collimed and aimed at the end proposed were the oblation and intercession of Jesus Christ, which are united, intending the same object, as was also cleared. Now, unless we will blasphemously ascribe want of wisdom, power, perfection, and sufficiency in working unto the agent, or affirm that the death and intercession of Christ were not suitable and proportioned for the attaining the end proposed by it to be effected, we must grant that the end of these is one and the same. Whatsoever the blessed Trinity intended by them, that was effected; and whatsoever we find in the issue ascribed unto them, that by them the blessed Trinity intended. So that we shall have no cause to consider these apart, unless it be sometimes to argue from the one to the other;—as, where we find any thing ascribed to the death of Christ, as the fruit thereof, we may conclude that *that* God intended to effect by it; and so also on the contrary.

Now, the end of the death of Christ is either *supreme* and ultimate, or *intermediate* and subservient to that last end.

1. The first is the glory of God, or the manifestation of his glorious attributes, especially of his justice, and mercy tempered with justice, unto us. The Lord doth necessarily aim at himself in the first place, as the chiefest good, yea, indeed, that alone which is good; that is, absolutely and simply so, and not by virtue of communication from another: and therefore in all his works, especially in this which we have in hand, the chiefest of all, he first intends the manifestation of his own glory; which also he fully accomplisheth in the close, to every point and degree by him intended. He "maketh all things for himself," Prov. xvi. 4; and every thing in the end must "redound to the glory of God," 2 Cor. iv. 15; wherein Christ himself is said to be "God's," 1 Cor. iii. 23, serving to his glory in that whole administration that was committed to him. So, Eph. i. 6, the whole end of all this dispensation, both of choosing us from eternity, redeeming us by Christ, blessing us with all spiritual blessings in him, is affirmed to be "the praise of the glory of his grace;" and, verse

12, "That we should be to the praise of his glory." This is the end of all the benefits we receive by the death of Christ; for "we are filled with the fruits of righteousness, which are by Jesus Christ, unto the glory and praise of God," Phil. i. 11;—which also is fully asserted, chap. ii. 11, "That every tongue should confess that Jesus Christ is Lord, to the glory of God the Father." This the apostle fully clears in the ninth to the Romans, where he so asserts the supreme dominion and independency of God in all his actions, his absolute freedom from taking rise, cause, or occasion to his purposes, from any thing among us sons of men, doing all things for his own sake, and aiming only at his own glory. And this is that which in the close of all shall be accomplished, when every creature shall say, "Blessing, and honour, and glory, and power, be unto him that sitteth upon the throne, and unto the Lamb for ever and ever," Rev. v. 13. But this is ἀναμφισβήτητον.

2. There is an *end* of the death of Christ which is *intermediate* and subservient to that other, which is the last and most supreme, even the effects which it hath in respect of us, and that is it of which we now treat; which, as we before affirmed, is the *bringing of us unto God.* Now, this, though in reference to the oblation and intercession of Christ it be one entire end, yet in itself, and in respect of the relation which the several acts therein have one to another, may be considered distinctly in two parts, whereof one is the *end* and the other the *means* for the attaining of that end; both the complete end of the mediation of Christ in respect of us. The ground and cause of this is the appointment of the Lord that there should be such a connection and coherence between the things purchased for us by Jesus Christ, that the one should be a means and way of attaining the other,—the one the condition, and the other the thing promised upon that condition, but both equally and alike procured for us by Jesus Christ; for if either be omitted in his purchase, the other would be vain and fruitless, as we shall afterward declare. Now, both these consist in a communication of God and his goodness unto us (and our participation of him by virtue thereof); and that either to *grace* or *glory*, holiness or blessedness, *faith* or *salvation*. In this last way they are usually called, *faith* being the means of which we speak, and *salvation* the end; *faith* the condition, *salvation* the promised inheritance. Under the name of *faith* we comprise all saving grace that accompanies it; and under the name of *salvation*, the whole "glory to be revealed," the liberty of the glory of the children of God, Rom. viii., 18, 21,—all that blessedness which consisteth in an eternal fruition of the blessed God. With *faith* go all the effectual means thereof, both external and internal;—the word and almighty sanctifying Spirit; all advancement of state and condition attending it, as justification, reconcilia-

tion, and adoption into the family of God; all fruits flowing from it in sanctification and universal holiness; with all other privileges and enjoyments of believers here, which follow the redemption and reconciliation purchased for them by the oblation of Christ. A real, effectual, and infallible bestowing and applying of all these things,— as well those that are the means as those that are the end, the condition as the thing conditioned about, faith and grace as salvation and glory,—unto all and every one for whom he died, do we maintain to be the end proposed and effected by the blood-shedding of Jesus Christ, with those other acts of his mediatorship which we before declared to be therewith inseparably conjoined: so that every one for whom he died and offered up himself hath, by virtue of his death or oblation, a right purchased for him unto all these things, which in due time he shall certainly and infallibly enjoy; or (which is all one), the end of Christ's obtaining grace and glory with his Father was, that they might be certainly bestowed upon all those for whom he died, some of them upon condition that they do believe, but faith itself absolutely upon no condition at all.   All which we shall farther illustrate and confirm, after we have removed some false ends assigned.

CHAPTER II.

Containing a removal of some mistakes and false assignations of the end of the death of Christ.

THAT the death, oblation, and blood-shedding of Jesus Christ is to be considered as the *means* for the compassing of an appointed *end* was before abundantly declared; and that such a *means* as is not in itself any way desirable but for the attaining of that end.   Now, because that which is the end of any thing must also be good, for unless it be so it cannot be an end (for *bonum et finis convertuntur*), it must be either his Father's good, or his own good, or our good, which was the end proposed.

I. That it was not merely *his own* is exceedingly apparent.   For in his divine nature he was eternally and essentially partaker of all that glory which is proper to the Deity; which though in respect of us it be capable of more or less manifestation, yet in itself it is always alike eternally and absolutely perfect.   And in this regard, at the close of all, he desires and requests no other glory but that which he had with his Father " before the world was," John xvii. 5.   And in respect of his human nature, as he was eternally predestinated, without any foresight of doing or suffering, to be personally united, from the instant of his conception, with the second person of the Trinity, so neither while he was in the way did he merit any thing for himself by his death and oblation. He needed not to suffer for himself, being perfectly and legally righteous; and the glory that he aimed at, by "enduring the cross, and despising the shame," was not so much his own, in respect of possession, by the exaltation of his own nature, as the bringing of many children to glory, even as it was in the promise set before him, as we before at large declared. His own exaltation, indeed, and power over all flesh, and his appointment to be Judge of the quick and the dead, was a consequent of his deep humiliation and suffering; but that it was the effect and product of it, procured *meritoriously* by it, that it was the end aimed at by him in his making satisfaction for sin, that we deny. Christ hath a power and dominion over all, but the foundation of this dominion is not in his death for all; for he hath dominion over all things, being appointed " heir of them, and upholding them all by the word of his power," Heb. i. 2, 3. "He is set over the works of God's hands, and all things are put in subjection under him," chap. ii. 7, 8. And what are those "all things," or what are amongst them, you may see in the place of the psalmist from whence the apostle citeth these words, Ps. viii. 5–8. And did he die for all these things? Nay, hath he not power over the angels? are not principalities and powers made subject to him? Shall he not at the last day judge the angels? for with him the saints shall do it, by giving attestation to his righteous judgments, 1 Cor. vi. 2, 3;—and yet, is it not expressly said that the angels have no share in the whole dispensation of God manifested in the flesh, so as to die for them to redeem them from their sins? of which some had no need, and the others are eternally excluded: Heb. ii. 16, "He took not on him the nature of angels; but he took on him the seed of Abraham." God setting him "king upon his holy hill of Zion," in despite of his enemies, to bruise them and to rule them "with a rod of iron," Ps. ii. 6, 9, is not the immediate effect of his death for them, but rather all things are given into his hand out of the immediate love of the Father to his Son, John iii. 35; Matt. xi. 27. That is the foundation of all this sovereignty and dominion over all creatures, with this power of judging that is put into his hand.

Besides, be it granted (which cannot be proved) that Christ by his death did procure this power of judging, would any thing hence follow that might be beneficial to the proving of the general ransom for all? No, doubtless; this dominion and power of judging is a power of condemning as well as saving; it is "all judgment" that is committed to him, John v. 22. "He hath authority given unto him to execute judgment, because he is the Son of man;" that is, at that hour " when all that are in their graves shall hear his voice and come forth; they that have done good, unto the resurrection of life; and they that have done evil, to the resurrection of condemnation," verses 27–29; 2 Cor. v. 10. Now, can it be reasonably asserted that Christ died for men to redeem them, that he might have power to condemn? Nay, do not these two overthrow one another? If he redeemed thee by his death, then he did not aim at the obtaining of any power to condemn thee; if he did the latter, then that former was not in his intention.

II. Nor, secondly, was it *his Father's good.* I speak now of the proximate and immediate end and product of the death of Christ, not of the ultimate and remote, knowing that the supreme end of Christ's oblation, and all the benefits purchased and procured by it, was "the praise of his glorious grace;" but for this other, it doth not directly tend to the obtaining of any thing unto God, but of all good things from God to us. Arminius, with his followers, with the other Universalists of our days, affirm this to be the end proposed, that God might, his justice being satisfied, save sinners, the hinderance being removed by the satisfaction of Christ. He had by his death obtained a right and liberty of pardoning sin upon what condition he pleased: so that, after the satisfaction of Christ yielded and considered, "integrum Deo fuit" (as his words are), it was wholly in God's free disposal whether he would save any or no; and upon what condition he would, whether of faith or of works. "God," say they, "had a good mind and will to do good to human kind, but could not by reason of sin, his justice lying in the way; whereupon he sent Christ to remove that obstacle, that so he might, upon the prescribing of what condition he pleased, and its being by them fulfilled, have mercy on them." Now, because in this they place the chief, if not the sole, end of the oblation of Christ, I must a little show the falseness and folly of it; which may be done plainly by these following reasons:—

First, The foundation of this whole assertion seems to me to be false and erroneous,—namely, that God could not have mercy on mankind unless satisfaction were made by his Son. It is true, indeed, supposing the decree, purpose, and constitution of God that so it should be, that so he would manifest his glory, by the way of vindicative justice, it was impossible that it should otherwise be; for with the Lord there is "no variableness, neither shadow of turning," James i. 17; 1 Sam. xv. 29: but to assert positively, that absolutely and antecedently to his constitution he could not have done it, is to me an unwritten tradition, the Scripture affirming no such thing, neither can it be gathered from thence in any good consequence. If any one shall deny this, we will try what the Lord will enable us to say unto it, and in the meantime rest contented in that of Augustine: "Though other ways of saving us were not wanting to his infinite wisdom, yet certainly the way which he did proceed in was the most convenient, because we find he proceeded therein."[1]

---

[1] The reader may be referred to the treatise by the author at the end of this volume, "De Divinâ Justitiâ," for the full and mature expression of his views on the necessity

Secondly, This would make the cause of sending his Son to die to be a common love, or rather wishing that he might do good or show mercy to all, and not an entire act of his will or purpose, of knowing, redeeming, and saving his elect; which we shall afterward disprove.

Thirdly, If the end of the death of Christ were to acquire a right to his Father, that notwithstanding his justice he might save sinners, then did he rather die to redeem a liberty unto God than a liberty from evil unto us,—that his Father might be enlarged from that estate wherein it was impossible for him to do that which he desired, and which his nature inclined him to, and not that we might be freed from that condition wherein, without this freedom purchased, it could not be but we must perish. If this be so, I see no reason why Christ should be said to come and redeem his people from their sins; but rather, plainly, to purchase this right and liberty for his Father. Now, where is there any such assertion, wherein is any thing of this nature in the Scripture? Doth the Lord say that he sent his Son out of love to himself, or unto us? Is God or are men made the immediate subject of good attained unto by this oblation? *Rep.* But it is said, that although immediately, and in the first place, this right did arise unto God by the death of Christ, yet that that also was to tend to our good, Christ obtaining that right, that the Lord might now bestow mercy on us, if we fulfilled the condition that he would propose. But I answer, that this utterly overthrows all the merit of the death of Christ towards us, and leaves not so much as the nature of merit unto it; for that which is truly meritorious indeed deserves that the thing merited, or procured and obtained by it, *shall* be done, or *ought* to be bestowed, and not only that it *may* be done. There is such a habitude and relation between merit and the thing obtained by it, whether it be absolute or arising on contract, that there ariseth a real right to the thing procured by it in them by whom or for whom it is procured. When the labourer hath wrought all day, do we say, "Now his wages *may* be paid," or rather, "Now they *ought* to be paid"? Hath he not a right unto it? Was ever such a merit heard of before, whose nature should consist in this, that the thing procured by it *might* be bestowed, and not that it *ought* to be? And shall Christ be said now to purchase by his meritorious oblation this only at his Father's hand, that he *might* bestow upon and apply the fulness of his death to some or all, and not that he *should* so do? "To him that worketh," saith the apostle, "is the reward not reckoned of grace, but of debt," Rom. iv. 4. Are not the fruits of the death of Christ by his death as truly procured for us as if they had been obtained by

of the atonement. In the statements above, it is implied that salvation might have been accomplished without the absolute necessity of such a satisfaction to the claims of justice as the death of Christ afforded. Dr Owen, it will be found in the treatise referred to, latterly changed his views on this point, and held the necessity for the satisfaction of divine justice by an atonement, in order to salvation, to be absolute.—ED.

our own working? And if so, though in respect of the persons on whom they are bestowed they are of free grace, yet in respect of the purchase, the bestowing of them is of debt.

Fourthly, That cannot be assigned as the complete end of the death of Christ, which being accomplished, it had not only been possible that not one soul might be saved, but also impossible that by virtue of it any sinful soul should be saved; for sure the Scripture is exceedingly full in declaring that through Christ we have remission of sins, grace, and glory (as afterward). But now, notwithstanding this, that Christ is said to have procured and purchased by his death such a right and liberty to his Father, that he might bestow eternal life upon all upon what conditions he would, it might very well stand that not one of those should enjoy eternal life: for suppose the Father would not bestow it, as he is by no engagement, according to this persuasion, bound to do (he had a right to do it, it is true, but that which is any one's right he may use or not use at his pleasure); again, suppose he had prescribed a condition of works which it had been impossible for them to fulfil;—the death of Christ might have had its full end, and yet not one been saved. Was this his coming to save sinners, to "save that which was lost?" or could he, upon such an accomplishment as this, pray as he did, "Father, I will that those whom thou hast given me be with me where I am; that they may behold my glory?" John xvii. 24. Divers other reasons might be used to evert this fancy, that would make the purchase of Christ, in respect of us, not to be the remission of sins, but a possibility of it; not salvation, but a salvability; not reconciliation and peace with God, but the opening of a door towards it;—but I shall use them in assigning the right end of the death of Christ.

Ask now of these, what it is that the Father can do, and will do, upon the death of Christ; by which means his justice, that before hindered the execution of his good-will towards them, is satisfied? and they tell you it is the entering into a new covenant of grace with them, upon the performance of whose condition they shall have all the benefits of the death of Christ applied to them. But to us it seemeth that Christ himself, with his death and passion, is the chief promise of the new covenant itself, as Gen. iii. 15; and so the covenant cannot be said to be procured by his death. Besides, the nature of the covenant overthrows this proposal, that they that are covenanted withal shall have such and such good things if they fulfil the condition, as though that all depended on this obedience, when that obedience itself, and the whole condition of it, is a promise of the covenant, Jer. xxxi. 33, which is confirmed and sealed by the blood of Christ. We deny not but that the death of Christ hath a proper end in respect of God,—to wit, the manifestation of his glory; whence he calls him "his servant, in whom he will be glorified," Isa. xlix. 3. And the bringing of many sons to glory, wherewith he was betrusted, was to the manifestation and praise of his glorious grace; that so his love to his elect might gloriously appear, his salvation being borne out by Christ to the utmost parts of the earth. And this full declaration of his glory, by the way of mercy tempered with justice (for "he set forth Christ to be a propitiation through faith in his blood, that he might be just, and the justifier of him that believeth in Jesus," Rom. iii. 25, 26), is all that which accrued to the Lord by the death of his Son, and not any right and liberty of doing that which before he would have done, but could not for his justice. In respect of us, the end of the oblation and blood-shedding of Jesus Christ was, not that God might if he would, but that he should, by virtue of that compact and covenant which was the foundation of the merit of Christ, bestow upon us all the good things which Christ aimed at and intended to purchase and procure by his offering of himself for us unto God; which is in the next place to be declared.

CHAPTER III.

More particularly of the immediate end of the death of Christ, with the several ways whereby it is designed.

WHAT the Scripture affirms in this particular we laid down in the entrance of the whole discourse; which now, having enlarged in explication of our sense and meaning therein, must be more particularly asserted, by an application of the particular places (which are very many) to our thesis as before declared, whereof this is the sum:— "Jesus Christ, according to the counsel and will of his Father, did offer himself upon the cross, to the procurement of those things before recounted; and maketh continual intercession with this intent and purpose, that all the good things so procured by his death might be actually and infallibly bestowed on and applied to all and every one for whom he died, according to the will and counsel of God." Let us now see what the Scripture saith hereunto, the sundry places whereof we shall range under these heads:—First, Those that hold out the *intention and counsel of God,* with our Saviour's own mind; whose will was one with his Father's in this business. Secondly, Those that lay down the *actual accomplishment or effect* of his oblation, what it did really procure, effect, and produce. Thirdly, Those that point out the *persons* for whom Christ died, as designed peculiarly to be the object of this work of redemption in the end and purpose of God.

I. For the first, or those which hold out the counsel, purpose, mind, intention, and will of God and our Saviour in this work: Matt. xviii.

11, "The Son of man is come to save that which was lost;" which words he repeateth again upon another occasion, Luke xix. 10. In the first place, they are in the front of the parable of seeking the lost sheep; in the other, they are in the close of the recovery of lost Zaccheus; and in both places set forth the end of Christ's coming, which was to do the will of his Father by the recovery of lost sinners: and that as Zaccheus was recovered by conversion, by bringing into the free covenant, making him a son of Abraham, or as the lost sheep which he lays upon his shoulder and bringeth home; so unless he findeth that which he seeketh for, unless he recover that which he cometh to save, he faileth of his purpose.

Secondly, Matt. i. 21, where the angel declareth the end of Christ's coming in the flesh, and consequently of all his sufferings therein, is to the same purpose. He was to "save his people from their sins." Whatsoever is required for a complete and perfect saving of his peculiar people from their sins was intended by his coming. To say that he did but in part or in some regard effect the work of salvation, is of ill report to Christian ears.

Thirdly, The like expression is that also of Paul, 1 Tim. i. 15, evidently declaring the end of our Saviour's coming, according to the will and counsel of his Father, namely, to "save sinners;"—not to open a door for them to come in if they will or can; not to make a way passable, that they may be saved; not to purchase reconciliation and pardon of his Father, which perhaps they shall never enjoy; but actually to save them from all the guilt and power of sin, and from the wrath of God for sin: which, if he doth not accomplish, he fails of the end of his coming; and if that ought not to be affirmed, surely he came for no more than towards whom that effect is procured. The compact of his Father with him, and his promise made unto him, of "seeing his seed, and carrying along the pleasure of the Lord prosperously," Isa. liii. 10–12, I before declared; from which it is apparent that the decree and purpose of giving actually unto Christ a believing generation, whom he calleth "The children that God gave him," Heb. ii. 13, is inseparably annexed to the decree of Christ's "making his soul an offering for sin," and is the end and aim thereof.

Fourthly, As the apostle farther declareth, Heb. ii. 14, 15, "Forasmuch as the children are partakers of flesh and blood, he also himself likewise took part of the same; that through death he might destroy him that had the power of death, that is, the devil; and deliver them who through fear of death," etc. Than which words nothing can more clearly set forth the entire end of that whole dispensation of the incarnation and offering of Jesus Christ,—even a deliverance of the children whom God gave him from the power of death, hell, and the devil, so bringing them nigh unto God. Nothing at all of the purchasing of a possible deliverance for all and every one; nay, all are not those children which God gave him, all are not delivered from death and him that had the power of it: and therefore it was not all for whom he then took flesh and blood.

Fifthly, The same purpose and intention we have, Eph. v. 25-27, "Christ loved the church, and gave himself for it; that he might sanctify and cleanse it with the washing of water by the word, that he might present it to himself a glorious church, not having spot, or wrinkle, or any such thing; but that it should be holy and without blemish:" as also, Tit. ii. 14, "He gave himself for us, that he might redeem us from all iniquity, and purify unto himself a peculiar people, zealous of good works." I think nothing can be clearer than these two places; nor is it possible for the wit of man to invent expressions so fully and livelily to set out the thing we intend, as it is in both these places by the Holy Ghost. What did Christ do? "He gave himself," say both these places alike: "For his church," saith one; "For us," saith the other; both words of equal extent and force, as all men know. To what end did he this? "To sanctify and cleanse it, to present it to himself a glorious church, not having spot or wrinkle," saith he to the Ephesians; "To redeem us from all iniquity, and to purify unto himself a peculiar people, zealous of good works," saith he to Titus. I ask now, Are all men of this church? Are all in that rank of men among whom Paul placeth himself and Titus? Are all purged, purified, sanctified, made glorious, brought nigh unto Christ? or doth Christ fail in his aim towards the greatest part of men? I dare not close with any of these.

Sixthly, Will you hear our Saviour Christ himself expressing this more evidently, restraining the object, declaring his whole design and purpose, and affirming the end of his death? John xvii. 19, "For their sakes I sanctify myself, that they also might be sanctified through the truth." "For their sakes." Whose, I pray? "The men whom thou hast given me out of the world," verse 6. Not the whole world, whom he prayed not for, verse 9. "I sanctify myself." Whereunto? "To the work I am now going about, even to be an oblation." And to what end? "Ἵνα καὶ αὐτοὶ ὦσιν ἡγιασμένοι ἐν ἀληθείᾳ· —"That they also may be truly sanctified." That Ἵνα there, "that they," signifies the intent and purpose of Christ,—it designs out the end he aimed at,—which our hope is (and that is the hope of the gospel), that he hath accomplished ("for the Deliverer that cometh out of Sion turneth away ungodliness from Jacob," Rom. xi. 26);—and that herein there was a concurrence of the will of his Father, yea, that this his purpose was to fulfil the will of his Father, which he came to do.

Seventhly, And that this also was his counsel is apparent, Gal. i. 4; for our Lord Jesus "gave himself for our sins, that he might deliver us from this present evil world, according to the will of God and our

Father;" which will and purpose of his the apostle farther declares, chap. iv. 4–6, " God sent forth his Son, made of a woman, made under the law, to redeem them that were under the law, that we might receive the adoption of sons;" and, because sons, our deliverance from the law, and thereby our freedom from the guilt of sin. Our adoption to sons, receiving the Spirit, and drawing nigh unto God, are all of them in the purpose of the Father giving his only Son for us.

Eighthly, I shall add but one place more, of the very many more that might be cited to this purpose, and that is 2 Cor. v. 21, " He hath made him to be sin for us, who knew no sin, that we might be made the righteousness of God in him." The purpose of God in making his Son to be sin is, that those for whom he was made sin might become righteousness; that was the end of God's sending Christ to be so, and Christ's willingness to become so. Now, if the Lord did not purpose what is not fulfilled, yea, what he knew should never be fulfilled, and what he would not work at all that it might be fulfilled (either of which are most atheistical expressions), then he made Christ sin for no more than do in the effect become actually righteousness in him: so that the counsel and will of God, with the purpose and intention of Christ, by his oblation and blood-shedding, was to fulfil that will and counsel, is from these places made apparent.

From all which we draw this argument:—That which the Father and the Son intended to accomplish in and towards all those for whom Christ died, by his death that is most certainly effected (if any shall deny this proposition, I will at any time, by the Lord's assistance, take up the assertion of it;) but the Father and his Son intended by the death of Christ to redeem, purge, sanctify, purify, deliver from death, Satan, the curse of the law, to quit of all sin, to make righteousness in Christ, to bring nigh unto God, all those for whom he died, as was above proved: therefore, Christ died for all and only those in and towards whom all these things recounted are effected;—which, whether they are all and every one, I leave to all and every one to judge that hath any knowledge in these things.

II. The second rank contains those places which lay down the actual accomplishment and effect of this oblation, or what it doth really produce and effect in and towards them for whom it is an oblation. Such are Heb. ix. 12, 14, " By his own blood he entered in once into the holy place, having obtained eternal redemption for us. . . . . The blood of Christ, who through the eternal Spirit offered himself without spot to God, purge your consciences from dead works to serve the living God." Two things are here ascribed to the blood of Christ;—one referring to God, " It obtains eternal redemption;" the other respecting us, "It purgeth our consciences from dead works:" so that justification with God, by procuring for us an eternal redemption from the guilt of our sins and his wrath due unto them, with sanctification in ourselves (or, as it is called, Heb. i. 3, a "purging our sins"), is the immediate product of that blood by which he entered into the holy place, of that oblation which, through the eternal Spirit, he presented unto God. Yea, this meritorious purging of our sins is peculiarly ascribed to his offering, as performed before his ascension: Heb. i. 3, "When he had by himself purged our sins, he sat down on the right hand of the Majesty on high;" and again, most expressly, chap. ix. 26, "He hath appeared to put away sin by the sacrifice of himself:" which expiation, or putting away of sin by the way of sacrifice, must needs be the actual sanctification of them for whom he was a sacrifice, even as "the blood of bulls and goats, and the ashes of an heifer sprinkling the unclean, sanctifieth to the purifying of the flesh," verse 13. Certain it is, that whosoever was either polluted or guilty, for whom there was an expiation and sacrifice allowed in those carnal ordinances, "which had a shadow of good things to come," had truly;—first, A legal cleansing and sanctifying, to the purifying of the flesh; and, secondly, Freedom from the punishment which was due to the breach of the law, as it was the rule of conversation to God's people: so much his sacrifice carnally accomplished for him that was admitted thereunto. Now, these things being but "shadows of good things to come," certainly the sacrifice of Christ did effect spiritually, for all them for whom it was a sacrifice, whatever the other could typify out; that is, spiritual cleansing by sanctification, and freedom from the guilt of sin: which the places produced do evidently prove. Now, whether this be accomplished in all and for them all, let all that are able judge.

Again; Christ, by his death, and in it, is said to "bear our sins:" so 1 Pet. ii. 24, "His own self bare our sins;"—where you have both what he did, "Bare our sins" (ἀνήνεγκε, he carried them up with him upon the cross); and what he intended, "That we, being dead unto sins, should live unto righteousness." And what was the effect? "By his stripes we are healed:" which latter, as it is taken from the same place of the prophet where our Saviour is affirmed to "bear our iniquities, and to have them laid upon him" (Isa. liii. 5, 6, 10–12), so it is expository of the former, and will tell us what Christ did by "bearing our sins;" which phrase is more than once used in the Scripture to this purpose. 1. Christ, then, so bare our iniquities by his death, that, by virtue of the stripes and afflictions which he underwent in his offering himself for us, this is certainly procured and effected, that we should go free, and not suffer any of those things which he underwent for us. To which, also, you may refer all those places which evidently hold out a commutation in this point of suffering between Christ and us: Gal. iii. 13, "He delivered us from the curse of the law, being made a curse for us;" with divers others which we shall have occasion afterward to mention.

Peace, also, and reconciliation with God,—that is, actual peace by the removal of all enmity on both sides, with all the causes of it,—is fully ascribed to this oblation: Col. i. 21, 22, "And you, that were sometime alienated and enemies in your mind by wicked works, yet now hath he reconciled in the body of his flesh through death, to present you holy and unblamable and unreprovable in his sight;" as also Eph. ii. 13–16, "Ye who sometimes were far off are made nigh by the blood of Christ: for he is our peace; having abolished in his flesh the enmity, even the law of commandments, that he might reconcile both unto God in one body by the cross, having slain the enmity thereby." To which add all those places wherein plenary deliverances from anger, wrath, death, and him that had the power of it, is likewise asserted as the fruit thereof, as Rom. v. 8–10, and ye have a farther discovery made of the immediate effect of the death of Christ. Peace and reconciliation, deliverance from wrath, enmity, and whatever lay against us to keep us from enjoying the love and favour of God,—a redemption from all these he effected for his church "with his own blood," Acts xx. 28. Whence all and every one for whom he died may truly say, "Who shall lay any thing to our charge? It is God that justifieth. Who is he that condemneth? It is Christ that died, yea rather, that is risen again, who is even at the right hand of God, who also maketh intercession for us," Rom. viii. 33, 34. Which that they are procured for all and every one of the sons of Adam, that they all may use that rejoicing in full assurance, cannot be made appear. And yet evident it is that so it is with all for whom he died,—that these are the effects of his death in and towards them for whom he underwent it: for by his being slain "he redeemed them to God by his blood, out of every kindred, and tongue, and people, and nation; and made them unto our God kings and priests," Rev. v. 9, 10; for "he made an end of their sins, he made reconciliation for their iniquity, and brought in everlasting righteousness," Dan. ix. 24.

Add also those other places where our life is ascribed to the death of Christ, and then this enumeration will be perfect: John vi. 33, He "came down from heaven to give life to the world." Sure enough he giveth life to that world for which he gave his life. It is the world of "his sheep, for which he layeth down his life," chap. x. 15, even that he might "give unto them eternal life, that they might never perish," verse 28. So he appeared "to abolish death, and to bring life and immortality to light," 2 Tim. i. 10; as also Rom. v. 6–10.

Now, there is none of all these places but will afford a sufficient strength against the general ransom, or the universality of the merit of Christ. My leisure will not serve for so large a prosecution of the subject as that would require, and, therefore, I shall take from the whole this general argument:—If the death and oblation of Jesus Christ (as a sacrifice to his Father) doth sanctify all them for whom it was a sacrifice; doth purge away their sin; redeem them from wrath, curse, and guilt; work for them peace and reconciliation with God; procure for them life and immortality; bearing their iniquities and healing all their diseases;—then died he only for those that are in the event sanctified, purged, redeemed, justified, freed from wrath and death, quickened, saved, etc.; but that all are not thus sanctified, freed, etc., is most apparent: and, therefore, they cannot be said to be the proper object of the death of Christ. The supposal was confirmed before; the inference is plain from Scripture and experience, and the whole argument (if I mistake not) solid.

III. Many places there are that point out the persons for whom Christ died, as designed peculiarly to be the object of this work of redemption, according to the aim and purpose of God; some of which we will briefly recount. In some places they are called *many:* Matt. xxvi. 28, "The blood of the new testament is shed for many, for the remission of sins." "By his knowledge shall my righteous servant justify many, for he shall bear their iniquities," Isa. liii. 11. "The Son of man came not to be ministered unto, but to minister, and give his life a ransom for many," Mark x. 45; Matt. xx. 28. He was to "bring many sons unto glory;" and so was to be the "captain of their salvation, through sufferings," Heb. ii. 10. And though perhaps the word *many* itself be not sufficient to restrain the object of Christ's death unto *some*, in opposition to *all*, because *many* is sometimes placed absolutely for *all*, as Rom. v. 19, yet these *many* being described in other places to be such as it is most certain all are not, so it is a full and evident restriction of it: for these many are the "sheep" of Christ, John x. 15; the "children of God that were scattered abroad," chap. xi. 52; those whom our Saviour calleth "brethren," Heb. ii. 11; "the children that God gave him," which were "partakers of flesh and blood," verses 13, 14; and frequently, "those who were given unto him of his Father," John xvii. 2, 6, 9, 11, who should certainly be preserved; the "sheep" whereof he was the "Shepherd, through the blood of the everlasting covenant," Heb. xiii. 20; his "elect," Rom. viii. 33; and his "people," Matt. i. 21; farther explained to be his "visited and redeemed people, Luke i. 68; even the people which he "foreknew," Rom. xi. 2; even such a people as he is said to have had at Corinth before their conversion; his people by election, Acts xviii. 10; the people that he "suffered for without the gate, that he might sanctify them," Heb. xiii. 12; his "church, which he redeemed by his own blood," Acts xx. 28, which "he loved and gave himself for," Eph. v. 25; the "many" whose sins he took away, Heb. ix. 28, with whom he made a covenant, Dan. ix. 27. Those many being thus described, and set forth with such qualifications as by no means are common to all, but proper only to the elect, do most evidently appear to be all and only those that are chosen of God to obtain eternal life through the offering and blood-shedding of Jesus Christ. Many things are here excepted with much confidence and clamour, that may easily be removed. And so you see the end of the death of Christ, as it is set out in the Scripture.

That we may have the clearer passage, we must remove the hinderances that are laid in the way by some pretended answers and evasions used to escape the force of the argument drawn from the Scripture, affirming Christ to have died for "many," his "sheep," his "elect," and the like. Now, to this it is replied, that this "reason," as it is called, is "weak and of no force, equivocal, subtile, fraudulent, false, ungodly, deceitful, and erroneous;" for all these several epithets are accumulated to adorn it withal, ("Universality of Free Grace," page xvi.) Now, this variety of terms (as I conceive) serves only to declare with what *copia verborum* the unlearned eloquence of the author is woven withal; for such terrible names imposed on that which we know not well how to gainsay is a strong argument of a weak cause. When the Pharisees were not able to resist the spirit whereby our Saviour spake, they call him "devil and Samaritan." Waters that make a noise are usually but shallow. It is a proverb among the Scythians, that the "dogs which bark most bite least." But let us see "quid dignum tanto feret hic responsor hiatu," and hear him speak in his own language. He says then,—

"First, This reason is weak and of no force: for the word *many* is oft so used, that it both signifies all and every man, and also amplifieth or setteth forth the greatness of that number; as in Dan. xii. 2, Rom. v. 19, and in other places, where *many* cannot, nor is by any Christian understood for less than all men."

Rep. 1. That if the proof and argument were taken merely from the word *many*, and not from the annexed description of those many, with the presupposed distinction of all men into several sorts by the purpose of God, this exception would bear some colour; but for this see our arguments following. Only by the way observe, that he that shall divide the inhabitants of any place, as at London, into poor and rich, those that want and those that abound, afterward affirming that he will bestow his bounty on many at London, on the poor, on those that want, will easily be understood to give it unto and bestow it upon them only. 2. Neither of the places quoted proves directly that *many* must necessarily in them be taken for *all*. In Dan. xii. 2, a distribution of the word to the several parts of the affirmation must be allowed, and not an application of it to the whole, as such; and so the sense is, the dead shall arise, many to life, and many to shame, as in another language it would have been expressed. Neither are such Hebraisms unusual. Besides, perhaps, it is not improbable that many are said to rise to life, because, as the apostle says, " All shall not die." The like, also, may be said of Rom. v. 19. Though the *many* there seem to be *all*, yet certainly they are not called so with any intent to denote all, " with an amplification" (which that *many* should be to *all* is not likely): for there is no comparison there instituted at all between number and number, of those that died by Adam's disobedience and those that were made alive by the righteousness of Christ, but only in the effects of the sin of Adam and the righteousness of Christ, together with the way and manner of communicating death and life from the one and the other; whereunto any consideration of the number of the participators of those effects is not inserted. 3. The other places whereby this should be confirmed, I am confident our author cannot produce, notwithstanding his free inclination of such a reserve, these being those which are in this case commonly urged by Arminians; but if he could, they would be no way material to infringe our argument, as appeareth by what was said before.

"Secondly, This reason," he adds, "is equivocal, subtile, and fraudulent; seeing where *all* men and *every* man is affirmed of, the death of Christ, as the ransom and propitiation, and the fruits thereof, only is assumed for them; but where the word *many* is in any place used in this business, there are more ends of the death of Christ than this one affirmed of."

Rep. 1. It is denied that the death of Christ, in any place of Scripture, is said to be for " all men" or for " every man;" which, with so much confidence, is supposed, and imposed on us as a thing acknowledged. 2. That there is any other end of the death of Christ, besides the fruit of his ransom and propitiation, directly intended, and not by accident attending it, is utterly false. Yea, what other end the ransom paid by Christ and the atonement made by him can have but the fruits of them, is not imaginable. The end of any work is the same with the fruit, effect, or product of it. So that this wild distinction of the ransom and propitiation of Christ, with the fruits of them, to be for all, and the other ends of his death to be only for many, is an assertion neither equivocal, subtile, nor fraudulent! But I speak to what I conceive the meaning of the place; for the words themselves bear no tolerable sense. 3. The observation, that where the word *many* is used many ends are designed, but where *all* are spoken of there only the ransom is intimated, is,—(1.) Disadvantageous to the author's persuasion, yielding the whole argument in hand, by acknowledging that where *many* are mentioned, there *all* cannot be understood, because more ends of the death of Christ than do belong to all are mentioned; and so confessedly all the other answers to prove that by *many*, *all* are to be understood, are against the author's own light. (2.) It is frivolous; for it cannot be proved that there are more ends of the death of Christ besides the fruit of his ransom. (3.) It is false; for where the death of Christ is spoken of as for *many*, he is said to "give his life a ransom" for them, Matt. xx. 28, which are the very words where he is said to die for *all*, 1 Tim. ii. 6. What difference is there in these? what ground for this observation? Even such as these are divers others of that author's observations, as his whole tenth chapter is spent to prove that whereever there is mention of the redemption purchased by the oblation of Christ, there they for whom it is purchased are always spoken of in the third person, as by "all the world," or the like; when yet, in chap. i. of his book, himself produceth many places to prove this general redemption where the persons for whom Christ is said to suffer are mentioned in the first or second person, 1 Pet. ii. 24, iii. 18; Isa. liii. 5, 6; 1 Cor. xv. 3; Gal. iii. 13, etc.

Thirdly, He proceeds, " This reason is false and ungodly; for it is nowhere in Scripture said that Christ died or gave himself a ransom but for many, or only for many, or only for his sheep; and it is ungodliness to add to or diminish from the word of God in Scripture."

Rep. To pass by the loving terms of the author, and allowing a grain to make the sense current, I say,—*First*, That Christ affirming that he gave his life for " many," for his " sheep," being said to die for his " church," and innumerable places of Scripture witnessing that all men are not of his sheep, of his church, we argue and conclude, by just and undeniable consequence, that he died not for those who are not so. If this be adding to the word of God (being only an exposition and unfolding of his mind therein), who ever spake from the word of God and was guiltless? *Secondly*, Let it be observed, that in the very place where our Saviour says that he " gave his life for his sheep," he presently adds, that some are not of his sheep, John x. 26; which, if it be not equivalent to his sheep only, I know not what is. *Thirdly*, It were easy to recriminate; but,—

Fourthly, " But," says he, " the reason is deceitful and erroneous, for the Scripture doth nowhere say,—2. [1]Those many he died for are his sheep (much less his elect, as the reason intends it). As for the place, John x. 15, usually instanced to this end, it is therein much abused: for our Saviour, John x., did not set forth the difference between such as he died for and such as he died not for, [b]or such as he died for so and so, and not so and so; [c]but the difference between those that believe on him and those who believe not on him, verses 4, 5, 14, 26, 27. One hear his voice and follow him, the other not. [d]Nor did our Saviour here set forth the privileges of all he died for, or for whom he died so and so, but of those that believe on him

---

[1] These figures are designed by the author to connect each argument which he is refuting with the answer he supplies to it in the succeeding paragraphs.—ED.

through the ministration of the gospel, and so do know him, and approach to God, and enter the kingdom by him, verses 3, 4, 9, 27. *Nor was our Saviour here setting forth the excellency of those for whom he died, or died for so only, wherein they are preferred before others; but the excellency of his own love, with the fruits thereof to those not only that he died for, but also that are brought in by his ministration to believe on him, verses 11, 27. ᶠNor was our Saviour here treating so much of his ransom-giving and propitiation-making as of his ministration of the gospel, and so of his love and faithfulness therein; wherein he laid down his life for those ministered to, and therein gave us example, not to make propitiation for sin, but to testify love in suffering."

Rep. I am persuaded that nothing but an acquaintedness with the condition of the times wherein we live can afford me sanctuary from the censure of the reader to be lavish of precious hours, in considering and transcribing such canting lines as these last repeated. But yet, seeing better cannot be afforded, we must be content to view such evasions as these, all whose strength is in incongruous expressions, in incoherent structure, cloudy, windy phrases, all tending to raise such a mighty fog as that the business in hand might not be perceived, being lost in this smoke and vapour, cast out to darken the eyes and amuse the senses of poor seduced souls. The argument undertaken to be answered being, that Christ is said to die for " many," and those many are described and designed to be his " sheep," as John x., what answer, I pray, or any thing like thereunto, is there to be picked out of this confused heap of words which we have recited? So that I might safely pass the whole evasion by without farther observation on it, but only to desire the reader to observe how much this one argument presseth, and what a nothing is that heap of confusion which is opposed to it! But yet, lest any thing should adhere, I will give a few annotations to the place, answering the marks wherewith we have noted it, leaving the full vindication of the place until I come to the pressing of our arguments.

I say then, First, ᵃThat the many Christ died for were his sheep, was before declared. Neither is the place of John x. at all abused, our Saviour evidently setting forth a difference between them for whom he died and those for whom he would not die, calling the first his " sheep," verse 15,—those to whom he would " give eternal life," verse 28,—those " given him by his Father," chap. xvii. 9 ; evidently distinguishing them from others who were not so. Neither is it material what was the primary intention of our Saviour in this place, from which we do not argue, but from the intention and aim of the words he uses, and the truth he reveals for the end aimed at; which was the consolation of believers.

Secondly, ᵇFor the difference between them he "died for so and so," and those he "died for so and so," we confess he puts none; for we suppose that this " *so and so* " doth neither express nor intimate any thing that may be suitable to any purpose of God, or intent of our Saviour in this business. To us for whom he died, he died in the same manner, and for the same end.

Thirdly, ° We deny that the primary difference that here is made by our Saviour is between believers and not believers, but between elect and not elect, sheep and not sheep; the thing wherein they are thus differenced being the believing of the one, called "hearing of his voice and knowing him," and the not believing of the other; the foundation of these acts being their different conditions in respect of God's purpose and Christ's love, as is apparent from the antithesis and opposition which we have in verses 26 and 27, "Ye believe not, because ye are not of my sheep," and, "My sheep hear my voice." First, there is a distinction put,—in the act of believing and hearing (that is, therewithal to obey); and then is the foundation of this distinction asserted, from their distinguished state and condition,—the one being not his sheep, the other being so, even them whom he loved and gave his life for.

Fourthly, ^d*First*, It is nothing to the business before us what privileges our Saviour here expresseth; our question is, for whom he says he would give his life? and that only. *Secondly*, This frequent repetition of that useless *so and so* serves for nothing but to puzzle the poor ignorant reader. *Thirdly*, We deny that Christ died for any but those who shall certainly be brought unto him by the ministration of the gospel. So that there is not a "Not only those whom he died for, but also those that are brought in unto him;" for he died for his sheep, and his sheep hear his voice. They for whom he died, and those that come in to him, may receive different qualifications, but they are not several persons.

Fifthly, ° *First*, The question is not at all, to what end our Saviour here makes mention of his death? but for whom he died? who are expressly said to be his "sheep;" which all are not. *Secondly*, His intention is, to declare the giving of his life for a ransom, and that according to the "commandment received of his Father," verse 18.

Sixthly, ' *First*, "The love and faithfulness of Jesus Christ in the ministration of the gospel,"—that is, his performing the office of the mediator of the new covenant,—are seen in nothing more than in giving his life for a ransom, John xv. 13. *Secondly*, Here is not one word of giving us an "example;" though in laying down his life he did that also, yet here it is not improved to that purpose. From these brief annotations, I doubt not but that it is apparent that that long discourse before recited is nothing but a miserable mistaking of the text and question; which the author perhaps perceiving, he adds divers other evasions, which follow.

" Besides," saith he, " the opposition appears here to be not so much between elect and not elect, as between Jews called and Gentiles uncalled."

Rep. The opposition is between sheep and not sheep, and that with reference to their election, and not to their vocation. Now, whom would he have signified by the " not sheep"? those that were not called,—the Gentiles? That is against the text terming them sheep, that is in designation, though not as yet called, verse 16. And who are the called? the Jews? True, they were then outwardly called; yet many of them were not sheep, verse 26. Now, truly, such evasions from the force of truth as this, by so foul corrupting of the word of God, is no small provocation of the eye of his glory. But he adds,—

" Besides, there is in Scripture great difference between sheep, and sheep of his flock and pasture, of which he here speaketh, verses 4, 5, 11, 15, 16."

Rep. 1. This unrighteous distinction well explained must needs, no doubt (if any know how), give a great deal of light to the business in hand. 2. If there be a distinction to be allowed, it can be nothing but this, that the " sheep" who are simply so called are those who are only so to Christ from the donation of his Father; and the " sheep of his pasture," those who, by the effectual working of the Spirit, are actually brought home to Christ. And then of both sorts we have mention in this chapter, verses 16, 27, both making up the number of those sheep for whom he gave his life, and to whom he giveth life. But he proceeds:—

" Besides, sheep, verses 4, 5, 11, 15, are not mentioned as all those for whom he died, but as those who by his ministration are brought in to believe and enjoy the benefit of his death, and to whom he ministereth and communicateth spirit."

Rep. 1. The substance of this and other exceptions is, that by sheep is meant believers; which is contrary to verse 16, calling them sheep who are not as yet gathered into his fold. 2. That his sheep are not mentioned as those for whom he died is in terms contradictory to verse 15, " I lay down my life for my sheep." 3. Between those for whom he died and those whom he brings in by the ministration of his Spirit, there is no more difference than is between Peter, James, and John, and the three apostles that were in the mount with our Saviour at his transfiguration. This is childish sophistry, to beg the thing in question, and thrust in the opinion controverted into the room of an answer. 4. That bringing in which is here mentioned, to believe and enjoy the benefit of the death of Christ, is a most special fruit and benefit of that death, certainly to be conferred on all them for whom he died, or else most certainly his death will do them no good at all. Once more, and we have done:—

" Besides, here are more ends of his death mentioned than ransom or propitiation only, and yet it is not said, ' Only for his sheep;' and when the ransom or propitiation only is mentioned, it is said, 'For all men.' So that this reason appears weak, fraudulent, ungodly, and erroneous."

Rep. 1. Here is no word mentioned nor intimated of the death of Christ, but only that which was accomplished by his being a propitiation, and making his death a ransom for us, with the fruits which certainly and infallibly spring therefrom. 2. If more ends than one of the death of Christ are here mentioned, and such as belong not unto all, why do you deny that he speaks here of his sheep only? Take heed, or you will see the truth. 3. Where it is said, "Of all men," I know not; but this I am sure, that Christ is said to "give his life a ransom," and that is only mentioned where it is not said for all; as Matt. xx. 28, Mark x. 45.

And so, from these brief annotations, I hope any indifferent reader will be able to judge whether the reason opposed, or the exceptions against it devised, be to be accounted " weak, fraudulent, ungodly, and erroneous."

Although I fear that in this particular I have already intrenched upon the reader's patience, yet I cannot let pass the discourse immediately following in the same author to those exceptions which we last removed, laid by him against the arguments we had in hand, without an obelisk; as also an observation of his great abilities to cast down a man of clouds, which himself had set up to manifest his skill in its direction. To the preceding discourse he adds another exception, which he imposeth on those that oppose universal redemption, as though it were laid by them against the understanding of the general expressions in the Scripture, in that way and sense wherein he conceives them; and it is, " That those words were fitted for the time of Christ and his apostles, having another meaning in them than they seem to import." Now, having thus gaily trimmed and set up this man of straw,—to whose framing I dare boldly say not one of his adversaries did ever contribute a penful of ink,—to show his rare skill, he chargeth it with I know not how many errors, blasphemies, lies, set on with exclamations and vehement outcries, until it tumble to the ground. Had he not sometimes answered an argument, he would have been thought a most unhappy disputant. Now, to make sure that for once he would do it, I believe he was very careful that the objection of his own framing should not be too strong for his own defacing. In the meantime, how blind are they who admire him for a combatant who is skilful only at fencing with his own shadow! and yet with such empty janglings as these, proving what none denies, answering what none objects, is the greatest part of Mr More's book stuffed.

CHAPTER IV.

Of the distinction of impetration and application—The use and abuse thereof;
with the opinion of the adversaries upon the whole matter in controversy unfolded; and the question on both sides stated.

THE farther reasons whereby the precedent discourse may be confirmed, I defer until I come to oppose some argument to the general
ransom. For the present, I shall only take away that general answer which is usually given to the places of Scripture produced, to
waive the sense of them; which is φάρμακον πάνσοφον to our adversaries, and serves them, as they suppose, to bear up all the weight
wherewith in this case they are urged:—

I. They say, then, that in the oblation of Christ, and concerning
the good things by him procured, two things are to be considered:—
First, The *impetration*, or obtaining of them; and, secondly, The
application of them to particular persons. " The first," say they, "is
general, in respect to all. Christ obtained and procured all good
things by his death of his Father,—reconciliation, redemption, forgiveness of sins,—for all and every man in the world, if they will believe and lay hold upon him: but in respect of *application*, they are
actually bestowed and conferred but on a few; because but a few
believe, which is the condition on which they are bestowed. And in
this latter sense are the texts of Scripture which we have argued,
all of them, to be understood. So that they do no whit impeach the
universality of merit, which they assert; but only the *universality
of application*, which they also deny." Now, this answer is commonly set forth by them in various terms and divers dresses, according as it seems best to them that use it, and most subservient to
their several opinions; for,—

First, Some of them say that Christ, by his death and passion,
did absolutely, according to the intention of God, purchase for all
and every man, dying for them, remission of sins and reconciliation
with God, or a restitution into a state of grace and favour; all which
shall be actually beneficial to them, provided that they do believe.
So the Arminians.

Secondly, Some,[1] again, that Christ died for all indeed, but *conditionally* for some, if they do believe, or will so do (which he knows
they cannot of themselves); and *absolutely* for his own, even them on
whom he purposeth to bestow faith and grace, so as actually to be
made possessors of the good things by him purchased. So Camero,
and the divines of France, which follow a new method by him devised.

Thirdly, Some[2] distinguish of a twofold reconciliation and redemp-

---

[1] Camero, Testardus, Amyraldus.   [2] More, with some others of late.

tion;—one wrought by Christ with God for man, which, say they, is general for all and every man; secondly, a reconciliation wrought by Christ in man unto God, bringing them actually into peace with him. And sundry other ways there are whereby men express their conceptions in this business. The sum of all comes to this, and the weight of all lies upon that distinction which we before recounted;—namely, that in respect of *impetration*, Christ obtained redemption and reconciliation for all; in respect of *application*, it is bestowed only on them who do believe and continue therein.

II. Their arguments whereby they prove the generality of the ransom and universality of the reconciliation must afterward be considered: for the present, we handle only the distinction itself, the meaning and misapplication whereof I shall briefly declare; which will appear if we consider,—

FIRST, The true nature and meaning of this distinction, and the true use thereof; for we do acknowledge that it may be used in a sound sense and right meaning, which way soever you express it, either by impetration and application, or by procuring reconciliation with God and a working of reconciliation in us. For by *impetration* we mean the meritorious purchase of all good things made by Christ for us with and of his Father; and by *application*, the actual enjoyment of those good things upon our believing;—as, if a man pay a price for the redeeming of captives, the paying of the price supplieth the room of the *impetration* of which we speak; and the freeing of the captives is as the application of it. Yet, then, we must observe,—

First, That this distinction hath no place in the *intention* and purpose of Christ, but only in respect of the things procured by him; for in his purpose they are both united, his full end and aim being to deliver us from all evil, and procure all good actually to be bestowed upon us. But in respect of the *things themselves*, they may be considered either as procured by Christ, or as bestowed on us.

Secondly, That the will of God is not at all *conditional* in this business, as though he gave Christ to obtain peace, reconciliation, and forgiveness of sins, upon condition that we do believe. There is a condition in the things, but none in the will of God; that is absolute that such things should be procured and bestowed.

Thirdly, That all the things which Christ obtained for us are not bestowed upon *condition*, but some of them *absolutely*. And as for those that are bestowed upon condition, the condition on which they are bestowed is actually purchased and procured for us, upon no condition but only by virtue of the purchase. For instance: Christ hath purchased remission of sins and eternal life for us, to be enjoyed on our believing, upon the condition of faith. But faith itself, which is the condition of them, on whose performance they are bestowed, that he hath procured for us absolutely, on no condition at all; for what condition soever can be proposed, on which the Lord should bestow faith, I shall afterward show it vain, and to run into a circle.

Fourthly, That both these, *impetration* and *application*, have for their objects the same individual persons; that, look, for whomsoever Christ obtained any good thing by his death, unto them it shall certainly be applied, upon them it shall actually be bestowed: so that it cannot be said that he obtained any thing for any one, which that one shall not or doth not in due time enjoy. For whomsoever he wrought reconciliation *with* God, in them doth he work reconciliation *unto* God. The one is not extended to some to whom the other doth not reach. Now, because this being established, the opposite interpretation and misapplication of this distinction vanisheth, I shall briefly confirm it with reasons:—

First, If the *application* of the good things procured be the end why they are procured, for whose sake alone Christ doth obtain them, then they must be applied to all for whom they are obtained; for otherwise Christ faileth of his end and aim, which must not be granted. But that this *application* was the end of the obtaining of all good things for us appeareth,—*First,* Because if it were otherwise, and Christ did not aim at the *applying* of them, but only at their *obtaining*, then might the death of Christ have had its full effect and issue without the application of redemption and salvation to any one soul, that being not aimed at, and so, notwithstanding all that he did for us, every soul in the world might have perished eternally; which, whether it can stand with the dignity and sufficiency of his oblation, with the purpose of his Father, and his own intention, who "came into the world to save sinners,—that which was lost," and to "bring many sons unto glory," let all judge. *Secondly,* God, in that action of sending his Son, laying the weight of iniquity upon him, and giving him up to an accursed death, must be affirmed to be altogether uncertain what event all this should have in respect of us. For, did he intend that we should be saved by it?—then the application of it is that which he aimed at, as we assert: did he not?—certainly, he was uncertain what end it should have; which is blasphemy, and exceeding contrary to Scripture and right reason. Did he appoint a Saviour without thought of them that were to be saved? a Redeemer, not determining who should be redeemed? Did he resolve of a means, not determining the end? It is an assertion opposite to all the glorious properties of God.

Secondly, If that which is obtained by any do, by virtue of that action whereby it is obtained, become his in right for whom it is obtained, then for whomsoever any thing is by Christ obtained, it is to them *applied;* for that must be made theirs in fact which is theirs in right. But it is most certain that whatsoever is obtained for any is theirs by right for whom it is obtained. The very sense of the word, whether you call it *merit, impetration, purchase, acquisition*, or *obtaining*, doth bespeak a right in them for whose good the merit is effected and the purchase made. Can that be said to be obtained for me which is no wise mine? When I obtain any thing by prayer or entreaty of any one, it being obtained, it is mine own. That which is *obtained* by one is *granted* by him of whom it is obtained; and if granted, it is granted by him to *them* for whom it is obtained. But they will say, " It is obtained upon condition; and until the condition be fulfilled no right doth accrue." I answer, If this condition be equally purchased and obtained, with other things that are to be bestowed on that condition, then this hinders not but that every thing is to be applied that is procured. But if it be uncertain whether this condition will be fulfilled or not, then,—*first*, This makes God uncertain what end the death of his Son will have; *secondly*, This doth not answer but deny the thing we are are in proving, which is confirmed.

Thirdly, Because the Scripture, perpetually conjoining these two things together, will not suffer us so to sever them as that the one should belong to some and not to others, as though they could have several persons for their objects: as Isa. liii. 11, " By his knowledge shall my righteous servant justify many,"—there is the application of all good things; " for he shall bear their iniquities,"—there is the impetration. He justifieth all whose iniquities he bore. As also verse 5 of that chapter, " But he was wounded for our transgressions, he was bruised for our iniquities: the chastisement of our peace was upon him; and by his stripes we are healed." His wounding and our healing, impetration and application, his chastisement and our peace, are inseparably associated. So Rom. iv. 25, " He was delivered for our offences, and was raised again for our justification." So chap. v. 18, " By the righteousness of one" (that is, his impetration), " the free gift came upon all men unto justification of life," in the application. See there who are called "All men," most clearly. Chap. viii. 32–34, " He that spared not his own Son, but delivered him up for us all, how shall he not with him also freely give us all things? Who shall lay any thing to the charge of God's elect? It is God that justifieth. Who is he that condemneth? It is Christ that died, yea rather, that is risen again, who is even at the right hand of God, who also maketh intercession for us." From which words we have these several reasons of our assertion:—*First*, That for whom God gives his Son, to them, in him, he freely gives all things; therefore, all things obtained by his death must be bestowed, and are, on them for whom he died, verse 32. *Secondly*, They for whom Christ died are justified, are God's elect, cannot be condemned, nor can any thing be laid to their charge; all that he hath purchased for them must be applied to them, for by virtue thereof it is that they are so saved, verses 33, 34. *Thirdly*, For whom Christ died, for them he maketh intercession. Now, his intercession is for the application of those things, as is confessed, and therein he is always heard. Those to whom the one belongs, theirs also is the other. So, John x. 10, the coming of Christ is, that "his might have life, and have it abundantly;" as also 1 John iv. 9. Heb. x. 10, " By the which will we are sanctified,"—that is the application; "through the offering of the body of Jesus Christ,"—that is the means of impetration: " for by one offering he hath perfected for ever them that are sanctified," verse 14. In brief, it is proved by all those places which we produced rightly to assign the end of the death of Christ. So that this may be rested on, as I conceive, as firm and immovable, that the impetration of good things by Christ, and the application of them, respect the same individual persons.

SECONDLY, We may consider the meaning of those who seek to maintain universal redemption by this distinction in it, and to what use they do apply it. " Christ," say they, " died for all men, and by his death purchased reconciliation with God for them and forgiveness of sins: which to some is applied, and they become actually reconciled to God, and have their sins forgiven them; but to others not, who, therefore, perish in the state of irreconciliation and enmity, under the guilt of their sins. This application," say they, " is not procured nor purchased by Christ,—for then, he dying for all, all must be actually reconciled and have their sins forgiven them and be saved,— but it attends the fulfilling of the condition which God is pleased to prescribe unto them, that is, believing:" which, say some, they can do by their own strength, though not in terms, yet by direct consequence; others not, but God must give it. So that when it is said in the Scripture, Christ hath reconciled us to God, redeemed us, saved us by his blood, underwent the punishment of our sins, and so made satisfaction for us, they assert that no more is meant but that Christ did that which upon the fulfilling of the condition that is of us required, these things will follow. To the death of Christ, indeed, they assign many glorious things; but what they give on the one hand they take away with the other, by suspending the enjoyment of them on a condition by us to be fulfilled, not by him procured; and in terms assert that the proper and full end of the death of Christ was the doing of that whereby God, his justice being satisfied, might save sinners if he would, and on what condition it pleased him,—that a door of grace might be opened to all that would come in, and not that actual justification and remission of sins, life, and immortality were procured by him, but only a possibility of those things, that so it might be. Now, that all the venom that lies under this exposition and abuse of this distinction may the better appear, I shall set down the whole mind of them that use it in a few assertions, that it may be clearly seen what we do oppose.

First, " God," say they, " considering all mankind as fallen from that grace and favour in Adam wherein they were created, and excluded utterly from the attainment of salvation by virtue of the covenant of works which was at the first made with him, yet by his infinite goodness was inclined to desire the happiness of them, all and every one, that they might be delivered from misery, and be brought unto himself;" which inclination of his they call his universal love and antecedent will, whereby he would desirously have them all to be saved; out of which love he sendeth Christ.

Obs. 1. That God hath any natural or necessary inclination, by his goodness, or any other property, to do good to us, or any of his creatures, we do deny. Every thing that concerns us is an act of his free will and good pleasure, and not a natural, necessary act of his Deity, as shall be declared.

Obs. 2. The ascribing an antecedent conditional will unto God, whose fulfilling and accomplishment should depend on any free, contingent act or work of ours, is injurious to his wisdom, power, and sovereignty, and cannot well be excused from blasphemy; and is contrary to Rom. ix. 19, " Who hath resisted his will?" I say,—

Obs. 3. A common affection and inclination to do good to all doth not seem to set out the freedom, fulness, and dimensions of that most intense love of God which is asserted in the Scripture to be the cause of sending his Son; as John iii. 16, " God so loved the world, that he gave his only-begotten Son." Eph. i. 9, " Having made known unto us the mystery of his will, according to his good pleasure which he hath purposed in himself." Col. i. 19, " It pleased the Father that in him should all fulness dwell." Rom. v. 8, " God commendeth his love toward us, in that, while we were yet sinners, Christ died for us." These two[1] I shall, by the Lord's assistance, fully clear, if the Lord give life and strength, and his people encouragement, to go through with the second part of this controversy.

Obs. 4. We deny that all mankind are the object of that love of God which moved him to send his Son to die; God having " made some for the day of evil," Prov. xvi. 4; " hated them before they were born," Rom. ix. 11, 13; " before of old ordained them to condemnation," Jude 4; being " fitted to destruction," Rom. ix. 22; " made to be taken and destroyed," 2 Pet. ii. 12; " appointed to wrath," 1 Thess. v. 9; to " go to their own place," Acts i. 25.

Secondly, " The justice of God being injured by sin, unless something might be done for the satisfaction thereof, that love of God whereby he wouldeth good to all sinners could no way be brought

---

[1] See book iv., chap. ii. and chap. iv., where John iii. 16, and Rom. v. 8, are very fully considered. These must be the two passages to which he refers.—ED.

forth into act, but must have its eternal residence in the bosom of God without any effect produced."

Obs. 1. That neither Scripture nor right reason will enforce nor prove an utter and absolute want of power in God to save sinners by his own absolute will, without satisfaction to his justice, supposing his purpose that so it should be; indeed, it could not be otherwise. But, without the consideration of that, certainly he could have effected it. It doth not imply any violating of his holy nature.

Obs. 2. An actual and necessary *velleity*, for the doing of any thing which cannot possibly be accomplished without some work fulfilled outwardly of him, is opposite to his eternal blessedness and all-sufficiency.

Thirdly, " God, therefore, to fulfil that general love and good-will of his towards all, and that it might put forth itself in such a way as should seem good to him, to satisfy his justice, which stood in the way, and was the only hinderance, he sent his Son into the world to die."

The failing of this assertion we shall lay forth, when we come to declare that love whereof the sending of Christ was the proper issue and effect.

Fourthly, " Wherefore, the proper and immediate end and aim of the purpose of God in sending his Son to die for all men was, that he might, what way it pleased him, save sinners, his justice which hindered being satisfied,"—as Arminius; or, "That he might will to save sinners,"—as Corvinus. " And the intention of Christ was, to make such satisfaction to the justice of God as that he might obtain to himself a power of saving, upon what conditions it seemed good to his Father to prescribe."

Obs. 1. Whether this was the intention of the Father in sending his Son or no, let it be judged. Something was said before, upon the examination of those places of Scripture which describe his purpose; let it be known from them whether God, in sending of his Son, intended to procure to himself a liberty to save us if he would, or to obtain certain salvation for his elect.

Obs. 2. That such a possibility of salvation, or, at the utmost, a velleity or willing of it, upon an uncertain condition, to be by us fulfilled, should be the full, proper, and only immediate end of the death of Christ, will yet scarcely down with tender spirits.

Obs. 3. The expression, of procuring to himself *ability* to save, upon a condition to be prescribed, seems not to answer that certain purpose of our Saviour in laying down his life, which the Scripture saith was to " save his sheep," and to " bring many sons to glory," as before; nor hath it any ground in Scripture.

Fifthly, " Christ, therefore, obtained for all and every one reconciliation with God, remission of sins, life and salvation; not that they should actually be partakers of these things, but that God (his justice now not hindering) might and would prescribe a condition to be by them fulfilled, whereupon he would actually apply it, and make them partake of all those good things purchased by Christ." And here comes their distinction of impetration and application, which we before intimated; and thereabout, in the explication of this assertion, they are wondrously divided.

Some say that this proceeds so far, that all men are thereby received into a new covenant, in which redemption Adam was a common person as well as in his fall from the old, and all we again restored in him; so that none shall be damned that do not sin actually against the condition wherein they are born, and fall from the state whereinto all men are assumed through the death of Christ. So Boræus, Corvinus; and one of late, in plain terms, that all are reconciled, redeemed, saved, and justified in Christ; though how he could not understand (More, p. 10). But others, more warily, deny this, and assert that *by nature we are all children of wrath*, and that until we come to Christ *the wrath of God abideth on all*, so that it is not actually removed from any: so the assertors of the efficacy of grace in France.

Again, some say that Christ by this satisfaction removed *original sin in all*, and, by consequent, that only; so that all infants, though of Turks and Pagans, out of the covenant, dying before they come to the use of reason, must undoubtedly be saved, that being removed in all, even the calamity, guilt, and alienation contracted by our first fall, whereby God may save all upon a new condition. But others of them, more warily, observing that the blood of Christ is said to "cleanse from all sin," (1 John i. 7; 1 Pet. i. 18, 19; Isa. liii. 6), say he died for all sinners alike; absolutely for none, but conditionally for all. Farther, some of them affirm that after the satisfaction of Christ, or the consideration of it in God's prescience, it was absolutely undetermined what condition should be prescribed, so that the Lord might have reduced all again to the law and covenant of works; so Corvinus: others, that a procuring of a new way of salvation by faith was a part of the fruit of the death of Christ; so More, p. 35.

Again, some of them, that the condition prescribed is by our own strength, with the help of such means as God at all times, and in all places, and unto all, is ready to afford, to be performed; others deny this, and affirm that effectual grace flowing peculiarly from election is necessary to believing: the first establishing the *idol* of *free-will* to maintain their own assertion; others overthrowing their own assertion for the establishment of grace. So Amyraldus, Camero, etc.

Moreover, some say that the love of God in the sending of Christ is equal to all: others go a strain higher, and maintain an inequality in the love of God, although he send his Son to die for all, and though greater love there cannot be than that whereby the Lord sent his Son to die for us, as Rom. viii. 32; and so they say that

Christ purchased a greater good for some, and less for others. And here they put themselves upon innumerable uncouth *distinctions*, or rather (as one calleth them), *extinctions*, blotting out all sense, and reason, and true meaning of the Scripture. Witness Testardus, Amyraldus, and, as every one may see that can but read English, in T. M[ore.] Hence that multiplicity of the several ends of the death of Christ,—some that are the fruits of his ransom and satisfaction, and some that are I know not what; besides his dying for some so and so, for others so and so, this way and that way;—hiding themselves in innumerable unintelligible expressions, that it is a most difficult thing to know what they mean, and harder to find out their mind than to answer their reasons.

In one particular they agree well enough,—namely, in denying that faith is procured or merited for us by the death of Christ. So far they are all of them constant to their own principles, for once to grant it would overturn the whole fabric of universal redemption; but in assigning the cause of faith they go asunder again.

Some say that God sent Christ to die for all men, but only conditionally, if they did and would believe;—as though, if they believed, Christ died for them; if not, he died not; and so make the act the cause of its own object: other some, that he died absolutely for all, to procure all good things for them, which yet they should not enjoy until they fulfil the condition that was to be prescribed unto them. Yet all conclude that in his death Christ had no more respect unto the elect than others, to sustain their persons, or to be in their room, but that he was a public person in the room of all mankind.

III. Concerning the close of all this, in respect of the event and immediate product of the death of Christ, divers have diversely expressed themselves; some placing it in the power, some in the will, of God; some in the opening of a door of grace; some in a right purchased to himself of saving whom he pleased; some that in respect of us he had no end at all, but that all mankind might have perished after he had done all. Others make divers and distinct ends, not almost to be reckoned, of this one act of Christ, according to the diversity of the persons for whom he died, whom they grant to be distinguished and differenced by a foregoing decree; but to what purpose the Lord should send his Son to die for them whom he himself had determined not to save, but at least to pass by and leave to remediless ruin for their sins, I cannot see, nor the meaning of the twofold destination by some invented. Such is the powerful force and evidence of truth that it scatters all its opposers, and makes them fly to several hiding-corners; who, if they are not willing to yield and submit themselves, they shall surely lie down in darkness and error. None of these, or the like intricate and involved impedite distinctions, hath [truth] itself need of; into none of such poor shifts and devices doth it compel its abettors; it needeth not any windings and turnings to bring itself into a defensible posture; it is not liable to contradictions in its own fundamentals: for, without any farther circumstances, the whole of it in this business may be thus summed up:—

" *God, out of his infinite love to his elect, sent his dear Son in the fulness of time, whom he had promised in the beginning of the world, and made effectual by that promise, to die, pay a ransom of infinite value and dignity, for the purchasing of eternal redemption, and bringing unto himself all and every one of those whom he had before ordained to eternal life, for the praise of his own glory.*"

So that freedom from all the evil from which we are delivered, and an enjoyment of all the good things that are bestowed on us, in our traduction from death to life, from hell and wrath to heaven and glory, are the proper issues and effects of the death of Christ, as the meritorious cause of them all; which may, in all the parts of it, be cleared by these few assertions:—

First, The fountain and cause of God's sending Christ is his eternal love to his elect, and to them alone; which I shall not now farther confirm, reserving it for the second general head of this whole controversy.

Secondly, The *value, worth,* and *dignity* of the ransom which Christ gave himself to be, and of the price which he paid, was infinite and immeasurable; fit for the accomplishing of any end and the procuring of any good, for all and every one for whom it was intended, had they been millions of men more than ever were created. Of this also afterward.   See Acts xx. 28, " God purchased his church with his own blood." 1 Pet. i. 18, 19, " Redeemed not with silver and gold, but with the precious blood of Christ;" and that answering the mind and intention of Almighty God, John xiv. 31, " As the Father gave me commandment, even so I do;" who would have such a price paid as might be the foundation of that economy and dispensation of his love and grace which he intended, and of the way whereby he would have it dispensed.   Acts xiii. 38, 39, " Through this man is preached unto you the forgiveness of sins; and by him all that believe are justified from all things, from which ye could not be justified by the law of Moses." 2 Cor. v. 20, 21, " We are ambassadors for Christ, as though God did beseech you by us: we pray you in Christ's stead, be ye reconciled to God.   For he hath made him to be sin for us, who knew no sin; that we might be made the righteousness of God in him."

Thirdly, The intention and aim of the Father in this great work was, a bringing of those many sons to glory,—namely, his elect, whom by his free grace he had chosen from amongst all men, of all sorts, nations, and conditions, to take them into a new covenant of grace with himself, the former being as to them, in respect of the event, null and abolished; of which covenant Jesus Christ is the first and chief promise, as he that was to procure for them all other good things promised therein, as shall be proved.

Fourthly, The *things purchased* or procured for those persons, —which are the proper effects of the death and ransom of Christ, in due time certainly to become theirs in possession and enjoyment,—are, remission of sin, freedom from wrath and the curse of the law, justification, sanctification, and reconciliation with God, and eternal life; for the will of his Father sending him for these, his own intention in laying down his life for them, and the truth of the purchase made by him, is the foundation of his intercession, begun on earth and continued in heaven; whereby he, whom his Father always hears, desires and demands that the good things procured by him may be actually bestowed on them, all and every one, for whom they were procured. So that the whole of what we assert in this great business is exceedingly clear and apparent, without any intricacy or the least difficulty at all; not clouded with strange expressions and unnecessary divulsions and tearings of one thing from another, as is the opposite opinion: which in the next place shall be dealt withal by arguments confirming the one and everting the other. But because the whole strength thereof lieth in, and the weight of all lieth on, that one distinction we before spoke of, by our adversaries diversely expressed and held out, we will a little farther consider that, and then come to our arguments, and so to the answering of the opposed objections.

CHAPTER V.

Of application and impetration.

THE allowable use of this distinction, how it may be taken in a sound sense, the several ways whereby men have expressed the thing which in these words is intimated, and some arguments for the overthrowing of the false use of it, however expressed, we have before intimated and declared. Now, seeing that this is the πρῶτον ψεῦδος of the opposite opinion, understood in the sense and according to the use they make of it, I shall give it one blow more, and leave it, I hope, a-dying.

I shall, then, briefly declare, that although these two things may admit of a distinction, yet they cannot of a separation, but that for whomsoever Christ obtained good, to them it might be applied; and for whomsoever he wrought reconciliation with God, they must actually unto God be reconciled. So that the blood of Christ, and his death in the virtue of it, cannot be looked on, as some do, as a medicine in a box, laid up for all that shall come to have any of it, and so applied now to one, then to another, without any respect or difference, as though it should be intended no more for one than for another; so that although he hath obtained all the good that he hath purchased for us, yet it is left indifferent and uncertain whether it shall ever be ours or no: for it is well known, that notwithstanding those glorious things that are assigned by the Arminians to the death of Christ, which they say he purchased for all, as remission of sins, reconciliation with God, and the like, yet they for whom this purchase and procurement is made may be damned, as the greatest part are, and certainly shall be. Now, that there should be such a distance between these two,—

First, It is contrary to common sense or our usual form of speaking, which must be wrested, and our understandings forced to apprehend it. When a man hath obtained an office, or any other obtained it for him, can it be said that it is uncertain whether he shall have it or no? If it be obtained for him, is it not his in right, though perhaps not in possession? That which is impetrated or obtained by petition is his by whom it is obtained. It is to offer violence to common sense to say a thing may be a man's, or it may not be his, when it is obtained for him; for in so saying we say it is his. And so it is in the purchase made by Jesus Christ, and the good things obtained by him for all them for whom he died.

Secondly, It is contrary to all reason in the world, that the death of Christ, in God's intention, should be applied to any one that shall have no share in the merits of that death. God's will that Christ should die for any, is his intention that he shall have a share in the death of Christ, that it should belong to him,—that is, be applied to him; for that is, in this case, said to be applied to any that is his in any respect, according to the will of God. But now the death of Christ, according to the opinion we oppose, is so applied to all, and yet the fruits of this death are never so much as once made known to far the greatest part of those all.

Thirdly, [It is contrary to reason] that a ransom should be paid for captives, upon compact for their deliverance, and yet upon the payment those captives not be made free and set at liberty. The death of Christ is a ransom, Matt. xx. 28, paid by compact for the deliverance of captives for whom it was a ransom; and the promise wherein his Father stood engaged to him at his undertaking to be a Saviour, and undergoing the office imposed on him, was their deliverance, as was before declared, upon his performance of these things: on that [being done, that] the greatest number of these captives should never be released, seems strange and very improbable.

Fourthly, It is contrary to Scripture, as was before at large declared. See [also book iii.] chap. x.

But now, all this our adversaries suppose they shall wipe away with one slight distinction, that will make, as they say, all we affirm in this kind to vanish; and that is this: " It is true," say they, " all things that are absolutely procured and obtained for any do presently become theirs in right for whom they are obtained; but things that are obtained upon condition become not theirs until the condition be fulfilled. Now, Christ hath purchased, by his death for all, all good things, not absolutely, but upon condition; and until that condition come to be fulfilled, unless they perform what is required, they have neither part nor portion, right unto nor possession of them." Also, what this condition is they give in, in sundry terms; some call it a *not resisting* of this redemption offered to them; some, a *yielding* to the invitation of the gospel; some, in plain terms, *faith.* Now, be it so that Christ purchaseth all things for us, to be bestowed on this condition, that we do believe it, then I affirm that,—

First, Certainly this condition ought to be revealed to all for whom this purchase is made, if it be intended for them in good earnest. All for whom he died must have means to know that his death will do them good if they believe; especially it being in his power alone to grant them these means who intends good to them by his death. If I should entreat a physician that could cure such a disease to cure all that came unto him, but should let many rest ignorant of the grant which I had procured of the physician, and none but myself could acquaint them with it, whereby they might go to him and be healed, could I be supposed to intend the healing of those people? Doubtless no. The application is easy.

Secondly, This condition of them to be required is in their power to perform, or it is not. If it be, then have all men power to believe; which is false: if it be not, then the Lord will grant them grace to perform it, or he will not. If he will, why then do not all believe? why are not all saved? if he will not, then this impetration, or obtaining salvation and redemption for all by the blood of Jesus Christ, comes at length to this:—*God intendeth that he shall die for all, to procure for them remission of sins, reconciliation with him, eternal redemption and glory; but yet so that they shall never have the least good by these glorious things, unless they perform that which he knows they are no way able to do, and which none but himself can enable them to perform, and which concerning far the greatest part of them he is resolved not to do.* Is this to intend that Christ should die for them for their good? or rather, that he should die for them to expose them to shame and misery? Is it not all one as if a man should promise a blind man a thousand pounds upon condition that he will see.

Thirdly, This condition of faith is procured for us by the death of Christ, or it is not. If they say it be not, then the chiefest grace, and without which redemption itself (express it how you please) is of no value, doth not depend on the grace of Christ as the meritorious procuring cause thereof;—which, *first*, is exceedingly injurious to our blessed Saviour, and serves only to diminish the honour and love due to him; *secondly*, is contrary to Scripture: Tit. iii. 5, 6; 2 Cor. v. 21, "He became sin for us, that we might be made the righteousness of God in him." And how we can become the righteousness of God but by believing, I know not. Yea, expressly saith the apostle, "It is given to us for Christ's sake, on the behalf of Christ, to believe in him," Phil. i. 29; "God blessing us with all spiritual blessings in him," Eph. i. 3, whereof surely faith is not the least. If it be a fruit of the death of Christ, why is it not bestowed on all, since he died for all, especially since the whole impetration of redemption is altogether unprofitable without it? If they do invent a condition upon which this is bestowed, the vanity of that shall be afterward discovered. For the present, if this condition be, *So they do not refuse or resist the means of grace*, then I ask, if the fruit of the death of Christ shall be applied to all that fulfil this condition of not refusing or not resisting the means of grace? If not, then why is that produced? If so, then all must be saved that have not, or do not resist, the means of grace; that is, all pagans, infidels, and those infants to whom the gospel was never preached.

Fourthly, This whole assertion tends to make Christ but a half mediator, that should procure the end, but not the means conducing thereunto. So that, notwithstanding this exception and new distinction, our assertion stands firm,—That the fruits of the death of Christ, in respect of impetration of good and application to us, ought not to be divided; and our arguments to confirm it are unshaken.

For a close of all; that which in this cause we affirm may be summed up in this: Christ did not die for any upon condition, *if they do believe;* but he died for all God's elect, *that they should believe*, and believing have eternal life. Faith itself is among the principal effects and fruits of the death of Christ; as shall be declared. It is nowhere said in Scripture, nor can it reasonably be affirmed, that if we believe, Christ died for us, as though our believing should make that to be which otherwise was not,—the act create the object; but Christ died for us that we might believe. Salvation, indeed, is bestowed conditionally; but faith, which is the condition, is absolutely procured. The question being thus stated, the difference laid open, and the thing in controversy made known, we proceed, in the next place, to draw forth some of those arguments, demonstrations, testimonies, and proofs, whereby the truth we maintain is established, in which it is contained, and upon which it is firmly founded: only desiring the reader to retain some notions in his mind of those funda-

mentals which in general we laid down before; they standing in such
relation to the arguments which we shall use, that I am confident
not one of them can be thoroughly answered before they be everted.

BOOK III.

CHAPTER I.

Arguments against the universality of redemption—The two first; from the nature
of the new covenant, and the dispensation thereof.

ARGUMENT I. The first argument may be taken from the nature
of the covenant of grace, which was established, ratified, and confirmed in and by the death of Christ; that was the testament whereof
he was the testator, which was ratified in his death, and whence his
blood is called "The blood of the new testament," Matt. xxvi. 28.
Neither can any effects thereof be extended beyond the compass of
this covenant.   But now this covenant was not made universally with
all, but particularly only with some, and therefore those alone were
intended in the benefits of the death of Christ.

The assumption appears from the nature of the covenant itself,
described clearly, Jer. xxxi. 31, 32, "I will make a new covenant
with the house of Israel, and with the house of Judah: not according
to the covenant that I made with their fathers in the day that I took
them by the hand to bring them out of the land of Egypt; which
my covenant they brake, though I was an husband to them, saith
the LORD;"—and Heb. viii. 9–11, "Not according to the covenant
that I made with their fathers in the day when I took them by the
hand to lead them out of the land of Egypt; because they continued
not in my covenant, and I regarded them not, saith the Lord.   For
this is the covenant that I will make with the house of Israel after
those days, saith the Lord; I will put my laws in their mind, and
write them in their hearts: and I will be to them a God, and they
shall be to me a people: and they shall not teach every man his
neighbour, and every man his brother, saying, Know the Lord: for
all shall know me, from the least to the greatest." Wherein, first,
the condition of the covenant is not said to be required, but it is
absolutely promised: "I will put my fear in their hearts."   And this
is the main difference between the old covenant of works and the
new one of grace, that in that the Lord did only require the fulfilling
of the condition prescribed, but in this he promiseth to effect it in
them himself with whom the covenant is made.   And without this

spiritual efficacy, the truth is, the new covenant would be as weak and unprofitable, for the end of a covenant (the bringing of us and binding of us to God), as the old. For in what consisted the weakness and unprofitableness of the old covenant, for which God in his mercy abolished it? Was it not in this, because, by reason of sin, we were no way able to fulfil the condition thereof, " Do this, and live?" Otherwise the connection is still true, that " he that doeth these things shall live." And are we of ourselves any way more able to fulfil the condition of the new covenant? Is it not as easy for a man by his own strength to fulfil the whole law, as to repent and savingly believe the promise of the gospel? This, then, is one main difference of these two covenants,—that the Lord did in the old only require the condition; now, in the new, he will also effect it in all the federates, to whom this covenant is extended. And if the Lord should only exact the obedience required in the covenant of us, and not work and effect it also in us, the new covenant would be a show to increase our misery, and not a serious imparting and communicating of grace and mercy. If, then, this be the nature of the new testament,—as appears from the very words of it, and might abundantly be proved, —that the condition of the covenant should certainly, by free grace, be wrought and accomplished in all that are taken into covenant, then no more are in this covenant than in whom those conditions of it are effected.

But thus, as is apparent, it is not with all; for "all men have not faith,"—it is " of the elect of God:" therefore, it is not made with all, nor is the compass thereof to be extended beyond the remnant that are according to election. Yea, every blessing of the new covenant being certainly common, and to be communicated to all the covenantees, either faith is none of them, or all must have it, if the covenant itself be general. But some may say that it is true God promiseth to write his law in our hearts, and put his fear in our inward parts; but it is upon condition. Give me that condition, and I will yield the cause. Is it if they do believe? Nothing else can be imagined. That is, if they have the law written in their hearts (as every one that believes hath), then God promiseth to write his law in their hearts! Is this probable, friends? is it likely? I cannot, then, be persuaded that God hath made a covenant of grace with all, especially those who never heard a word of covenant, grace, or condition of it, much less received grace for the fulfilling of the condition; without which the whole would be altogether unprofitable and useless. The covenant is made with Adam, and he is acquainted with it, Gen. iii. 15,—renewed with Noah, and not hidden from him,—again established with Abraham, accompanied with a full and rich declaration of the chief promises of it, Gen. xii.; which is most certain not to be effected towards all, as afterwards will appear.

Yea, that first distinction between the seed of the woman and the seed of the serpent is enough to overthrow the pretended universality of the covenant of grace; for who dares affirm that God entered into a covenant of grace with the seed of the serpent?

Most apparent, then, it is that the new covenant of grace, and the promises thereof, are all of them of distinguishing mercy, restrained to the people whom God did foreknow; and so not extended universally to all. Now, the blood of Jesus Christ being the blood of this covenant, and his oblation intended only for the procurement of the good things intended and promised thereby,—for he was the surety thereof, Heb. vii. 22, and of that only,—it cannot be conceived to have respect unto all, or any but only those that are intended in this covenant.

Arg. II. If the Lord intended that he should, and [he] by his death did, procure pardon of sin and reconciliation with God for all and every one, to be actually enjoyed upon condition that they do believe, then ought this good-will and intention of God, with this purchase in their behalf by Jesus Christ, to be made known to them by the word, that they might believe; "for faith cometh by hearing, and hearing' by the word of God," Rom. x. 17 : for if these things be not made known and revealed to all and every one that is concerned in them, namely, to whom the Lord intends, and for whom he hath procured so great a good, then one of these things will follow;—either, first, That they may be saved without faith in, and the knowledge of, Christ (which they cannot have unless he be revealed to them), which is false, and proved so ; or else, secondly, That this good-will of God, and this purchase made by Jesus Christ, is plainly in vain, and frustrate in respect of them, yea, a plain mocking of them, that will neither do them any good to help them out of misery, nor serve the justice of God to leave them inexcusable, for what blame can redound to them for not embracing and well using a benefit which they never heard of in their lives? Doth it become the wisdom of God to send Christ to die for men that they might be saved, and never cause these men to hear of any such thing; and yet to purpose and declare that unless they do hear of it and believe it, they shall never be saved? What wise man would pay a ransom for the delivery of those captives which he is sure shall never come to the knowledge of any such payment made, and so never be the better for it? Is it answerable to the goodness of God, to deal thus with his poor creatures? to hold out towards them all in pretence the most intense love imaginable, beyond all compare and illustration,—as his love in sending his Son is set forth to be,—and yet never let them know of any such thing, but in the end to damn them for not believing it? Is it answerable to the love and kindness of Christ to us, to assign unto him at his death such a resolution as this :—"I will now, by the oblation of myself, obtain for all and every one peace and reconciliation with God, redemption and everlasting salvation, eternal glory in the high heavens, even for all those poor, miserable, wretched worms, condemned caitiffs, that every hour ought to expect the sentence of condemnation ; and all these shall truly and really be communicated to them if they will believe. But yet, withal, I will so order things that innumerable souls shall never hear one word of all this that I have done for them, never be persuaded to believe, nor have the object of faith that is to be believed proposed to them, whereby they might indeed possibly partake of these things?" Was this the mind and will, this the design and purpose, of our merciful high priest? God forbid. It is all one as if a prince should say and proclaim, that whereas there be a number of captives held in sore bondage in such a place, and he hath a full treasure, he is resolved to redeem them every one, so that every one of them shall come out of prison that will thank him for his good-will, and in the meantime never take care to let these poor captives know his mind and pleasure; and yet be fully assured that unless he effect it himself it will never be done. Would not this be conceived a vain and ostentatious flourish, without any good intent indeed towards the poor captives? Or as if a physician should say that he hath a medicine that will cure all diseases, and he intends to cure the diseases of all, but lets but very few know his mind, or any thing of his medicine; and yet is assured that without his relation and particular information it will be known to very few. And shall he be supposed to desire, intend, or aim at the recovery of all?

Now, it is most clear, from the Scripture and experience of all ages, both under the old dispensation of the covenant and the new, that innumerable men, whole nations, for a long season, are passed by in the declaration of this mystery. The Lord doth not procure that it shall, by any means, in the least measure be made out to all; they hear not so much as a rumour or report of any such thing. Under the Old Testament, "In Judah was God known, and his name was great in Israel; in Salem was his tabernacle, and his dwelling-place in Zion," Ps. lxxvi. 1, 2. "He showed his word unto Jacob, and his statutes and his judgments unto Israel. He hath not dealt so with any nation: and as for his judgments, they have not known them," Ps. cxlvii. 19, 20. Whence those appellations of the heathen, and imprecations also: as Jer. x. 25, "Pour out thy fury upon the heathen that know thee not, and upon the families that call not upon thy name;" of whom you have a full description, Eph. ii. 12, "Without Christ, aliens from the commonwealth of Israel, and strangers from the covenants of promise, having no hope, and without God in the world." And under the New Testament, though the church have "lengthened her

cords, and strengthened her stakes," and " many nations are come up
to the mountain of the LORD,"—so many as to be called " all people,"
"all nations," yea, the "world," the "whole world," in comparison
of the small precinct of the church of the Jews,—yet now also Scripture and experience do make it clear that many are passed by, yea,
millions of souls, that never hear a word of Christ, nor of reconciliation
by him; of which we can give no other reason, but, " Even so, Father,
for so it seemed good in thy sight," Matt. xi. 26. For the Scripture,
ye have the Holy Ghost expressly forbidding the apostles to go to
sundry places with the word, but sending them another way, Acts
xvi. 6, 7, 9, 10; answerable to the former dispensation in some particulars, wherein "he suffered all nations to walk in their own ways,"
chap. xiv. 16. And for experience, not to multiply particulars, do
but ask any of our brethren who have been but any time in the
Indies, and they will easily resolve you in the truth thereof.

The exceptions against this argument are poor and frivolous,
which we reserve for reply. In brief; how is it revealed to those
thousands of the offspring of infidels, whom the Lord cuts off in their
infancy, that they may not pester the world, persecute his church,
nor disturb human society? how to their parents, of whom Paul
affirms, that by the works of God they might be led to the knowledge of his eternal power and Godhead, but that they should know
any thing of redemption or a Redeemer was utterly impossible?

CHAPTER II.

Containing three other arguments.

ARG. III. If Jesus Christ died for all men,—that is, purchased
and procured for them, according to the mind and will of God, all
those things which we recounted, and the Scripture setteth forth, to
be the effects and fruits of his death, which may be summed up in
this one phrase, " *eternal redemption*,"—then he did this, and that
according to the purpose of God, either *absolutely* or upon some *condition* by them to be fulfilled. If *absolutely*, then ought all and
every one, absolutely and infallibly, to be made actual partakers of
that eternal redemption so purchased; for what, I pray, should hinder
the enjoyment of that to any which God absolutely intended, and
Christ absolutely purchased for them? If upon *condition*, then he
did either procure this condition for them, or he did not? If he did
procure this condition for them,—that is, that it should be bestowed
on them and wrought within them,—then he did it either absolutely
again, or upon a condition. If *absolutely*, then are we as we were
before; for to procure any thing for another, to be conferred on him

upon such a condition, and withal to procure that condition absolutely to be bestowed on him, is equivalent to the absolute procuring of the thing itself. For so we affirm, in this very business: Christ procured salvation for us, to be bestowed conditionally, if we do believe; but faith itself, *that* he hath absolutely procured, without prescribing of any condition. Whence we affirm, that the purchasing of salvation for us is equivalent to what it would have been if it had been so purchased as to have been absolutely bestowed, in respect of the event and issue. So that thus also must all be absolutely saved. But if this *condition* be procured upon *condition*, let that be assigned, and we will renew our *quære* concerning the procuring of that, whether it were absolute or conditional, and so never rest until they come to fix somewhere, or still run into a circle.

But, on the other side, is not this *condition* procured by him on whose performance all the good things purchased by him are to be actually enjoyed? Then, first, This condition must be made known to all, as Arg. ii. Secondly, All men are able of themselves to perform this condition, or they are not. If they are, then, seeing that condition is faith in the promises, as is on all sides confessed, are all men of themselves, by the power of their own free-will, able to believe; which is contrary to the Scriptures, as, by the Lord's assistance, shall be declared. If they cannot, but that this faith must be bestowed on them and wrought within them by the free grace of God, then when God gave his Son to die for them, to procure eternal redemption for them all, upon condition that they did believe, he either purposed to work faith in them all by his grace, that they might believe, or he did not? If he did, why doth not he actually perform it, seeing "he is of one mind, and who can turn him?" why do not all believe? why have not all men faith? Or doth he fail of his purpose? If he did not purpose to bestow faith on them all, or (which is all one) if he purposed not to bestow faith on all (for the will of God doth not consist in a pure negation of any thing,—what he doth not will that it should be, he wills that it should not be), then the sum of it comes to this:—That God gave Christ to die for all men, but upon this condition, that they perform that which of themselves without him they cannot perform, and purposed that, for his part, he would not accomplish it in them.

Now, if this be not extreme madness, to assign a will unto God of doing that which himself knows and orders that it shall never be done, of granting a thing upon a condition which without his help cannot be fulfilled, and which help he purposed not to grant, let all judge. Is this any thing but to delude poor creatures? Is it possible that any good at all should arise to any by such a purpose as this, such a giving of a Redeemer? Is it agreeable to the goodness of God to intend so great a good as is the redemption purchased by Christ, and to pretend that he would have it profitable for them, when he knows that they can no more fulfil the condition which he requires, that it may be by them enjoyed, than Lazarus could of himself come out of the grave? Doth it beseem the wisdom of God, to purpose that which he knows shall never be fulfilled? If a man should promise to give a thousand pounds to a blind man upon condition that he will open his eyes and see,—which he knows well enough he cannot do,—were that promise to be supposed to come from a heart-pitying of his poverty, and not rather from a mind to illude and mock at his misery? If the king should promise to pay a ransom for the captives at Algiers, upon condition that they would conquer their tyrants and come away,—which he knows full well they cannot do,—were this a kingly act? Or, as if a man should pay a price to redeem captives, but not that their chains may be taken away, without which they cannot come out of prison; or promise dead men great rewards upon condition they live again of themselves;—are not these to as much end as the obtaining of salvation for men upon condition that they do believe, without obtaining that condition for them? Were not this the assigning such a will and purpose as this to Jesus Christ:—" I will obtain eternal life to be bestowed on men, and become theirs, by the application of the benefits of my death; but upon this condition, that they do believe. But as I will not reveal my mind and will in this business, nor this condition itself, to innumerable of them, so concerning the rest I know they are no ways able of themselves,—no more than Lazarus was to rise, or a blind man is to see,—to perform the condition that I do require, and without which none of the good things intended for them can ever become theirs; neither will I procure that condition ever to be fulfilled in them. That is, I do will that that shall be done which I do not only know shall never be done, but that it cannot be done, because I will not do that without which it can never be accomplished"? Now, whether such a will and purpose as this beseem the wisdom and goodness of our Saviour, let the reader judge. In brief; an intention of doing good unto any one upon the performance of such a condition as the intender knows is absolutely above the strength of him of whom it is required,—especially if he know that it can no way be done but by his concurrence, and he is resolved not to yield that assistance which is necessary to the actual accomplishment of it,—is a vain fruitless flourish. That Christ, then, should obtain of his Father eternal redemption, and the Lord should through his Son intend it for them who shall never be made partakers of it, because they cannot perform, and God and Christ have purposed not to bestow, the condition on which alone it is to be made actually theirs, is unworthy of Christ, and unprofitable to them for whom it is obtained; which that any thing that Christ obtained for the sons of men should be

unto them, is a hard saying indeed. Again; if God through Christ
purpose to save all if they do believe, because he died for all, and
this faith be not purchased by Christ, nor are men able of themselves
to believe, how comes it to pass that any are saved?

[If it be answered], " God bestows faith on some, not on others," I
reply, Is this distinguishing grace purchased for those some comparatively, in respect of those that are passed by without it? If it be, then
did not Christ die equally for all, for he died that some might have
faith, not others; yea, in comparison, he cannot be said to die for those
other some at all, not dying that they might have faith, without which
he knew that all the rest would be unprofitable and fruitless. But is
it *not* purchased for them by Christ? Then have those that be saved
no more to thank Christ for than those that are damned; which were
strange, and contrary to Rev. i. 5, 6, " Unto him that loved us, and
washed us from our sins in his own blood, and hath made us kings and
priests unto God and his Father," etc. For my part, I do conceive
that Christ hath obtained salvation for men, not upon condition if they
would receive it, but so fully and perfectly that certainly they *should*
receive it. He purchased *salvation*, to be bestowed on them that do
believe; but withal *faith*, that they might believe. Neither can it be
objected, that, according to our doctrine, God requires any thing of
men that they cannot do, yea, faith to believe in Christ: for,—First,
Commands do not signify what is God's intention should be done, but
what is our duty to do; which may be made known to us whether
we be able to perform it or not: it signifieth no intention or purpose
of God. Secondly, For the promises which are proposed together
with the command to believe:—*First*, they do not hold out the intent and purpose of God, that Christ should die for us if we do
believe; which is absurd,—that the act should be the constituter of
its own object, which must be before it, and is presupposed to be
before we are desired to believe it: nor, *secondly*, the purpose of God
that the death of Christ should be profitable to us if we do believe;
which we before confuted: but, *thirdly*, only that faith is the way
to salvation which God hath appointed; so that all that do believe
shall undoubtedly be saved, these two things, faith and salvation,
being inseparably linked together, as shall be declared.

ARG. IV. If all mankind be, in and by the eternal purpose of God,
distinguished into two sorts and conditions, severally and distinctly
described and set forth in the Scripture, and Christ be peculiarly
affirmed to die for one of these sorts, and nowhere for them of the
other, then did he not die for all; for of the one sort he dies for all
and every one, and of the other for no one at all. But,—

First, There is such a discriminating distinguishment among men,
by the eternal purpose of God, as those whom he " loves" and those
whom he "hates," Rom. ix. 13; whom he " knoweth," and whom

he "knoweth not:" John x. 14, "I know my sheep;" 2 Tim. ii. 19,
"The Lord knoweth them that are his;" Rom. viii. 29, "Whom he did
foreknow;" chap. xi. 2, "His people which he foreknew;" "I know
you not," Matt. xxv. 12: so John xiii. 18, "I speak not of you all; I
know whom I have chosen." Those that are appointed to life and
glory, and those that are appointed to and fitted for destruction,—
"elect"and "reprobate;" those that were "ordained to eternal life,"and
those who "before were of old ordained to condemnation:" as Eph. i. 4,
"He hath chosen us in him;" Acts xiii. 48, "Ordained to eternal life;"
Rom. viii. 30, "Whom he did predestinate, them he also called: and
whom he called, them he also justified: and whom he justified, them
he also glorified." So, on the other side, 1 Thess. v. 9, "God hath not
appointed us to wrath, but to obtain salvation;" Rom. ix. 18-21,
"He hath mercy on whom he will have mercy, and whom he will he
hardeneth. Thou wilt say then unto me, Why doth he yet find fault?
For who hath resisted his will? Nay but, O man, who art thou that
repliest against God? Shall the thing formed say to him that formed
it, Why hast thou made me thus? Hath not the potter power over
the clay, of the same lump to make one vessel to honour, and another
to dishonour?" Jude 4, "Ordained to this condemnation;" 2 Pet. ii. 12,
"Made to be taken and destroyed;" "Sheep and goats," Matt.
xxv. 32; John x. passim. Those on whom he hath "mercy," and
those whom he "hardeneth," Rom. ix. 18. Those that are his
"peculiar people" and "the children of promise," that are "not
of the world," his "church;" and those that, in opposition to them,
are "the world," "not prayed for," "not his people:" as Tit. ii. 14;
Gal. iv. 28; John xv. 19, xvii. 9; Col. i. 24; John xi. 52; Heb. ii.
10, 12, 13. Which distinction of men is everywhere ascribed to
the purpose, will, and good pleasure of God: Prov. xvi. 4, "The LORD
hath made all things for himself, even the wicked for the day of evil."
Matt. xi. 25, 26, "I thank thee, O Father, because thou hast hid these
things from the wise and prudent, and hast revealed them unto babes.
Even so, Father; for so it seemed good in thy sight." Rom. ix. 11, 12,
"The children being not yet born, neither having done any good or
evil, that the purpose of God according to election might stand, not
of works, but of him that calleth; it was said unto her, The elder
shall serve the younger." Verses 16, 17, "So then it is not of him
that willeth, nor of him that runneth, but of God that showeth
mercy. For the scripture saith unto Pharaoh, Even for this same
purpose have I raised thee up, that I might show my power in thee,
and that my name might be declared throughout all the earth."
chap. viii. 28-30, "Who are the called according to his purpose. For
whom he did foreknow, he also did predestinate to be conformed to
the image of his Son, that he might be the first-born among many
brethren. Moreover, whom he did predestinate, them he also called:

and whom he called, them he also justified: and whom he justified them he also glorified." So that the first part of the proposition is clear from the Scripture.

Now, Christ is said expressly and punctually to die for them on the one side: for his "people," Matt. i. 21; his "sheep," John x. 11, 14; his "church," Acts xx. 28, Eph. v. 25, as distinguished from the world, Rom. v. 8, 9, John xi. 51, 52; his "elect," Rom. viii. 32–34; his "children," Heb. ii. 12, 13;—as before more at large. Whence we may surely conclude that Christ died not for all and every one,—to wit, not for those he "never knew," whom he "hateth," whom he "hardeneth," on whom he "will not show mercy," who "were before of old ordained 'to condemnation;" in a word, for a reprobate, for the world, for which he would not pray. That which some except, that though Christ be said to die for his "sheep," for his "elect," his "chosen," yet he is not said to die for them only,—that term is nowhere expressed, is of no value; for is it not, without any forced interpretation, in common sense, and according to the usual course of speaking, to distinguish men into two such opposite conditions as elect and reprobate, sheep and goats, and then affirm that he died for his elect, [is it not] equivalent to this, he died for his elect only? Is not the sense as clearly restrained as if that restrictive term had been added? Or is that term always added in the Scripture in every indefinite assertion, which yet must of necessity be limited and restrained as if it were expressly added? as where our Saviour saith, "I am the way, the truth, and the life," John xiv. 6;—he doth not say that he *only* is so, and yet of necessity it must be so understood. As also in that, Col. i. 19, "It pleased the Father that in him should all fulness dwell;"—he doth not express the limitation "only," and yet it were no less than blasphemy to suppose a possibility of extending the affirmation to any other. So that this exception, notwithstanding this argument, is, as far as I can see, unanswerable; which also might be farther urged by a more large explication of God's purpose of election and reprobation, showing how the death of Christ was a means set apart and appointed for the saving of his elect, and not at all undergone and suffered for those which, in his eternal counsel, he did determine should perish for their sins, and so never be made partakers of the benefits thereof. But of this more must be spoken, if the Lord preserve us, and give assistance for the other part of this controversy, concerning the cause of sending Christ.

ARG. V. That is not to be asserted and affirmed which the Scripture doth not anywhere go before us in; but the Scripture nowhere saith Christ died *for all men*, much less for all and every man (between which two there is a wide difference, as shall be declared): therefore, this is not to be asserted. It is true, Christ is said to give his life "a ransom for all," but nowhere for all men. And because it is affirmed expressly in other places that he died for *many*, for his *church*, for them that *believe*, for the *children* that God gave him, for *us*, some of all sorts, though not expressly, yet clearly in terms equivalent, Rev. v. 9, 10, it must be clearly proved that where *all* is mentioned, it cannot be taken for all believers, all his elect, his whole church, all the children that God gave him, some of all sorts, before a universal affirmative can be thence concluded. And if men will but consider the particular places, and contain themselves until they have done what is required, we shall be at quiet, I am persuaded, in this business.

CHAPTER III.

Containing two other arguments from the person Christ sustained in this business.

ARG. VI. For whom Christ died, he died as a *sponsor*, in their stead, as is apparent, Rom. v. 6–8, "For when we were yet without strength, in due time Christ died for the ungodly. For scarcely for a righteous man will one die: yet peradventure for a good man some would even dare to die. But God commendeth his love toward us, in that, while we were yet sinners, Christ died for us." Gal. iii. 13, "He was made a curse for us." 2 Cor. v. 21, "He hath made him to be sin for us." All which places do plainly signify and hold out a change or commutation of persons, one being accepted in the room of the other. Now, if he died as the sponsor or surety of them for whom he died, in their stead, then these two things at least will follow:—First, That he freed them from that anger, and wrath, and guilt of death, which he underwent for them, that they should in and for him be all reconciled, and be freed from the bondage wherein they are by reason of death; for no other reason in the world can be assigned why Christ should undergo any thing in another's stead, but that that other might be freed from undergoing that which he underwent for him. And all justice requires that so it should be ; which also is expressly intimated, when our Saviour is said to be ἔγγυος, "a surety of a better testament," Heb. vii. 22; that is, by being our priest, undergoing the "chastisement of our peace," and the burden of our "iniquities," Isa. liii. 5, 6. He was "made sin for us, that we might be made the righteousness of God in him," 2 Cor. v. 21. But now all are not freed from wrath and the guilt of death, and actually reconciled to God,—which is to be justified through an imputation of righteousness, and a non-imputation of iniquities;—for until men come to Christ "the wrath of God abideth on them," John iii. 36; which argueth and intimateth a non-removal of wrath, by reason of not believing. He doth not say, it *comes* on them, as though by Christ's death they were freed from being under a state and condition of wrath, which we are all in by nature, Eph. ii. 3; but μένει, "it remaineth," or abideth: it was never removed. And to them the gospel is a savour of death unto death,—bringing a new death and a sore condemnation, by its being despised, unto that death the guilt whereof they before lay under. Some have, indeed, affirmed that all and every one are redeemed, restored, justified, and made righteous in Christ, and by his death; but truly this is so wretched, I will not say perverting of the Scriptures, which give no colour to any such assertion, but so direct an opposition to them, as I judge it fruitless, and lost labour, to go about to remove such exceptions (More, p. 45). Secondly, It follows that Christ made satisfaction for the sins of all and every man, if he died for them; for the reason why he underwent death for us as a surety was, to make satisfaction to God's justice for our sins, so to redeem us to himself, neither can any other be assigned. But Christ hath not satisfied the justice of God for all the sins of all and every man: which may be made evident by divers reasons ; for,—

First, For whose sins he made satisfaction to the justice of God, for their sins justice is satisfied, or else his satisfaction was rejected as insufficient, for no other reason can be assigned of such a fruitless attempt ; which to aver is blasphemy in the highest degree. But now the justice of God is not satisfied for all the sins of all and every man; which also is no less apparent than the former: for they that must undergo eternal punishment themselves for their sins, that the justice of God may be satisfied for their sins, the justice of God was not satisfied without their own punishment, by the punishment of Christ; for they are not healed by his stripes. But that innumerable souls shall to eternity undergo the punishment due to their own sins, I hope needs, with Christians, no proving. Now, how can the justice of God require satisfaction of them for their sins, if it were before satisfied for them in Christ? To be satisfied, and to require satisfaction that it may be satisfied, are contradictory, and cannot be affirmed of the same in respect of the same; but that the Lord will require of some "the uttermost farthing" is most clear, Matt. v. 26.

Secondly, Christ, by undergoing death for us, as our surety, satisfied for no more than he intended so to do. So great a thing as satisfaction for the sins of men could not accidentally happen besides his intention, will, and purpose; especially considering that his intention and good-will, sanctifying himself to be an oblation, was of absolute necessity to make his death an acceptable offering. But now Christ did not intend to satisfy for the sins of all and every man for innumerable souls were in hell, under the punishment and weight of their own sins; from whence there is no redemption before, nor actually then when our Saviour made himself an oblation for sin. Now, shall we suppose that Christ would make himself an offering for their sins whom he knew to be past recovery, and that it was utterly impossible that ever they should have any fruit or benefit by his offering? Shall we think that the blood of the covenant was cast away upon them for whom our Saviour intended no good at all? To intend good to them he could not, without a direct opposition to the eternal decree of his Father, and therein of his own eternal Deity. Did God send his Son, did Christ come to die, for Cain and Pharaoh, damned so many ages before his suffering? "Credat Apella?" The exception, that Christ died for them, and his death would have been available to them if they had believed and fulfilled the condition required, is, in my judgment, of no force at all; for,—First, For the most part they never heard of any such condition. Secondly, Christ at his death knew full well that they had not fulfilled the condition, and were actually cut off from any possibility ever so to do, so that any intention to do them good by his death must needs be vain and frustrate; which must not be assigned to the Son of God. Thirdly, This redemption, conditionate, if they believe, we shall reject anon.

Neither is that other exception, that Christ might as well satisfy for them that were eternally damned at the time of his suffering (for whom it could not be useful), as for them that were then actually saved (for whom it was not needful), of any more value. For,—First, Those that were saved were saved upon this ground, that Christ should certainly suffer for them in due time; which suffering of his was as effectual in the purpose and promise as in the execution and accomplishment. It was in the mind of God accounted for them as accomplished, the compact and covenant with Christ about it being surely ratified upon mutual, unchangeable promises (according to our conception); and so our Saviour was to perform it, and so it was needful for them that were actually saved: but for those that were actually damned, there was no such inducement to it, or ground for it, or issue to be expected out of it. Secondly, A simile will clear the whole:—If a man should send word to a place where captives were in prison, that he would pay the price and ransom that was due for their delivery, and to desire the prisoners to come forth, for he that detains them accepts of his word and engagement; when he comes to make payment, according to his promise, if he find some to have gone forth according as was proposed, and others continued obstinate in their dungeon, some hearing of what he had done, others not, and that according to his own appointment, and were now long since dead; doth he, in the payment of his promised ransom, intend it for them that died stubbornly and obstinately in the prison, or only for them who went forth? Doubtless, only for these last. No more can the passion of Christ be supposed to be a price paid for them that died in the prison of sin and corruption before the payment of his ransom; though it might full well be for them that were delivered by virtue of his engagement for the payment of such a ransom. *Thirdly,* If Christ died in the stead of all men, and made satisfaction for their sins, then he did it for all their sins, or only for some of their sins. If for some only, who then can be saved? If for all, why then are all not saved? They say it is because of their unbelief; they will not believe, and therefore are not saved. That unbelief, is it a sin, or is it not? If it be not, how can it be a cause of damnation? If it be, Christ died for it, or he did not. If he did not, then he died not for all the sins of all men. If he did, why is this an obstacle to their salvation? Is there any new shift to be invented for this? or must we be contented with the old, namely, because they do not believe? that is, Christ did not die for their unbelief, or rather, did not by his death remove their unbelief, because they would not believe, or because they would not themselves remove their unbelief; or he died for their unbelief conditionally, that they were not unbelievers. These do not seem to me to be sober assertions.

ARG. VII. For whom Christ died, for them he is a *mediator:* which is apparent; for the oblation or offering of Christ, which he made of himself unto God, in the shedding of his blood, was one of the chiefest acts of his mediation. But he is not a mediator for all and every one; which also is no less evident, because as mediator he is the priest for them for whom he is a mediator. Now, to a priest it belongs, as was declared before, to sacrifice and intercede, to procure good things, and to apply them to those for whom they are procured; as is evident, Heb. ix., and was proved before at large: which, confessedly, Christ doth not for all. Yea, that Christ is not a mediator for every one needs no proof. Experience sufficiently evinceth it, besides innumerable places of Scripture. It is, I confess, replied by some, that Christ is a mediator for some in respect of some acts, and not in respect of others; but truly, this, if I am able to judge, is a dishonest subterfuge, that hath no ground in Scripture, and would make our Saviour a half mediator in respect of some, which is an unsavoury expression. But this argument was vindicated before.

CHAPTER IV.

Of sanctification, and of the cause of faith, and the procurement thereof by the death of Christ.

ARG. VIII. Another argument may be taken from the *effect* and *fruit* of the death of Christ unto *sanctification,* which we thus propose:—If the blood of Jesus Christ doth *wash, purge, cleanse,* and *sanctify* them for whom it was shed, or for whom he was a sacrifice, then certainly he died, shed his blood, or was a sacrifice, only for them that in the event are *washed, purged, cleansed,* and *sanctified;*—which that all or every one is not is most apparent, faith being the first principle of the heart's purification, Acts xv. 9, and "all men have not faith," 2 Thess. iii. 2; it is " of the elect of God," Tit. i. 1. The consequence, I conceive, is undeniable, and not to be avoided with any distinctions. But now we shall make it evident that the blood of Christ is effectual for all those ends of washing, purging, and sanctifying, which we before recounted. And this we shall do;—first, from the *types* of it; and, secondly, by plain *expressions* concerning the thing itself:—

First, For the *type,* that which we shall now consider is the sacrifice of expiation, which the apostle so expressly compareth with the sacrifice and oblation of Christ. Of this he affirmeth, Heb. ix. 13, that it legally sanctified them for whom it was a sacrifice. "For," saith he, " the blood of bulls and goats, and the ashes of an heifer sprinkling the unclean, sanctifieth to the purifying of the flesh." Now, that which was done carnally and legally in the type must be spiritually effected in the antitype,—the sacrifice of Christ, typified by that bloody sacrifice of beasts. This the apostle asserteth in the verse following. "How much more," saith he, "shall the blood of Christ, who through the eternal Spirit offered himself without spot to God, purge your conscience from dead works to serve the living God?" If I know any thing, that answer of Arminius and some others to this,—namely, that the sacrifice did sanctify, not as offered but as sprinkled, and the blood of Christ, not in respect of the oblation, but of its application, answereth it,—is weak and unsatisfactory; for it only asserts a division between the *oblation* and *application* of the blood of Christ, which, though we allow to be distinguished, yet such a division we are now disproving. And to weaken our argument, the same division which we disprove is proposed; which, if any, is an easy, facile way of answering. We grant that the blood of Christ sanctifieth in respect of the application of the good things procured by it, but withal prove that it is so applied to all for whom it was an oblation; and that because it is said to sanctify and purge, and must answer the type, which did sanctify to the purifying of the flesh.

Secondly, It is expressly, in divers places, *affirmed* of the blood-shedding and death of our Saviour, that it doth effect these things, and that it was intended for that purpose. Many places for the clearing of this were before recounted. I shall now repeat so many of them as shall be sufficient to give strength to the argument in hand, omitting those which before were produced, only desiring that all those places which point out the end of the death of Christ may be considered as of force to establish the truth of this argument. Rom. vi. 5, 6, "For if we have been planted together in the likeness of his death, we shall be also in the likeness of his resurrection: knowing this, that our old man is crucified with him, that the body of sin might be destroyed, that henceforth we should not serve sin." The words of the latter verse yield a reason of the former assertion in verse 5,—namely, that a participation in the death of Christ shall certainly be accompanied with conformity to him in his resurrection; that is, both to life spiritual, as also to eternal: "Because our old man is crucified with him, that the body of sin might be destroyed." That is, our sinful corruption and depravation of nature are, by his death and crucifying, effectually and meritoriously slain, and disabled from such a rule and dominion over us as that we should be servants any longer unto them; which is apparently the sense of the place, seeing it is laid as a foundation to press forward unto all degrees of sanctification and freedom from the power of sin.

The same apostle also tells us, 2 Cor. i. 20, that "all the promises of God are in him yea, and in him Amen, unto the glory of God by us." "Yea, and Amen,"—confirmed, ratified, unchangeably established, and irrevocably made over to us. Now, this was done "in him,"—that is, in his death and blood-shedding for the confirmation of the testament, whereof these promises are the conveyance of the legacies to us,—confirmed by the "death of him, the testator," Heb. ix. 16: for he was "the surety of this better testament," chap. vii. 22; which testament or "covenant he confirmed with many," by his being "cut off" for them, Dan. ix. 26, 27. Now, what are the promises that are thus confirmed unto us, and established by the blood of Christ? The sum of them you have, Jer. xxxi. 33, 34; whence they are repeated by the apostle, Heb. viii. 10–12, to set out the nature of that covenant which was ratified in the blood of Jesus, in which you have a summary description of all that free grace towards us, both in sanctification, verses 10, 11, and in justification, verse 12. Amongst these promises, also, is that most famous one of circumcising our hearts, and of giving new hearts and spirits unto us: as Deut. xxx. 6; Ezek. xxxvi. 26. So that our whole sanctification, holiness, with justification and reconciliation unto God, is procured by, and established unto us with, unchangeable promises in the death and blood-shedding of Christ, "the heavenly or spiritual things being purified with that sacrifice of his, Heb. ix. 23; "For we have redemption through his blood, even the forgiveness of sins," Col. i. 14; "By death he destroyed him that had the power of death, that is, the devil," that he might "deliver them who, through fear of death, were all their lifetime subject to bondage," Heb. ii. 14, 15.

Do but take notice of those two most clear places, Tit. ii. 14, Eph.

v. 25, 26: in both which our cleansing and sanctification is assigned
to be the end and intendment of Christ the worker; and therefore
the certain effect of his death and oblation, which was the work, as
was before proved. And I shall add but one place more to prove that
which I am sorry that I need produce any one to do,—to wit, that
the blood of Christ purgeth us from all our sin, and it is, 1 Cor. i.
30, " Who of God is made unto us wisdom, and righteousness, and
sanctification, and redemption." Of which, because it is clear enough,
I need not spend time to prove that he was thus made unto us of
God, inasmuch as he set him forth to be " a propitiation through faith
in his blood;" as Rom. iii. 25. So that our sanctification, with all
other effects of free grace, are the immediate procurement of the
death of Christ. And of the things that have been spoken this is
the sum:—Sanctification and holiness is the certain fruit and effect of
the death of Christ in all them for whom he died; but all and every
one are not partakers of this sanctification, this purging, cleansing,
and working of holiness: therefore, Christ died not for all and every
one, " quod erat demonstrandum."

It is altogether in vain to except, as some do, that the death of
Christ is not the sole cause of these things, for they are not actually
wrought in any without the intervention of the Spirit's working in
them, and faith apprehending the death of Christ: for,—First,
Though many total causes of the same kind cannot concur to the
producing of the same effect, yet several causes of several kinds may
concur to one effect, and be the sole causes in that kind wherein they
are causes. The Spirit of God is the cause of sanctification and holiness; but what kind of cause, I pray? Even such an one as is immediately and really efficient of the effect. Faith is the cause of pardon
of sin; but what cause? in what kind? Why, merely as an instrument,
apprehending the righteousness of Christ. Now, do these causes,
whereof one is efficient, the other instrumental, both natural and
real, hinder that the blood of Christ may not only concur, but also
be the sole cause, moral and meritorious, of these things? Doubtless, they do not. Nay, they do suppose it so to be, or else they
would in this work be neither instrumental nor efficient, that being
the sole foundation of the Spirit's operation and efficience, and
the sole cause of faith's being and existence. A man is detained
captive by his enemy, and one goes to him that detains him, and
pays a ransom for his delivery; who thereupon grants a warrant to
the keepers of the prison that they shall knock off his shackles, take
away his rags, let him have new clothes, according to the agreement,
saying, " Deliver him, for I have found a ransom." Because the
jailer knocks off his shackles, and the warrant of the judge is brought
for his discharge, shall he or we say that the price and ransom which
was paid was not the cause, yea, the sole cause of his delivery?

Considering that none of these latter had been, had not the ransom been paid, they are no less the effect of that ransom than his own delivery. In our delivery from the bondage of sin, it is true, there are other things, in other kinds, which do concur besides the death of Christ, as the operation of the Spirit and the grace of God; but these being in one kind, and that in another, these also being no less the fruit and effect of the death of Christ than our deliverance wrought by them, it is most apparent that that is the only main cause of the whole. Secondly, To take off utterly this exception, with all of the like kind, we affirm that faith itself is a proper immediate fruit and procurement of the death of Christ in all them for whom he died; which (because, if it be true, it utterly overthrows the general ransom, or universal redemption; and if it be not true, I will very willingly lay down this whole controversy, and be very indifferent which way it be determined, for go it which way it will, free-will must be established), I will prove apart by itself in the next argument.

ARG. IX. Before I come to press the argument intended, I must premise some few things; as,—

1. Whatever is freely bestowed upon us, in and through Christ, that is all wholly the procurement and merit of the death of Christ. Nothing is bestowed through him on those that are his which he hath not purchased; the price whereby he made his purchase being his own blood, 1 Pet. i. 18, 19; for the covenant between his Father and him, of making out all spiritual blessings to them that were given unto him, was expressly founded on this condition, " That he should make his soul an offering for sin," Isa. liii. 10.

2. That confessedly, on all sides, faith is, in men of understanding, of such absolute indispensable necessity unto salvation,—there being no sacrifice to be admitted for the want of it under the new covenant,—that, whatever God hath done in his love, sending his Son, and whatever Christ hath done or doth, in his oblation and intercession for all or some, without this in us, is, in regard of the event, of no value, worth, or profit unto us, but serveth only to increase and aggravate condemnation; for, whatsoever is accomplished besides, that is most certainly true, " He that believeth not shall be damned," Mark xvi. 16. (So that if there is in ourselves a power of believing, and the act of it do proceed from that power, and is our own also, then certainly and undeniably it is in our power to make the love of God and death of Christ effectual towards us or not, and that by believing we actually do the one by an act of our own; which is so evident that the most ingenious and perspicacious of our adversaries have in terms confessed it, as I have declared elsewhere).[1] Such being, then, the absolute necessity of faith, it seems to me that the cause of that must needs be the prime and principal cause of salva-

[1] Display of Arminianism.

tion, as being the cause of that without which the whole would not be, and by which the whole is, and is effectual.

3. I shall give those that to us in this are contrary-minded their choice and option, so that they will answer directly, categorically, and without uncouth, insignificant, cloudy distinctions, whether our Saviour, by his death and intercession (which we proved to be conjoined), did merit or procure faith for us, or no? or, which is all one, whether faith be a fruit and effect of the death of Christ, or no? And according to their answer I will proceed.

First, If they answer affirmatively, that it is, or that Christ did procure it by his death (provided always that they do not wilfully equivocate, and when I speak of faith as it is a grace in a particular person, taking it subjectively, they understand faith as it is the doctrine of faith, or the way of salvation declared in the gospel, taking it objectively, which is another thing, and beside the present question; although, by the way, I must tell them that we deny the granting of that new way of salvation, in bringing life and immortality to light by the gospel in Christ, to be procured for us by Christ, himself being the chiefest part of this way, yea, the way itself: and that he should himself be procured by his own death and oblation is a very strange, contradictory assertion, beseeming them who have used it (More, p. 35.) It is true, indeed, a full and plenary carrying of his elect to life and glory by that way we ascribe to him, and maintain it against all; but the granting of that way was of the same free grace and unprocured love which was also the cause of granting himself unto us, Gen. iii. 15.);—if, I say, they answer thus affirmatively, then I demand whether Christ procured faith for all for whom he died absolutely, or upon some condition on their part to be fulfilled? If *absolutely*, then surely, if he died for all, they must all absolutely believe; for that which is absolutely procured for any is absolutely his, no doubt. He that hath absolutely procured an inheritance, by what means soever, who can hinder, that it should not be his? But this is contrary to that of the apostle, " All men have not faith," 2 Thess. iii. 2; and, " Faith is of the elect of God," Tit. i. 1. If they say that he procured it for them, that is, to be bestowed on them *conditionally*, I desire that they would answer *bona fide*, and roundly, in terms without equivocation or blind distinctions, assign that condition, that we may know what it is, seeing it is a thing of so infinite concernment to all our souls. Let me know this condition which ye will maintain, and *en herbam amici!*[1] the cause is yours. Is it, as some say, if they do not resist the grace of God? Now, what is it not to resist the grace of God? is it not to obey it? And what is it to obey the grace of God? is it not to believe? So the condition of faith is faith itself. *Christ procured that they should believe, upon condition that they do believe!* Are these things so? But they

<hr>

[1] " I own myself conquered," Facciolati.—Ed.

can assign a condition, on our part required, of faith, that is not faith itself. Can they do it? Let us hear it, then, and we will renew our inquiry concerning that condition, whether it be procured by Christ or no. If not, then is the cause of faith still resolved into ourselves; Christ is not the author and finisher of it. If it be, then are we just where we were before, and must follow with our queries whether that condition was procured absolutely or upon condition. *Depinge ubi sistam.*

But, secondly, if they will answer negatively, as, agreeably to their own principles, they ought to do, and deny that faith is procured by the death of Christ, then,—

1. They must maintain that it is an act of our own wills, so our own as not to be wrought in us by grace; and that it is wholly situated in our power to perform that spiritual act, nothing being bestowed upon us by free grace, in and through Christ (as was before declared), but what by him, in his death and oblation, was procured: which is contrary,—(1.) To express Scripture in exceeding many places, which I shall not recount: (2.) To the very nature of the being of the new covenant, which doth not prescribe and require the condition of it, but effectually work it in all the covenantees, Jer. xxxi. 33, 34; Ezek. xxxvi. 26; Heb. viii. 10, 11: (3.) To the advancement of the free grace of God, in setting up the power of free-will, in the state of corrupted nature, to the slighting and undervaluing thereof. (4.) To the received doctrine of our natural depravedness and disability to any thing that is good; yea, by evident unstrained consequence, overthrowing that fundamental article of original sin: yea, (5.) To right reason, which will never grant that the natural faculty is able of itself, without some spiritual elevation, to produce an act purely spiritual; as 1 Cor. ii. 14.

2. They must resolve almost the sole cause of our salvation into ourselves ultimately, it being in our own power to make all that God and Christ do unto that end effectual, or to frustrate their utmost endeavours for that purpose : for all that is done, whether in the Father's loving us and sending his Son to die for us, or in the Son's offering himself for an oblation in our stead, or for us (in our behalf), is confessedly, as before, of no value nor worth, in respect of any profitable issue, unless we believe; which that we shall do, Christ hath not effected nor procured by his death, neither can the Lord so work it in us but that the sole casting voice (if I may so say), whether we will believe or no, is left to ourselves. Now, whether this be not to assign unto ourselves the cause of our own happiness, and to make us the chief builders of our own glory, let all judge.

These things being thus premised, I shall briefly prove that which is denied, namely, that faith is procured for us by the death of Christ; and so, consequently, he died not for all and every one, for "all men have not faith:" and this we may do by these following reasons:—

1. The death of Jesus Christ purchased holiness and sanctification for us, as was at large proved, Arg. viii.; but faith, as it is a grace of the Spirit inherent in us, is formally a part of our sanctification and holiness: therefore he procured faith for us. The assumption is most certain, and not denied; the proposition was sufficiently confirmed in the foregoing argument; and I see not what may be excepted against the truth of the whole. If any shall except, and say that Christ might procure for us some part of holiness (for we speak of parts, and not of degrees and measure), but not all, as the sanctification of hope, love, meekness, and the like, I ask,—first, What warrant have we for any such distinction between the graces of the Spirit, that some of them should be of the purchasing of Christ, others of our own store? secondly, Whether we are more prone of ourselves to believe, and more able, than to love and hope? and where may we have a ground for that?

2. All the fruits of election are purchased for us by Jesus Christ; for "we are chosen in him," Eph. i. 4, as the only cause and fountain of all those good things which the Lord chooseth us to, for the praise of his glorious grace, that in all things he might have the pre-eminence. I hope I need not be solicitous about the proving of this, that the Lord Jesus is the only way and means by and for whom the Lord will certainly and actually collate upon his elect all the fruits and effects or intendments of that love whereby he chose them. But now faith is a fruit, a principal fruit, of our election; for saith the apostle, "We are chosen in him before the foundation of the world, that we should be holy," Eph. i. 4,—of which holiness, faith, purifying the heart, is a principal share. "Moreover, whom he did predestinate, them he also called," Rom. viii. 30; that is, with that calling which is according to his purpose, effectually working faith in them by the mighty operation of his Spirit, "according to the exceeding greatness of his power," Eph. i. 19. And so they "believe" (God making them differ from others, 1 Cor. iv. 7, in the enjoyment of the means) "who are ordained to eternal life," Acts xiii. 48. Their being ordained to eternal life was the fountain from whence their faith did flow; and so "the election hath obtained, and the rest were blinded," Rom. xi. 7.

3. All the blessings of the new covenant are procured and purchased by him in whom the promises thereof are ratified, and to whom they are made; for all the good things thereof are contained in and exhibited by those promises, through the working of the Spirit of God. Now, concerning the promises of the covenant, and their being confirmed in Christ, and made unto his, as Gal. iii. 16, with what is to be understood in those expressions, was before declared. Therefore, all the good things of the covenant are the effects, fruits, and purchase of the death of Christ, he and all things for

him being the substance and whole of it. Farther; that faith is of the good things of the new covenant is apparent from the description thereof, Jer. xxxi. 33, 34; Heb. viii. 10–12; Ezek. xxxvi. 25–27, with divers other places, as might clearly be manifested if we affected copiousness in *causa facili*.

4. That without which it is utterly impossible that we should be saved must of necessity be procured by him by whom we are fully and effectually saved. Let them that can, declare how he can be said to procure salvation fully and effectually for us, and not be the author and purchaser of that (for he is the author of our salvation by the way of purchase) without which it is utterly impossible we should attain salvation. Now, without faith it is utterly impossible that ever any should attain salvation, Heb. xi. 6, Mark xvi. 16; but Jesus Christ, according to his name, doth perfectly save us, Matt. i. 21, procuring for us " eternal redemption," Heb. ix. 12, being " able to save to the uttermost them that come unto God by him," chap. vii. 25: and therefore must faith also be within the compass of those things that are procured by him.

5. The Scripture is clear, in express terms, and such as are so equivalent that they are not liable to any evasion; as Phil. i. 29, " It is given unto us, ὑπὲρ Χριστοῦ, on the behalf of Christ, for Christ's sake, to believe on him." Faith, or belief, is the gift, and Christ the procurer of it: "God hath blessed us with all spiritual blessings in him in heavenly places," Eph. i. 3. If faith be a spiritual blessing, it is bestowed on us " in him," and so also for his sake; if it be not, it is not worth contending about in this sense and way: so that, let others look which way they will, I desire to look unto Jesus as the " author and finisher of our faith," Heb. xii. 2. Divers other reasons, arguments, and places of Scripture might be added for the confirmation of this truth; but I hope I have said enough, and do not desire to say all. The sum of the whole reason may be reduced to this head, —namely, if the fruit and effect procured and wrought by the death of Christ absolutely, not depending on any condition in man to be fulfilled, be not common to all, then did not Christ die for all; but the supposal is true, as is evident in the grace of faith, which being procured by the death of Christ, to be absolutely bestowed on them for whom he died, is not common to all: therefore, our Saviour did not die for all.

ARG. X. We argue from the type to the antitype, or the thing signified by it; which will evidently restrain the oblation of Christ to God's elect. The people of Israel were certainly, in all remarkable things that happened unto them, typical of the church of God; as the apostle at large [declares], 1 Cor. x. 11. Especially, their institutions and ordinances were all representative of the spiritual things of the gospel; their priests, altar, sacrifices, were but all shadows of the good things to come in Jesus Christ; their Canaan was a type of heaven, Heb. iv. 3, 9; as also Jerusalem or Sion, Gal. iv. 26, Heb. xii. 22. The whole people itself was a type of God's church, his elect, his chosen and called people: whence as they were called a "holy people, a royal priesthood;" so also, in allusion to them, are believers, 1 Pet. ii. 5, 9. Yea, God's people are in innumerable places called his "Israel," as it is farther expounded, Heb. viii. 8. A true Israelite is as much as a true believer, John i. 47; and he is a Jew who is so in the hidden man of the heart. I hope it need not be proved that that people, as delivered from bondage, preserved, taken nigh unto God, brought into Canaan, was typical of God's spiritual church, of elect believers. Whence we thus argue:—Those only are really and spiritually redeemed by Jesus Christ who were designed, signified, typified by the people of Israel in their carnal, typical redemption (for no reason in the world can be rendered why some should be typed out in the same condition, partakers of the same good, and not others); but by the people of the Jews, in their deliverance from Egypt, bringing into Canaan, with all their ordinances and institutions, only the elect, the church of God, was typed out, as was before proved. And, in truth, it is the most senseless thing in the world, to imagine that the Jews were under a type to all the whole world, or indeed to any but God's chosen ones, as is proved at large, Heb. ix. x. Were the Jews and their ordinances types to the seven nations whom they destroyed and supplanted in Canaan? were they so to Egyptians, infidels, and haters of God and his Christ? We conclude, then, assuredly, from that just proportion that ought to be observed between the types and the things typified, that only the elect of God, his church and chosen ones, are redeemed by Jesus Christ.

CHAPTER V.

Being a continuance of arguments from the nature and description of the thing in hand; and first, of redemption.

ARG. XI. That doctrine which will not by any means suit with nor be made conformable to the thing signified by it, and the expression, literal and deductive, whereby in Scripture it is held out unto us, but implies evident contradictions unto them, cannot possibly be sound and sincere, as is the milk of the word. But now such is this persuasion of universal redemption; it can never be suited nor fitted to the thing itself, or redemption, nor to those expressions whereby in the Scripture it is held out unto us. Universal redemption, and yet many to die in captivity, is a contradiction irreconcilable in itself.

To manifest this, let us consider some of the chiefest words and phrases whereby the matter concerning which we treat is delivered in the Scripture, such as are, *redemption, reconciliation, satisfaction, merit, dying for us,* bearing our sins, suretiship,—his being God, a common person, a Jesus, saving to the utmost, a sacrifice putting away sin, and the like; to which we may add the importance of some prepositions and other words used in the original about this business: and doubt not but we shall easily find that the general ransom, or rather universal redemption, will hardly suit to any of them; but it is too long for the bed, and must be cropped at the head or heels.

Begin we with the word REDEMPTION itself, which we will consider, name and thing. Redemption, which in the Scripture is λύτρωσις sometimes, but most frequently ἀπολύτρωσις, is the delivery of any one from captivity and misery by the intervention λύτρου, of a price or ransom. That this ransom, or price of our deliverance, was the blood of Christ is evident; he calls it λύτρον, Matt. xx. 28; and [it is called] ἀντίλυτρον, 1 Tim. ii. 6,—that is, the price of such a redemption, that which was received as a valuable consideration for our dismission. Now, that which is aimed at in the payment of this price is, the deliverance of those from the evil wherewith they were oppressed for whom the price is paid; it being in this spiritual redemption as it is in corporal and civil, only with the alteration of some circumstances, as the nature of the thing enforceth. This the Holy Spirit manifesteth by comparing the "blood of Christ" in this work of redemption with "silver and gold," and such other things as are the intervening ransom in civil redemption, 1 Pet. i. 18, 19. The evil wherewith we were oppressed was the punishment which we had deserved;—that is, the satisfaction required when the debt is sin; which also we are, by the payment of this price, delivered from; so Gal. iii. 13: for we are "justified freely by his grace, through the redemption that is in Christ Jesus," Rom. iii. 24; "in whom we have redemption through his blood, the forgiveness of sins," Eph. i. 7; Col. i. 14. Free justification from the guilt, and pardon of sin, in the deliverance from the punishment due unto it, is the effect of the redemption procured by the payment of the price we before mentioned: as if a man should have his friend in bondage, and he should go and lay out his estate to pay the price of his freedom that is set upon his head by him that detains him, and so set him at liberty. Only, as was before intimated, this spiritual redemption hath some supereminent things in it, that are not to be found in other deliverances; as,—

First, He that receives the ransom doth also give it. Christ is a propitiation to appease and atone the Lord, but the Lord himself set him forth so to be, Rom. iii. 24, 25; whence he himself is often said to redeem us. His love is the cause of the price in respect of its procurement, and his justice accepts of the price in respect of its merit; for Christ " came down from heaven to do the will of him that sent him," John vi. 38; Heb. x. 9, 10. It is otherwise in the redemption amongst men, where he that receives the ransom hath no hand in the providing of it.

Secondly, The captive or prisoner is not so much freed from his power who detains him as brought into his favour. When a captive amongst men is redeemed, by the payment of a ransom, he is instantly to be set free from the power and authority of him that did detain him; but in this spiritual redemption, upon the payment of the ransom for us, which is the blood of Jesus, we are not removed from God, but are " brought nigh" unto him, Eph. ii. 13,—not delivered from his power, but restored to his favour,—our misery being a punishment by the way of banishment as well as thraldom.

Thirdly, As the judge was to be satisfied, so the jailer was to be conquered; God, the judge, giving him leave to fight for his dominion, which was wrongfully usurped, though that whereby he had it was by the Lord justly inflicted, and his thraldom by us rightly deserved, Heb. ii. 14; Col. ii. 15. And he lost his power, as strong as he was, for striving to grasp more than he could hold; for the foundation of his kingdom being sin, assaulting Christ who did no sin, he lost his power over them that Christ came to redeem, having no part in him. So was the strong man bound, and his house spoiled.

In these and some few other circumstances is our spiritual redemption diversified from civil; but for the main it answers the word in the propriety thereof, according to the use that it hath amongst men. Now, there is a twofold way whereby this is in the Scripture expressed: for sometimes our Saviour is said to die for our redemption, and sometimes for the redemption of our transgressions; both tending to the same purpose,—yea, both expressions, as I conceive, signify the same thing. Of the latter you have an example, Heb. ix. 15. He died εἰς ἀπολύτρωσιν παραβάσεων· which, say some, is a metonymy, transgressions being put for transgressors; others, that it is a proper expression for the paying of a price whereby we may be delivered from the evil of our transgressions. The other expression you have, Eph. i. 7, and in divers other places, where the words λύτρον and ἀπολύτρωσις do concur; as also Matt. xx. 28, and Mark x. 45. Now, these words, especially that of αντίλυτρον, 1 Tim. ii. 6, do always denote, by the not-to-be-wrested, genuine signification of them, the payment of a price, or an equal compensation, in lieu of something to be done or grant made by him to whom that price is paid. Having given these few notions concerning redemption in general, let us now see how applicable it is unto general redemption.

Redemption is the freeing of a man from misery by the intervention of a ransom, as appeareth. Now, when a ransom is paid for the liberty of a prisoner, is it not all the justice in the world that he should have and enjoy the liberty so purchased for him by a valuable consideration? If I should pay a thousand pounds for a man's deliverance from bondage to him that detains him, who hath power to set him free, and is contented with the price I give, were it not injurious to me and the poor prisoner that his deliverance be not accomplished? Can it possibly be conceived that there should be a redemption of men, and those men not redeemed? that a price should be paid, and the purchase not consummated? Yet all this must be made true, and innumerable other absurdities, if universal redemption be asserted. A price is paid for all, yet few delivered; the redemption of all consummated, yet few of them redeemed; the judge satisfied, the jailer conquered, and yet the prisoners inthralled! Doubtless, "*universal*" and "*redemption*," where the greatest part of men perish, are as irreconcilable as "*Roman*" and "*Catholic.*" If there be a universal redemption of all, then all men are redeemed. If they are redeemed, then are they delivered from all misery, virtually or actually, whereunto they were inthralled, and that by the intervention of a ransom. Why, then, are not all saved? In a word, the redemption wrought by Christ being the full deliverance of the persons redeemed from all misery, wherein they were inwrapped, by the price of his blood, it cannot possibly be conceived to be universal unless all be saved: so that the opinion of the Universalists is unsuitable to redemption.

CHAPTER VI.

Of the nature of reconciliation, and the argument taken from thence.

ARG. XII. Another thing ascribed to the death of Christ, and, by the consent of all, extending itself unto all for whom he died, is RECONCILIATION. This in the Scripture is clearly proposed under a double notion; first, of God to us; secondly, of us to God;—both usually ascribed to the death and blood-shedding of Jesus Christ: for those who were "enemies he reconciled in the body of his flesh through death," Col. i. 21, 22. And, doubtless, these things do exactly answer one another. All those to whom he hath reconciled God, he doth also reconcile unto God: for unless both be effected, it cannot be said to be a perfect reconciliation; for how can it be, if peace be made only on the one side? Yea, it is utterly impossible that a division of these two can be rationally apprehended: for if God be reconciled, not man, why doth not he reconcile him, seeing it is confessedly in his power; and if man should be reconciled, not God, how can he be ready to receive all that come unto him? Now, that God and all and every one in the world are actually reconciled, and made at peace in Jesus Christ, I hope will not be affirmed. But to clear this, we must a little consider the nature of *reconciliation* as it is proposed to us in the gospel; unto which, also, some light may be given from the nature of the thing itself, and the use of the word in civil things.

Reconciliation is the renewing of friendship between parties before at variance, both parties being properly said to be reconciled, even both he that offendeth and he that was offended. God and man were set at distance, at enmity and variance, by sin. Man was the party offending, God offended, and the alienation was mutual, on either side;—but yet with this difference, that man was alienated in respect of affections, the ground and cause of anger and enmity; God in respect of the effects and issue of anger and enmity. The word in the New Testament is καταλλαγή, and the verb καταλλάσσω, *reconciliation, to reconcile;* both from ἀλλάττω, *to change*, or to turn from one thing, one mind, to another: whence the first native signification of those words is *permutatio*, and *permutare*, (so Arist. Eth. 3, Τὸν βίον πρὸς μιχρὰ κέρδη—καταλλάττονται,[1]) because most commonly those that are reconciled are changed in respect of their affections, always in respect of the distance and variance, and in respect of the effects; thence it signifieth reconciliation, and to reconcile. And the word may not be affirmed of any business, or of any men, until both parties are actually reconciled, and all differences removed in respect of any former grudge and ill-will. If one be well pleased with the other, and that other continue ἀκατάλλακτος, unappeased and implacable, there is no reconciliation. When our Saviour gives that command, that he that brought his gift to the altar, and there remembered that his brother had aught against him,—was offended with him for any cause, —he should go and be reconciled to him, [he] fully intendeth a mutual returning of minds one to another, especially respecting the appeasing and atoning of him that was offended. Neither are these words used among men in any other sense, but always denote, even in common speech, a full redintegration of friendship between dissenting parties, with reference most times to some compensation made to the offended party. The reconciling of the one party and the other may be distinguished, but both are required to make up an entire reconciliation.

As, then, the folly of Socinus and his sectaries is remarkable, who would have the reconciliation mentioned in the Scripture to be nothing but our conversion to God, without the appeasing of his anger and turning away his wrath from us,—which is a reconciliation hopping on one leg,—so that distinction of some between the reconciliation of God to man, making that to be universal towards all, and

---

[1] Aristotle is speaking of soldiers who "barter their life for small gains." The quotation is exceedingly apt and felicitous when the reference is understood.—Ed.

the reconciliation of man to God, making that to be only of a small number of those to whom God is reconciled, is a no less monstrous figment. Mutual alienation must have mutual reconciliation, seeing they are *correlata*. The state between God and man, before the reconciliation made by Christ, was a state of enmity. Man was at enmity with God; we were his "enemies," Col. i. 21; Rom. v. 10; hating him and opposing ourselves to him, in the highest rebellion, to the utmost of our power. God also was thus far an enemy to us, that his "wrath" was on us, Eph. ii. 3; which remaineth on us until we do believe, John iii. 36. To make perfect reconciliation (which Christ is said in many places to do), it is required, first, That the wrath of God be turned away, his anger removed, and all the effects of enmity on his part towards us; secondly, That we be turned away from our opposition to him, and brought into voluntary obedience. Until both these be effected, reconciliation is not perfected. Now, both these are in the Scripture assigned to our Saviour, as the effects of his death and sacrifice.

1. He turned away the wrath of God from us, and so appeased him towards us; that was the reconciling of God by his death: for "when we were enemies, we were reconciled to God by the death of his Son," Rom. v. 10. That here is meant the reconciling of God, as that part of reconciliation which consisteth in turning away his wrath from us, is most apparent, it being that whereby God chiefly commendeth his love to us, which certainly is in the forgiveness of sin, by the aversion of his anger due to it; as also being opposed to our being saved from the wrath to come, in the latter end of the verse, which compriseth our conversion and whole reconciliation to God. Besides, verse 11, we are said to receive τὴν καταλλαγήν, this "reconciliation" (which, I know not by what means, we have translated " atonement"); which cannot be meant of our reconciliation to God, or conversion, which we cannot properly be said to accept or receive, but of him to us, which we receive when it is apprehended by faith.

2. He turneth us away from our enmity towards God, redeeming and reconciling us to God by "the blood of his cross," Col. i. 20;—to wit, then meritoriously, satisfactorily, by the way of acquisition and purchase; accomplishing it in due time actually and efficiently by his Spirit. Both these ye have jointly mentioned, 2 Cor. v. 18–20; where we may see, first, God being reconciled to us in Christ, which consisteth in a non-imputation of iniquities, and is the subject-matter of the ministry, verses 18, 19; secondly, the reconciling of us to God, by accepting the pardon of our sins, which is the end of the ministry, verse 20;—as the same is also at large declared, Eph. ii. 13–15. The actual, then, and effectual accomplishment of both these, "simul et semel," in respect of procurement, by continuance, and in process of time, in the ordinances of the gospel, in respect of final accomplish-

ment on the part of men, do make up that reconciliation which is the effect of the death of Christ; for so it is in many places assigned to be: " We are reconciled to God by the death of his Son," Rom. v. 10; " And you, that were sometime alienated, hath he reconciled in the body of his flesh through death," Col. i. 21, 22: which is in sundry places so evident in the Scripture, that none can possibly deny reconciliation to be the immediate effect and product of the death of Christ.

Now, how this reconciliation can possibly be reconciled with universal redemption, I am no way able to discern; for if reconciliation be the proper effect of the death of Christ, as is confessed by all, then if he died for all, I ask how cometh it to pass,—First, That God is not reconciled to all? as he is not, for his wrath abideth on some, John iii. 36, and reconciliation is the aversion of wrath. Secondly, That all are not reconciled to God? as they are not, for " by nature all are the children of wrath," Eph. ii. 3; and some all their lives do nothing but "treasure up wrath against the day of wrath," Rom. ii. 5. Thirdly, How, then, can it be that reconciliation should be wrought between God and all men, and yet neither God reconciled to all nor all reconciled to God? Fourthly, If God be reconciled to all, when doth he begin to be unreconciled towards them that perish? by what alteration is it? in his will or nature? Fifthly, If all be reconciled by the death of Christ, when do they begin to be unreconciled who perish, being born children of wrath? Sixthly, Seeing that reconciliation on the part of God consists in the turning away of his wrath and not imputing of iniquity, 2 Cor. v. 18, 19, which is justification, rendering us blessed, Rom. iv. 6–8, why, if God be reconciled to all, are not all justified and made blessed through a non-imputation of their sin? They who have found out a redemption where none are redeemed, and a reconciliation where none are reconciled, can easily answer these and such other questions; which to do I leave them to their leisure, and in the meantime conclude this part of our argument. That reconciliation which is the renewing of lost friendship, the slaying of enmity, the making up of peace, the appeasing of God, and turning away of his wrath, attended with a non-imputation of iniquities; and, on our part, conversion to God by faith and repentance;—this, I say, being that reconciliation which is the effect of the death and blood of Christ, it cannot be asserted in reference to any, nor Christ said to die for any other, but only those concerning whom all the properties of it, and acts wherein it doth consist, may be truly affirmed; which, whether they may be of all men or not, let all men judge.

CHAPTER VII.

Of the nature of the satisfaction of Christ, with arguments from thence.

ARG. XIII. A third way whereby the death of Christ for sinners is expressed is SATISFACTION,—namely, that by his death he made satisfaction to the justice of God for their sins for whom he died, that so they might go free. It is true, the word *satisfaction* is not found in the Latin or English Bible applied to the death of Christ. In the New Testament it is not at all, and in the Old but twice, Num. xxxv. 31, 32; but the thing itself intended by that word is everywhere ascribed to the death of our Saviour, there being also other words in the original languages equivalent to that whereby we express the thing in hand. Now, that Christ did thus make satisfaction for all them, or rather for their sins, for whom he died, is (as far as I know) confessed by all that are but outwardly called after his name, the wretched Socinians excepted, with whom at this time we have not to do. Let us, then, first see what this satisfaction is; then how inconsistent it is with universal redemption.

Satisfaction is a term borrowed from the law, applied properly to things, thence translated and accommodated unto persons; and it is *a full compensation of the creditor from the debtor.* To whom any thing is due from any man, he is in that regard that man's creditor; and the other is his debtor, upon whom there is an obligation to pay or restore what is so due from him, until he be freed by a lawful breaking of that obligation, by making it null and void; which must be done by yielding *satisfaction* to what his *creditor* can require by virtue of that obligation: as, if I owe a man a hundred pounds, I am his debtor, by virtue of the bond wherein I am bound, until some such thing be done as recompenseth him, and moveth him to cancel the bond; which is called *satisfaction.* Hence, from things *real*, it was and is translated to things *personal*. Personal debts are injuries and faults; which when a man hath committed, he is liable to punishment. He that is to inflict that punishment, or upon whom it lieth to see that it be done, is, or may be, the creditor; which he must do, unless satisfaction be made. Now, there may be a twofold satisfaction:—First, By a solution, or paying the *very thing* that is in the obligation, either by the party himself that is bound, or by some other in his stead: as, if I owe a man twenty pounds, and my friend goeth and payeth it, my creditor is fully satisfied. Secondly, By a solution, or paying of so much, although in another kind, not the same that is in the obligation, which, by the creditor's acceptation, stands in the lieu of it; upon which, also, freedom from the obligation followeth, not necessarily, but by virtue of an act of favour.

In the business in hand,—First, the *debtor* is *man;* he oweth the ten thousand talents, Matt. xviii. 24. Secondly, The *debt* is *sin:* "Forgive us our debts," Matt. vi. 12. Thirdly, That which is required in lieu thereof to make satisfaction for it, is *death:* "In the day that thou eatest thereof, thou shalt surely die," Gen. ii. 17; "The wages of sin is death," Rom. vi. 23. Fourthly, The *obligation* whereby the debtor is tied and bound is the *law,* "Cursed is every one," etc., Gal. iii. 10; Deut. xxvii. 26; the justice of God, Rom. i. 32; and the truth of God, Gen. iii. 3. Fifthly, The *creditor* that requireth this of us is *God,* considered as the party offended, severe Judge, and supreme Lord of all things. Sixthly, That which interveneth to the destruction of the obligation is the *ransom* paid by Christ: Rom. iii. 25, "God set him forth to be a propitiation through faith in his blood."

I shall not enter upon any long discourse of the satisfaction made by Christ, but only so far clear it as is necessary to give light to the matter in hand. To this end two things must be cleared:—First, That Christ did make such satisfaction as whereof we treat; as also wherein it doth consist. Secondly, What is that act of God towards man, the debtor, which doth and ought to follow the satisfaction made. For the FIRST, I told you the word itself doth not occur in this business in the Scripture, but the thing signified by it (being a compensation made to God by Christ for our debts) most frequently. For to make satisfaction to God for our sins, it is required only that he undergo the punishment due to them; for that is the satisfaction required where sin is the debt. Now, this Christ has certainly effected; for "his own self bare our sins in his own body on the tree," 1 Pet. ii. 24; "By his knowledge shall my righteous servant justify many, for he shall bear their iniquities," Isa. liii. 11. The word נָשָׂא (*nasa*), also, verse 12, arguing a taking of the punishment of sin from us and translating it to himself, signifieth as much, yea all that we do by the word *satisfaction.* So also doth that of ἀνήνεγχεν, used by Peter in the room thereof: for to bear iniquity, in the Scripture language, is to undergo the punishment due to it, Lev. v. 1; which we call to *make satisfaction* for it;—which is farther illustrated by a declaration how he bare our sins, even by being "wounded for our transgressions, and bruised for our iniquities," Isa. liii. 5; whereunto is added, in the close, that "the chastisement of our peace was upon him." Every chastisement is either νουθετική, for instruction, or παραδειγματική, for example, punishment and correction. The first can have no place in our Saviour; the Son of God had no need to be taught with such thorns and briers. It must, therefore, be for punishment and correction, and that for our sins then upon him; whereby our peace or freedom from punishment was procured.

Moreover, in the New Testament there be divers words and expressions concerning the death of our Saviour, holding out that thing which by *satisfaction* we do intend; as when, first, it is termed προσφορά· Eph. v. 2, Παρέδωκεν ἑαυτὸν προσφορὰν καὶ θυσίαν,—an oblation or sacrifice of expiation; as appeareth by that type of it with which it is compared, Heb. ix. 13, 14. Of the same force also is the word אָשָׁם (*ascham*), Isa. liii. 10; Lev. vii. 2. "He made his soul an offering for sin,"—a piacular sacrifice for the removing of it away; which the apostle abundantly cleareth, in saying that he was made ἁμαρτία, "sin" itself, 2 Cor. v. 21, sin being there put for the adjunct of it, or the punishment due unto it. So also is he termed ἱλασμός, 1 John ii. 2. Whereunto answers the Hebrew *chitte*, used Gen. xxxi. 39, אָנֹכִי אֲחַטֶּנָּה, "Ego illud expiabam," which is to undergo the debt, and to make compensation for it; which was the office of him who was to be Job's goël, chap. xix. 25. All which and divers other words, which in part shall be afterward considered, do declare the very same thing which we intend by *satisfaction;* even a taking upon him the whole punishment due to sin, and in the offering of himself doing that which God, who was offended, was more delighted and pleased withal, than he was displeased and offended with all the sins of all those that he suffered and offered himself for. And there can be no more complete satisfaction made to any than by doing that which he is more contented with, than discontented and troubled with that for which he must be satisfied. God was more pleased with the obedience, offering, and sacrifice of his Son, than displeased with the sins and rebellions of all the elect. As if a good king should have a company of his subjects stand out in rebellion against him, and he were thereby moved to destroy them, because they would not have him reign over them, and the only son of that king should put in for their pardon, making a tender to his father of some excellent conquest by him lately achieved, beseeching him to accept of it, and be pleased with his poor subjects, so as to receive them into favour again; or, which is nearer, should offer himself to undergo that punishment which his justice had allotted for the rebels, and should accordingly do it;—he should properly make satisfaction for their offence, and in strict justice they ought to be pardoned. This was Christ, as that one *hircus,* ἀποπομπαῖος, sent-away goat, that bare and carried away all the sins of the people of God, to fall himself under them, though with assurance to break all the bonds of death, and to live for ever. Now, whereas I said that there is a twofold satisfaction, whereby the debtor is freed from the obligation that is upon him,—the one being *solutio ejusdem,* payment of the same thing that was in the obligation; the other, *solutio tantidem,* of that which is not the same, nor equivalent unto it, but only in the gracious acceptation of the creditor,—it is worth our inquiry which of these it was that our Saviour did perform.

He[1] who is esteemed by many to have handled this argument
with most exactness, denieth that the payment made by Christ for us
(by the payment of the debt of sin understand, by analogy, the undergoing of the punishment due unto it) was *solutio ejusdem*, or of the
same thing directly which was in the obligation: for which he giveth
some reasons; as,—First, Because such a solution, satisfaction, or
payment, is attended with actual freedom from the obligation. Secondly, Because, where such a solution is made, there is no room for
remission or pardon. "It is true,"saith he, "deliverance followeth upon
it; but this deliverance cannot be by way of gracious pardon, for
there needeth not the interceding of any such act of grace. But
now," saith he, "that satisfaction whereby some other thing is offered
than that which was in the obligation may be admitted or refused,
according as the creditor pleaseth; and being admitted for any, it is
by an act of grace ; and such was the satisfaction made by Christ."
Now, truly, none of these reasons seem of so much weight to me as
to draw me into that persuasion.

For the first reason rests upon that, for the confirmation of it,
which cannot be granted,—namely, that actual freedom from the
obligation doth not follow the satisfaction made by Christ; for by
death he did deliver us from death, and that actually, so far as that
the elect are said to die and rise with him. He did actually, or *ipso
facto*, deliver us from the curse, by being made a curse for us; and
the hand-writing that was against us, even the whole obligation,
was taken out of the way and nailed to his cross. It is true, all for
whom he did this do not instantly actually apprehend and perceive
it, which is impossible: but yet that hinders not but that they have
all the fruits of his death in actual right, though not in actual possession, which last they cannot have until at least it be made known
to them. As, if a man pay a ransom for a prisoner detained in a
foreign country, the very day of the payment and acceptation of it
the prisoner hath right to his liberty, although he cannot enjoy it
until such time as tidings of it are brought unto him, and a warrant
produced for his delivery. So that that reason is nothing but a beg-
ging τοῦ ἐν ἀρχῇ.

Secondly, The satisfaction of Christ, by the payment of the same
thing that was required in the obligation, is no way prejudicial to
that free, gracious condonation of sin so often mentioned. God's
gracious pardoning of sin compriseth the whole dispensation of grace
towards us in Christ, whereof thēre are two parts:—First, The laying of our sin on Christ, or making him to be sin for us; which was

---

[1] The allusion is to Grotius, among whose varied and elaborate theological works
there is a treatise entitled, "Defensio Fidei Catholicæ de Satisfactione Christi, contra
F. Socinum." The distinguished reputation of Grotius in legal science explains some
references which Owen makes in discussing his views.--ED.

merely and purely an act of free grace, which he did for his own sake. *Secondly,* The gracious imputation of the righteousness of Christ to us, or making us the righteousness of God in him; which is no less of grace and mercy, and that because the very merit of Christ himself hath its foundation in a free compact and covenant. However, that remission, grace, and pardon, which is in God for sinners, is not opposed to Christ's merits, but ours. He pardoneth all to us; but he spared not his only Son, he bated him not one farthing. The freedom, then, of pardon hath not its foundation in any defect of the merit or satisfaction of Christ, but in three other things:—*First,* The will of God freely appointing this satisfaction of Christ, John iii. 16; Rom. v. 8; 1 John iv. 9. *Secondly,* In a gracious acceptation of that decreed satisfaction in our steads; for so many, no more. *Thirdly,* In a free application of the death of Christ unto us.

Remission, then, excludes not a full satisfaction by the solution of the very thing in the obligation, but only the solution or satisfaction by him to whom pardon and remission are granted. So that, notwithstanding any thing said to the contrary, the death of Christ made satisfaction in the very thing that was required in the obligation. He took away the curse, by "being made a curse," Gal. iii. 13. He delivered us from sin, being "made sin," 2 Cor. v. 21. He underwent death, that we might be delivered from death. All our debt was in the curse of the law, which he wholly underwent. Neither do we read of any relaxation of the punishment in the Scripture, but only a commutation of the person; which being done, "God condemned sin in the flesh of his Son," Rom. viii. 3, Christ standing in our stead: and so reparation was made unto God, and satisfaction given for all the detriment that might accrue to him by the sin and rebellion of them for whom this satisfaction was made. His justice was violated, and he "sets forth Christ to be a propitiation" for our sins, "that he might be just, and the justifier of him which believeth in Jesus," Rom. iii. 25, 26. And never, indeed, was his justice more clearly demonstrated than in causing "the iniquity of us all to meet upon him." His law was broken; therefore Christ comes to be "the end of the law for righteousness," Rom. x. 4. Our offence and disobedience was to him distasteful; in the obedience of Christ he took full pleasure, Rom. v. 17; Matt. iii. 16.

Now from all this, thus much (to clear up the nature of the satisfaction made by Christ) appeareth,—namely, It was a full, valuable compensation, made to the justice of God, for all the sins of all those for whom he made satisfaction, by undergoing that same punishment which, by reason of the obligation that was upon them, they themselves were bound to undergo. When I say *the same,* I mean essentially the same in weight and pressure, though not in all accidents of duration and the like; for it was impossible that he should be detained by death. Now, whether this will stand in the justice of God, that any of these should perish eternally for whom Jesus Christ made so full, perfect, and complete satisfaction, we shall presently inquire; and this is the first thing that we are to consider in this business.

SECONDLY, We must look what act of God it is that is exercised either towards us or our Saviour in this business. That God in the whole is the party offended by our sins is by all confessed. It is his law that is broken, his glory that is impaired, his honour that is abased by our sin: "If I be a father," saith he, "where is mine honour?" Mal. i. 6. Now, the law of nature and universal right requireth that the party offended be recompensed in whatsoever he is injured by the fault of another. Being thus offended, the Lord is to be considered under a twofold notion:—First, In respect of *us*, he is as a creditor, and all we miserable debtors; to him we owe the "ten thousand talents," Matt. xviii. 24. And our Saviour hath taught us to call our sins our "debts," Matt. vi. 12; and the payment of this debt the Lord requireth and exacteth of us. Secondly, In respect of *Christ*,—on whom he was pleased to lay the punishment of us all, to make our iniquity to meet upon him, not sparing him, but requiring the debt at his hands to the utmost farthing,—God is considered as the supreme Lord and Governor of all, the only Lawgiver, who alone had power so far to relax his own law as to have the name of a surety put into the obligation, which before was not there, and then to require the whole debt of that surety; for he alone hath power of life and death, James iv. 12. Now, these two acts are eminent in God in this business:—First, An act of severe justice, as a creditor exacting the payment of the debt at the hands of the debtor; which, where sin is the debt, is punishment, as was before declared: the justice of God being repaired thereby in whatsoever it was before violated. Secondly, An act of sovereignty or supreme dominion, in translating the punishment from the principal debtor to the surety, which of his free grace he himself had given and bestowed on the debtor: "He spared not his own Son, but delivered him up to death for us all." Hence, let these two things be observed:—

1. That God accepteth of the punishment of Christ as a creditor accepteth of his due debt, when he spares not the debtor, but requires the uttermost farthing. It is true of punishment, as punishment, there is no creditor properly; for, "Delicta puniri publicè interest." But this punishment being considered also as a price, as it is, 1 Cor. vi. 20, it must be paid to the hands of some creditor, as this was into the hands of God; whence Christ is said to come to do God's will, Heb. x. 9, and to satisfy him, as John vi. 38. Neither, indeed, do the arguments that some have used to prove that God, as a creditor,

cannot inflict punishment, nor yet by virtue of supreme dominion, seem to me of any great weight. Divers I find urged by him whose great skill in the law, and such terms as these, might well give him sanctuary from such weak examiners as myself; but he that hath so foully betrayed the truth of God in other things, and corrupted his word, deserves not our assent in any thing but what by evidence of reason is extorted. Let us, then, see what there is of that in this which we have now in hand:—

First, then, he tells us that " The right of punishing in the rector or lawgiver can neither be a right of absolute dominion nor a right of a creditor; because these things belong to him, and are exercised for his own sake, who hath them, but the right of punishing is for the good of community."

Ans. Refer this reason unto God, which is the aim of it, and it will appear to be of no value; for we deny that there is any thing in him or done by him primarily for the good of any but himself. His αὐτάρκεια, or self-sufficiency, will not allow that he should do any thing with an ultimate respect to any thing but himself. And whereas he saith that the right of punishing is for the good of community, we answer, that " bonum universi," the good of community, is the glory of God, and that only. So that these things in him cannot be distinguished.

Secondly, He addeth, " Punishment is not in and for itself desirable, but only for community's sake. Now, the right of dominion and the right of a creditor are things in themselves expetible and desirable, without the consideration of any public aim."

Ans. First, That the comparison ought not to be between punishment and the right of dominion, but between the right of punishment and the right of dominion; the fact of one is not to be compared with the right of the other.

Secondly, God desireth nothing, neither is there any thing desirable to him, but only for himself. To suppose a good desirable to God for its own sake is intolerable

Thirdly, There be some acts of supreme dominion, in themselves and for their own·sake, as little desirable as any act of punishment; as the annihilation of an innocent creature, which Grotius will not deny but that God may do.

Thirdly, He proceedeth, " Any one may, without any wrong, go off from the right of supreme dominion or creditorship; but the Lord cannot omit the act of punishment to some sins, as of the impenitent."

Ans. God may, by virtue of his supreme dominion, omit punishment without any wrong or prejudice to his justice. It is as great a thing to impute sin where it is not, and to inflict punishment upon that imputation, as not to impute sin where it is, and to remove or not to inflict punishment upon that non-imputation. Now, the first of these God did towards Christ; and, therefore, he may do the latter.

Secondly, The wrong or injustice of not punishing any sin or sins doth not arise from any natural obligation, but the consideration of an affirmative positive act of God's will, whereby he hath purposed that he will do it.

Fourthly, He adds, "None can be called just for using his own right or lordship; but God is called just for punishing or not remitting sin," Rev. xvi. 5.

Ans. First, However it be in other causes, yet in this God may certainly be said to be just in exacting his debt or using his dominion, because his own will is the only rule of justice.

Secondly, We do not say punishing is an act of dominion, but an act of exacting a due debt; the requiring this of Christ in our stead supposing the intervention of an act of supreme dominion.

Fifthly, His last reason is, "Because that virtue whereby one goeth off from his dominion or remitteth his debt, is liberality; but that virtue whereby a man abstaineth from punishing is clemency: so that punishment can be no act of exacting a debt or acting a dominion."

Ans. The virtue whereby a man goeth off from the exacting of that which is due, universally considered, is not always liberality; for, as Grotius himself confesseth, a debt may arise and accrue to any by the injury of his fame, credit, or name, by a lie, slander, or otherwise. Now, that virtue whereby a man is moved not to exact payment by way of reparation, is not in this case liberality, but either clemency, or that grace of the gospel for which moralists have no name; and so it is with every party offended, so often as he hath a right of requiring punishment from his offender, which yet he doth not. So that, notwithstanding these exceptions, this is eminently seen in this business of satisfaction,—that God, as a creditor, doth exactly require the payment of the debt by the way of punishment.

2. The second thing eminent in it is, an act of supreme sovereignty and dominion, requiring the punishment of Christ, for the full, complete answering of the obligation and fulfilling of the law, Rom. viii. 3, x. 4.

Now, these things being thus at large unfolded, we may see, in brief, some natural consequences following and attending them as they are laid down; as,—First, That the full and due debt of all those for whom Jesus Christ was responsible was fully paid in to God, according to the utmost extent of the obligation. Secondly, That the Lord, who is a just creditor, ought in all equity to cancel the bond, to surcease all suits, actions, and molestations against the debtors, full payment being made unto him for the debt. Thirdly, That the debt thus paid was not this or that sin, but all the sins of all those for whom and in whose name this payment was made, 1 John i. 7, as was before demonstrated. Fourthly, That a second payment of a debt once paid, or a requiring of it, is not answerable to the justice which God demonstrated in setting forth Christ to be a propitiation for our sins, Rom. iii. 25. Fifthly, That whereas to receive a discharge from farther trouble is equitably due to a debtor who hath been in obligation, his debt being paid, the Lord, having accepted of the payment from Christ in the stead of all them for whom he died, ought in justice, according to that obligation which, in free grace, he hath put upon himself, to grant them a discharge. Sixthly, That considering that relaxation of the law which, by the supreme power of the lawgiver, was effected, as to the persons suffering the punishment required, such actual satisfaction is made thereto, that it can lay no more to their charge for whom Christ died than if they had really fulfilled, in the way of obedience, whatsoever it did require, Rom. viii. 32–34.

Now, how consistent these things (in themselves evident, and clearly following the doctrine of Christ's satisfaction, before declared) are with universal redemption is easily discernible; for,—First, If the full debt of all be paid to the utmost extent of the obligation, how comes it to pass that so many are shut up in prison to eternity, never freed from their debts? Secondly, If the Lord, as a just creditor, ought to cancel all obligations and surcease all suits against such as have their debts so paid, whence is it that his wrath smokes against some to all eternity? Let none tell me that it is because they walk not worthy of the benefit bestowed; for that not walking worthy is part of the debt which is fully paid, for (as it is in the third inference) the debt so paid is all our sins. Thirdly, Is it probable that God calls any to a second payment, and requires satisfaction of them for whom, by his own acknowledgment, Christ hath made that which is full and sufficient? Hath he an after-reckoning that he thought not of? for, for what was before him he spared him not, Rom. viii. 32. Fourthly, How comes it that God never gives a discharge to innumerable souls, though their debts be paid? Fifthly, Whence is it that any one soul lives and dies under the condemning power of the law, never released, if that be fully satisfied in his behalf, so as it had been all one as if he had done whatsoever it could require? Let them that can, reconcile these things. I am no Œdipus for them. The poor beggarly distinctions whereby it is attempted, I have already discussed. And so much for satisfaction.

CHAPTER VIII.

A digression, containing the substance of an occasional conference concerning the satisfaction of Christ.

MUCH about the time that I was composing that part of the last argument which is taken from the satisfaction of Christ, there came one (whose name, and all things else concerning him, for the respect I bear to his parts and modesty, shall be concealed) to the place where I live, and, in a private exercise about the sufferings of Christ, seemed to those that heard him to enervate, yea overthrow, the satisfaction of Christ: which I apprehending to be of dangerous consequence, to prevent a farther inconvenience, set myself briefly and plainly to oppose; and also, a little after, willingly entertained a conference and debate (desired by the gentleman) about the point in question: which being carried along with that quietness and sobriety of spirit which beseemed lovers of and searchers after truth, I easily perceived not only what was his persuasion in the thing in hand, but also what was the ground and sole cause of his misapprehension; and it was briefly this:—That the eternal, unchangeable love of God to his elect did actually instate them in such a condition as wherein they were in an incapacity of having any satisfaction made for them: the end of that being to remove the wrath due unto them, and to make an atonement for their sins; which, by reason of the former love of God, they stood in no need of, but only wanted a clear manifestation of that love unto their souls, whereby they might be delivered from all that dread, darkness, guilt, and fear, which was in and upon their consciences, by reason of a not-understanding of this love, which came upon them through the fall of Adam. Now, to remove this, Jesus Christ was sent to manifest this love, and declare this eternal good-will of God towards them, so bearing and taking away their sins, by removing from their consciences that misapprehension of God and their own condition which, by reason of sin, they had before, and not to make any satisfaction to the justice of God for their sins, he being eternally well-pleased with them. The sum is, election is asserted to the overthrow of redemption. What followed in our conference, with what success by God's blessing it did obtain, shall, for my part, rest in the minds and judgments of those that heard it, for whose sake alone it was intended. The things themselves being, first, of great weight and importance, of singular concernment to all Christians; secondly, containing in them a mixture of undoubted truth and no less undoubted errors, true propositions and false inferences, assertions of necessary verities to the exclusion of others no less necessary; and, thirdly, directly belonging to the business in hand,—I shall briefly declare and confirm the whole truth in this business, so far as occasion was given by the exercise and debate before mentioned, beginning with the first part of it, concerning the eternal love of God to his elect, with the state and condition they are placed in thereby: concerning which you may observe,—

First, That which is now by some made to be a new doctrine of free grace is indeed an old objection against it. That a non-necessity of satisfaction by Christ, as a consequent of eternal election, was more than once, for the substance of it, objected to Austin by the old Pelagian heretics, upon his clearing and vindicating that doctrine, is most apparent. The same objection, renewed by others, is also answered by Calvin, Institut. lib. ii. cap. 16; as also divers schoolmen had before, in their way, proposed it to themselves, as Thom. iii. g. 49, a. 4. Yet, notwithstanding the apparent senselessness of the thing itself, together with the many solid answers whereby it was long before removed, the Arminians, at the Synod of Dort, greedily snatched it up again, and placed it in the very front of their arguments against the effectual redemption of the elect by Jesus Christ. Now, that which was in them only an objection is taken up by some amongst us as a truth, the absurd inconsequent consequence of it owned as just and good, and the conclusion deemed necessary, from the granting of election to the denial of satisfaction.

Secondly, Observe that there is the same reason of election and reprobation (in things so opposed, so it must be): "Jacob have I loved, but Esau have I hated," Rom. ix. 13. By the one, men are "ordained to eternal life," Acts xiii. 48; by the other, "before of old ordained unto condemnation," Jude 4. Now, if the elect are justified, and sanctified, and saved, because of God's decree that so they shall be, whereby they need nothing but the manifestation thereof, then likewise are the reprobates, as soon as they are finally impenitent, damned, burned, and want nothing but a manifestation thereof; which, whether it be true or no, consult the whole dispensation of God towards them.

Thirdly, Consider what is the eternal love of God. Is it an affection in his eternal nature, as love is in ours? It were no less than blasphemy once so to conceive. His pure and holy nature, wherein there is neither change nor shadow of turning, is not subject to any such passion; it must be, then, an eternal act of his will, and that alone. In the Scripture it is called, his "good pleasure," Matt. xi. 26; his "purpose according to election," Rom. ix. 11; the "foundation of God," 2 Tim. ii. 19. Now, every eternal act of God's will is immanent in himself, not really distinguished from himself; whatever is so in God is God. Hence, it puts nothing into the creature concerning whom it is, nor alteration of its condition at all; producing, indeed, no effect until some external act of God's power do make it

out. For instance: God decreed from eternity that he would make
the world, yet we know the world was not made until about five
thousand five hundred years ago. But ye will say, "It was made in
God's purpose." That is, say I, he purposed to make it. So he purposeth there shall be a day of judgment; is there therefore actually
a universal day of judgment already? God purposeth that he will,
in and through Christ, justify and save such and such certain persons;
are they therefore justified because God purposeth it? It is true,
they shall be so, because he hath purposed it; but that they are so is
denied. The consequence is good from the divine purpose to the
futurition of any thing, and the certainty of its event, not to its actual
existence. As when the Lord, in the beginning, went actually to make
the world, there was no world; so when he comes to bestow faith and
actually to justify a man, until he hath so done he is not justified.
The sum is,—

First, The eternal love of God towards his elect is nothing but
his purpose, good pleasure, a pure act of his will, whereby he deter-
mines to do such and such things for them in his own time and way.
Secondly, No purpose of God, no immanent eternal act of his will,
doth produce any outward effect, or change any thing in nature and
condition of that thing concerning which his purpose is; but only
makes the event and success necessary in respect of that purpose.
Thirdly, The wrath and anger of God that sinners lie under is not
any passion in God, but only the outward effects of anger, as guilt,
bondage, etc. *Fourthly,* An act of God's eternal love, which is immanent in himself, doth not exempt the creature from the condition
wherein he is under anger and wrath, until some temporal act of
free grace do really change its state and condition. For example:
God holding the lump of mankind in his own power, as the clay
in the hand of the potter, determining to make some vessels unto
honour, for the praise of his glorious grace, and others to dishonour,
for the manifestation of his revenging justice, and to this end suffer
them all to fall into sin and the guilt of condemnation, whereby
they became all liable to his wrath and curse; his purpose to save
some of these doth not at all exempt or free them from the common
condition of the rest, in respect of themselves and the truth of their
estate, until some actual thing be accomplished for the bringing of
them nigh unto himself: so that notwithstanding his eternal purpose, his wrath, in respect of the effects, abideth on them until that
eternal purpose do make out itself in some distinguishing act of free
grace; which may receive farther manifestation by these ensuing
arguments:—

1. If the sinner want nothing to acceptation and peace but a
manifestation of God's eternal love, then evangelical justification is
nothing but an apprehension of God's eternal decree and purpose.

But this cannot be made out from the Scripture,—namely, that God's justifying of a person is his making known unto him his decree of election; or [that] man's justification [is] an apprehension of that decree, purpose, or love. Where is any such thing in the book of God? It is true, there is a discovery thereof made to justified believers, and therefore it is attainable by the saints, " God shedding abroad his love in their hearts by the Holy Ghost which is given unto them," Rom. v. 5; but it is after they are "justified by faith," and have " peace with God," verse 1. Believers are to give "all diligence to make their calling and election sure;" but that justification should consist herein is a strange notion. Justification, in the Scripture, is an act of God, pronouncing an ungodly person, upon his believing, to be absolved from the guilt of sin, and interested in the all-sufficient righteousness of Christ: so God "justifieth the ungodly," Rom. iv. 5, " by the righteousness of God which is by the faith of Jesus Christ unto them," chap. iii. 22; making Christ to become righteousness to them who were in themselves sin. But of this manifestation of eternal love there is not the least foundation, as to be the form of justification; which yet is not without sense and perception of the love of God, in the improvement thereof.

2. The Scripture is exceeding clear in making all men, before actual reconciliation, to be in the like state and condition, without any real difference at all, the Lord reserving to himself his distinguishing purpose of the alteration he will afterward by his free grace effect: " There is none that doeth good, no, not one," Rom. iii. 12; for " we have proved both Jews and Gentiles that they are all under sin," verse 9. All mankind are in the same condition, in respect of themselves and their own real state: which truth is not at all prejudiced by the relation they are in to the eternal decrees; for " every mouth is stopped, and all the world is become guilty before God," Rom. iii. 19,—ὑπόδικος, obnoxious to his judgment. " Who maketh thee to differ from another? and what hast thou that thou didst not receive?" 1 Cor. iv. 7. All distinguishment, in respect of state and condition, is by God's actual grace; for even believers are "by nature children of wrath, even as others," Eph. ii. 3. The condition, then, of all men, during their unregeneracy, is one and the same, the purpose of God concerning the difference that shall be being referred to himself. Now, I ask whether reprobates in that condition lie under the effects of God's wrath, or no? If ye say "No," who will believe you? If so, why not the elect also? The same condition hath the same qualifications; an actual distinguishment we have proved there is not. Produce some difference that hath a real existence, or the cause is lost.

3. Consider what it is to lie under the effects of God's wrath, according to the declaration of the Scripture, and then see how the elect are delivered therefrom, before their actual calling. Now, this

consists in divers things; as,—(1.) To be in such a state of alienation
from God as that none of their services are acceptable to him: "The
prayer of the wicked is an abomination to the LORD," Prov. xxviii. 9.
(2.) To have no outward enjoyment sanctified, but to have all things
unclean unto them, Tit. i. 15. (3.) To be under the power of Satan,
who rules at his pleasure in the children of disobedience, Eph. ii. 2.
(4.) To be in bondage unto death, Heb. ii. 15. (5.) To be under the
curse and condemning power of the law, Gal. iii. 13. (6.) To be obnoxious to the judgment of God, and to be guilty of eternal death
and damnation, Rom. iii. 19. (7.) To be under the power and
dominion of sin, reigning in them, Rom. vi. 19. These and such like
are those which we call the effects of God's anger.

Let now any one tell me what the reprobates, in this life, lie under
more? And do not all the elect, until their actual reconciliation, in
and by Christ, lie under the very same? for,—(1.) Are not their prayers
an abomination to the Lord? can they without faith please God? Heb.
xi. 6. And faith we suppose them not to have; for if they have, they
are actually reconciled. (2.) Are their enjoyments sanctified unto
them? hath any thing a sanctified relation without faith? See 1 Cor.
vii. 14. (3.) Are they not under the power of Satan? If not, how
comes Christ, in and for them, to destroy the works of the devil?
Did not he come to deliver his from him that had the power of death,
that is, the devil? Heb. ii. 14; Eph. ii. 2. (4.) Are they not under
bondage unto death? The apostle affirms plainly that they are so all
their lives, until they are actually freed by Jesus Christ, Heb. ii. 14, 15.
(5.) Are they not under the curse of the law? How are they freed
from it? By Christ being made a curse for them, Gal. iii. 13. (6.)
Are they not obnoxious unto judgment, and guilty of eternal death?
How is it, then, that Paul says that there is no difference, but that
all are subject to the judgment of God, and are guilty before him?
Rom. iii. 9; and that Christ saves them from this wrath, which, in
respect of merit, was to come upon them? Rom v. 9; 1 Thess. i. 10.
(7.) Are they not under the dominion of sin? " God be thanked,"
says Paul, "that ye were the servants of sin, but ye have obeyed,"
etc., Rom. vi. 17. In brief, the Scripture is in nothing more plentiful than in laying and charging all the misery and wrath of and due
to an unreconciled condition upon the elect of God, until they actually
partake in the deliverance by Christ.

But now some men think to wipe away all that hath been said in
a word, and tell us that all this is so but only in their own apprehension; not that those things are so indeed and in themselves. But
if these things be so to them only in their apprehension, why are
they otherwise to the rest of the whole world? The Scripture gives
us no difference nor distinction between them. And if it be so with
all, then let all get this apprehension as fast as they can, and all

shall be well with the whole world, now miserably captived under
a misapprehension of their own condition; that is, let them say the
Scripture is a fable, and the terror of the Almighty a scarecrow to
fright children; that sin is only in conceit; and so square their conversation to their blasphemous fancies. Some men's words eat as a
canker.

4. Of particular places of Scripture, which might.abundantly be
produced to our purpose, I shall content myself to name only one:
John iii. 36, "He that believeth not the Son, the wrath of God
abideth on him." It abideth: there it was, and there it shall remain, if
unbelief be continued; but upon believing it is removed. "But is not
God's love unchangeable, by which we shall be freed from his wrath?"
Who denies it? But is an apprentice free because he shall be so at
the end of seven years? Because God hath purposed to free his in
his own time, and will do it, are they therefore free before he doth
it? "But are we not in Christ from all eternity?" Yes, chosen in him
we are; therefore, in some sense, in him. But how? Even as we
are. Actually, a man cannot be in Christ until he be. Now, how
are we from eternity? are we eternal? No; only God from eternity hath purposed that we shall be. Doth this give us an eternal
being? Alas! we are of yesterday; our being in Christ respecteth
only the like purpose, and therefore from thence can be made only
the like inference.

This, then, being cleared, it is, I hope, apparent to all how miserable
a strained consequence it is, to argue from God's decree of election to
the overthrow of Christ's merit and satisfaction; the redemption
wrought by Jesus Christ being, indeed, the chief means of carrying
along that purpose unto execution, the pleasure of the Lord prosper-
ing in his hand. Yea, the argument may be retorted, κατὰ τὸ βίαιον,
and will hold undeniable on the other side, the consequence being
evident, from the purpose of God to save sinners, to the satisfaction
of Christ for those sinners. The same act of God's will which sets us
apart from eternity for the enjoyment of all spiritual blessings in
heavenly places, sets also apart Jesus Christ to be the purchaser and
procurer of all those spiritual blessings, as also to make satisfaction
for all their sins; which that he did (being the main thing opposed)
we prove by these ensuing arguments.

CHAPTER IX.

Being a second part of the former digression—Arguments to prove the
satisfaction of Christ.

I. IF Christ so took our sins, and had them by God so laid and
imposed on him, as that he underwent the punishment due unto

them in our stead, then he made satisfaction to the justice of God for them, that the sinners might go free; but Christ so took and bare our sins, and had them so laid upon him, as that he underwent the punishment due unto them, and that in our stead: therefore, he made satisfaction to the justice of God for them. The consequent of the proposition is apparent, and was before proved. Of the assumption there be three parts, severally to be confirmed:—First, That Christ took and bare our sins, God laying them on him. Secondly, That he so took them as to undergo the punishment due unto them. Thirdly, That he did this in our stead.

For the first, that he took and bare our sins, ye have it, John i. 29, 'Ο αἴρων,[1] etc.,—" Who taketh away the sin of the world;" 1 Pet. ii. 24, 'Ος ἀνήνεγκεν,—"Who his own self bare our sins in his own body;" Isa. liii. 11, הוּא יִסְבֹּל,—" He shall bear their iniquities;" and verse 12, נָשָׂא,—" He bare the sin of many." That God also laid or imposed our sins on him is no less apparent: Isa. liii. 6, " The LORD, הִפְגִּיעַ, made to meet on him the iniquity of us all;" 2 Cor. v. 21, 'Αμαρτίαν ἐποίησε,—" He hath made him to be sin for us."

The second branch is, that in thus doing our Saviour underwent the punishment due to the sins which he bare, which were laid upon him; which may be thus made manifest:—Death and the curse of the law contain the whole of the punishment due to sin, Gen. ii. 17, מוֹת תָּמוּת, " Dying thou shalt die," is that which was threatened. Death was that which entered by sin, Rom. v. 12: which word in these places is comprehensive of all misery due to our transgressions; which also is held out in the curse of the law, Deut. xxvii. 26, " Cursed be he that confirmeth not all the words of this law to do them." That all evils of punishment whatsoever are comprised in these is unquestionably evident. Now, Jesus Christ in bearing our sins underwent both these: for " by the grace of God he tasted death," Heb. ii. 9; by death delivering from death, verse 14. He was not "spared, but given up to death for us all," Rom. viii. 32. So also the curse of the law: Gal. iii. 13, Γενόμενος κατάρα,—he " was made a curse for us;" and ἐπικατάρατος, " cursed." And this by the way of undergoing the punishment that was in death and curse: for by these " it pleased the LORD to bruise him, and put him to grief," Isa. liii. 10; yea, οὐκ ἐφείσατο, "he spared him not," Rom. viii. 32, but " condemned sin in his flesh," verse 3. It remaineth only to show that he did this in our stead, and the whole argument is confirmed.

Now, this also our Saviour himself maketh apparent, Matt. xx. 28. He came δοῦναι τὴν ψυχὴν αὐτοῦ λύτρον ἀντὶ πολλῶν,—"to give himself a ransom for many." The word ἀντί always supposeth a commutation, and change of one person or thing instead of another, as

[1] Aufert, sustulit, tulit.

shall be afterward declared: so Matt. ii. 22; so 1 Tim. ii. 6; 1 Pet. iii. 18, "He suffered for us, the just for the unjust;" and Ps. lxix. 4, "I restored" (or paid) "that which I took not away,"—namely, our debt, so far as that thereby we are discharged, as Rom. viii. 34, where it is asserted, upon this very ground, that he died in our stead. And so the several parts of this first argument are confirmed.

II. If Jesus Christ paid into his Father's hands a valuable price and ransom for our sins, as our surety, so discharging the debt that we lay under, that we might go free, then did he bear the punishment due to our sins, and make satisfaction to the justice of God for them (for to pay such a ransom is to make such satisfaction); but Jesus Christ paid such a price and ransom, as our surety, into his Father's hands, etc.: *ergo*,—

There be four things to be proved in the assumption, or second proposition:—First, That Christ paid such a price and ransom. Secondly, That he paid it into the hands of his Father. Thirdly, That he did it as our surety. Fourthly, That we might go free. All which we shall prove in order:—

First, For the first, our Saviour himself affirms it, Matt. xx. 28. He "came to give his life λύτρον," a ransom or price of redemption "for many," Mark x. 45; which the apostle terms ἀντίλυτρον, 1 Tim. ii. 6, a ransom to be accepted in the stead of others: whence we are said to have deliverance διὰ τῆς ἀπολυτρώσεως, "by the ransom-paying of Christ-Jesus," Rom. iii. 24. "He bought us with a price," 1 Cor. vi. 20; which price was his own blood, Acts xx. 28; compared to and exalted above silver and gold in this work of redemption, 1 Pet. i. 18. So that this first part is most clear and evident.

Secondly, He paid this price into the hands of his Father. A price must be paid to somebody in the case of deliverance from captivity by it; it must be paid to the judge or jailer,—that is, to God or the devil. To say the latter were the highest blasphemy; Satan was to be conquered, not satisfied. For the former, the Scripture is clear: It was his "wrath" that was on us, John iii. 36. It was he that had "shut us all up under sin," Gal. iii. 22. He is the great king to whom the debt is owing, Matt. xviii. 23-34. He is the only "law-giver, who is able to save and to destroy," James iv. 12. Nay, the ways whereby this ransom-paying is in the Scripture expressed abundantly enforce the payment of it into the hands of his Father; for his death and blood-shedding is said to be προσφορά and θυσία, "an oblation and sacrifice," Eph. v. 2; and his soul to be אָשָׁם, a sacrifice or "offering for sin," Isa. liii. 10. Now, certainly offerings and sacrifices are to be directed unto God alone.

Thirdly, That he did this as surety, we are assured, Heb. vii. 22. He was made ἔγγυος, a "surety of a better testament;" and, in performance of the duty which lay upon him as such, "he paid that

which he took not away," Ps. lxix. 4. All which could not possibly
have any other end but that we might go free.

III. To make an atonement for sin, and to reconcile God unto
the sinners, is in effect to make satisfaction unto the justice of God
for sin, and all that we understand thereby; but Jesus Christ, by
his death and oblation, did make an atonement for sin, and reconcile
God unto sinners: *ergo*,—

The first proposition is in itself evident; the assumption is confirmed, Rom. iii. 24, 25. We are justified freely by the ransom-paying that is in Christ, whom God hath set forth to be ἱλαστήριον, a
propitiation, an atonement, a mercy-seat, a covering of iniquity; and
that εἰς ἔνδειξιν τῆς δικαιοσύνης, for the manifestation of his justice, declared in the going forth and accomplishment thereof. So likewise
Heb. ii. 17, he is said to be a " merciful high priest, εἰς τὸ ἱλάσκεσθαι
τὰς ἁμαρτίας τοῦ λαοῦ,"—" to make reconciliation for the sins of the
people," to reconcile God unto the people: the meaning of the words
being, ἱλάσκεσθαι τὸν Θεὸν περὶ τῶν ἁμαρτιῶν τοῦ λαοῦ,—to reconcile God,
who was offended with the sins of the people; which reconciliation we
are said to " receive," Rom. v. 11 (the word καταλλαγή there, in our
common translation rendered "atonement," is in other places in the
same rendered "reconciliation," being, indeed, the only word used for
it in the New Testament.) And all this is said to be accomplished δι'
ἑνὸς δικαιώματος,—by one righteousness or satisfaction ; that is of Christ,
(the words will not bear that sense wherein they are usually rendered,
" By the righteousness of one," for then must it have been διὰ δικαιώματος τοῦ ἑνός.) And hereby were we delivered from that from which
it was impossible we should be otherwise delivered, Rom. viii. 3.

IV. That wherein the exercise of the priestly office of Jesus Christ
whilst he was on earth doth consist, cannot be rejected nor denied
without damnable error; but the exercise of the priestly office of
Jesus Christ whilst he was upon the earth consisted in this, to bear
the punishment due to our sins, to make atonement with God, by
undergoing his wrath, and reconciling him to sinners upon the satisfaction made to his justice: therefore cannot these things be denied
without damnable error.

That in the things before recounted the exercise of Christ's priestly
office did consist is most apparent,—first, From all the types and
sacrifices whereby it was prefigured, their chief end being propitiation and atonement; secondly, From the very nature of the sacerdotal
office, appointed for sacrificing, Christ having nothing to offer but his
own blood, through the eternal Spirit; and, thirdly, From divers, yea,
innumerable texts of Scripture affirming the same. It would be too
long a work to prosecute these things severally and at large, and therefore I will content myself with one or two places wherein all those
testimonies are comprised ; as Heb. ix. 13, 14, " If the blood of bulls

and of goats," etc., " how much more shall the blood of Christ, who through the eternal Spirit offered himself without spot to God?" etc. Here the death of Christ is compared to, exalted above, and in the antitype answereth, the sacrifices of expiation which were made by the blood of bulls and goats; and so must, at least spiritually, effect what they did carnally accomplish and typically prefigure,—namely, deliverance from the guilt of sin by expiation and atonement: for as in them the life and blood of the sacrifice was accepted in the stead of the offerer, who was to die for the breach of the law, according to the rigour of it, so in this of Christ was his blood accepted as an atonement and propitiation for us, himself being priest, altar, and sacrifice. So, Heb. x. 10–12, he is said expressly, in the room of all the old, insufficient, carnal sacrifices, which could not make the comers thereunto perfect, to offer up his own body a sacrifice for sins, for the remission and pardon of sins through that offering of himself; as it is verse 19. And in the performance also do we affirm that our Saviour underwent the wrath of God which was due unto us. This, because it is by some questioned, I shall briefly confirm, and that with these following reasons:—

First, The punishment due to sin is the wrath of God: Rom. i. 18, " The wrath of God is revealed against all ungodliness;" chap. ii. 5, " The day of wrath and revelation of the righteous judgment of God;" Eph. ii. 3, " Children of wrath;" John iii. 36. But Jesus Christ underwent the punishment due to sin: 2 Cor. v. 21, " Made sin for us;" Isa. liii. 6, " Iniquity was laid upon him;" 1 Pet. ii. 24, " He bare our sins in his own body on the tree." Therefore he underwent the wrath of God.

Secondly, The curse of the law is the wrath of God taken passively, Deut. xxix. 20, 21. But Jesus Christ underwent the curse of the law: Gal. iii. 13, " Made a curse for us," the curse that they lie under who are out of Christ, who are " of the works of the law," verse 10. Therefore he underwent the wrath of God.

Thirdly, The death that sinners are to undergo is the wrath of God. Jesus Christ did taste of that death which sinners for themselves were to undergo; for he died as " our surety," Heb. vii. 22, and in our stead, Matt. xx. 28. Hence his fear, Heb. v. 7; agony, Luke xxii. 44; astonishment and amazement, Mark xiv. 33; dereliction, Matt. xxvii. 46; sorrow, heaviness, and inexpressible pressures, chap. xxvi. 37–39.

V. That doctrine cannot be true nor agreeable to the gospel which strikes at the root of gospel faith, and plucks away the foundation of all that strong consolation which God is so abundantly willing we should receive; but such is that of denying the satisfaction made by Christ, his answering the justice and undergoing the wrath of his Father. It makes the poor soul to be like Noah's dove in its distress, not knowing where to rest the soles of her feet. When a soul is turned out of its self-righteousness, and begins to look abroad, and view the heaven and earth for a resting place, and perceives an ocean, a flood, an inundation of wrath, to cover all the world, the wrath of God revealing itself from heaven against all ungodliness, so that it can obtain no rest nor abiding,—heaven it cannot reach by its own flight, and to hell it is unwilling to fall;—if now the Lord Jesus Christ do not appear as an ark in the midst of the waters, upon whom the floods have fallen, and yet has got above them all for a refuge, alas! what shall it do? When the flood fell there were many mountains glorious in the eye, far higher than the ark; but yet those mountains were all drowned, whilst the ark still kept on the top of the waters. Many appearing hills and mountains of self-righteousness and general mercy, at the first view, seem to the soul much higher than Jesus Christ, but when the flood of wrath once comes and spreads itself, all those mountains are quickly covered; only the ark, the Lord Jesus Christ, though the flood fall on him also, yet he gets above it quite, and gives safety to them that rest upon him.

Let me now ask any of those poor souls who ever have been wandering and tossed with the fear of the wrath to come, whether ever they found a resting-place until they came to this:—God spared not his only Son, but gave him up to death for us all; that he made him to be sin for us; that he put all the sins of all the elect into that cup which he was to drink of; that the wrath and flood which they feared did fall upon Jesus Christ (though now, as the ark, he be above it, so that if they could get into him they should be safe). The storm hath been his, and the safety shall be theirs. As all the waters which would have fallen upon them that were in the ark fell upon the ark, they being dry and safe, so all the wrath that should have fallen upon them fell on Christ; which alone causeth their souls to dwell in safety? Hath not, I say, this been your bottom, your foundation, your resting-place? If not (for the substance of it), I fear you have but rotten bottoms. Now, what would you say if a man should come and pull this ark from under you, and give you an old rotten post to swim upon in the flood of wrath? It is too late to tell you no wrath is due unto you; the word of truth and your own consciences have given you other information. You know the "wages of sin is death," in whomsoever it be; he must die in whomsoever it is found. So that truly the soul may well say, "Bereave me of the satisfaction of Christ, and I am bereaved. If he fulfilled not justice, I must; if he underwent not wrath, I must to eternity. O rob me not of my only pearl!" Denying the satisfaction of Christ destroys the foundation of faith and comfort.

VI. Another argument we may take from some few particular places of Scripture, which, instead of many, I shall produce:—

As, first, 2 Cor. v. 21, "He made him to be sin for us, who knew

no sin." " He made him to be sin for us ;" how could that be ? are
not the next words, " He knew no sin ?" was he not a Lamb without
blemish, and without spot ? Doubtless; " he did no sin, neither was
guile found in his mouth." What then is this, "God made him
to be sin?" It cannot be that God made him sinful, or a sinner by
any inherent sin; that will not stand with the justice of God, nor
with the holiness of the person of our Redeemer. What is it, then ?
"He made him to be sin who knew no sin ?" Why, clearly, by dispensation and consent, he laid that to his charge whereof he was not
guilty. He charged upon him and imputed unto him all the sins
of all the elect, and proceeded against him accordingly. He stood
as our surety, really charged with the whole debt, and was to pay
the utmost farthing, as a surety is to do if it be required of him;
though he borrow not the money, nor have one penny of that which
is in the obligation, yet if he be sued to an execution, he must
pay all. The Lord Christ (if I may so say) was sued by his
Father's justice unto an execution, in answer whereunto he underwent all that was due to sin; which we proved before to be death,
wrath, and curse.

If it be excepted (as it is) " That God was always well pleased with
his Son,—he testified it again and again from heaven,—how, then,
could he lay his wrath upon him?" *Ans.* It is true he was always
well pleased with him; yet it "pleased him to bruise him and put him
to grief." He was always well pleased with the holiness of his person,
the excellency and perfectness of his righteousness, and the sweetness
of his obedience, but he was displeased with the sins that were charged
on him: and therefore it pleased him to bruise and put him to grief
with whom he was always well pleased.

Nor is that other exception of any more value, " That Christ underwent no more than the elect lay under; but they lay not under wrath
and the punishment due to sin." *Ans.* The proposition is most false,
neither is there any more truth in the assumption; for,—First, Christ
underwent not only that wrath (taking it passively) which the elect
were under, but that also which they should have undergone had not
he borne it for them: he "delivered them from the wrath to come."
Secondly, The elect do, in their several generations, lie under all the
wrath of God in respect of merit and procurement, though not in respect of actual endurance,—in respect of guilt, not present punishment. So that, notwithstanding these exceptions, it stands firm that
"he was made sin for us, who knew no sin."

Isa. liii. 5, "He was wounded for our transgressions, he was bruised
for our iniquities: the chastisement of our peace was upon him; and
with his stripes we are healed." Of this place something was said
before; I shall add some small enlargements that conduce to discover
the meaning of the words. "The chastisement of our peace was upon

him;" that is, he was chastised or punished that we might have peace, that we might go free, our sins being the cause of his wounding, and our iniquities of his being bruised, all our sins meeting upon him, as verse 6; that is, he "bare our sins," in Peter's interpretation. He bare our sins (not, as some think, by declaring that we were never truly sinful, but) by being wounded for them, bruised for them, undergoing the chastisement due unto them, consisting in death, wrath, and curse, so making his soul an offering for sin. "He bare our sins;" that is, say some, he declared that we have an eternal righteousness in God, because of his eternal purpose to do us good. But is this to interpret Scripture, or to corrupt the word of God? Ask the word what it means by Christ's bearing of sin; it will tell you, his being "stricken" for our transgressions, Isa. liii. 8,— his being "cut off" for our sins, Dan. ix. 26. Neither hath the expression of bearing sins any other signification in the word: Lev. v. 1, "If a soul hear the voice of swearing, if he do not utter it, then he shall bear his iniquity." What is that? he shall declare himself or others to be free from sin? No, doubtless; but, he shall undergo the punishment due to sin, as our Saviour did in bearing our iniquities. He must be a cunning gamester indeed that shall cheat a believer of this foundation.

More arguments or texts on this subject I shall not urge or produce, though the cause itself will enforce the most unskilful to abound. I have proceeded as far as the nature of a digression will well bear. Neither shall I undertake, at this time, the answering of objections to the contrary; a full discussion of the whole business of the satisfaction of Christ, which should cause me to search for, draw forth, and confute all objections to the contrary, being not by me intended. And for those which were made at that debate which gave occasion to this discourse, I dare not produce them, lest haply I should not be able to restrain the conjectures of men that I purposely framed such weak objections, that I might obtain an easy conquest over a man of straw of mine own erection, so weak were they, and of so little force to the shaking of so fundamental a truth as that is which we do maintain. So of this argument hitherto.

CHAPTER X.

Of the merit of Christ, with arguments from thence.

ARG. XIV. A fourth thing ascribed to the death of Christ is MERIT, or that worth and value of his death whereby he purchased and procured unto us, and for us, all those good things which we find in the Scripture for his death to be bestowed upon us. Of this,

much I shall not speak, having considered the thing itself under
the notion of impetration already; only, I shall add some few observations proper to that particular of the controversy which we have
in hand. The word *merit* is not at all to be found in the New Testament, in no translation out of the original that I have seen. The
vulgar Latin once reads *promeretur*, Heb. xiii. 16; and the Rheimists,
to preserve the sound, have rendered it promerited. But these words
in both languages are uncouth and barbarous, besides that they no
way answer *εὐαρεστεῖται*, the word in the original, which gives no
colour to merit, name or thing. Nay, I suppose it will prove a
difficult thing to find out any one word, in either of the languages
wherein the holy Scripture was written, that doth properly and immediately, in its first native importance, signify merit. So that about
the name we shall not trouble ourselves, if the thing itself intended
thereby be made apparent, which it is both in the Old and New Testament; as Isa. liii. 5, " The chastisement of our peace was upon him,
and with his stripes we are healed." The procurement of our peace
and healing was the merit of his chastisement and stripes. So Heb.
ix. 12, Διὰ τοῦ ἰδίου αἵματος αἰωνίαν λύτρωσιν εὑράμενος, "Obtaining by
his blood eternal redemption," is as much as we intend to signify by
the merit of Christ. The word which comes nearest it in signification we have, Acts xx. 28, Περιεποιήσατο, "Purchased with his own
blood;" purchase and impetration, merit and acquisition, being in
this business terms equivalent: which latter word is used in divers
other places, as 1 Thess. v. 9; Eph. i. 14; 1 Pet. ii. 9. Now, that
which by this name we understand is, the performance of such an
action as whereby the thing aimed at by the agent is due unto him,
according to the equity and equality required in justice; as, " To him
that worketh, is the reward not reckoned of grace, but of debt,"
Rom. iv. 4. That there is such a merit attending the death of Christ
is apparent from what was said before; neither is the weight of any
operose proving [of] it imposed on us, by our adversaries seeming to
acknowledge it no less themselves; so that we may take it for granted
(until our adversaries close with the Socinians in this also).

Christ then, by his death, did merit and purchase, for all those for
whom he died, all those things which in the Scripture are assigned
to be the fruits and effects of his death. These are the things purchased and merited by his blood-shedding and death; which may be
referred unto two heads:—First, Such as are *privative; as,*—1. Deliverance from the hand of our enemies, Luke i. 74; from the wrath to
come, 1 Thess. i. 10. 2. The destruction and abolition of death in his
power, Heb. ii. 14; 3. Of the works of the devil, 1 John iii. 8. 4. Deliverance from the curse of the law, Gal. iii. 13; 5. From our vain conversation, 1 Pet. i. 18; 6. From the present evil world, Gal. i. 4;
7. From the earth, and from among men, Rev. xiv. 3, 4. 8. Purging

of our sins, Heb. i. 3, Secondly, *Positive;* as,—1. Reconciliation with God, Rom. v. 10; Eph. ii. 16; Col. i. 20. 2. Appeasing or atoning of God by propitiation, Rom. iii. 25; 1 John ii. 2. 3. Peace-making, Eph. ii. 14. 4. Salvation, Matt. i. 21. All these hath our Saviour by his death merited and purchased for all them for whom he died; that is, so procured them of his Father that they ought, in respect of that merit, according to the equity of justice, to be bestowed on them for whom they were so purchased and procured. It was absolutely of free grace in God that he would send Jesus Christ to die for any; it was of free grace for whom he would send him to die; it is of free grace that the good things procured by his death be bestowed on any person, in respect of those persons on whom they are bestowed: but considering his own appointment and constitution, that Jesus Christ by his death should merit and procure grace and glory for those for whom he died, it is of debt in respect of Christ that they be communicated to them. Now, that which is thus merited, which is of debt to be bestowed, we do not say that it *may* be bestowed, but it *ought* so to be, and it is injustice if it be not.

Having said this little of the nature of merit, and of the merit of Christ, the procurement of his death for them in whose stead he died, it will quickly be apparent how irreconcilable the general ransom is therewith; for the demonstration whereof we need no more but the proposing of this one question,—namely, If Christ hath merited grace and glory for all those for whom he died, if he died for all, how comes it to pass that these things are not communicated to and bestowed upon all? Is the defect in the merit of Christ, or in the justice of God? How vain it is to except, that these things are not bestowed absolutely upon us, but upon condition, and therefore were so procured; seeing that the very condition itself is also merited and procured, as Eph. i. 3, 4, Phil. i. 29,—hath been already declared.

ARG. XV. Fifthly, The very phrases of "DYING FOR US," "bearing our sins," being our "surety," and the like, whereby the death of Christ for us is expressed, will not stand with the payment of a ransom for all. To die for another is, in Scripture, to die in that other's stead, that he might go free; as Judah besought his brother Joseph to accept of him for a bondman instead of Benjamin, that he might be set at liberty, Gen. xliv. 33, and that to make good the engagement wherein he stood bound to his father to be a surety for him. He that is surety for another (as Christ was for us, Heb. vii. 22), is to undergo the danger, that the other may be delivered. So David, wishing that he had died for his son Absalom, 2 Sam. xviii. 33, intended, doubtless, a commutation with him, and a substitution of his life for his, so that he might have lived. Paul also, Rom. v. 7, intimates the same, supposing that such a thing might be found among men that one should die for another; no doubt alluding to the Decii,

Menœceus, Euryalus, and such others, whom we find mentioned in the stories of the heathen, who voluntarily cast themselves into death for the deliverance of their country or friends, continuing their liberty and freedom from death who were to undergo it, by taking it upon themselves, to whom it was not directly due. And this plainly is the meaning of that phrase, "Christ died for us;" that is, in the undergoing of death there was a subrogation of his person in the room and stead of ours. Some, indeed, except that where the word ὑπέρ is used in this phrase, as Heb. ii. 9, "That he by the grace of God should taste death for every man," there only the good and profit of them for whom he died is intended, not enforcing the necessity of any commutation. But why this exception should prevail I see no reason, for the same preposition being used in the like kind in other cases doth confessedly intimate a commutation; as Rom. ix. 3, where Paul affirms that he "could wish himself accursed from Christ ὑπέρ τῶν ἀδελφῶν,"—"for his brethren,"—that is, in their stead, that they might be united to him. So also, 2 Cor. v. 20, 'Ὑπὲρ Χριστοῦ πρεσ⸂εύομεν, "We are ambassadors in Christ's stead." So the same apostle, 1 Cor. i. 13, asking, and strongly denying by way of interrogation, Μὴ Παῦλος ἐσταυρώθη ὑπὲρ ὑμῶν; "Was Paul crucified for you?" plainly showeth that the word ὑπέρ, used about the crucifying of Christ for his church, doth argue a commutation or change, and not only designs the good of them for whom he died · for, plainly, he might himself have been crucified for the good of the church; but in the stead thereof, he abhorreth the least thought of it. But concerning the word ἀντί, which also is used, there is no doubt, nor can any exception be made; it always signifieth a commutation and change, whether it be applied to things or persons: so Luke xi. 11, "Ὄφις ἀντὶ ἰχθύος, "A serpent instead of a fish;" so Matt. v. 38, 'Ὀφθαλμὸς ἀντὶ ὀφθαλμοῦ, "An eye for an eye;" so Heb. xii. 16;—and for persons, Archelaus is said to reign ἀντὶ Ἡρώδου τοῦ πατρός, "instead of his father," Matt. ii. 22. Now, this word is used of the death of our Saviour, Matt. xx. 28, "The Son of man came δοῦναι τὴν ψυχὴν αὐτοῦ λύτρον ἀντὶ πολλῶν,"—which words are repeated again, Mark x. 45,—that is, to give his life a ransom in the stead of the lives of many. So that, plainly, Christ dying for us, as a surety, Heb. vii. 22, and thereby and therein "bearing our sins in his own body," 1 Pet. ii. 24, being made a curse for us, was an undergoing of death, punishment, curse, wrath, not only for our good, but directly in our stead; a commutation and subrogation of his person in the room and place of ours being allowed, and of God accepted. This being cleared, I demand,—First, Whether Christ died thus for all? that is, whether he died in the room and stead of all, so that his person was substituted in the room of theirs? as, whether he died in the stead of Cain and Pharaoh, and the rest, who long before his

death were under the power of the second death, never to be delivered? Secondly, Whether it be justice that those, or any of them,
in whose stead Christ died, bearing their iniquities, should themselves also die and bear their own sins to eternity? Thirdly, What
rule of equity is there, or example for it, that when the surety hath
answered and made satisfaction to the utmost of what was required
in the obligation wherein he was a surety, they for whom he
was a surety should afterwards be proceeded against? Fourthly,
Whether Christ hung upon the cross in the room or stead of reprobates? Fifthly, Whether he underwent all that which was due unto
them for whom he died? If not, how could he be said to die in
their stead? If so, why are they not all delivered? I shall add no
more but this, that to affirm Christ to die for all men is the readiest
way to prove that he died for no man, in the sense Christians have
hitherto believed, and to hurry poor souls into the bottom of Socinian blasphemies.

CHAPTER XI.

The last general argument.

ARG. XVI. Our next argument is taken from some particular
places of Scripture, clearly and distinctly in themselves holding out
the truth of what we do affirm. Out of the great number of them I
shall take a few to insist upon, and therewith to close our arguments.

1. The first that I shall begin withal is the first mentioning of
Jesus Christ, and the first revelation of the mind of God concerning a
discrimination between the people of Christ and his enemies: Gen. iii.
15, " I will put enmity between thee" (the serpent) " and the woman,
and between thy seed and her seed." By the seed of the woman is
meant the whole body of the elect, Christ in the first place as the
head, and all the rest as his members; by the seed of the serpent, the
devil, with all the whole multitude of reprobates, making up the malig-
nant state, in opposition to the kingdom and body of Jesus Christ.

That by the first part, or the seed of the woman, is meant Christ
with all the elect, is most apparent; for they in whom all the things
that are here foretold of the seed of the woman do concur, are
the seed of the woman (for the properties of any thing do prove
the thing itself.) But now in the elect, believers in and through
Christ, are to be found all the properties of the seed of the woman;
for, for them, in them, and by them, is the head of the serpent
broken, and Satan trodden down under their feet, and the devil dis-
appointed in his temptations, and the devil's agents frustrated in
their undertakings. Principally and especially, this is spoken of

Christ himself, collectively of his whole body, which beareth a continual hatred to the serpent and his seed.

Secondly, By the seed of the serpent is meant all the reprobate, men of the world, impenitent, unbelievers. For,

First, The enmity of the serpent lives and exerciseth itself in them. They hate and oppose the seed of the woman; they have a perpetual enmity with it; and every thing that is said of the seed of the serpent belongs properly to them.

Secondly, They are often so called in the Scripture: Matt. iii. 7, "O generation of vipers," or seed of the serpent; so also chap. xxiii. 33. So Christ telleth the reprobate Pharisees, "Ye are of your father the devil, and the lusts of your father ye will do," John viii. 44. So again, "Child of the devil," Acts xiii. 10,—that is, the seed of the serpent; for "he that committeth sin is of the devil," 1 John iii. 8.

These things being undeniable, we thus proceed:—Christ died for no more than God promised unto him that he should die for. But God did not promise him to all, as that he should die for them; for he did not promise the seed of the woman to the seed of the serpent, Christ to reprobates, but in the first word of him he promiseth an enmity against them. In sum, the seed of the woman died not for the seed of the serpent.

2. Matt. vii. 23, "I will profess unto them, I never knew you." Christ at the last day professeth to some he never knew them. Christ saith directly that he knoweth his own, whom he layeth down his life for, John x. 14–17. And surely he knows whom and what he hath bought. Were it not strange that Christ should die for them, and buy them that he will not own, but profess he never knew them? If they are "bought with a price," surely they are his own? 1 Cor. vi. 20. If Christ did so buy them, and lay out the price of his precious blood for them, and then at last deny that he ever knew them, might they not well reply, "Ah, Lord! was not thy soul heavy unto death for our sakes? Didst thou not for us undergo that wrath that made thee sweat drops of blood? Didst thou not bathe thyself in thine own blood, that our blood might be spared? Didst thou not sanctify thyself to be an offering for us as well as for any of thy apostles? Was not thy precious blood, by stripes, by sweat, by nails, by thorns, by spear, poured out for us? Didst thou not remember us when thou hungest upon the cross? And now dost thou say, thou never knewest us? Good Lord, though we be unworthy sinners, yet thine own blood hath not deserved to be despised. Why is it that none can lay any thing to the charge of God's elect? Is it not because thou diedst for them? And didst thou not do the same for us? Why, then, are we thus charged, thus rejected? Could not thy blood satisfy thy Father, but we ourselves must be punished? Could not justice content itself with that sacrifice, but we must now hear, 'Depart, I

never knew you?'" What can be answered to this plea, upon the
granting of the general ransom, I know not.

3. Matt. xi. 25, 26, " I thank thee, O Father, Lord of heaven and
earth, because thou hast hid these things from the wise and prudent,
and hast revealed them unto babes. Even so, Father: for so it
seemed good in thy sight." Those men from whom God in his
sovereignty, as Lord of heaven and earth, of his own good pleasure,
hideth the gospel, either in respect of the outward preaching of it, or
the inward revelation of the power of it in their hearts, those certainly
Christ died not for; for to what end should the Father send his only
Son to die for the redemption of those whom he, for his own good
pleasure, had determined should be everlasting strangers from it, and
never so much as hear of it in the power thereof revealed to them?
Now, that such there are our Saviour here affirms; and he thanks his
Father for that dispensation at which so many do at this day repine.

4. John x. 11, 15, 16, 27, 28. This clear place, which of itself is
sufficient to evert the general ransom, hath been a little considered
before, and, therefore, I shall pass it over the more briefly. First,
That all men are not the sheep of Christ is most apparent; for,—
First, He himself saith so, verse 26, " Ye are not of my sheep."
Secondly, The distinction at the last day will make it evident, when
the sheep and the goats shall be separated. *Thirdly*, The properties
of the sheep are, that they hear the voice of Christ, that they know
him; and the like are not in all. Secondly, That the sheep here
mentioned are all his elect, as well those that were to be called as
those that were then already called. Verse 16, Some were not as
yet of his fold of called ones; so that they are sheep by election, and
not believing. Thirdly, That Christ so says that he laid down his life
for his sheep, that plainly he excludes all others; for,—*First*, He lays
down his life for them as sheep. Now, that which belongs to them
as such belongs only to such. If he lays down his life for sheep, as
sheep, certainly he doth it not for goats, and wolves, and dogs.
Secondly, He lays down his life as a shepherd, verse 11; therefore,
for them as the sheep. What hath the shepherd to do with the
wolves, unless it be to destroy them? *Thirdly*, Dividing all into
sheep and others, verse 26, he saith he lays down his life for his
sheep; which is all one as if he had said he did it for them only.
Fourthly, He describes them for whom he died by this, " My Father
gave them me," verse 29; as also chap. xvii. 6, " Thine they were,
and thou gavest them me:" which are not all; for " all that the
Father giveth him shall come to him," chap. vi. 37, and he " giveth
unto them eternal life, and they shall never perish," chap. x. 28. Let
but the sheep of Christ keep close to this evidence, and all the world
shall never deprive them of their inheritance. Farther to confirm
this place, add Matt. xx. 28; John xi. 52.

5. Rom. viii. 32–34. The intention of the apostle in this place is, to hold out consolation to believers in affliction or under any distress; which he doth, verse 31, in general, from the assurance of the presence of God with them, and his assistance at all times, enough to conquer all oppositions, and to make all difficulty indeed contemptible, by the assurance of his loving-kindness, which is better than life itself. " If God be for us, who can be against us?" To manifest this his presence and kindness, the apostle minds them of that most excellent, transcendent, and singular act of love towards them, in sending his Son to die for them, not sparing him, but requiring their debt at his hand; whereupon he argues from the greater to the less, —that if he have done that for us, surely he will do every thing else that shall be requisite. If he did the greater, will he not do the less? If he give his Son to death, will he not also freely give us all things? Whence we may observe,—First, That the greatest and most eximious expression of the love of God towards believers is in sending his Son to die for them, not sparing him for their sake; this is made the chief of all. Now, if God sent his Son to die for all, he had [done] as great an act of love, and hath made as great a manifestation of it, to them that perish as to those that are saved. Secondly, That for whomsoever he hath given and not spared his Son, unto them he will assuredly freely give all things; but now he doth not give all things that are good for them unto all, as faith, grace, and glory: from whence we conclude that Christ died not for all. Again, verse 33, he gives us a description of those that have a share in the consolation here intended, for whom God gave his Son, to whom he freely gives all things; and that is, that they are his " elect,"—not all, but only those whom he hath chosen before the foundation of the world, that they should be holy; which gives another confirmation of the restraint of the death of Christ to them alone: which he yet farther confirms, verse 34, by declaring that those of whom he speaks shall be freely justified and freed from condemnation; whereof he gives two reasons,— first, Because Christ died for them; secondly, Because he is risen, and makes intercession for them for whom he died: affording us two invincible arguments to the business in hand. The first, taken from the infallible effects of the death of Christ: Who shall lay any thing to their charge? who shall condemn them? Why, what reason is given? "It is Christ that died." So that his death doth infallibly free all them from condemnation for whom he died. The second, from the connection that the apostle here makes between the death and intercession of Jesus Christ: For whom he died, for them he makes intercession; but he saveth to the utmost them for whom he intercedeth, Heb. vii. 25. From all which it is undeniably apparent that the death of Christ, with the fruits and benefits thereof, belongeth only to the elect of God.

6. Eph. i. 7, " In whom we have redemption." If his blood was

shed for all, then all must have a share in those things that are to
be had in his blood. Now, amongst these is that redemption that
consists in the forgiveness of sins; which certainly all have not, for
they that have are "blessed," Rom. iv. 7, and shall be blessed for
evermore: which blessing comes not upon all, but upon the seed of
righteous Abraham, verse 16.

7. 2 Cor. v. 21, "He hath made him to be sin for us, that we might
be made the righteousness of God in him." It was in his death that
Christ was made sin, or an offering for it. Now, for whomsoever he
was made sin, they are made the righteousness of God in him: "By
his stripes we are healed," Isa. liii. 5; John xv. 13, "Greater love hath
no man than this, that a man lay down his life for his friends."
Then, to intercede is not of greater love than to die, nor any thing
else that he doth for his elect. If, then, he laid down his life for all,
which is the greatest, why doth he not also the rest for them, and
save them to the uttermost?

8. John xvii. 9, "I pray for them: I pray not for the world, but
for them which thou hast given me; for they are thine." And verse
19, "For their sakes I sanctify myself."

9. Eph. v. 25, "Husbands, love your wives, even as Christ also
loved the church, and gave himself for it;" as [also] Acts xx. 28. The
object of Christ's love and his death is here asserted to be his bride,
his church; and that as properly as a man's own wife is the only
allowed object of his conjugal affections. And if Christ had a love
to others so as to die for them, then is there in the exhortation a
latitude left unto men, in conjugal affections, for other women besides
their wives.

I thought to have added other arguments, as intending a clear
discussing of the whole controversy; but, upon a review of what hath
been said, I do with confidence take up and conclude that those
which have been already urged will be enough to satisfy them who
will be satisfied with any thing, and those that are obstinate will
not be satisfied with more. So of our arguments here shall be an
end.

BOOK IV.

CHAPTER I.

Things previously to be considered, to the solution of objections.

THERE being sundry places in holy Scripture wherein the ransom
and propitiation made by the blood of Christ is set forth in general
and indefinite expressions; as also a fruitlessness or want of success in

respect of some, through their own default, for whom he died, seemingly intimated; with general proffers, promises, and exhortations, made for the embracing of the fruits of the death of Christ, even to them who do never actually perform it,—whence some have taken occasion to maintain *a universality of redemption*, equally respecting all and every one, and that with great confidence, affirming that the contrary opinion cannot possibly be reconciled with those places of Scripture wherein the former things are proposed;—these three heads being the only fountains from whence are drawn (but with violence) all the arguments that are opposed to the peculiar effectual redemption of the elect only, I shall, before I come to the answering of objections arising from a wrested interpretation of particular places, lay down some such fundamental principles as are agreeable to the word, and largely held forth in it, and no way disagreeable to our judgment in this particular, which do and have given occasion to those general and indefinite affirmations as they are laid down in the word, and upon which they are founded, having their truth in them, and not in a universal ransom for all and every one; with some distinctions conducing to the farther clearing of the thing in question, and waiving of many false imputations of things and consequences, erroneously or maliciously imposed on us.

1. The first thing that we shall lay down is concerning the dignity, worth, preciousness, and infinite value of the blood and death of Jesus Christ. The maintaining and declaring of this is doubtless especially to be considered; and every opinion that doth but seemingly clash against it is exceedingly prejudiced, at least deservedly suspected, yea, presently to be rejected by Christians, if upon search it be found to do so really and indeed, as that which is injurious and derogatory to the merit and honour of Jesus Christ. The Scripture, also, to this purpose is exceeding full and frequent in setting forth the excellency and dignity of his death and sacrifice, calling his blood, by reason of the unity of his person, " God's own blood," Acts xx. 28; exalting it infinitely above all other sacrifices, as having for its principle " the eternal Spirit," and being itself " without spot," Heb. ix. 14; transcendently more precious than silver, or gold, or corruptible things, 1 Pet. i. 18; able to give justification from all things, from which by the law men could not be justified, Acts xiii. 28. Now, such as was the sacrifice and offering of Christ in itself, such was it intended by his Father it should be. It was, then, the purpose and intention of God that his Son should offer a sacrifice of infinite worth, value, and dignity, sufficient in itself for the redeeming of all and every man, if it had pleased the Lord to employ it to that purpose; yea, and of other worlds also, if the Lord should freely make them, and would redeem them. Sufficient we say, then, was the sacrifice of Christ for the redemption of the whole world, and for the expiation of all

the sins of all and every man in the world.   This sufficiency of his sacrifice hath a twofold rise :—First, The dignity of the person that did offer and was offered.   Secondly, The greatness of the pain he endured, by which he was able to bear, and did undergo, the whole curse of the law and wrath of God due to sin.   *And this sets out the innate, real, true worth and value of the blood-shedding of Jesus Christ.*   This is its own true internal perfection and sufficiency. That it should be applied unto any, made a price for them, and become beneficial to them, according to the worth that is in it, is external to it, doth not arise from it, but merely depends upon the intention and will of God.   It was in itself of infinite value and sufficiency to *have been made a price* to have bought and purchased all and every man in the world.   That it did formally become a price for any is solely to be ascribed to the purpose of God, intending their purchase and redemption by it.   The intention of the offerer and accepter that it should be for *such, some,* or *any,* is that which gives the formality of a price unto it; this is external.   But the value and fitness of it to be made a price ariseth from its own internal sufficiency.   Hence may appear what is to be thought of that old distinction of the schoolmen, embraced and used by divers protestant divines, though by others again rejected,—namely, " That Christ died for all in respect of the sufficiency of the ransom he paid, but not in respect of the efficacy of its application;" or, " The blood of Christ was a sufficient price for the sins of all the world;"—which last expression is corrected by some, and thus asserted, " That the blood of Christ was sufficient to have been made a price for all;" which is most true, as was before declared: for its being a price for all or some doth not arise from its own sufficiency, worth, or dignity, but from the intention of God and Christ using it to that purpose, as was declared; and, therefore, it is denied that the blood of Christ was a sufficient price and ransom for all and every one, not because it was not sufficient, but because it was not a ransom.   And so it easily appears what is to be owned in the distinction itself before expressed.   If it intend no more but that the blood of our Saviour was of sufficient value for the redemption of all and every one, and that Christ intended to lay down a price which should be sufficient for their redemption, it is acknowledged as most true.   But the truth is, that expression, "To die for them," holds out the intention of our Saviour, in the laying down of the price, to have been their redemption; which we deny, and affirm that then it could not be but that they must be made actual partakers of the eternal redemption purchased for them, unless God failed in his design, through the defect of the ransom paid by Christ, his justice refusing to give a dismission upon the delivery of the ransom.

Now, the infinite value and worth which we assert to be in the death of Christ we conceive to be exceedingly undervalued by the assertors of universal redemption; for that it should be extended to this or that object, fewer or more, we showed before to be extrinsical to it. But its true worth consists in the immediate effects, products, and issues of it, with what in its own nature it is fit and able to do; which they openly and apparently undervalue, yea, almost annihilate. Hence those expressions concerning it:—First, That by it a *door of grace was opened for sinners:* where, I suppose, they know not; but that any were [ever] effectually carried in at the door by it, that they deny. Secondly, *That God might, if he would, and upon what condition he pleased, save those for whom Christ died.* That a right of salvation was by him purchased for any, they deny. Hence they grant, that after the death of Christ,—first, *God might have dealt with man upon a legal condition again;* secondly, *That all and every man might have been damned, and yet the death of Christ have had its full effect;* as also, moreover, *That faith and sanctification are not purchased by his death,* yea, no more *for any* (as before) *than what he may go to hell withal.* And divers other ways do they express their low thoughts and slight imaginations concerning the innate value and sufficiency of the death and blood-shedding of Jesus Christ. To the honour, then, of Jesus Christ our Mediator, God and man, our all-sufficient Redeemer, we affirm, such and so great was the dignity and worth of his death and blood-shedding, of so precious a value, of such an infinite fulness and sufficiency was this oblation of himself, that it was every way able and perfectly sufficient to redeem, justify, and reconcile and save all the sinners in the world, and to satisfy the justice of God for all the sins of all mankind, and to bring them every one to everlasting glory. Now, this fulness and sufficiency of the merit of the death of Christ is a foundation unto two things:—

First, The general publishing of the gospel unto "all nations," with the right that it hath to be preached to " every creature," Matt. xxviii. 19; Mark xvi. 15; because the way of salvation which it declares is wide enough for all to walk in. There is enough in the remedy it brings to light to heal all their diseases, to deliver them from all their evils. If there were a thousand worlds, the gospel of Christ might, upon this ground, be preached to them all, there being enough in Christ for the salvation of them all, if so be they will derive virtue from him by touching him in faith; the only way to draw refreshment from this fountain of salvation. It is, then, altogether in vain which some object, that the preaching of the gospel to all is altogether needless and useless, if Christ died not for all; yea, that it is to make God call upon men to believe that which is not true,—namely, that Christ died for them: for, first, besides that amongst those nations whither the gospel is sent there are some to be saved (" I have much people,") which they cannot be, in the way that God hath appointed to do it, unless the gospel be preached to others as well as themselves; and besides, secondly, that in the economy and dispensation of the new covenant, by which all external differences and privileges of people, tongues, and nations being abolished and taken away, the word of grace was to be preached without distinction, and all men called everywhere to repent; and, thirdly, that when God calleth upon men to believe, he doth not, in the first place, call upon them to believe that Christ died for them, but that there is no name under heaven given unto men whereby they might be saved, but only of Jesus Christ, through whom salvation is preached;—I say, besides these certain truths, fully taking off that objection, this one thing of which we speak is a sufficient basis and ground for all those general precepts of preaching the gospel unto all men, even that sufficiency which we have described.

Secondly, That the preachers of the gospel, in their particular congregations, being utterly unacquainted with the purpose and secret counsel of God, being also forbidden to pry or search into it, Deut. xxix. 29, may from hence justifiably call upon every man to believe, with assurance of salvation to every one in particular upon his so doing, knowing, and being fully persuaded of this, that there is enough in the death of Christ to save every one that shall so do; leaving the purpose and counsel of God, on whom he will bestow faith, and for whom in particular Christ died (even as they are commanded), to himself.

And this is one principal thing, which, being well observed, will crush many of the vain flourishes of our adversaries; as will in particular hereafter appear.

2. A second thing to be considered is, the *economy or administration of the new covenant* in the times of the gospel, with the amplitude and enlargement of the kingdom and dominion of Christ after his appearance in the flesh; whereby, all external differences being taken away, the name of Gentiles removed, the partition-wall broken down, the promise to Abraham that he should be heir of the world, as he was father of the faithful, was now fully to be accomplished. Now, this administration is so opposite to that dispensation which was restrained to one people and family, who were God's peculiar, and all the rest of the world excluded, that it gives occasion to many general expressions in the Scripture; which are far enough from comprehending a universality of all individuals, but denote only a removal of all such restraining exceptions as were before in force. So that a consideration of the end whereunto these general expressions are used, and of what is aimed at by them, will clearly

manifest their nature, and how they are to be understood, with whom they are that are intended by them and comprehended in them. For it being only this enlargement of the visible kingdom of Christ to all nations in respect of right, and to many in respect of fact (God having elect in all those nations to be brought forth, in the several generations wherein the means of grace are in those places employed), that is intended, it is evident that they import only a *distribution* of men through all differences whatsoever, and not a *universal collection* of all and every one; the thing intended by them requiring the one and not the other. Hence, those objections which are made against the particularity of the ransom of Christ, and the restraining of it only to the elect, from the terms of *all, all men, all nations, the world, the whole world,* and the like, are all of them exceeding weak and invalid, as wresting the general expressions of the Scripture beyond their aim and intent, they being used by the Holy Ghost only to evidence the removal of all personal and national distinctions,—the breaking up of all the narrow bounds of the Old Testament, the enlarging the kingdom of Christ beyond the bounds of Jewry and Salem, abolishing all old restrictions, and opening a way for the elect amongst all people (called "The fulness of the Gentiles,") to come in; there being now "neither Greek nor Jew, circumcision nor uncircumcision, Barbarian, Scythian, bond nor free, but Christ is all, and in all," Col. iii. 11. Hence the Lord promiseth to "pour out his Spirit upon all flesh," Joel ii. 28; which Peter interpreteth to be accomplished by the filling of the apostles with the gifts of the Spirit, that they might be enabled to preach to several nations, Acts ii. 17, "having received grace and apostleship for obedience to the faith among all nations" Rom. i. 5;—not the Jews only, but some among all nations, "the gospel being the power of God unto salvation to every one that believeth, to the Jew first, and also to the Greek," verse 16; intending only, as to salvation, the peculiar bought by Christ, which he "redeemed out of every kindred, and tongue, and people, and nation," Rev. v. 9, where ye have an evident distribution of that which in other places is generally set down; the gospel being commanded to be preached to all these nations, Matt. xxviii. 19, that those bought and redeemed ones amongst them all might be brought home to God, John xi. 52. And this is that which the apostle so largely sets forth, Eph. ii. 14–17. Now, in this sense, which we have explained, and no other, are those many places to be taken which are usually urged for universal grace and redemption, as shall afterward be declared in particular.

3. We must exactly distinguish between man's duty and God's purpose, there being no connection between them. The purpose and decree of God is not the rule of our duty; neither is the perform-

ance of our duty in doing what we are commanded any declaration of what is God's purpose to do, or his decree that it should be done. Especially is this to be seen and considered in the duty of the ministers of the gospel, in the dispensing of the word, in exhortations, invitations, precepts, and threatenings, committed unto them; all which are perpetual declaratives of our duty, and do manifest the approbation of the thing exhorted and invited to, with the truth of the connection between one thing and another, but not of the counsel and purpose of God, in respect of individual persons, in the ministry of the word. A minister is not to make inquiry after, nor to trouble himself about, those secrets of the eternal mind of God, namely,— whom he purposeth to save, and whom he hath sent Christ to die for in particular. It is enough for them to search his revealed will, and thence take their *directions*, from whence they have their *commissions*. Wherefore, there is no sequel between the universal precepts from the word concerning the *things*, unto God's purpose in himself concerning *persons*. They command and invite all to repent and believe; but they know not in particular on whom God will bestow repentance unto salvation, nor in whom he will effect the work of faith with power. And when they make proffers and tenders in the name of God to all, they do not say to all, "It is the purpose and intention of God that ye should believe," (who gave them any such power?) but, that it is his command, which makes it their duty to do what is required of them; and they do not declare his mind, what himself in particular will do. The external offer is such as from which every man may conclude his own duty; none, God's purpose, which yet may be known upon performance of his duty. Their objection, then, is vain, who affirm that God hath given Christ for all to whom he offers Christ in the preaching of the gospel; for his offer in the preaching of the gospel is not declarative to any in particular, neither of what God hath done nor of what he will do in reference to him, but of what he ought to do, if he would be approved of God and obtain the good things promised. Whence it will follow,—

First, That God always intends to save some among them to whom he sends the gospel in its power. And the ministers of it being, *first*, unacquainted with his particular purpose; *secondly*, bound to seek the good of all and every one, as much as in them lies; *thirdly*, to hope and judge well of all, even as it is meet for them,—they may make a proffer of Jesus Christ, with life and salvation in him, notwithstanding that the Lord hath given his Son only to his elect.

Secondly, That this offer is neither vain nor fruitless, being declarative of their duty, and of what is acceptable to God if it be performed as it ought to be, even as it is required. And if any ask, What it is of the mind and will of God that is declared and made known when men are commanded to believe for whom Christ did not die? I answer, *first*, What they ought to do, if they will do that which is acceptable to God; *secondly*, The sufficiency of salvation that is in Jesus Christ to all that believe on him; *thirdly*, The certain, infallible, inviolable connection that is between faith and salvation, so that whosoever performs the one shall surely enjoy the other, for whoever comes to Christ he will in no wise cast out. Of which more afterward.

4. The ingraffed erroneous persuasion of the Jews, which for a while had a strong influence upon the apostles themselves, restraining salvation and deliverance by the Messiah, or promised seed, to themselves alone, who were the offspring of Abraham according to the flesh, must be considered as the ground of many general expressions and enlargements of the objects of redemption; which yet, being so occasioned, give no colour of any unlimited universality. That the Jews were generally infected with this proud opinion, that all the promises belonged only to them and theirs, towards whom they had a universality, exclusive of all others, whom they called "dogs, uncircumcised," and poured out curses on them, is most apparent. Hence, when they saw the multitudes of the Gentiles coming to the preaching of Paul, they were "filled with envy, contradicting, blaspheming, and raising up persecution against them," Acts xiii. 45–50; which the apostle again relates of them, 1 Thess. ii. 15, 16. "They please not God," saith he, "and are contrary to all men; forbidding us to speak to the Gentiles that they might be saved;" being not with any thing more enraged in the preaching of our Saviour than his prediction of letting out his vineyard to others.

That the apostles themselves, also, had deeply drunk in this opinion, learned by tradition from their fathers, appeareth, not only in their questioning about the restoration of the kingdom unto Israel, Acts i. 6, but also most evidently in this, that after they had received commission to teach and baptize all nations, Matt. xxviii. 19, or every creature, Mark xvi. 15, and were endued with power from above so to do, according to promise, Acts i. 8; yet they seem to have understood their commission to have extended only to the lost sheep of the house of Israel, for they went about and preached only to the Jews, chap. xi. 19: and when the contrary was evidenced and demonstrated to them, they glorified God, saying, "Then hath God also to the Gentiles granted repentance unto life," verse 18; admiring at it, as a thing which before they were not acquainted with. And no wonder that men were not easily nor soon persuaded to this, it being the great mystery that was not made known in former ages, as it

was then revealed to God's holy apostles and prophets by the Spirit
—namely, "That the Gentiles should be fellow-heirs, and of the
same body, and partakers of his promise in Christ by the gospel,"
Eph. iii. 5, 6.

But now, this being so made known unto them by the Spirit, and
that the time was come wherein the little sister was to be considered,
the prodigal brought home, and Japheth persuaded to dwell in the
tents of Shem, they laboured by all means to root it out of the minds
of their brethren according to the flesh, of whom they had a special
care;—as also, to leave no scruple in the mind of the eunuch, that he
was a dry tree; or of the Gentile, that he was cut off from the people
of God. To which end they use divers general expressions, carrying a
direct opposition to that former error, which was absolutely destructive to the kingdom of Jesus Christ. Hence are those terms of the
world, all men, all nations, every creature, and the like, used in the
business of redemption and preaching of the gospel; these things
being not restrained, according as they supposed, to one certain
nation and family, but extended to the universality of God's people
scattered abroad in every region under heaven. Especially are these
expressions used by John, who, living to see the first coming of the
Lord, in that fearful judgment and vengeance which he executed upon
the Jewish nation some forty years after his death, is very frequent
in the asserting of the benefit of the world by Christ, in opposition,
as I said before, to the Jewish nation,—giving us a rule how to understand such phrases and locutions: John xi. 51, 52, " He signified
that Jesus should die for that nation; and not for that nation only,
but that also he should gather together in one the children of God
that were scattered abroad;" conformably whereunto he tells the
believing Jews that Christ is not a propitiation for them only, " but
for the sins of the whole world," 1 John ii. 2, or the people of God
scattered throughout the whole world, not tied to any one nation, as
they sometime vainly imagined. And this may and doth give much
light into the sense and meaning of those places where the words
world and *all* are used in the business of redemption. They do not
hold out a collective universality, but a general distribution into
men of all sorts, in opposition to the before-recounted erroneous persuasion.

5. The extent, nature, and signification of those general terms
which we have frequently used indefinitely in the Scripture, to set
out the object of the redemption by Christ, must seriously be
weighed. Upon these expressions hangs the whole weight of the
opposite cause, the chief if not the only argument for the universality
of redemption being taken from words which seem to be of a latitude
in their signification equal to such an assertion, as the *world,* the

whole world, all, and the like; which terms, when they have once fastened upon, they run with, "Io triumphe," as though the victory were surely theirs. *The world, the whole world, all, all men!*—who can oppose it? Call them to the context in the several places where the words are; appeal to rules of interpretation; mind them of the circumstances and scope of the place, the sense of the same words in other places; with other fore-named helps and assistances which the Lord hath acquainted us with for the discovery of his mind and will in his word,—they presently cry out, the *bare word,* the letter is theirs: "Away with the gloss and interpretation; give us leave to believe what the word expressly saith;"—little (as I hope) imagining, being deluded with the love of their own darling, that if this assertion be general, and they will not allow us the gift of interpretation agreeable to the proportion of faith, that, at one clap, they confirm the cursed madness of the Anthropomorphites,—assigning a human body, form and shape, unto God, who hath none; and the alike cursed figment of transubstantiation, overthrowing the body of Christ, who hath one; with divers other most pernicious errors. Let them, then, as long as they please, continue such empty clamours, fit to terrify and shake weak and unstable men; for the truth's sake we will not be silent: and I hope we shall very easily make it appear that the general terms that are used in this business will indeed give no colour to any argument for universal redemption, whether absolute or conditionate.

Two words there are that are mightily stuck upon or stumbled at;—first, The *world;* secondly, *All.* The particular places wherein they are, and from which the arguments of our adversaries are urged, we shall afterward consider, and for the present only show that the words themselves, according to the Scripture use, do not necessarily hold out any collective universality of those concerning whom they are affirmed, but, being words of various significations, must be interpreted according to the scope of the place where they are used and the subject-matter of which the Scripture treateth in those places.

First, then, for the word *world,* which in the New Testament is called χόσμος (for there is another word sometimes translated world, namely, αἰών, that belongs not to this matter, noting rather the duration of time than the thing in that space continuing) : he that doth not acknowledge it to be πολύσημον, need say no more to manifest his unacquaintedness in the book of God. I shall briefly give you so many various significations of it as shall make it apparent that from the bare usage of a word so exceedingly equivocal, no argument can be taken, until it be distinguished, and the meaning thereof in that particular place evinced from whence the argument is taken.

THE SCHEME.

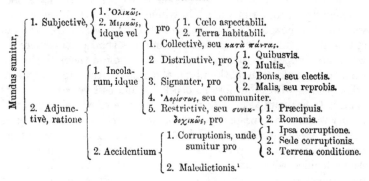

All these distinctions of the use of the word are made out in the following observations:—

The word *world* in the Scripture is in general taken five ways:—

First, *Pro mundo continente;* and that,—*First,* generally, ὅλως, for the whole fabric of heaven and earth, with all things in them contained, which in the beginning were created of God: so Job xxxiv. 13; Acts xvii. 24; Eph. i. 4, and in very many other places. *Secondly,* Distinctively, first, for the heavens, and all things belonging to them, distinguished from the earth, Ps. xc. 2; secondly, The habitable earth, and this very frequently, as Ps. xxiv. 1, xcviii. 7; Matt. xiii. 38; John i. 9, iii. 17, 19, vi. 14, xvii. 11; 1 Tim. i. 15, vi. 7.

Secondly, *For the world contained,* especially men in the world; and that either,—*First,* universally for all and every one, Rom. iii. 6, 19, v. 12. *Secondly,* Indefinitely for men, without restriction

¹ The following is a translation of the above scheme :—

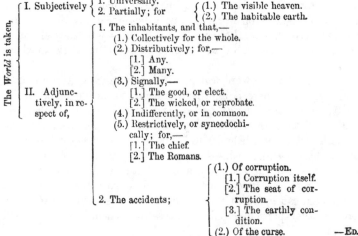

—ED.

or enlargement, John vii. 4; Isa. xiii. 11. *Thirdly,* Exegetically, for many, which is the most usual acceptation of the word, Matt. xviii. 7; John iv. 42, xii. 19, xvi. 8, xvii. 21; 1 Cor. iv. 9; Rev. xiii. 3. *Fourthly,* Comparatively, for a great part of the world, Rom. i. 8; Matt. xxiv. 14, xxvi. 13; Rom. x. 18. *Fifthly,* Restrictively, for the inhabitants of the Roman empire, Luke ii. 1. *Sixthly,* For men distinguished in their several qualifications, as,—1*st,* For the good, God's people, either in designation or possession, Ps. xxii. 27; John iii. 16, vi. 33, 51; Rom. iv. 13, xi. 12, 15; 2 Cor. v. 19; Col. i. 6; 1 John ii. 2. 2*dly,* For the evil, wicked, rejected men of the world, Isa. xiii. 11; John vii. 7, xiv. 17, 22, xv. 19, xvii. 25; 1 Cor. vi. 2, xi. 32; Heb. xi. 38; 2 Pet. ii. 5; 1 John v. 19; Rev. xiii. 3.

Thirdly, *For the world corrupted,* or that universal corruption which is in all things in it, as Gal. i. 4, vi. 14; Eph. ii. 2; James i. 27, iv. 4; 1 John ii. 15–17; 1 Cor. vii. 31, 33; Col. ii. 8; 2 Tim. iv. 10; Rom. xii. 2; 1 Cor. i. 20, 21, iii. 18, 19.

Fourthly, *For a terrene worldly estate or condition* of men or things, Ps. lxxiii. 12; Luke xvi. 8; John xviii. 36; 1 John iv. 5, and very many other places.

Fifthly, *For the world accursed,* as under the power of Satan, John vii. 7, xiv. 30, xvi. 11, 33; 1 Cor. ii. 12; 2 Cor. iv. 4; Eph. vi. 12. And divers other significations hath this word in holy writ, which are needless to recount.

These I have rehearsed to show the vanity of that clamour wherewith some men fill their mouths, and frighten unstable souls with the Scripture mentioning *world* so often in the business of redemption, as though some strength might be taken thence for the upholding of the general ransom. "Parvas habet spes Troja, si tales habet." If their greatest *strength be but sophistical craft, taken from the ambiguity of an equivocal word, their whole endeavour is like to prove fruitless.* Now, as I have declared that it hath divers other acceptations in the Scripture, so when I come to a consideration of their objections that use the word for this purpose, I hope, by God's assistance, to show that in no one place wherein it is used in this business of redemption, it is or can be taken for all and every man in the world, as, indeed, it is in very few places besides. So that, forasmuch as concerning this word our way will be clear, if to what hath been said ye add these observations,—

First, That as in other words, so in these, this is in the Scripture usually an ἀντανάκλασις, whereby the same word is ingeminated in a different sense and acceptation. So Matt. viii. 22, " Let the dead bury their dead;"—dead in the first place denoting them that are spiritually dead in sin; in the next, those that are naturally dead by a dissolution of soul and body. So John i. 11, He came εἰς τὰ ἴδια,

" to his own," even all things that he had made; καὶ οἱ ἴδιοι, " his own," that is, the greatest part of the people, " received him not." So, again, John iii. 6, " That which is born of the Spirit is spirit." Spirit in the first place is the almighty Spirit of God; in the latter, a spiritual life of grace received from him. Now, in such places as these, to argue that as such is the signification of the word in one place, therefore in the other, were violently to pervert the mind of the Holy Ghost. Thus also is the word *world* usually changed in the meaning thereof. So John i. 10, " He was in the world, and the world was made by him, and the world knew him not." He that should force the same signification upon the *world* in that triple mention of it would be an egregious glosser: for in the first, it plainly signifieth some part of the habitable earth, and is taken *subjectivè* μερικῶς· in the second, the whole frame of heaven and earth, and is taken *subjectivè* ὁλικῶς· and, in the third, for some men living in the earth,—namely, unbelievers, who may be said to be the world *adjunctivè*. So, again, John iii. 17, " God sent not his Son into the world to condemn the world, but that the world through him might be saved;" where, by the *world* in the first, is necessarily to be understood that part of the habitable world wherein our Saviour conversed; in the second, all men in the world, as some suppose (so also there is a truth in it, for our Saviour came not to condemn all men in the world: for, *first*, condemnation of any was not the prime aim of his coming; *secondly*, he came to save his own people, and so not to condemn all); in the third, God's elect, or believers living in the world, in their several generations, who were they whom he intended to save, and none else, or he faileth of his purpose, and the endeavour of Christ is insufficient for the accomplishment of that whereunto it is designed.

Secondly, That no argument can be taken from a phrase of speech in the Scripture, in any particular place, if in other places thereof where it is used the signification pressed from that place is evidently denied, unless the scope of the place or subject-matter do enforce it. For instance: God is said to love the *world,* and send his Son; to be in Christ reconciling the *world* to himself; and Christ to be a propitiation for the sins of the *whole world.* If the scope of the places where these assertions are, or the subject-matter of which they treat, will enforce a universality of all persons to be meant by the word *world,* so let it be, without control. But if not, if there be no enforcement of any such interpretation from the places themselves, why should the *world* there signify all and every one, more than in John i. 10, " The world knew him not," which, if it be meant of all without exception, then no one did believe in Christ, which is contrary to verse 12; or in Luke ii. 1, " That all the world should be taxed," where none but the chief inhabitants of the Roman empire can be understood; or in John viii. 26, " I speak to the world those things which I have heard of him," understanding the Jews to whom he spake, who then lived in the world, and not every one, to whom he was not sent; or in John xii. 19, " Behold, the world is gone after him!" which world was nothing but a great multitude of one small nation; or in 1 John v. 19, "The whole world lieth in wickedness," from which, notwithstanding, all believers are to be understood as exempted; or in Rev. xiii. 3, " All the world wondered after the beast," which, whether it be affirmed of the whole universality of individuals in the world, let all judge? That *all nations*, an expression of equal extent with that of *the world*, is in like manner to be understood, is apparent, Rom. i. 5; Rev. xviii. 3, 23; Ps. cxviii. 10; 1 Chron. xiv. 17; Jer. xxvii. 7. It being evident that the words *world, all the world, the whole world*, do, where taken adjunctively for men in the world, usually and almost always denote only some or many men in the world, distinguished into good or bad, believers or unbelievers, elect or reprobate, by what is immediately in the several places affirmed of them, I see no reason in the world why they should be wrested to any other meaning or sense in the places that are in controversy between us and our opponents. The particular places we shall afterward consider.

Now, as we have said of the word *world*, so we may of the word *all*, wherein much strength is placed, and many causeless boastings are raised from it. That it is nowhere affirmed in the Scripture that Christ died for *all men*, or gave himself a ransom for all men, much less for all and every man, we have before declared. That he " gave himself a ransom for all" is expressly affirmed, 1 Tim. ii. 6. But now, who this *all* should be, whether all believers, or all the elect, or some of all sorts, or all of every sort, is in debate. Our adversaries affirm the last; and the main reason they bring to assert their interpretation is from the importance of the word itself: for, that the circumstances of the place, the analogy of faith, and other helps for exposition, do not at all favour their gloss, we shall show when we come to the particular places urged. For the present, let us look upon the word in its usual acceptation in the Scripture, and search whether it always necessarily requires such an interpretation.

That the word *all*, being spoken of among all sorts of men, speaking, writing, any way expressing themselves, but especially in holy writ, is to be taken either *collectively* for all in general, without exception, or *distributively* for some of all sorts, excluding none, is more apparent than that it can require any illustration. That it is sometimes taken in the first sense, for all collectively, is granted, and I need not prove it, they whom we oppose affirming that this is the only sense of the word,—though I dare boldly say it is not once in ten times so to be understood in the usage of it through the whole book of God; but that it is commonly, and indeed properly, used in the latter sense, for some of all sorts, concerning whatsoever it is affirmed, a few instances, for many that might be urged, will make it clear. Thus, then, ye have it, John xii. 32, "And I, if I be lifted up from the earth, will draw all unto me." That we translate it "all men," as in other places (for though I know the sense may be the same, yet the word *men* being not in the original, but only πάντας), I cannot approve. But who, I pray, are these *all?* Are they all and every one? Then are all and every one drawn to Christ, made believers, and truly converted, and shall be certainly saved; for those that come unto him by his and his Father's drawing, "he will in no wise cast out," John vi. 37. *All,* then, can here be no other than many, some of all sorts, no sort excluded, according as the word is interpreted in Rev. v. 9, "Thou hast redeemed us out of every kindred, and tongue, and people, and nation." These are the *all* he draws to him: which exposition of this phrase is with me of more value and esteem than a thousand glosses of the sons of men. So also, Luke xi. 42, where our translators have made the word to signify immediately and properly (for translators are to keep close to the propriety and native signification of every word) what we assert to be the right interpretation of it; for they render πᾶν λάχανον (which ῥητῶς is "every herb"), "all manner of herbs," taking the word (as it must be) *distributively,* for herbs of all sorts, and not for any individual herb, which the Pharisees did not, could not tithe. And in the very same sense is the word used again, Luke xviii. 12, "I give tithes of all that I possess;" where it cannot signify every individual thing, as is apparent. Most evident, also, is this restrained signification of the word, Acts ii. 17, "I will pour out of my Spirit, ἐπὶ πᾶσαν σάρκα·" which, whether it compriseth every man or no, let every man judge, and not rather men of several and sundry sorts. The same course of interpretation as formerly is followed by our translators, Acts x. 12, rendering πάντα τὰ τετράποδα, (literally, "all beasts or four-footed creatures,") "all manner of beasts," or beasts of sundry several sorts. In the same sense also must it be understood, Rom. xiv. 2, "One believeth that he may eat all things;" that is, what he pleaseth of things to be eaten of. See, moreover, 1 Cor. i. 5. Yea, in that very chapter where men so eagerly contend that the word *all* is to be taken for all and every one (though fruitlessly and falsely, as shall be demonstrated),—namely, 1 Tim. ii. 4, where it is said that "God will have all men to be saved,"—in that very chapter confessedly the word is to be expounded according to the sense we give, namely, verse 8, "I will, therefore, that men pray ἐν παντὶ τόπῳ·" which, that it cannot signify every individual place in heaven, earth, and hell, is of all confessed, and needeth no proof; no more than when our Saviour is said to cure πᾶσαν νόσον, as Matt. ix. 35, there is need to prove that he did not cure every disease of every man, but only all sorts of diseases.

Sundry other instances might be given to manifest that this is the most usual and frequent signification of the word *all* in the holy Scripture; and, therefore, from the bare word nothing can be inferred to enforce an absolute unlimited universality of all individuals to be intimated thereby. The particular places insisted on we shall afterward consider. I shall conclude all concerning these general expressions that are used in the Scripture about this business in these observations:—

First, The word *all* is certainly and unquestionably sometimes restrained, and to be restrained, to *all of some sorts*, although the qualification be not expressed which is the bond of the limitation: so for all believers, 1 Cor. xv. 22; Eph. iv. 6; Rom. v. 18, " The free gift came upon all men to justification of life:" which " all men," that are so actually justified, are no more nor less than those that are Christ's,—that is, believers; for certainly justification is not without faith.

Secondly, The word *all* is sometimes used for *some of all sorts*, Jer. xxxi. 34. The word כֻּלָּם is by Paul rendered πάντες, Heb. viii. 11; so John xii. 32; 1 Tim. ii. 1–3; which is made apparent by the mention of "kings," as one sort of people there intended. And I make no doubt but it will appear to all that the word must be taken in one of these senses in every place where it is used in the business of redemption; as shall be proved.

Thirdly, Let a diligent comparison be made between the general expressions of the New with the predictions of the Old Testament, and they will be found to be answerable to, and expository of, one another; the Lord affirming in the New that that was done which in the Old he foretold should be done. Now, in the predictions and prophecies of the Old Testament, that *all nations, all flesh, all people, all the ends, families*, or *kindreds of the earth, the world, the whole earth*, the *isles*, shall be converted, look up to Christ, come to the mountain of the Lord, and the like, none doubts but that the elect of God in all nations are only signified, knowing that in them alone those predictions have the truth of their accomplishment. And why should the same expressions used in the Gospel, and many of them aiming directly to declare the fulfilling of the other, be wire-drawn to a large extent, so contrary to the mind of the Holy Ghost? In fine, as when the Lord is said to wipe tears from all faces, it hinders not but that the reprobates shall be cast out to eternity where there is weeping and wailing, etc.; so when Christ is said to die for all, it hinders not but that those reprobates may perish to eternity for their sins, without any effectual remedy intended for them, though occasionally proposed to some of them.

6. Observe that the Scripture often speaketh of things and persons according to the appearance they have, and the account that is of

them amongst men, or that esteem that they have of them to whom it speaketh,—frequently speaking of men and unto men as in the condition wherein they are according to outward appearance, upon which human judgment must proceed, and not what they are indeed. Thus, many are called and said to be *wise, just,* and *righteous,* according as they are so esteemed, though the Lord knows them to be foolish sinners. So Jerusalem is called "The holy city," Matt. xxvii. 53, because it was so in esteem and appearance, when indeed it was a very "den of thieves." And 2 Chron. xxviii. 23, it is said of Ahaz, that wicked king of Judah, that " he sacrificed to the gods of Damascus that smote him." It was the Lord alone that smote him, and those idols to which he sacrificed were but stocks and stones, the work of men's hands, which could no way help themselves, much less smite their enemies; yet the Holy Ghost useth an expression answering his idolatrous persuasion, and saith, "They smote him." Nay, is it not said of Christ, John v. 18, that he had broken the Sabbath, which yet he only did in the corrupt opinion of the blinded Pharisees?

Add, moreover, to what hath been said, that which is of no less an undeniable truth,—namely, that many things which are proper and peculiar to the children of God are oft and frequently assigned to them who live in the same outward communion with them, and are partakers of the same external privileges, though indeed aliens in respect of the participation of the grace of the promise. Put, I say, these two things, which are most evident, together, and it will easily appear that those places which seem to express a possibility of perishing and eternal destruction to them who are said to be redeemed by the blood of Christ, are no ways advantageous to the adversaries of the effectual redemption of God's elect by the blood of Christ; because such may be said to be redeemed κατὰ τὴν δόξαν, not κατὰ τὴν ἀλήθειαν,—κατὰ τὸ φαίνεσθαι, not κατὰ τὸ εἶναι,—in respect of appearance, not reality, as is the use of the Scripture in divers other things.

7. That which is spoken according to the *judgment of charity* on our parts must not always be exactly squared and made answerable to *verity* in respect of them of whom any thing is affirmed. For the rectitude of our judgment, it sufficeth that we proceed according to the rules of judging that are given us; for what is out of our cognizance, whether that answer to our judgments or no, belongs not to us. Thus, oftentimes the apostles in the Scriptures write unto men, and term them "holy," "saints," yea, "elected;" but from thence positively to conclude that they were all so indeed, we have no warrant. So Peter, 1 Epist. i. 1, 2, calls all the strangers to whom he wrote, scattered throughout Pontus, Galatia, Cappadocia, Asia, and Bithynia, "elect according to the foreknowledge of God the Father," etc.; and yet that I have any warrant to conclude, *de fide,* that all were such, none

dare affirm.   So Paul tells the Thessalonians, the whole church to
whom he wrote, that he "knew their election of God," 1 Thess. i. 4;
2 Thess. ii. 13, he blesseth God "who had chosen them to salvation."   Now, did not Paul make this judgment of them by the rule
of charity? according as he affirms in another place, "It is meet
for me to think so of you all," Phil. i. 7; and can it, ought it, hence
to be infallibly concluded that they were all elected?   If some of
these should be found to fall away from the gospel and to have
perished, would an argument from thence be valid that the elect
might perish? would we not presently answer, that they were said
to be elected according to the judgment of charity, not that they
were so indeed?   And why is not this answer as sufficient and satis-
fying when it is given to the objection taken from the perishing of
some who were said to be redeemed merely in the judgment of charity,
as when they were said to be elected?

8. The *infallible connection*, according to God's purpose and will,
of faith and salvation, which is frequently the thing intended in
gospel proposals, must be considered.   The Lord hath in his counsel
established it, and revealed in his word, that there is an indissoluble
bond between these two things, so that " he that believeth shall be
saved," Mark xvi. 16; which, indeed, is the substance of the gospel, in
the outward promulgation thereof.   This is the testimony of God,
that eternal life is in his Son; which whoso believeth, he sets to his
seal that God is true; he who believes not doing what in him lieth
to make God a liar, 1 John v. 9–11.   Now, this connection of the
means and the end, faith and life, is the only thing which is signified
and held out to innumerable to whom the gospel is preached, all
the commands, proffers, and promises that are made unto them intimating no more than this will of God, that believers shall certainly
be saved; which is an unquestionable divine verity and a sufficient
object for supernatural faith to rest upon, and which being not closed
with is a sufficient cause of damnation: John viii. 24, " If ye believe not that I am he" (that is, "the way, the truth, and the life"),
" ye shall die in your sins."

It is a vain imagination of some, that when the command and
promise of believing are made out to any man, though he be of
the number of them that shall certainly perish, yet the Lord hath a
conditional will of his salvation, and intends that he shall be saved,
on condition that he will believe; when the condition lieth not at all
in the will of God, which is always absolute, but is only between the
things to them proposed, as was before declared.   And those poor
deluded things, who will be standing upon their own legs before
they are well able to crawl, and might justly be persuaded to hold
by men of more strength, do exceedingly betray their own conceited
ignorance, when, with great pomp, they hold out the broken pieces of

an old Arminian sophism with acclamations of grace to this *new* discovery (for so they think of all that is new to them),—namely, "As is God's proffer, so is his intention; but he calls to all to believe and be saved: therefore he intends it to all." For,—

First, God doth not proffer life to *all* upon the condition of faith, passing by a great part of mankind without any such proffer made to them at all.

Secondly, If by God's *proffer* they understand his command and promise, who told them that these things were declarative of his will and purpose or intention? He commands Pharaoh to let his people go; but did he intend he should so do according to his command? had he not foretold that he would so order things that he should not let them go? I thought always that God's commands and promises had revealed our duty, and not his purpose; what God would have us to do, and not what he will do. His promises, indeed, as *particularly* applied, hold out his mind to the *persons* to whom they are applied; but as *indefinitely* proposed, they reveal no other intention of God but what we before discovered, which concerns *things*, not *persons*, even his determinate purpose infallibly to connect faith and salvation.

Thirdly, If the proffer be (as they say) universal, and the intention of God be answerable thereunto,—that is, he intends the salvation of them to whom the tender of it upon faith is made, or may be so; then,—*First*, What becomes of election and reprobation? Neither of them, certainly, can consist with this universal purpose of saving us all. *Secondly*, If he intend it, why is it, then, not accomplished? doth he fail of his purpose? "Dum vitant stulti vitia, in contraria currunt." Is not this certain *Scylla* worse than the other feared *Charybdis?* But they say, "He intendeth it only upon condition; and the condition being not fulfilled, he fails not in his purpose, though the thing be not conferred." But did the Lord foreknow whether the condition would be fulfilled by them to whom the proposal was made, or not? If not, where is his prescience, his omniscience? If he did, how can he be said to intend salvation to them of whom he certainly knew that they would never fulfil the condition on which it was to be attained; and, moreover, knew it with this circumstance, that the condition was not to be attained without his bestowing, and that he had determined not to bestow it? Would they ascribe such a will and purpose to a wise man as they do ignorantly and presumptuously to the only wise God,—namely, that he should intend to have a thing done upon the performance of such a condition as he knew full well without him could never be performed, and he had fully resolved not to effect it: for instance, to give his daughter in marriage to such a one, upon condition he would give unto him such a jewel as he hath not, nor can have, unless he bestow it upon him, which he is resolved never to do? Oh, whither will blindness and ignorance, esteemed light and knowledge, carry poor deluded souls? This, then, is the main thing demonstrated and held out in the promulgation of the gospel, especially for what concerns unbelievers, even the strict connection between the duty of faith assigned and the benefit of life promised; which hath a truth of universal extent, grounded upon the plenary sufficiency of the death of Christ, towards all that shall believe. And I see no reason why this should be termed part of *the mystery of the Universalists*, though the lowest part (as it is by M—— S——, page 202), *that the gospel could not be preached to all unless Christ died for all;* which, with what is mentioned before concerning another and higher part of it, is an old, rotten, carnal, and long-since-confuted sophism, arising out of the ignorance of the word and right reason, which are no way contrary.

9. The mixed distribution of the elect and reprobates, believers and unbelievers, according to the purpose and mind of God, throughout the whole world, and in the several places thereof, in all or most of the single congregations, is another ground of holding out a tender of the blood of Jesus Christ to them for whom it was never shed, as is apparent in the event by the ineffectualness of its proposals. The ministers of the gospel, who are stewards of the mysteries of Christ, and to whom the word of reconciliation is committed, being acquainted only with revealed things (the Lord lodging his purposes and intentions towards particular persons in the secret ark of his own bosom, not to be pryed into), are bound to admonish all, and warn all men, to whom they are sent; giving the same commands, proposing the same promises, making tenders of Jesus Christ in the same manner, to all, that the elect, whom they know not but by the event, may obtain, whilst the rest are hardened. Now, these things being thus ordered by Him who hath the supreme disposal of all,—namely, First, That there should be such a mixture of elect and reprobate, of tares and wheat, to the end of the world; and, secondly, That Christ, and reconciliation through him, should be preached by men ignorant of his eternal discriminating purposes; there is an absolute necessity of two other things: First, That the promises must have a kind of unrestrained generality, to be suitable to this dispensation before recounted. Secondly, That they must be proposed to them towards whom the Lord never intended the good things of the promises, they having a share in this proposal by their mixture in this world with the elect of God. So that, from the general proposition of Christ in the promises, nothing can be concluded concerning his death for all to whom it is proposed, as having another rise and occasion. The sum is:—The word of reconciliation being committed to men unacquainted with God's distinguishing counsels, to be

preached to men of a various, mixed condition in respect of his purpose, and the way whereby he hath determined to bring his own
home to himself being by exhortations, entreaties, promises, and
the like means, accommodated to the reasonable nature whereof all
are partakers to whom the word is sent, which are suited also to
the accomplishment of other ends towards the rest, as conviction,
restraint, hardening, inexcusableness, it cannot be but the proposal
and offer must necessarily be made to some upon condition, who in-
tentionally, and in respect of the purpose of God, have no right unto
it in the just aim and intendment thereof. Only, for a close, observe
these two things:—First, That the proffer itself neither is nor ever
was absolutely universal to all, but only indefinite, without respect
to outward differences. Secondly, That Christ being not to be received without faith, and God giving faith to whom he pleaseth, it
is manifest that he never intendeth Christ to them on whom he will
not bestow faith.

10. The faith which is enjoined and commanded in the gospel
hath divers several acts and different degrees, in the exercise whereof it proceedeth orderly, according to the natural method of the
proposal of the objects to be believed: the consideration whereof is
of much use in the business in hand, our adversaries pretending that
if Christ died not for all, then in vain are they exhorted to believe,
there being, indeed, no proper object for the faith of innumerable,
because Christ did not die for them; as though the gospel did hold
out this doctrine in the very entrance of all, that Christ died for every
one, elect and reprobate; or as though the first thing which any
one living under the means of grace is exhorted to believe were,
that Christ died for him in particular;—both which are notoriously
false, as I hope, in the close of our undertaking, will be made manifest
to all. For the present I shall only intimate something of what I
said before, concerning the order of exercising the several acts of
faith; whereby it will appear that no one in the world is commanded or invited to believe, but that he hath a sufficient object to
fix the act of faith on, of truth enough for its foundation, and latitude
enough for its utmost exercise, which is enjoined him.

First, then, The first thing which the gospel enjoineth sinners,
and which it persuades and commands them to believe, is, that salvation is not to be had in themselves, inasmuch as all have sinned
and come short of the glory of God; nor by the works of the law, by
which no flesh living can be justified. Here is a saving gospel truth
for sinners to believe, which the apostle dwells upon wholly, Rom. i.
ii. iii., to prepare a way for justification by Christ. Now, what num-
berless numbers are they to whom the gospel is preached who never
come so far as to believe so much as this! amongst whom you may
reckon almost the whole nation of the Jews, as is apparent, Rom. ix.,

x. 3, 4. Now, not to go one step farther with any proposal, a contempt of this object of faith is the sin of infidelity.

Secondly, The gospel requires faith to this, that there is salvation to be had in the promised seed,—in Him who was before ordained to be a captain of salvation to them that do believe. And here also at this trial some millions of the great army of men, outwardly called, drop off, and do never believe, with true divine faith, that God hath provided a way for the saving of sinners.

Thirdly, That Jesus of Nazareth, who was crucified by the Jews, was this Saviour, promised before; and that there is no name under heaven given whereby they may be saved besides his. And this was the main point upon which the Jews broke off, refusing to accept of Christ as the Saviour of men, but rather prosecuted him as an enemy of God; and are thereupon so oft charged with infidelity and damnable unbelief. The question was not, between Christ and them, whether he died for them all or no? but, whether he was that Messiah promised? which they denied, and perished in their unbelief.

Now, before these three acts of faith be performed, in vain is the soul exhorted farther to climb the uppermost steps, and miss all the bottom foundation ones.

Fourthly, The gospel requires a resting upon this Christ, so discovered and believed on to be the promised Redeemer, as an all-sufficient Saviour, with whom is plenteous redemption, and who is able to save to the utmost them that come to God by.him, and to bear the burden of all weary labouring souls that come by faith to him; in which proposal there is a certain infallible truth, grounded upon the superabundant sufficiency of the oblation of Christ in itself, for whomsoever (fewer or more) it be intended. Now, much self-knowledge, much conviction, much sense of sin, God's justice, and free grace, is required to the exercise of this act of faith. Good Lord! how many thousand poor souls within the pale of the church can never be brought unto it! The truth is, without the help of God's Spirit none of those three before, much less this last, can be performed; which worketh freely, when, how, and in whom he pleaseth.

Fifthly, These things being firmly seated in the soul (and not before), we are every one called in particular to believe the efficacy of the redemption that is in the blood of Jesus towards our own souls in particular: which every one may assuredly do in whom the free grace of God hath wrought the former acts of faith, and doth work this also, without either doubt or fear of want of a right object to believe if they should so do; for certainly Christ died for every one in whose heart the Lord, by his almighty power, works effectually faith to lay hold on him and assent unto him, according to that orderly proposal that is held forth in the gospel. Now, according to this order (as by some it is observed) are the articles of our faith disposed in the apostles' creed (that ancient summary of Christian religion commonly so called), the remission of our sins and life eternal being in the last place proposed to be believed; for before we attain so far the rest must be firmly rooted. So that it is a senseless vanity to cry out of the nullity of the object to be believed, if Christ died not for all, there being an absolute truth in every thing which any is called to assent unto, according to the order of the gospel.

And so I have proposed the general foundations of those answers which we shall give to the ensuing objections; whereunto to make particular application of them will be an easy task, as I hope will be made apparent unto all.

CHAPTER II.

An entrance to the answer unto particular arguments.

Now we come to the consideration of the objections wherewith the doctrine we have, from the word of God, undeniably confirmed is usually, with great noise and clamour, assaulted; concerning which I must give you these three cautions, before I come to lay them down:—

The first whereof is this, that for mine own part I had rather they were all buried than once brought to light, in opposition to the truth of God, which they seem to deface; and therefore, were it left to my choice, I would not produce any one of them: not that there is any difficulty or weight in them, that the removal should be operose or burdensome, but only that I am not willing to be any way instrumental to give breath or light to that which opposeth the truth of God. But because, in these times of liberty and error, I suppose the most of them have been objected to the reader already by men lying in wait to deceive, or are likely to be, I shall therefore show you the poison, and withal furnish you with an antidote against the venom of such self-seekers as our days abound withal.

Secondly, I must desire you, that when ye hear an objection, ye would not be carried away with the sound of words, nor suffer it to take impression on your spirits, remembering with how many demonstrations and innumerable places of Scripture the truth opposed by them hath been confirmed, but rest yourselves until the places be well weighed, the arguments pondered, the answers set down; and then the Lord direct you to "prove all things, and hold fast that which is good."

Thirdly, That you would diligently observe what comes near the stress of the controversy, and the thing wherein the difference lieth, leaving all other flourishes and swelling words of vanity, as of no weight, of no importance.

Now, the objections laid against the truth maintained are of two sorts;—the first, taken from Scripture perverted; the other, from reason abused.

We begin with the first, the OBJECTIONS TAKEN FROM SCRIPTURE; all the places whereof that may any way seem to contradict our assertion are, by our [1]strongest adversaries, in their greatest strength, referred to three heads:—First, Those places that affirm that Christ died for the *world*, or that otherwise make mention of the word *world* in the business of redemption. Secondly, Those that mention *all* and *every man*, either in the work of Christ's dying for them, or where God is said to will their salvation. Thirdly, Those which affirm Christ *bought* or died for them that perish. Hence they draw out three principal arguments or sophisms, on which they much insist. All which we shall, by the Lord's assistance, consider in their several order, with the places of Scripture brought to confirm and strengthen them.

I. The first whereof is taken from the word " *world*," and is thus proposed by them, to whom our poor pretenders are indeed very children:—

" He that is given out of the love wherewith God loved the world, as John iii. 16; that gave himself for the life of the world, as John vi. 51; and was a propitiation for the sins of the whole world, as 1 John ii. 2" (to which add, John i. 29, iv. 42; 2 Cor. v. 19, cited by Armin. pp. 530, 531, and Corv. ad Molin. p. 442, chap. 29); "he was given and died for every man in the world;—but the first is true of Christ, as appears by the places before alleged: therefore he died for all and every one," Remon. Act. Synod. p. 300. And to this they say their adversaries have not any colour of answer.

But granting them the liberty of boasting, we flatly deny, without seeking for colours, the consequent of the first proposition, and will, by the Lord's help, at any time, put it to the trial whether we have not just cause so to do. There be two ways whereby they go about to prove this consequent from the *world* to *all* and *every one;*—first, By reason and the sense of the word; secondly, From the consideration of the particular places of Scripture urged. We will try them in both.

First, If they will make it out by the way of reasoning, I conceive they must argue thus:—

The whole world contains all and every man in the world; Christ died for the whole world: therefore, etc.

Ans. Here are manifestly four terms in this syllogism, arising from the ambiguity of the word "world," and so no true *medium* on which the weight of the conclusion should hang; the *world*, in the first proposition, being taken for the world containing; in the second, for the world contained, or men in the world, as is too apparent to be made a thing to be proved. So that unless ye render the conclusion, *Therefore Christ died for that which contains all the men in the world,* and assert in the *assumption* that Christ died for the *world containing,* or the fabric of the habitable earth (which is a frenzy), this syllogism is most sophistically false. If, then, ye will take any proof from the word "world," it must not be from the thing itself, but from the signification of the word in the Scripture; as thus:—

This word "world" in the Scripture signifieth all and every man in the world; but Christ is said to die for the world: ergo, etc.

Ans. The first proposition, concerning the signification and meaning of the word *world* is either *universal,* comprehending all places where it is used, or particular, intending only some. If the first, the proposition is apparently false, as was manifested before; if in the second way, then the argument must be thus formed:—

In some places in Scripture the word "world" signifieth all and every man in the world, of all ages, times, and conditions; but Christ is said to die for the world: ergo, etc.

Ans. That this *syllogism* is no better than the former is most evident, a universal conclusion being inferred from a particular proposition. But now the first proposition being rightly formed, I have one question to demand concerning the second, or the assumption, —namely, whether in every place where there is mention made of the death of Christ, it is said he died for the world, or only in some? If ye say in every place, that is apparently false, as hath been already discovered by those many texts of Scripture before produced, restraining the death of Christ to his elect, his sheep, his church, in comparison whereof these are but few. If the second, then the argument must run thus:—

In some few places of Scripture the word "world" doth signify all and every man in the world; but in some few places Christ is said to die for the world (though not in express words, yet in terms equivalent): ergo, etc.

Ans. This argument is so weak, ridiculous, and sophistically false, that it cannot but be evident to any one; and yet clearly, from the word ˈworld itself, it will not be made any better, and none need desire that it should be worse. It concludes a universal upon particular affirmatives, and, besides, with four terms apparently in the syllogism; unless the *some places* in the *first* be proved to be the very *some places* in the *assumption,* which is the thing in question. So that if any strength be taken from this word, it must be an argument in this form:—

If the word "world" doth signify all and every man that ever were or shall be, in those places where Christ is said to die for the world, then Christ died for all and every man; but the word "world," in all those places where Christ is said to die for the world, doth signify all and every man in the world: therefore Christ died for them.

Ans. First, That it is but *in one place* said that Christ gave his life for the world, or died for it, which holds out the intention of our Saviour; all the other places seem only to hold out the sufficiency of his oblation for all, which we also maintain. Secondly, We absolutely deny the assumption, and appeal for trial to a consideration of all those particular places wherein such mention is made.

Thus have I called this argument to rule and measure, that it might be evident where the great strength of it lieth (which is indeed very weakness), and that for their sakes who, having caught hold of the word *world*, run presently away with the bait, as though all were clear for universal redemption; when yet, if ye desire them to lay out and manifest the strength of their reason, they know not what to say but *the world* and *the whole world*, understanding, indeed, neither what they say nor whereof they do affirm. And now, *quid dignum tanto?* what cause of the great boast mentioned in the entrance? A weaker argument, I dare say, was never by rational men produced in so weighty a cause; which will farther be manifested by the consideration of the several particular places produced to give it countenance, which we shall do in order :—

1. The first place we pitch upon is that which by our adversaries is first propounded, and not a little rested upon ; and yet, notwithstanding their clamorous claim, there are not a few who think that very text as fit and ready to overthrow their whole opinion as Goliath's sword to cut off his own head, many unanswerable arguments against the universality of redemption being easily deduced from the words of that text. The great peaceable King of his church guide us to make good the interest of truth to the place in controversy which through him we shall attempt;—first, by opening the words; and, secondly, by balancing of reasonings and arguments from them. And this place is John iii. 16, "God so loved the world, that he gave his only-begotten Son, that whosoever believeth in him should not perish, but have everlasting life."

This place, I say, the Universalists exceedingly boast in; for which we are persuaded they have so little cause, that we doubt not but, with the Lord's assistance, to demonstrate that it is destructive to their whole defence: to which end I will give you, in brief, a double paraphrase of the words, the first containing their sense, the latter ours. Thus, then, our adversaries explain these words:—" '*God so loved*,' had such a natural inclination, velleity, and propensity to the good of '*the world*,' Adam, with all and every one of his posterity, of all ages, times, and conditions (whereof some were in heaven, some in hell long before), '*that he gave his only-begotten Son,*' causing him to be incarnate in the fulness of time, to die, not with a purpose and resolution to save any, but '*that whosoever,*' what persons soever of those which he had propensity unto, '*believeth in him should not perish, but have everlasting life,*' should have this fruit and issue, that he should escape death and hell, and live eternally." In which explication of the sense of the place these things are to be observed:—

First, What is that *love* which was the cause of the sending or giving of Christ; which they make to be a *natural propensity to the good of all.* Secondly, Who are the objects of this love; *all and every man of all generations.* Thirdly, Wherein this giving consisteth; of which I cannot find whether they mean by it the appointment of Christ to be a recoverer, or his actual exhibition in the flesh for the accomplishment of his ministration. Fourthly, *Whosoever*, they make distributive of the persons in the world, and so not restrictive in the intention to some. Fifthly, That life eternal *is the fruit obtained by believers,* but not the end intended by God.

Now, look a little, in the second place, at what we conceive to be the mind of God in those words; whose aim we take to be the advancement and setting forth of the free love of God to lost sinners, in sending Christ to procure for them eternal redemption, as may appear in this following paraphrase:—

" '*God*' the Father '*so loved,*' had such a peculiar, transcendent love, being an unchangeable purpose and act of his will concerning their salvation, towards '*the world,*' miserable, sinful, lost men of all sorts, not only Jews but Gentiles also, which he peculiarly loved, '*that,*' intending their salvation, as in the last words, for the praise of his glorious grace, '*he gave,*' he prepared a way to prevent their everlasting destruction, by appointing and sending '*his only-begotten Son*' to be an all-sufficient Saviour to all that look up unto him, '*that whosoever believeth in him,*' all believers whatsoever, and only they, '*should not perish, but have everlasting life,*' and so effectually be brought to the obtaining of those glorious things through him which the Lord in his free love had designed for them."

In which enlargement of the words, for the setting forth of what we conceive to be the mind of the Holy Ghost in them, these things are to be observed:—

First, What we understand by the "*love*" of God, even that act of his will which was the cause of sending his Son Jesus Christ, being the most eminent act of love and favour to the creature; for love is *velle alicui bonum,* "to will good to any." And never did God will greater good to the creature than in appointing his Son for their redemption. Notwithstanding, I would have it observed that I do not make the purpose of sending or giving Christ to be absolutely sub-ordinate to God's love to his elect, as though that were the end of the other absolutely, but rather that they are both co-ordinate to the same supreme end, or the manifestation of God's glory by the way of mercy tempered with justice; but in respect of our appre-hension, that is the relation wherein they stand one to another. Now, this love we say to be that, greater than which there is none.

Secondly, By the "*world*," we understand the elect of God only, though not considered in this place as such, but under such a notion as, being true of them, serves for the farther exaltation of God's love towards them, which is the end here designed; and this is, as they are poor, miserable, lost creatures in the world, of the world, scattered abroad in all places of the world, not tied to Jews or Greeks, but dispersed in any nation, kindred, and language under heaven.

Thirdly, Ἵνα πᾶς ὁ πιστεύων, is to us, "*that every believer*," and is declarative of the intention of God in sending or giving his Son, con-taining no distribution of the world beloved, but a direction to the persons whose good was intended, that love being an unchangeable intention of the chiefest good.

Fourthly, "*Should not perish, but have life everlasting*," contains an expression of the particular aim and intention of God in this busi-ness; which is, the certain salvation of believers by Christ. And this, in general, is the interpretation of the words which we adhere unto, which will yield us sundry arguments, sufficient each of them to evert the general ransom; which, that they may be the better bottomed, and the more clearly convincing, we will lay down and compare the several words and expressions of this place, about whose interpreta-tion we differ, with the reason of our rejecting the one sense and embracing the other:—

The first difference in the interpretation of this place is about the cause of sending Christ; called here *love*. The second, about the object of this love; called here the *world*. Thirdly, Concerning the intention of God in sending his Son; said to be that believers might be *saved*.

For the FIRST, By "love" in this place, all our adversaries agree that *a natural affection and propensity in God to the good of the crea-ture, lost under sin, in general, which moved him to take some way whereby it might possibly be remedied*, is intended. We, on the con-trary, say that by *love* here is not meant an inclination or propensity of his nature, but an *act of his will* (where we conceive his love to be seated), *and eternal purpose to do good to man, being the most trans-cendent and eminent act of God's love to the creature.*

That both these may be weighed, to see which is most agreeable to the mind of the Holy Ghost, I shall give you, first, some of the reasons whereby we oppose the former interpretation; and, secondly, those whereby we confirm our own.

First, If *no natural affection*, whereby he should necessarily be carried to any thing without himself, can or ought to be ascribed unto God, then no such thing is here intended in the word *love;* for that cannot be here intended which is not in God at all. But now, that there neither is nor can be any such natural affection in God is most apparent, and may be evidenced by many demonstrations. I shall briefly recount a few of them:—

First, Nothing that includes any imperfection is to be assigned to Almighty God: he *is God all-sufficient;* he is our *rock, and his work is perfect.* But a natural affection in God to the good and salvation of all, being never completed nor perfected, carrieth along with it a great deal of imperfection and weakness; and not only so, but it must also needs be exceedingly prejudicial to the absolute blessedness and happiness of Almighty God. Look, how much any thing wants of the fulfilling of that whereunto it is carried out with any desire, natural or voluntary, so much it wanteth of blessedness and happiness. So that, without impairing of the infinite blessedness of the ever-blessed God, no natural affection unto any thing never to be accomplished can be ascribed unto him, such as this general love to all is supposed to be.

Secondly, If the Lord hath such a natural affection to all, as to love them so far as to send his Son to die for them, whence is it that this affection of his doth not receive accomplishment? whence is it that it is hindered, and doth not produce its effects? why doth not the Lord engage his power for the fulfilling of his desire? " It doth not seem good to his infinite wisdom," say they, "so to do." Then is there an affection in God to that which, in his wisdom, he cannot prosecute. This among the sons of men, the worms of the earth, would be called a brutish affection.

Thirdly, No affection or natural propensity to good is to be ascribed to God which the Scripture nowhere assigns to him, and is contrary to what the Scripture doth assign unto him. Now, the Scripture doth nowhere assign unto God any natural affection whereby he should be naturally inclined to the good of the creature; the place to prove it clearly is yet to be produced. And that it is contrary to what the Scripture assigns him is apparent; for it describes him to be free in showing mercy, every act of it being by him performed freely, even as he pleaseth, for " he hath mercy on whom he will have mercy." Now, if every act of mercy showed unto any do proceed from the free distinguishing will of God (as is apparent), certainly there can be in him no such natural affection. And the truth is, if the Lord should not show mercy, and be carried out towards the creature, merely upon his own distinguishing will, but should naturally be moved to show mercy to the miserable, he should, first, be no more merciful to men than to devils, nor, secondly, to those that are saved than to those that are damned: for that which is natural must be equal in all its operations; and that which is natural to God must be eternal. Many more effectual reasons are produced by our divines for the denial of this natural affection in God, in the resolution of the Arminian distinction (I call it so, as now by them abused) of God's antecedent and consequent will, to whom the learned reader may repair for satisfaction. So that the love mentioned in this place is not that natural affection to all in general, which is not. But,—

Secondly, It is the *special love of God to his elect*, as we affirm, and so, consequently, not any such thing as our adversaries suppose to be intended by it,—namely, a *velleity* or *natural inclination to the good of all*. For,—

First, The love here intimated is absolutely the most eminent and transcendent love that ever God showed or bare towards any miserable creature; yea, the intention of our Saviour is so to set it forth, as is apparent by the emphatical expression of it used in this place. The particles " so," " that," declare no less, pointing out an eximiousness peculiarly remarkable in the thing whereof the affirmation is [made], above any other thing in the same kind. Expositors usually lay weight upon almost every particular word of the verse, for the exaltation and demonstration of the love here mentioned. " *So*," that is, in such a degree, to such a remarkable, astonishable height: " *God*," the glorious, all-sufficient God, that could have manifested his justice to eternity in the condemnation of all sinners, and no way wanted them to be partakers of his blessedness: " *loved*," with such an earnest, intense affection, consisting in an eternal, unchangeable act and purpose of his will, for the bestowing of the chiefest good (the choicest effectual love): " *the world*," men in the world, of the world, subject to the iniquities and miseries of the world, lying in their blood, having nothing to render them commendable in his eyes, or before him : " *that he gave*," did not, as he made all the world at first, speak the word and it was done, but proceeded higher, to the performance of a great deal more and longer work, wherein he was to do more than exercise an act of his almighty power, as before; and therefore gave " *his Son;*" not any favourite or other well-pleasing creature; not sun, moon, or stars; not the rich treasure of his creation (all too mean, and coming short of expressing this love); but his Son: " *begotten Son*," and that not so called by reason of some near approaches to him, and *filial, obediential* reverence of him, as the angels are called the sons of God; for it was not an angel that he gave, which yet had been an expression of most intense love; nor yet any son by adoption, as believers are the sons of God; but his begotten Son, begotten of his own person from eternity; and that "*his only-begotten Son;*" not any one of his sons, but whereas he had or hath but one only-begotten Son, always in his bosom, his Isaac, he gave him:—than which how could the infinite wisdom of God make or give any higher testimony of his love? especially if ye will add what is here evidently included, though the time was not as yet come that it should be openly expressed, namely whereunto he gave his Son, his only one; not to be a king, and worshipped in the first place,—but he "spared him not, but delivered him up" to death "for us all," Rom. viii. 32. Whereunto, for a close of all, cast your eyes upon his design and purpose in this whole business, and ye shall find that it was that believers, those whom he thus loved, "*might not perish,*"—that is, undergo the utmost misery and wrath to eternity, which they had deserved,—"*but have everlasting life,*" eternal glory with himself, which of themselves they could no way attain; and ye will easily grant that "greater love hath no man than this." Now, if the love here mentioned be the greatest, highest, and chiefest of all, certainly it cannot be that common affection towards all that we discussed before; for the love whereby men are actually and eternally saved is greater than that which may consist with the perishing of men to eternity.

Secondly, The Scripture positively asserts this very love as the chiefest act of the love of God, and that which he would have us take notice of in the first place: Rom. v. 8, "God commendeth his love toward us, in that, while we were yet sinners, Christ died for us;" and fully, 1 John iv. 9, 10, "In this was manifested the love of God toward us, because that God sent his only-begotten Son into the world, that we might live through him. Herein is love, not that we loved God, but that he loved us, and sent his Son to be the propitiation for our sins." In both which places the eminency of this love is set forth exceeding emphatically to believers, with such expressions as can no way be accommodated to a natural velleity to the good of all.

Thirdly, That seeing all love in God is but *velle alicui bonum,* to will good to them that are beloved, *they* certainly are the object of his love to whom he intends that good which is the issue and effect of that love; but now the issue of this love or good intended, being *not perishing,* and *obtaining eternal life* through Christ, happens alone to, and is bestowed on, only elect believers: therefore, they certainly are the object of this love, and they alone;—which was the thing we had to declare.

Fourthly, That love which is the cause of giving Christ is also always the cause of the bestowing of all other good things: Rom. viii. 32, "He that spared not his own Son, but delivered him up for us all, how shall he not with him also freely give us all things?"

Therefore, if the love there mentioned be the cause of sending Christ, as it is, it must also cause all other things to be given with him, and so can be towards none but those who have those things bestowed on them; which are only the elect, only believers. Who else have grace here, or glory hereafter?

Fifthly, The word here, which is ἠγάπησε, signifieth, in its native importance, *valde dilexit,*—to love so as to rest in that love; which how it can stand with hatred, and an eternal purpose of not bestowing effectual grace, which is in the Lord towards some, will not easily be made apparent. And now let the Christian reader judge, whether by the love of God, in this place mentioned, be to be understood a natural velleity or inclination in God to the good of all, both elect and reprobate, or the peculiar love of God to his elect, being the fountain of the chiefest good that ever was bestowed on the sons of men. This is the first difference about the interpretation of these words.

SECONDLY, The second thing controverted is the *object of this love,* pressed by the word "world;" which our adversaries would have to signify all and every man; we, the elect of God scattered abroad in the world, with a tacit opposition to the nation of the Jews, who alone, excluding all other nations (some few proselytes excepted), before the actual exhibition of Christ in the flesh, had all the benefits of the promises appropriated to them, Rom. ix. 4; in which privilege now all nations were to have an equal share. To confirm the exposition of the word as used by the Universalists, nothing of weight, that ever yet I could see, is brought forth, but only the word itself; for neither the love mentioned in the beginning, nor the design pointed at in the end of the verse, will possibly agree with the sense which they impose on that word in the middle. Besides, how weak and infirm an inference from the word *world,* by reason of its ambiguous and wonderful various acceptations, is, we have at large declared before.

Three poor shifts I find in the great champions of this course, to prove that the word *world* doth not signify the *elect.* Justly we might have expected some reasons to prove that it signified or implied *all* and *every man* in the world, which was their own assertion; but of this ye have a deep silence, being conscious, no doubt, of their disability for any such performance. Only, as I said, three pretended arguments they bring to disprove that which none went about to prove,—namely, that by the *world* is meant the *elect* as such; for though we conceive the persons here designed directly men in and of the world, to be all and only God's elect, yet we do not say that they are here so considered, but rather under another notion, as men scattered over all the world, in themselves subject to misery and sin. So that whosoever will oppose our exposition of this place must either, first, prove that by the *world* here must be necessarily under-

stood all and every man in the world; or, secondly, that it cannot
be taken indefinitely for men in the world which materially are
elect, though not considered under that formality. So that all those
vain flourishes which some men make with these words, by putting the
word *elect* into the room of the word *world*; and then coining absurd
consequences, are quite beside the business in hand. Yet, farther,
we deny that by a supply of the word *elect* into the text any absurdity
or untruth will justly follow. Yea, and that flourish which is usually
so made is but a bugbear to frighten weak ones; for, suppose we
should read it thus, "God so loved the elect, that he gave his only-
begotten Son, that whosoever believeth in him should not perish,"
what inconvenience will now follow? "Why," say they, "that
some of the elect, whom God so loved as to send his Son for, may
perish." Why, I pray? Is it because he sent his Son that they
might not perish? or what other cause? "No; but because it is
said, that whosoever of them believeth on him should not perish;
which intimates that some of them might not believe." Very good!
But where is any such intimation? God designs the salvation of all
them in express words for whom he sends his Son; and certainly
all that shall be saved shall believe. But it is in the word *whosoever*,
which is distributive of the world into those that believe and those
that believe not. *Ans.* First, If this word *whosoever* be distributive, then it is restrictive of the love of God to some, and not to
others,—to one part of the distribution, and not to the other. And if
it do not restrain the love of God, intending the salvation of some,
then it is not distributive of the fore-mentioned object of it; and if
it do restrain it, then all are not intended in the love which moved
God to give his Son. Secondly, I deny that the word here is distributive of the object of God's love, but only declarative of his end
and aim in giving Christ in the pursuit of that love,—to wit, that
all believers might be saved. So that the sense is, "God so loved his
elect throughout the world, that he gave his Son with this intention,
that by him believers might be saved." And this is all that is by
any (besides a few worthless cavils) objected from this place to disprove our interpretation; which we shall now confirm both positively
and negatively:—

First, Our first reason is taken from what was before proved concerning the nature of that love which is here said to have the world
for its object, which cannot be extended to all and every one in the
world, as will be confessed by all. Now, such is the world, here, as
is beloved with that love which we have here described, and proved
to be here intended;—even such a love as is, first, the most transcendent and remarkable; secondly, an eternal act of the will of God;
thirdly, the cause of sending Christ; fourthly, of giving all good
things in and with him; fifthly, an assured fountain and spring of

salvation to all beloved with it. So that the world beloved with this love cannot possibly be all and every one in the world.

Secondly, The word *world* in the next verse, which carries along the sense of this, and is a continuation of the same matter, being a discovery of the intention of God in giving his Son, must needs signify the elect and believers, at least only those who in the event are saved; therefore so also in this. It is true, the word *world* is three times used in that verse in a dissonant sense, by an inversion not unusual in the Scripture, as was before declared. It is the latter place that this hath reference to, and is of the same signification with the *world* in verse 16, " That the world through him might be saved,"—*ἵνα σωθῇ*, " that it should be saved." It discovers the aim, purpose, and intention of God, what it was towards the world that he so loved, even its salvation. Now, if this be understood of any but believers, God fails of his aim and intention, which as yet we dare not grant.

Thirdly, It is not unusual with the Scripture to call God's chosen people by the name of the *world*, as also of *all flesh, all nations, all families of the earth*, and the like general expressions; and therefore no wonder if here they are so called, the intention of the place being to exalt and magnify the love of God towards them, which receives no small advancement from their being every way a world. So are they termed where Christ is said to be their Saviour, John iv. 42; which certainly he is only of them who are saved. A Saviour of men not saved is strange. Also John vi. 51, where he is said to give himself for their life. Clearly, verse 33 of the same chapter, he " giveth life unto the world:" which whether it be any but his elect let all men judge; for Christ himself affirms that he gives life only to his "sheep," and that those to whom he gives life "shall never perish," chap. x. 27, 28. So Rom. iv. 13, Abraham is said by faith to be "heir of the world;" who, verse 11, is called to be father of the faithful. And Rom. xi. 12, the fall of the Jews is said to be "the riches of the world;" which world compriseth only believers of all sorts in the world, as the apostle affirmed that the word bare fruit "in all the world," Col. i. 6. This is that "world" which "God reconcileth to himself, not imputing their trespasses unto them," 2 Cor. v. 19; which is attended with blessedness in all them to whom that non-imputation belongeth, Rom. iv. 8. And for divers evident reasons is it that they have this appellation; as,—First, to distinguish the object of this love of God from the nature angelical, which utterly perished in all the fallen individuals; which the Scripture also carefully doth in express terms, Heb. ii. 16, and by calling this love of God *φιλανθρωπία*, Tit. iii. 4. Secondly, To evert and reject the boasting of the Jews, as though all the means of grace and all the benefits intended were to them appropriated. Thirdly, To denote that great difference and distinction between the old administration of the covenant, when it was tied up to one people, family, and nation, and the new, when all boundaries being broken up, the fulness of the Gentiles and the corners of the world were to be made obedient to the sceptre of Christ. Fourthly, To manifest the condition of the elect themselves, who are thus beloved, for the declaration of the free grace of God towards them, they being divested of all qualifications but only those that bespeak them terrene, earthly, lost, miserable, corrupted. So that thus much at least may easily be obtained, that from the word itself nothing can be opposed justly to our exposition of this place, as hath been already declared, and shall be farther made manifest.

Fourthly, If every one in the world be intended, why doth not the Lord, in the pursuit of this love, reveal Jesus Christ to every one whom he so loved? Strange! that the Lord should so love men as to give his only-begotten Son for them, and yet not once by any means signify this his love to them, as to innumerable he doth not!—that he should love them, and yet order things so, in his wise dispensation, that this love should be altogether in vain and fruitless!—love them, and yet determine that they shall receive no good by his love, though his love indeed be a willing of the greatest good to them!

Fifthly, Unless ye will grant,—first, Some to be beloved and hated also from eternity; secondly, The love of God towards innumerable to be fruitless and vain; thirdly, The Son of God to be given to them who, *first*, never hear word of him; *secondly*, have no power granted to believe in him; fourthly, That God is mutable in his love, or else still loveth those that be in hell; fifthly, That he doth not give all things to them to whom he gives his Son, contrary to Rom. viii. 32; sixthly, That he knows not certainly beforehand who shall believe and be saved;—unless, I say, all these blasphemies and absurdities be granted, it cannot be maintained that by the *world* here is meant all and every one of mankind, but only men in common scattered throughout the world, which are the elect.

The THIRD difference about these words is, concerning the *means* whereby this love of the Father, whose object is said to be the *world* is made out unto them. Now, this is *by believing*, ἵνα πᾶς ὁ πιστεύων, —"that whosoever believeth," or "that every believer." The intention of these words we take to be, the designing or manifesting of the way whereby the elect of God come to be partakers of the fruits of the love here set forth,—namely, by faith in Christ, God having appointed that for the only way whereby he will communicate unto us the life that is in his Son. To this something was said before, having proved that the term *whosoever* is not distributive of the object of the love of God; to which, also, we may add these following reasons:—

First, If the object be here restrained, so that some only believe and are saved of them for whose sake Christ is sent, then this restriction and determination of the fruits of this love dependeth on the will of God, or on the persons themselves. If on the persons themselves, then make they themselves to differ from others; contrary to 1 Cor. iv. 7. If on the will of God, then you make the sense of the place, as to this particular, to be, " God so loved all as that but some of them should partake of the fruits of his love." To what end, then, I pray, did he love those other some? Is not this, " Out with the sword, and run the dragon through with the spear?"

Secondly, Seeing that these words, *that whosoever believeth*, do peculiarly point out the aim and intention of God in this business, if it do restrain the object beloved, then *the salvation of believers* is confessedly the aim of God in this business, and that distinguished from others; and if so, the general ransom is an empty sound, having no dependence on the purpose of God, his intention being carried out in the giving of his Son only to the salvation of believers, and that determinately, unless you will assign unto him a *nescience* of them that should believe.

These words, then, *whosoever believeth*, containing a designation of *the means* whereby the Lord will bring us to a participation of life through his Son, whom he gave for us; and the following words, of *having life everlasting*, making out the whole counsel of God in this matter, subordinate to his own glory; it followeth,—

That God gave not his Son,—1. For them who never do believe; 2. Much less for them who never hear of him, and so evidently want means of faith; 3. For them on whom he hath determined not to bestow effectual grace, that they might believe.

Let now the reader take up the several parts of these opposite expositions, weigh all, try all things, especially that which is especially to be considered, the *love of God*, and so inquire seriously whether it be only a general affection, and a natural velleity to the good of all, which may stand with the perishing of all and every one so beloved, or the peculiar, transcendent love of the Father to his elect, as before laid down; and then determine whether a general ransom, fruitless in respect of the most for whom it was paid, or the effectual redemption of the elect only, have the firmest and strongest foundation in these words of our Saviour; withal remembering that they are produced as the strongest supportment of the adverse cause, with which, it is most apparent, both the cause of sending Christ and the end intended by the Lord in so doing, as they are here expressed, are altogether inconsistent.

CHAPTER III.

An unfolding of the remaining texts of Scripture produced for the confirmation
of the first general argument for universal redemption.

NEXT to the place before considered, that which is urged with
most confidence and pressed with most importunity, for the defence
of the general ransom, in the prosecution of the former argument, is,—

2. 1 John ii. 1, 2, " If any man sin, we have an advocate with
the Father, Jesus Christ the righteous: and he is the propitiation for
our sins: and not for ours only, but also for the sins of the whole
world." Now, these words, and the deductions from thence, have
been set out in various dresses, with great variety of observations, to
make them appear advantageous to the cause in hand. The weight
of the whole hangs upon this, that the apostle affirms Christ to be the
"propitiation for the sins of the whole world;" "which," say they,
" manifestly appears to be all and every one in the world," and that,—

First, " From the words themselves without any wresting; for
what can be signified by *the whole world,* but all men in the world?"

Secondly, " From the opposition that is made between world and
believers, all believers being comprised in the first part of the apostle's
assertion, that Christ is a propitiation for our sins; and therefore by
the world, opposed unto them, all others are understood." If there
be any thing of moment farther excepted, we shall meet with it in
our following opening of the place.

Before I come to the farther clearing of the mind of the Holy
Ghost in these words, I must tell you that I might answer the objection from hence very briefly, and yet so solidly as quite to cut off
all the cavilling exceptions of our adversaries,—namely, that as by
the world, in other places, men living in the world are denoted, so by
the whole world in this can nothing be understood but men living
throughout the whole world, in all the parts and regions thereof (in
opposition to the inhabitants of any one nation, place, or country, as
such), as the redeemed of Christ are said to be, Rev. v. 9. But because they much boast of this place, I shall, by God's assistance, so
open the sense and meaning of it, that it shall appear to all how
little reason they have to place any confidence in their wrested interpretation thereof.

To make out the sense of this place, three things are to be considered:—(1.) To whom the apostle writes. (2.) What is his purpose
and aim in this particular place. (3.) The meaning of these two
expressions,—[1.] Christ being a "propitiation;" [2.] " The whole
world." Which having done, according to the analogy of faith, the
scope of this and other parallel places, with reference to the things

and use of the words themselves, we shall easily manifest, by undeniable reasons, that the text cannot be so understood (as by right) as
it is urged and wrested for universal redemption.

(1.) A discovery *of them to whom the epistle was peculiarly directed*
will give some light into the meaning of the apostle. This is one of
those things which, in the investigation of the right sense of any
place, is exceeding considerable; for although this and all other parts
of divine Scripture were given for the use, benefit, and direction of
the whole church, yet that many parts of it were directed to peculiar
churches, and particular persons, and some distinct sorts of persons,
and so immediately aiming at some things to be taught, reproved,
removed, or established, with direct reference to those peculiar persons and churches, needs no labour to prove. Now, though we have
nothing written expressly denominating *them* to whom this epistle
was primarily directed, to make an assertion thereof infallibly true
and *de fide*, yet, by clear and evident deduction, it may be made
more than probable that it was intended to the Jews, or believers of
the circumcision; for,—

First, John was in a peculiar manner a minister and an apostle to
the Jews, and therefore they were the most immediate and proper
objects of his care: "James, Cephas, and John gave to Paul and
Barnabas the right hand of fellowship, that they should go unto the
heathen, and themselves unto the circumcision," Gal. ii. 9. Now, as
Peter and James (for it was that James of whom Paul there speaks
who wrote the epistle, the brother of John being slain before), in the
prosecution of their apostleship towards them, wrote epistles unto
them in their dispersion, James i. 1, 1 Pet. i. 1; as Paul did to all
the chief churches among the Gentiles by him planted; so it is more
than probable that John, writing the epistle, directed it, chiefly and
in the first place, unto them who, chiefly and in the first place, were
the objects of his care and apostleship.

Secondly, He frequently intimates that those to whom he wrote
were of them who heard of and received the word from the beginning; so twice together in this chapter, verse 7, " I write an old commandment, which ye had from the beginning, ... which ye heard
from the beginning." Now, that the promulgation of the gospel had
its beginning among the Jews, and its first entrance with them, before
the conversion of any of the Gentiles,—which was a mystery for a
season,—is apparent from the story of the Acts of the Apostles, chap.
i.-v., x., xi. "To the Jew first, and also to the Greek," was the order
divinely appointed, Rom. i. 16.

Thirdly, The opposition that the apostle makes between *us* and
the *world* in this very place is sufficient to manifest unto whom he
wrote. As a Jew, he reckoneth himself with and among the believing Jews to whom he wrote, and sets himself with them in opposition

to the residue of believers in the world; and this is usual with this apostle, wherein how he is to be understood, he declares in his Gospel, chap. xi. 51, 52.

Fourthly, The frequent mention and cautions that he makes and gives of *false teachers, seducers, antichrists* (which in those first days were, if not all of them, yet for the greatest part, of the Circum-·cision, as is manifest from Scripture and ecclesiastical story; of whom the apostle said that "they went out from them," 1 John ii. 19), evidently declare that to them in especial was this epistle directed, who lay more open, and were more obnoxious to, the seducements of their countrymen than others.

Now, this being thus cleared, if withal ye will remind what was said before concerning the inveterate hatred of that people towards the Gentiles, and the ingrafted opinion they had concerning their own sole interest in the redemption procured and purchased by their Messiah, it will be no difficult thing for any to discern the aim of the apostle in this place, in the expression so much stuck at. " He," saith he, " is the propitiation for our sins,"—that is, our sins who are believers of the Jews; and lest by this assertion they should take occasion to confirm themselves in their former error, he adds, " And not for ours only, but for the sins of the whole world," or, "The children of God scattered abroad," as John xi. 51, 52, of what nation, kindred, tongue, or language soever they were. So that we have not here an opposition between the effectual salvation of all believers and the ineffectual redemption of all others, but an extending of the same effectual redemption which belonged to the Jewish believers to all other believers, or children of God throughout the whole world.

(2.) For the aim and intention of the apostle in these words, it is *to give consolation to believers* against their sins and failings : " If any man sin, we have an advocate with the Father, Jesus Christ the righteous: and he is the propitiation for our sins." The very order and series of the words, without farther enlargement, proves this to be so. That they were believers only to whom he intended this consolation, that they should not despair nor utterly faint under their infirmities, because of a sufficient, yea, effectual remedy provided, is no less evident: for,—First, They only have an *advocate;* it is confessed that believers only have an interest in Christ's advocation. Secondly, Comfort, in such a case, belongs to none but them; unto others in a state and condition of alienation, wrath is to be denounced, John iii. 36. Thirdly, They are the "little children" to whom he writes, 1 John ii. 1; whom he describes, verses 12, 13, to have "their sins forgiven them for his name's sake," and to "know the Father." So that the aim of the apostle being to make out consolation to believers in their failings, he can speak of none but them only. And if he should extend that whereof he speaks, namely,—that Christ was a propitiation to all and every one,—I cannot conceive how this can possibly make any thing to the end proposed, or the consolation of believers; for what comfort can arise from hence to them, by telling them that Christ died for innumerable that shall be damned? Will that be any refreshment unto me which is common unto me with them that perish eternally? Is not this rather a pumice-stone than a breast of consolation? If you ask how comfort can be given to all and every one, unless Christ died for them? I say, If by all and every one you mean all believers, Christ is, as in the text asserted, a propitiation and an advocate for them all. If all others, reprobates and unbelievers, we say that there is neither in the death of Christ nor in the word of God any solid spiritual consolation prepared for them; the children's bread must not be cast to dogs.

(3.) The meaning and purport of the word " propitiation," which Christ is said to be for " us," and " the whole world," is next to be considered:—

First, The word in the original is ἱλασμός, twice only used in the New Testament,—here, and chap. iv. 10 of this same epistle. The verb also, ἱλάσκομαι, is as often used;—namely, Heb. ii. 17, translated there (and that properly, considering the construction it is in) " to make reconciliation;" and Luke xviii. 13, it is the word of the publican, 'Ιλάσθητί μοι, " Be merciful to me." There is also another word of the same original and a like signification, namely, ἱλαστήριον, twice also used;—Rom. iii. 25, there translated " a propitiation;" and Heb. ix. 5, where it is used for, and also rendered, " the mercy-seat:" which will give some light into the meaning of the word. That which, Exod. xxv. 17, is called capporeth, from caphar, properly to cover, is here called ἱλαστήριον, that which Christ is said to be, Rom. iii. 25. Now, this mercy-seat was a plate of pure gold, two cubits and a half long, and a cubit and a half broad, like the uppermost plate or board of a table; that was laid upon the ark, shadowed over with the wings of the cherubim. Now, this word כַּפֹּרֶת comes, as was said, from כָּפַר, whose first native and genuine sense is " to cover," (though most commonly used [for] "to expiate.") This plate or mercy-seat was so called because it was placed upon the ark, and covered it, as the wings of the cherubim hovered over that; the mystical use hereof being to hide, as it were, the law or rigid tenor of the covenant of works which was in the ark, God thereby declaring himself to be pacified or reconciled, the cause of anger and enmity being hidden. Hence the word cometh to have its second acceptation, even that which is rendered by the apostle ἱλαστήριον, " placamen," or " placamentum,"—that whereby God is appeased. This that did plainly signify, being shadowed with the wings of the cherubim, denoting God's presence in power and goodness; which were made crouching over it, as the wings of a hen over her chickens. Hence

222 THE DEATH OF DEATH. [BOOK IV.

that prayer of David, to be "hid under the shadow of God's wings,"
Ps. xxxvi. 7, lvii. 1, lxi. 4, lxiii. 7, xci. 4 (and perhaps that allusion of
our Saviour, Matt. xxiii. 37), intimating the favourable protection of
God in mercy, denoted by the wings of the cherubim covering the propitiatory, embracing that which covered the bill of accusation; which,
typically, was that table, or golden plate or covering, before described;
truly and really Jesus Christ, as is expressly affirmed, Rom. iii. 25.

Now, all this will give us some light into the meaning of the word,
and so, consequently, into the sense of this place, with the mind of
the Holy Ghost therein. Ἱλασμός and ἱλαστήριον, both translated " a
propitiation," with the verb of the same original (the bottom of them
all being ἱλάω, not used in the New Testament, which in Eustathius
is from ἴεμαι λάειν, "intently and with care to look upon any thing,"
like the oracle on the mercy-seat), do signify that which was done or
typically effected by the mercy-seat,—namely, to appease, pacify, and
reconcile God in respect of aversation for sin. Hence that phrase,
Heb. ii. 17, Ἱλάσκεσθαι τὰς ἁμαρτίας τοῦ λαοῦ, which the Latinists
render " Expiare peccata populi," " To expiate the sins of the people."
(" Expiare" is, in this business, to turn away anger by an atonement.
So the historian, " Solere reges ostenta cœlestia cæde aliquâ illustri
expiare, atque a semet in capita procerum depellere," Suet. in Neron.
36.) We render it, "To make reconciliation for the sins of the people."
The word will bear both, the meaning being, to appease, or pacify, or
satisfy God for sin, that it might not be imputed to them towards
whom he was so appeased. Ἱλάσκεσθαι τὰς ἁμαρτίας τοῦ λαοῦ is as
much as Ἱλάσκεσθαι τὸν Θεὸν περὶ τῶν ἁμαρτιῶν, " To pacify God concerning sin." Hence the word receiveth another signification, that
wherein it is used by the publican, Luke xviii. 13, Ἱλάσθητί μοι, " Be
merciful to me;" that is, " Let me enjoy that mercy from whence
flows the pardon of sin, by thy being appeased towards me, and reconciled unto me." From all which it appeareth that the meaning
of the word ἱλασμός, or " propitiation," which Christ is said to be, is
that whereby the law is covered, God appeased and reconciled, sin
expiated, and the sinner pardoned; whence pardon, and remission of
sin is so often placed as the product and fruit of his blood-shedding,
whereby he was a " propitiation," Matt. xxvi. 28; Eph. i. 7; Col. i. 14;
Heb. ix. 22; Rom. iii. 25, v. 9; 1 John i. 7; 1 Pet. i. 2; Rev. i. 5.

From that which hath been said, the sense of the place is evident
to be, that Christ hath so expiated sin, and reconciled to God, that
the sinner is pardoned and received to mercy for his sake, and that
the law shall never be produced or brought forth for his condemnation. Now, whether this can be tolerably applied to the *whole world*
(taking it for all and every man in the world), let all the men in the
world that are able judge. Are the sins of every one expiated? Is
God reconciled to every one? Is every sinner pardoned? Shall no one

have the transgression of the law charged on him? Why, then, is not every one saved? Doubtless, all these are true of every believer, and of no one else in the whole world. For them the apostle affirmed that Christ is a *propitiation;* that he might show from whence ariseth, and wherein chiefly, if not only, that advocation for them, which he promiseth as the fountain of their consolation, did consist,—even in a presentation of the atonement made by his blood. He is also a propitiation only by faith, Rom. iii. 25; and surely none have faith but believers: and, therefore, certainly it is they only throughout the world for whom alone Christ is a propitiation. Unto them alone God says, ʹΙλεως ἔσομαι, "I will be propitious,"—the great word of the new covenant, Heb. viii. 12, they alone being covenanters.

Secondly, Let us consider the phrase ὅλου τοῦ κόσμου,—" of the whole world." I shall not declare how the word *world* is in the Scripture πολύσημον, of divers significations; partly because I have in some measure already performed it; partly because it is not in itself so much here insisted on, but only with reference to its general adjunct, *whole,* " the whole world:" and, therefore, we must speak to the whole phrase together. Now, concerning this expression, I say,—

First, That whereas, with that which is equivalent unto it, *all the world,* it is used seven or eight times in the New Testament, it cannot be made appear, clearly and undeniably, that in any place (save perhaps one, where it is used in *re necessariâ*) it compriseth all and every man in the world; so that unless some circumstance in this place enforce that sense (which it doth not), it will be a plain wresting of the words to force that interpretation upon them. Let us, then, briefly look upon the places, beginning with the last, and so ascending. Now, that is, Rev. iii. 10, " I will keep thee from the hour of temptation, which shall come ἐπὶ τῆς οἰκουμένης ὅλης,"—" upon all the world," (the word *world* is other in the original here than in the place we have before us, there being divers words to express the same thing, considered under several notions); where that it cannot signify all and every one is evident, because some are promised to be preserved from that which is said to come upon it. Passing the place of which we treat, the next is, Col. i. 6, "Which is come unto you καθὼς καὶ ἐν παντὶ τῷ κόσμῳ,"—" as in all the world." Where,—1. All and every man cannot be understood; for they had not all then received the gospel. 2. Only believers are here signified, living abroad in the world; because the gospel is said to " bring forth fruit" in them to whom it comes, and there is no true gospel fruit without faith and repentance. Another place is Rom. i. 8, " Your faith is spoken of ἐν ὅλῳ τῷ κόσμῳ,"—"throughout the whole world." Did every one in the world hear and speak of the Roman faith? You have it also Luke ii. 1, " There went out a decree from Cæsar Augustus, ἀπογράφεσθαι πᾶσαν τὴν οἰκουμένην,"—" that all the world should be taxed;" which yet was but the Roman empire, short enough of comprising all singular persons in the world.   It were needless to repeat the rest, being all of the same indefinite importance and signification.   If, then, the expression itself doth not hold out any such universality as is pretended, unless the matter concerning which it is used and the circumstances of the place do require it (neither of which enforcements has any appearance in this place), there is no colour to fasten such an acceptation upon it; rather may we conclude that *all the world,* and *the whole world,* being in other places taken indefinitely for men of all sorts throughout the world, the same words are no otherwise here to be understood.   So that ὅλος ὁ κόσμος is here no more than ἐκκλησία καθολική.

Secondly, The *whole world* can signify no more than *all nations, all the families of the earth, all flesh, all men, all the ends of the world.*   These surely are expressions equivalent unto, and as comprehensive of particulars as the whole world; but now all these expressions we find frequently to bear out believers only, but as of all sorts, and throughout the world.   And why should not this phrase also be affirmed to be, in the same matter, of the same and no other importance?   We may instance in some places: "All the ends of the earth have seen the salvation of our God," Ps. xcviii. 3; "All the ends of the world shall remember and turn unto the LORD, and all the kindreds of the nations shall worship before thee," Ps. xxii. 27; "All nations shall serve thee," Ps. lxxii. 11;—which general expressions do yet denote no more but only the believers of all the several nations of the world, who alone see the salvation of God, remember and turn to him and serve him.   So Joel ii. 28, "I will pour out of my Spirit upon all flesh;" as the words are again repeated on the accomplishment of the promise, Acts ii. 17;—Luke using the same expression, as part of a sermon of John Baptist, "All flesh shall see the salvation of God."   What a conquest should we have had proclaimed, if it had been anywhere affirmed that Christ died for *all flesh, all nations, all kindreds,* etc.! which yet are but liveries of believers, though garments as wide and large as this expression, *the whole world.*   Believers are called "all nations," Isa. ii. 2, lxvi. 18; yea, "all men," Tit. ii. 11: for to them alone the salvation-bringing grace of God is manifest.   If they, then, the children of God, be, as is apparent in the Scripture phrase, *all flesh, all nations, all kindreds, all the ends of the world, all the ends of the earth, all men,* why not also *the whole world?*

Thirdly, The *whole world* doth sometimes signify the worser part of the world; and why may it not, by a like synecdoche, signify the better part thereof?   Rev. xii. 9, "The Devil, and Satan, which deceiveth the whole world, is cast out;" that is, the wicked and reprobate in the whole world, others rejoicing in his overthrow, verse 10.

1 John v. 19, 'Ο κόσμος ὅλος, "The whole world lieth in wickedness;" where " the whole world" is opposed to them which are " of God," in the beginning of the verse. The contrary sense you have Col. i. 6. This, then, being spoken, to clear the signification of the expression here insisted on, will make it evident that there is nothing at all in the words themselves that should enforce any to conceive that all and every man in the world are denoted by them, but rather believers, even all that did or should believe, throughout the whole world, in opposition only to believers of the Jewish nation: which, that it is the meaning of the place, besides what hath been clearly demonstrated, I prove by these reasons:—

First, This place treateth not of the ransom of Christ in respect of *impetration*, but of *application;* for it affirms Christ to be that by his death which he is only by faith, as was manifested from Rom. iii. 25. Also, from application only ariseth consolation; now, never any said that the application of the death of Christ was universal: therefore, this place cannot have regard to all and every one.

Secondly, Christ is here said to be a propitiation only for such as are intended in the place, which is apparent; but now believers only are here intended, for it is to give them consolation in their failings (in which case consolation belongeth to them alone): therefore, it is believers only, though of all sorts, times, places, and conditions, for whom Christ is said to be a propitiation.

Thirdly, This kind of phrase and expression in other places cannot possibly be tortured to such an extension as to comprehend all and every one, as was apparent from the places before alleged; to which add, Matt. iii. 5, "Then went out to him πᾶσα ἡ 'Ιουδαία, καὶ πᾶσα ἡ περίχωρος τοῦ 'Ιορδάνου,"—" all Judea, and all the region round about Jordan;" among whom, notwithstanding, the Pharisees rejected his baptism. Why, then, should it be so understood here, especially all circumstances (as hath been showed) being contrary to such an interpretation?

Fourthly, The most clear parallel places in the Scripture are opposite to such a sense as is imposed. See Col. i. 6; John xi. 51, 52.

Fifthly, If the words are to be understood to signify all and every one in the world, then is the whole assertion useless as to the chief end intended,—namely, to administer consolation to believers; for what consolation can arise from hence unto any believer, that Christ was a propitiation for them that perish? Yea, to say that he was a *sufficient propitiation* for them, though not effectual, will yield them no more comfort than it would have done Jacob and his sons to have heard from Joseph that he had corn enough, sufficient to sustain them, but that he would do so was altogether uncertain; for had he told them he would sustain them sufficiently, though not effectually, they might have starved notwithstanding his courtesy. "The whole world," then, in this place, is the whole people of God (opposed to the Jewish nation), scattered abroad throughout the *whole world*, of what nation, kindred, tongue, or family soever, who are some of all sorts, not all of every sort. So that *this place makes nothing for general redemption.*

Some few objections there are which are usually laid against our interpretation of *this* passage of the apostle, but they are all prevented or removed in the explication itself; so that it shall suffice us to name one or two of them:—

Obj. 1. "It is the intention of the apostle to comfort all in their fears and doubts; but every one in the world may be in fears and doubts: therefore, he proposeth this, that they all may be comforted."

Ans. The *all* that may be in fears and doubts, in the business of consolation, must of necessity be restrained to believers, as was before declared.

Obj. 2. "All believers are comprehended in the first branch, 'For our sins;' and, therefore in the increase and extension of the assertion, by adding, 'For the sins of the whole world,' all others are intended."

Ans. 1. In the first part, the believing *Jews* alone are intended, of whom John was one; and the addition is not an extending of the propitiation of Christ to *others than believers*, but only to *other believers*. 2. If it might be granted that in the first branch all believers then living were comprehended, who might presently be made partakers of this truth, yet the increase or accession must be, by analogy, only those who *were to be* in after ages and remoter places than the name of Christ had then reached unto,—even all those who, according to the prayer of our Saviour, John xvii. 20, should believe on his name to the end of the world. And thus the two main places produced for the confirmation of the first argument are vindicated from the false glosses and violent wrestings of our adversaries; the rest will be easily cleared.

3. The next place urged in the argument is John vi. 51, where our Saviour affirms that he will give his "flesh for the life of the world." This giving of himself was the sanctifying and offering up of himself an acceptable oblation for the sins of them for whom he suffered; his intention being, that they for whom in dying he so offered himself might have life eternal thereby: which, because it was not for the Jews only, but also for all the elect of God everywhere, he calleth them "the world." That the *world* here cannot signify all and every one that ever were or should be, is as manifest as if it were written with the beams of the sun; and that because it is made the object of Christ's intendment, to purchase for them, and bestow upon them, life and salvation. Now, I ask, Whether any man, not bereaved of all spiritual and natural sense, can imagine that Christ, in

his oblation, intended to purchase life and salvation for all them whom he knew to be damned many ages before, the irreversible decree of wrath being gone forth against them? Or who dares once affirm that Christ gave himself for the life of them who, notwithstanding that, by his appointment, do come short of it to eternity? So that if we had no other place to manifest that the word *world* doth not always signify *all*, but only some of all sorts, as the elect of God are, but this one produced by our adversaries to the contrary, I hope with all equitable readers our defence would receive no prejudice.

4. Divers other places I find produced by Thomas More, chap. xiv. of the "Universality of Free Grace," to the pretended end in hand; which, with that whole chapter, shall be briefly considered.

The first insisted on by him is 2 Cor v. 19, "God was in Christ reconciling the world unto himself, not imputing their trespasses unto them."

Ans. 1. Really he must have no small confidence of his own strength and his reader's weakness, who from this place shall undertake to conclude the universality of redemption, and that the *world* doth here signify all and every one therein. They who are called the "world," verse 19, are termed "us," verse 18, "He hath reconciled us to himself by Jesus Christ;" as also verse 21, where they are farther described by Christ's being "made sin for them," and their being "made the righteousness of God in him." Are these things true of all in the world? If this text may receive any light from what is antecedent and consequent unto it,—if the word any interpretation from those expressions which are directly expository of it,—by the *world* here can be meant none but elect believers. 2. God's reconciling the world unto himself is described evidently either to consist in, or necessarily to infer, a *non-imputation of sin* to them, or that *world;* which is farther interpreted to be an imputation of the righteousness of Christ, verse 21. Now, in these two things consisteth the blessedness of justification in Christ, Rom. iv. 6, 7; therefore this *whole world*, which God in Christ reconcileth to himself, is a blessed, justified world,—not all and every one of the sons of men that ever were, are, or shall be in the world, the greatest part of whom *lie in evil*. 3. This *God in Christ reconciling*, holdeth out an effectual work of reconciliation. Now, this must be either an absolute reconciliation or a conditionate. If *absolute*, why are not all actually and absolutely reconciled, pardoned, justified? If conditionate, then,— First, How can a *conditionate reconciliation* be reconciled with that which is actual? Secondly, Why is no condition here mentioned? Thirdly, What is that condition? Is it faith and believing? Then the sense of the words must be either,—first, "God was in Christ, reconciling a believing world unto himself," of which there is no need, for believers are reconciled; or, secondly, "God was in Christ recon-

ciling an unbelieving world unto himself, upon condition that it do
believe;" that is, upon condition that it be not unbelieving; that is,
that it be reconciled. Is this the mind of the Holy Spirit? Fourthly,
If this reconciliation of the world consist (as it doth) in a non-imputation of sin, then this is either of all their sins, or only of some sins.
If of some only, then Christ saves only from some sins. If of all,
then of unbelief also, or it is no sin; then all the men in the world
must needs be saved, as whose unbelief is pardoned. The *world*
here, then, is only the world of blessed, pardoned believers, who are
" made the righteousness of God in Christ."

That which Thomas More bringeth to enforce the opposite signification of the word is, in many words, very little. Much time he spends,
with many uncouth expressions, to prove a twofold reconciliation intimated in the text,—the first of God to us by Christ, the other of us to
God by the Spirit; which we also grant, though we do not divide them,
but make them several parts of the same reconciliation, the former
being the rule of the latter: for look, to whomsoever God is reconciled
in and by Christ, they shall certainly every one of them be reconciled
to God by the Spirit;—God's reconciliation to them consisting in a
non-imputation of their sins; their reconciliation unto him, in an
acceptance of that non-imputation in Jesus Christ. And as it is the
rule of, so is it the chief motive unto, the latter, being the subject or
matter of the message in the gospel whereby it is effected. So that
the assertion of this twofold reconciliation, or rather two branches of
the same complete work of reconciliation, establisheth our persuasion
that the *world* can be taken only for the elect therein.

But he brings farther light from the context to strengthen his
interpretation. " For," saith he, "those of the world here are called
' men,' verse 11; men that must ' appear before the judgment-seat of
Christ,' verse 10; that were ' dead,' verse 14; that ought to live unto
Christ, verse 15: therefore, *all* men." Now, "homini homo quid
interest?" How easy is it for some men to prove what they please!
Only let me tell you, one thing more is to be done that the cause may
be yours,—namely, a proving that the elect of God are not men;
that they must not appear before the judgment-seat of Christ; that
they were not dead; that they ought not to live to Christ. This do,
or ye lose the reward.

But he adds,—First, " Of these, some are reconciled to God," verse
18. *Ans.* Most false, that there is any limitation or restriction of
reconciliation to some of those concerning whom he treats; it is
rather evidently extended to all of them. Secondly, " But some
are not reconciled," verse 11. *Ans.* Not a word of any such thing
in the text, nor can the least colour be possibly wrested thence for
any such assertion. "Many corrupt the word of God."

A second place he urgeth is John i. 9, " That was the true Light, which lighteth every man that cometh into the world." "This *world*," saith he, "is the world of mankind, verse 4, made by Christ, verse 3; which was his own by creation, mercy, and purchase, yet 'received him not,' verses 5, 10, 11. therefore, it is manifest that there is life, and that Christ died for all."

Ans. That by the *world* here is meant, not men in the world, all or some, but the habitable part of the earth, is more apparent than can well admit of proof or illustration. The phrase of *coming into the world* cannot possibly be otherwise apprehended. It is as much as *born*, and coming to breathe the common air. Now, among the expositions of this place, that seems most consonant and agreeable to the discourse of the apostle, with other expressions here used, which refers the word ἐρχόμενον, "coming," unto φῶς, "light," and not to ἄνθρωπον, "man," with which it is vulgarly esteemed to agree; so that the words should be rendered, "That was the true Light, which, coming into the world, lighteth every man." So John iii. 19, "Light is come into the world;" and chap. xii. 46, "I am come a light into the world;"—parallel expressions unto this. So that from the word *world* nothing can hence be extorted for the universality of grace or ransom. The whole weight must lie on the words "every man," which yet Thomas More doth not at all insist upon; and if any other should, the word, holding out actual illumination, can be extended in its subject to no more than indeed are illuminated.

Christ, then, coming into the world, is said to enlighten every man, partly because every one that hath any light hath it from him, partly because he is the only true light and fountain of illumination; so that he doth enlighten every one that is enlightened: which is all the text avers, and is by none denied. But whether all and every one in the world, before and after his incarnation, were, are, and shall be actually enlightened with the knowledge of Christ by his coming into the world, let Scripture, experience, reason, and sense determine. And this, in brief, may suffice to manifest the weakness of the argument for universal redemption from this place; waiving for the present, not denying or opposing, another interpretation of the words, rendering the enlightening here mentioned to be that of reason and understanding, communicated to all, Christ being proposed as, in his divine nature, the light of all, even the eternal wisdom of his Father.

A third place is John i. 29, "Behold the Lamb of God, which taketh away the sin of the world;" and this, saith he, is spoken of the world in general.

Ans. 1. If it should be spoken of the world in general, yet nothing could thence be inferred to a universality of individuals. 2. That Christ is he, ὁ αἴρων, that taketh away, beareth, purgeth, pardoneth, as the word is used, 2 Sam. xxiv. 10 (taketh away by justification that it should not condemn, by sanctification that it should not reign,

by glorification that it should not be), τὴν ἁμαρτίαν, " the sin," great
sin, original sin, τοῦ κόσμου, " of the world," common to all, is most
certain; but that he taketh it away from, beareth it for, pardoneth it
unto, purgeth it out of, all and every man in the world, is not in the
least manner intimated in the text, and is in itself exceeding false.

John iii. 17 is by him in the next place urged, " God sent not his
Son into the world to condemn the world, but that the world through
him might be saved."

Ans. A notable ἀντανάκλασις, or eminent inversion of the word
world in this place was before observed; like that of chap. i. 10, " He
was in the world," or on the earth, a part of it, " and the world was
made by him," the whole world, with all things therein contained,
" and the world knew him not," or the most of men living in the
world. So here, by the *world*, in the first place, that part of the
world wherein our Saviour conversed hath the name of the whole
assigned unto it. In the second, you may take it for all and every
one in the world, if you please (though from the text it cannot be
enforced); for the prime end of our Saviour's coming was not to
condemn any, but to save his own, much less to condemn all and
every one in the world, out of which he was to save his elect. In
the third place, they only are designed whom God sent his Son on
purpose to save, as the words eminently hold out. The saving of
them who then are called the *world* was the very purpose and design of God in sending his Son. Now, that these are not all men,
but only believers of Jews and Gentiles throughout the world, is
evident:—1. Because all are not saved, and the Lord hath said " he
will do all his pleasure, and his purpose shall stand." 2. Because the
most of men were at the instant actually damned. Did he send his
Son that they might be saved? 3. Because Christ was appointed for
the fall of some, Luke ii. 34, and, therefore, not that all and every
one might be saved. 4. The end of Christ's actual exhibition and
sending in the flesh is not opposite to any of God's eternal decrees,
which were eternally fixed concerning the condemnation of some for
their sins. Did he send his Son to save such? Doth he act contrary to his own purposes, or fail in his undertakings? *The saved
world is the people of God scattered abroad throughout the world.*

John iv. 42, and 1 John iv. 14, with John vi. 51 (which was before considered), are also produced by Thomas More; in all which
places Christ is called the " Saviour of the world."

Ans. Christ is said to be the Saviour of the *world*, either, first,
because there is no other Saviour for any in the world, and because
he saves all that are saved, even the people of God (not the Jews only),
all over the world; or, secondly, because he doth actually save all the
world, and every one in it. If in this latter way, *vicisti*, Mr More;
if in the former, μένομεν ὥσπερ ἐσμέν,—" we are still where we were."

The urging of John xii. 46, " I am come a light into the world," in this business, deserves to be noted, but not answered. The following places of John iii. 16, 17, 1 John ii. 1, 2, have been already considered. Some other texts are produced, but so exceedingly wrested, strangely perverted, and so extremely useless to the business in hand, that I dare not make so bold with the reader's patience as once to give him a repetition of them.

And this is our defence and answer to the first principal argument of our opposers, our explication of all those texts of Scripture which they have wrested to support it, the bottom of their strength being but the ambiguity of one word. Let the Christian reader " Prove all things, and hold fast that which is good."

CHAPTER IV.

Answer to the second general argument for the universality of redemption.

II. THE second argument, wherewith our adversaries make no less flourish than with the former, is raised from those places of Scripture where there is mention made of *all men* and *every man*, in the business of redemption. With these bare and naked words, attended with swelling, vain expressions of their own, they commonly rather proclaim a victory than study how to prevail. Their argument needs not to be drawn to any head or form, seeing they pretend to plead from express words of Scripture. Wherefore we shall only consider the several places by them in this kind usually produced, with such enforcements of their sense from them as by the ablest of that persuasion have been used. The chief places insisted on are, 1 Tim. ii. 4, 6; 2 Pet. iii. 9; Heb. ii. 9; 2 Cor. v. 14, 15; 1 Cor. xv. 22; Rom. v. 18.

For the use and signification of the word *all* in Scripture, so much hath been said already by many that it were needless for me to insist upon it. Something also to this purpose hath been spoken before, and that abundantly sufficient to manifest that no strength of argument can be taken from the word itself; wherefore I shall apply myself only to the examination of the particular places urged, and the objections from them raised:—

1. The first and chief place is, 1 Tim. ii. 4, 6, " God will have all men to be saved, and come to the knowledge of the truth. . . . . . Christ gave himself a ransom for all, to be testified in due time." Hence they draw this argument, Rem. Act. Synod:—" If God will have all men to be saved, then Christ died for all; but God will have all men to be saved, and come to the knowledge of the truth: therefore, Christ died for all men."

Ans. The whole strength of this argument lies in the ambiguity of the word *all*, which being of various significations, and to be interpreted suitably to the matter in hand and the things and persons whereof it is spoken, the whole may be granted, or several propositions denied, according as the acceptation of the word is enforced on us   That *all* or *all men* do not always comprehend all and every man that were, are, or shall be, may be made apparent by near five hundred instances from the Scripture. Taking, then, *all* and *all men distributively*, for some of all sorts, we grant the whole; taking them *collectively*, for all of all sorts, we deny the minor,—namely, that God will have them all to be saved. To make our denial of this appear to be an evident truth, and agreeable to the mind of the Holy Ghost in this place, two things must be considered:—1. What is that will of God here mentioned, whereby he willeth all to be saved. 2. Who are the *all* of whom the apostle is in this place treating.

1. The will of God is usually distinguished into his *will intending* and his *will commanding;* or rather, that word is used in reference unto God in this twofold notion,—(1.) For his purpose, what he will do; (2.) For his approbation of what we do, with his command thereof. Let now our opposers take their option in whether signification the will of God shall be here understood, or how he willeth the salvation of all.

First, If they say he doth it " voluntate signi," with his will commanding, requiring, approving, then the sense of the words is this:—" God commandeth all men to use the means whereby they may obtain the end, or salvation, the performance whereof is acceptable to God in any or all;" and so it is the same with that of the apostle in another place, " God commandeth all men everywhere to repent." Now, if this be the way whereby God willeth the salvation of all here mentioned, then certainly those *all* can possibly be no more than to whom he granteth and revealeth the means of grace; which are indeed a great many, but yet not the one hundredth part of the posterity of Adam. Besides, taking God's *willing* the salvation of men in this sense, we deny the *sequel* of the first proposition, —namely, that Christ died for as many as God thus willeth should be saved. The foundation of God's command unto men to use the *means* granted them is not Christ's dying for them in particular, but the *connection* which himself, by his decree, hath fixed between these two things, faith and salvation; the death of Christ being abundantly sufficient for the holding out of that *connection* unto all, there being enough in it to save all believers.

Secondly, If the will of God be taken for his efficacious will, the will of his purpose and good pleasure (as truly to me it seems exceedingly evident that that is here intended, because the will of

God is made the ground and bottom of our supplications; as if in these our prayers we should say only, "Thy will be done,"—which is to have them all to be saved: now, we have a promise to receive of God "whatsoever we ask according to his will," 1 John iii. 22, v 14; and therefore this will of God, which is here proposed as the ground of our prayers, must needs be his effectual or rather efficacious will, which is always accomplished);—if it be, I say, thus taken, then certainly it must be fulfilled, and all those saved whom he would have saved; for whatsoever God can do and will do, that shall certainly come to pass and be effected. That God can save all (not considering his decree) none doubts; and that he will save all it is here affirmed: therefore, if these *all* here be all and every one, all and every one shall certainly be saved. "Let us eat and drink, for tomorrow we shall die." "Who hath resisted God's will?" Rom. ix. 19. "He hath done whatsoever he hath pleased," Ps. cxv. 3. "He doeth according to his will in the army of heaven, and among the inhabitants of the earth," Dan. iv. 35. If *all*, then, here be to be understood of all men universally, one of these two things must of necessity follow:—either that God faileth of his purpose and intention, or else that all men universally shall be saved; which puts us upon the second thing considerable in the words, namely, who are meant by *all men* in this place.

2. By *all men* the apostle here intendeth all sorts of men indefinitely living under the gospel, or in these latter times, under the enlarged dispensation of the means of grace. That men of these times only are intended is the acknowledgment of Arminius himself, treating with Perkins about this place. The scope of the apostle, treating of the amplitude, enlargement, and extent of grace, in the outward administration thereof, under the gospel, will not suffer it to be denied. This he lays down as a foundation of our praying for all,—because the means of grace and the habitation of the church is now no longer confined to the narrow bounds of one nation, but promiscuously and indefinitely extended unto all people, tongues, and languages; and to all sorts of men amongst them, high and low, rich and poor, one with another. We say, then, that by the words *all men* are here intended only of all sorts of men, suitable to the purpose of the apostle, which was to show that all external difference between the sons of men is now taken away; which *ex abundanti* we farther confirm by these following reasons:—

First, The word *all* being in the Scripture most commonly used in this sense (that is, for many of all sorts), and there being nothing in the subject-matter of which it is here affirmed that should in the least measure impel to another acceptation of the word, especially for a universal collection of every individual, we hold it safe to cleave to the most usual sense and meaning of it. Thus, our Saviour is said to cure all diseases, and the Pharisees to tithe πᾶν λάχανον, Luke xi. 42.

Secondly, Paul himself plainly leadeth us to this interpretation of it; for after he hath enjoined us to pray for all, because the Lord will have all to be saved, he expressly intimates that by *all men* he understandeth men of all sorts, ranks, conditions, and orders, by distributing those *all* into several kinds, expressly mentioning some of them, as "kings and all in authority." Not unlike that expression we have, Jer. xxix. 1, 2, "Nebuchadnezzar carried away all the people captive to Babylon, Jeconiah the king, and the queen, and the eunuchs, the princes of Judah and Jerusalem, the carpenters, and the smiths;" where *all the people* is interpreted to be some of all sorts, by a distribution of them into the several orders, classes, and conditions whereof they were. No otherwise doth the apostle interpret the *all men* by him mentioned, in giving us the names of some of those orders and conditions whom he intendeth. "Pray for all men," saith he; that is, all sorts of men, as magistrates, all that are in authority, the time being now come wherein, without such distinctions as formerly have been observed, the Lord will save some of all sorts and nations.

Thirdly, We are bound to pray for all whom God would have to be saved. Now, we ought not to pray for all and every one, as knowing that some are reprobates and sin unto death; concerning whom we have an express caution not to pray for them.

Fourthly, All shall be saved whom God will have to be saved; this we dare not deny, for "who hath resisted his will?" Seeing, then, it is most certain that all shall not be saved (for some shall stand on the left hand), it cannot be that the universality of men should be intended in this place.

Fifthly, God would have no more to be "saved" than he would have "come to the knowledge of the truth." These two things are of equal latitude, and conjoined in the text. But it is not the will of the Lord that all and every one, in all ages, should come to the knowledge of the truth. Of old, "he showed his word unto Jacob, his statutes and his judgments unto Israel. He hath not dealt so with any nation: and as for his judgments, they have not known them," Ps. cxlvii. 19, 20. If he would have had them all come to the knowledge of the truth, why did he show his word to some and not to others, without which they could not attain thereunto? "He suffered all nations" in former ages "to walk in their own ways," Acts xiv. 16, and "winked at the time of this ignorance," Acts xvii. 30, hiding the mystery of salvation from those former ages, Col. i. 26, continuing the same dispensation even until this day in respect of some; and that because "so it seemeth good in his sight," Matt. xi. 25, 26. It is, then, evident that God doth not will that all and every one in the world, of all ages and times, should come to the knowledge of the truth, but only all sorts of men without difference; and, therefore, they only are here intended.

These, and the like reasons, which compel us to understand by *all men*, verse 4, whom God would have to be saved, men of all sorts, do also prevail for the same acceptation of the word *all*, verse 6, where Christ is said to give himself " a ransom for all;" whereunto you may also add all those whereby we before declared that it was of absolute necessity and just equity that all they for whom a ransom was paid should have a part and portion in that ransom, and, if that be accepted as sufficient, be set at liberty. Paying and accepting of a ransom intimate a commutation and setting free of all them for whom the ransom is paid and accepted. By *all*, then, can none be understood but the redeemed, ransomed ones of Jesus Christ,—such as, for him and by virtue of the price of his blood, are vindicated into the glorious liberty of the children of God; which, as some of all sorts are expressly said to be, Rev. v. 9 (which place is interpretative of this), so that all in the world universally are so is confessedly false.

Having thus made evident the meaning of the words, our answer to the objection (whose strength is a mere fallacy, from the ambiguous sense of the word *all*) is easy and facile. For if by *all men*, you mean the *all* in the text, that is, all sorts of men, we grant the whole, —namely, that Christ died for *all;* but if by *all men*, you mean all universally, we absolutely deny the minor, or assumption, having sufficiently proved that there is no *such all* in the text.

The enforcing of an objection from this place, Thomas More, in his " Universality of Free Grace," makes the subject of one whole chapter. It is also *one* of the two places which he lays for the bottom and foundation of the whole building, and whereunto at a dead lift he always retires. Wherefore, I thought to have considered that chapter of his at large; but, upon second considerations, have laid aside that resolution, and that for three reasons:—

First, Because I desired not *actum agere*, to do that which hath already been done, especially the thing itself being such as scarce deserveth to be meddled with at all. Now, much about the time that I was proceeding in this particular, the learned work of Mr Rutherford,[1] about the death of Christ, and the drawing of sinners thereby, came to my hand; wherein he hath fully answered that chapter of Mr More's book; whither I remit the reader.

Secondly, I find that he hath not once attempted to meddle with any of those reasons and arguments whereby we confirm our answer

---

[1] He refers to the eminent Scotch divine, Samuel Rutherford, 1600–1661. The work mentioned above was published in 1647, and is entitled, " Christ Dying, and Drawing to Himself; or, a survey of our Saviour in his soul's suffering," etc. The opinions of More are discussed in it from page 375 to 410.—ED.

to the objection from the place, and prove undeniably that by *all men* is meant only men of all sorts.

Thirdly, Because, setting aside those bare naked assertions of his own, whereby he seeks to strengthen his argument from and inter-pretation of this place, the residue wherewith he flourisheth is a poor fallacy running through the whole; the strength of all his argu-mentations consisting in this, that by the *all* we are to pray for are not meant only all who are at present believers; which as no man in his right wits will affirm, so he that will conclude from thence, that because they are not only all present believers, therefore they are all the individuals of mankind, is not to be esteemed very sober. Pro-ceed we, then, to the next place urged for the general ransom, from the word *all*, which is,—

2. 2 Pet. iii. 9, "The Lord is long-suffering to us-ward, not willing that any should perish, but that all should come to repentance." "The will of God," say some, "for the salvation of *all*, is here set down both *negatively*, that he would not have any perish, and *posi-tively*, that he would have all come to repentance; now, seeing there is no coming to repentance nor escaping destruction, but only by the blood of Christ, it is manifest that that blood was shed for *all*."

Ans. Many words need not be spent in answer to this objection, wrested from the misunderstanding and palpable corrupting of the sense of these words of the apostle. That indefinite and general ex-pressions are to be interpreted in an answerable proportion to the things whereof they are affirmed, is a rule in the opening of the Scripture. See, then, of whom the apostle is here speaking. "The Lord," saith he, "is long-suffering to us-ward, not willing that any should perish." Will not common sense teach us that *us* is to be repeated in both the following clauses, to make them up complete and full,—namely, "Not willing that any of *us* should perish, but that all of *us* should come to repentance?" Now, who are these of whom the apostle speaks, to whom he writes? Such as had received "great and precious promises," chap. i. 4, whom he calls "beloved," chap. iii. 1; whom he opposeth to the "scoffers" of the "last days," verse 3; to whom the Lord hath respect in the disposal of these days; who are said to be "elect," Matt. xxiv. 22. Now, truly, to argue that because God would have none of those to perish, but all of them to come to repentance, therefore he hath the same will and mind towards all and every one in the world (even those to whom he never makes known his will, nor ever calls to repentance, if they never once hear of his way of salvation), comes not much short of extreme madness and folly. Neither is it of any weight to the contrary, that they were not all elect to whom Peter wrote: for in the judgment of charity he es-teemed them so, desiring them "to give all diligence to make their calling and election sure," chap. i. 10; even as he expressly calleth those to whom he wrote his former epistle, "elect," chap. i. 2, and a "chosen generation," as well as a "purchased people," chap. ii. 9. I shall not need add any thing concerning the contradictions and inextricable difficulties wherewith the opposite interpretation is accompanied (as, that God should will such to come to repentance as he cuts off in their infancy out of the covenant, such as he hateth from eternity, from whom he hideth the means of grace, to whom he will not give repentance, and yet knoweth that it is utterly impossible they should have it without his bestowing). The text is clear, that it is all and only the elect whom he would not have to perish. A place supposed parallel to this we have in Ezek. xviii. 23, 32, which shall be afterward considered. The next is,—

3. Heb. ii. 9, "That he by the grace of God should taste death for every man."

Ans. That ὑπὲρ παντός, "for every one," is here used for ὑπὲρ πάντων, "for all," by an enallage of the number, is by all acknowledged. The whole question is, who these *all* are, whether all men universally, or only all those of whom the apostle there treateth. That this expression, *every man*, is commonly in the Scripture used to signify men under some restriction, cannot be denied. So in that of the apostle, "Warning every man, and teaching every man," Col. i. 28; that is, all those to whom he preached the gospel, of whom he is there speaking. "The manifestation of the Spirit is given to every man to profit withal," 1 Cor. xii. 7; namely, to all and every one of those who were endued with the gifts there mentioned, whether in the church at Corinth or elsewhere. The present place I have frequently met withal produced in the behalf of universal redemption, but never once had the happiness to find any endeavour to prove from the text, or any other way, that *all* here is to be taken for all and every one, although they cannot but know that the usual acceptation of the word is against their purpose. Mr More spends a whole chapter about this place; which I seriously considered, to see if I could pick out any thing which might seem in the least measure to tend that way,—namely, to the proving that all and every one are in that place by the apostle intended,—but concerning any such endeavour you have deep silence. So that, with abundance of smooth words, he doth nothing in that chapter but humbly and heartily beg the thing in question; unto which his petition, though he be exceeding earnest, we cannot consent, and that because of these following reasons:—

First, To *taste death*, being to *drink up the cup* due to sinners, certainly for whomsoever our Saviour did taste of it, he left not one drop for them to drink after him; he tasted or underwent death in their stead, that the cup might pass from them which passed not from him. Now, the cup of death passeth only from the elect, from believers; for whomsoever our Saviour tasted death, he swallowed it up into victory.

Secondly, We see an evident appearing cause that should move the apostle here to call those for whom Christ died *all*,—namely, because he wrote to the Hebrews, who were deeply tainted with an erroneous persuasion that all the benefits purchased by Messiah belonged alone to men of their nation, excluding all others; to root out which pernicious opinion, it behoved the apostle to mention the extent of free grace under the gospel, and to hold out a universality of God's elect throughout the world.

Thirdly, The present description of the *all* for whom Christ tasted death by the grace of God will not suit to all and every one, or any but only the elect of God. For, verse 10, they are called, "many sons to be brought to glory;" verse 11, those that are "sanctified," his "brethren;" verse 13, the "children that God gave him;" verse 15, those that are "delivered from the bondage of death;"—none of which can be affirmed of them who are born, live, and die the "children of the wicked one." Christ is not a captain of salvation, as he is here styled, to any but those that "obey him," Heb. v. 9; righteousness coming by him "unto all and upon all them that believe," Rom. iii. 22. For these and the like reasons we cannot be induced to hearken to our adversaries' petition, being fully persuaded that by *every one* here is meant all and only God's elect, in whose stead Christ, by the grace of God, tasted death.

4. Another place is 2 Cor. v. 14, 15, " For the love of Christ constraineth us; because we thus judge, that if one died for all, then were all dead: and that he died for all, that they which live should not henceforth live unto themselves, but unto him that died for them." "Here," say they, " verse 14, you have two *alls*, which must be both of an equal extent. If *all* were dead, then Christ died for *all*,—that is, for as many as were dead. Again; he died for all that must live unto him; but that is the duty of every one in the world: and therefore he died for them all. Farther; that *all* are all individuals is clear from verse 10, where they are affirmed to be all that must 'appear before the judgment-seat of Christ;' from which appearance not any shall be exempted."

Ans. 1. Taking the words, as to this particular, in the sense of some of our adversaries, yet it doth not appear from the texture of the apostle's arguing that the two *alls* of verse 14 are of equal extent. He doth not say that Christ died for all that were dead; but only, that all were dead which Christ died for: which proves no more than this, that all they for whom Christ died for were dead, with that kind of death of which he speaks. The extent of the words is to be taken from the first *all*, and not the latter. The apostle affirms so many to be dead as Christ died for; not that Christ died for so many as were dead. This the words plainly teach us: "If he died for all, then were all dead,"—that is, *all* he died for; so that the *all that were dead* can give no light to the extent of the *all that Christ died for*, being merely regulated by this. 2. That all and every one are *morally* bound to live unto Christ, *virtute præcepti*, we deny; only *they* are bound to live to him to whom he is revealed,—indeed only they who live by him, that have a spiritual life in and with him: all others are under previous obligations. 3. It is true, all and every one must appear before the judgment-seat of Christ,—he is ordained to be judge of the world; but that they are intended, verse 10 of this chapter, is not true. The apostle speaks of *us all, all believers*, especially all preachers of the gospel; neither of which all men are. Notwithstanding, then, any thing that hath been said, it no way appears that by *all* here is meant any but the elect of God, *all believers;* and that they only are intended I prove by these following reasons, drawn from the text:—

First, The resurrection of Christ is here conjoined with his death: "He died for them, and rose again." Now, for whomsoever Christ riseth, he riseth for their "justification," Rom. iv. 25; and they must be justified, chap. viii. 34. Yea, our adversaries themselves have always confessed that the fruits of the resurrection of Christ are peculiar to believers.

Secondly, He speaks only of those who, by virtue of the death of Christ, "live unto him," verse 15; who are "new creatures," verse 17; "to whom the Lord imputeth not their trespasses," verse 19; who "become the righteousness of God in Christ," verse 21;—which are only believers. All do not attain hereunto.

Thirdly, The article οἱ joined with πάντες evidently restraineth that *all* to all of some sort. "Then were they all" (or rather *all these*) "dead." These *all;*—what all? Even all those believers of whom he treats, as above.

Fourthly, All those of whom the apostle treats are proved to be dead, because Christ died for them: "If one died for all, then were all dead." What death is it which here is spoken of? Not a death natural, but spiritual; and of deaths which come under that name, not that which is *in sin*, but that which is *unto sin*. For,—*First*, The greatest champions of the Arminian cause, as Vorstius and Grotius (on the place), convinced by the evidence of truth, acknowledge that it is a death unto sin, by virtue of the death of Christ, that is here spoken of; and accordingly held out that for the sense of the place. *Secondly*, It is apparent from the text; the intention of the apostle being to prove that those for whom Christ died are so dead to sin, that henceforth they should live no more thereunto, but to him that died for them. The subject he hath in hand is the same with that he handleth more at large, Rom. vi. 5–8, where we are said to be "dead unto sin," by being "planted together in the likeness of the death of Christ;" from whence, *there* as *here*, he presseth them to "newness of life." These words, then, "If Christ died for all, then were all dead," are concerning the death of them unto sin for whom Christ died, at least of those concerning whom he there speaketh; and what is this to the general ransom?

Fifthly, The apostle speaks of the death of Christ in respect of application. The effectualness thereof towards those for whom he died, to cause them to live unto him, is insisted on. That Christ died for all in respect of application hath not yet by any been affirmed. Then must all live unto him, yea, live with him for evermore, if there be any virtue or efficacy in his applied oblation for that end. In sum, here is no mention of Christ's dying for any, but those that are dead to sin and live to him.

5. A fifth place urged to prove universal redemption from the word *all*, is 1 Cor. xv. 22, "For as in Adam all die, even so in Christ shall all be made alive."

Ans. There being another place, hereafter to be considered, wherein the whole strength of the argument usually drawn from these words is contained, I shall not need to speak much to this, neither will I at all turn from the common exposition of the place. Those concerning whom Paul speaketh in this chapter are in this verse called *all*. Those are they who are implanted into Christ, joined to him, as the members to the head, receiving a glorious resurrection by virtue of his; thus are they by the apostle described. That Paul, in this whole chapter, discourseth of the resurrection of believers is manifest from the arguments which he bringeth to confirm it, being such as are of force only with believers. Taken they are from the resurrection of Christ, the hope, faith, customs, and expected rewards of Christians; all which, as they are of unconquerable power to confirm and establish believers in the faith of the resurrection, so they would have been, all and every one of them, exceedingly ridiculous had they been held out to the men of the world to prove the resurrection of the dead in general. Farther; the very word ζωοποιηθήσονται denotes such a living again as is to a good life and glory, a blessed resurrection; and not the quickening of them who are raised to a second death. The Son is said ζωοποιεῖν, John v. 21, to "quicken" and make alive (not all, but) "whom he will." So he useth the word again, chap. vi. 63, "It is the Spirit, τὸ ζωοποιοῦν, that" (thus) "quickeneth;" in like manner, Rom. iv. 17. And not anywhere is it used to show forth that common resurrection which all shall have at the last day. *All*, then, who by virtue of the resurrection of Christ shall be made alive, are all those who are partakers of the nature of Christ; who, verse 23, are expressly called "they that are Christ's," and of whom, verse 20, Christ is said to be the "first-fruits;" and certainly

Christ is not the first-fruits of the damned. Yea, though it be true that all and every one died in Adam, yet that it is here asserted (the apostle speaking of none but believers) is not true; and yet, if it were so to be taken here, it could not prove the thing intended, because of the express limitation of the sense in the clause following. Lastly; granting all that can be desired,—namely, the universality of the word *all* in both places,—yet I am no way able to discern a medium that may serve for an argument to prove the general ransom.

6. Rom. v. 18 is the last place urged in this kind, and by some most insisted on: "As by the offence of one judgment came upon all men to condemnation; even so by the righteousness of one the free gift came upon all men unto justification of life." It might suffice us briefly to declare that by *all men* in the latter place can none be understood but those whom the free gift actually comes upon unto justification of life; who are said, verse 17, to "receive abundance of grace and of the gift of righteousness," and so to "reign in life by one, Jesus Christ;" and by his obedience to be "made righteous," verse 19; which certainly, if any thing be true and certain in the truth of God, all are not. Some believe not,—"all men have not faith;" on some "the wrath of God abideth," John iii. 36; upon whom, surely, grace doth not reign through righteousness to eternal life by Jesus Christ, as it doth upon all those on whom the free gift comes to justification, verse 17. We might, I say, thus answer only; but seeing some, contrary to the clear, manifest intention of the apostle, comparing Adam and Christ, in the efficacy of the sin of the one unto condemnation, and of the righteousness of the other unto justification and life, in respect of those who are the natural seed of the one by propagation, and the spiritual seed of the other by regeneration, have laboured to wrest this place to the maintenance of the error we oppose with more than ordinary endeavours and confidence of success, it may not be unnecessary to consider what is brought by them to this end and purpose:—

Verse 14. Adam is called τύπος, the type and "figure of him that was to come;" not that he was an *instituted type*, ordained for that only end and purpose, but only that in what he was, and what he did, with what followed thereupon, there was a *resemblance* between him and Jesus Christ. Hence by him and what he did, by reason of the resemblance, many things, by way of opposition, concerning the obedience of Christ and the efficacy of his death, may be well represented. That which the apostle here prosecuteth this resemblance in (with the showing of many diversities, in all which he exalteth Christ above his type) is this, that an alike though not an equal efficacy (for there is more merit and efficacy required to save one than to lose ten thousand) of the demerit, sin,

disobedience, guilt, transgression of the one, to condemn, or bring
the guilt of condemnation upon all them in whose room he was a
public person (being the head and natural fountain of them all, they
all being wrapped up in the same condition with him by divine
institution), and the righteousness, obedience, and death of the other,
for the absolution, justification, and salvation of all them to whom
he was a spiritual head by divine institution, and in whose room he
was a public person, is by him in divers particulars asserted. That
these last were all and every one of the first, there is not the least
mention. The comparison is solely to be considered intensively, in
respect of efficacy, not extensively, in respect of object; though the
all of Adam be called his *many*, and the *many* of Christ be called
his *all*, as indeed they are, even all the seed which is given unto
him.

Thomas More, in his "Universality of Free Grace," chap. viii.
p. 41, lays down this comparison, instituted by the apostle, between
Adam and Christ, as one of the main foundations of his universal redemption; and this (after some strange mixtures of truth and errors
premised, which, to avoid tediousness, we let pass) he affirmeth to
consist in four things:—

First, "That Adam, in his first sin and transgression, was a public
person, in the room and place of all mankind, by virtue of the covenant between God and him; so that whatever he did therein, all
were alike sharers with him. So also was Christ a public person in
his obedience and death, in the room and place of all mankind, represented by him, even every one of the posterity of Adam."

Ans. To that which concerneth Adam, we grant he was a public
person in respect of all his that were to proceed from him by natural
propagation; that Christ also was a public person in the room of his,
and herein prefigured by Adam. But that Christ, in his obedience,
death, and sacrifice, was a public person, and stood in the room and
stead of all and every one in the world, of all ages and times (that
is, not only of his elect and those who were given unto him of God,
but also of reprobate persons, hated of God from eternity; of those
whom he never knew, concerning whom, in the days of his flesh, he
thanked his Father that he had hid from them the mysteries of salvation; whom he refused to pray for; who were, the greatest part of
them, already damned in hell, and irrevocably gone beyond the
limits of redemption, before he actually yielded any obedience), is to
us such a monstrous assertion as cannot once be apprehended or
thought on without horror or detestation. That any should perish
in whose room or stead the Son of God appeared before his Father
with his perfect obedience; that any of those for whom he is a mediator and advocate, to whom he is a king, priest, and prophet (for all
these he is, as he was a public person, a sponsor, a surety, and under-

taker for them), should be taken from him, plucked out of his arms, his satisfaction and advocation in their behalf being refused;—I suppose is a doctrine that will scarce be owned among those who strive to preserve the witness and testimony of the Lord Jesus.

But let us a little consider the reasons whereby Mr More undertakes to maintain this strange assertion; which, as far as I can gather, are these, page 44:—First, He stood not in the room only of the elect, because Adam lost not election, being not intrusted with it. Secondly, If he stood not in the room of all, then he had come short of his figure. Thirdly, It is said he was to restore all men, lost by Adam, Heb. ii. 9. Fourthly, He took flesh, was subjected to mortality, became under the law, and bare the sins of mankind. Fifthly, He did it in the room of all mankind, once given unto him, Rom. xiv. 9; Phil. ii. 8–11. Sixthly, Because he is called the "last Adam;"—and, Seventhly, Is said to be a public person, in the room of all, ever since the "first Adam," 1 Cor. xv. 45, 47; 1 Tim. ii. 5; Rom. v.

Ans. Never, surely, was a rotten conclusion bottomed upon more loose and tottering principles, nor the word of God more boldly corrupted for the maintenance of any error, since the name of Christian was known. A man would think it quite lost, but that it is so very *easy* a labour to remove such hay and stubble. I answer, then, to the first, that though Adam lost not election, and the eternal decrees of the Almighty are not committed to the keeping of the sons of men, yet in him all the elect were lost, whom Christ came to seek, whom he found,—in whose room he was a public person. To the second, Christ is nowhere compared to Adam in respect of the *extent of the object* of his death, but only of the *efficacy of his obedience.* The third is a false assertion;—see our foregoing consideration of Heb. ii. 9. Fourthly, For his taking of flesh, etc., it was necessary he should do all this for the saving of his elect. He took flesh and blood because the children were partakers of the same. Fifthly, No such thing is once affirmed in the whole book of God, that all the sons of men were given unto Christ to redeem, so that he should be a public person in their room. Nay, himself plainly affirms the contrary, John xvii. 6, 9. Some only are given him out of the world, and those he saved; not one of them perisheth. The places urged hold out no such thing, nor any thing like it. They will also afterward come under farther consideration. Sixthly, He is called the "last Adam" in respect of the efficacy of his death unto the justification of the seed promised and given unto him, as the sin of the "first Adam" was effectual to bring the guilt of condemnation on the seed propagated from him; which proves not at all that he stood in the room of all those to whom his death was never known, nor any ways profitable. Seventhly, That he was a public person is confessed: that he was so in the room of all is not proved, neither by what hath been already said, nor by the texts, that there follow, alleged, all which have been considered. This being all that is produced by Mr More to justify his assertion, it may be an instance what weighty inferences he usually asserts from such weak, invalid premises. We cannot also but take notice, by the way, of one or two strange passages which he inserts into this discourse; whereof the first is, that Christ by his death brought all men out of that death whereinto they were fallen by Adam. Now, the death whereinto all fell in Adam being a death in sin, Eph. ii. 1–3, and the guilt of condemnation thereupon, if Christ freed all from this death, then must all and every one be made alive with life spiritual, which only is to be had and obtained by Jesus Christ; which, whether that be so or not, whether to live by Christ be not the peculiar privilege of believers, the gospel hath already declared, and God will one day determine. Another strange assertion is, his affirming the end of the death of Christ to be his presenting himself alive and just before his Father; as though it were the ultimate thing by him intended, the Holy Ghost expressly affirming that " he loved the church, and gave himself for it, that he might present it to himself a glorious church," Eph. v. 25–27.

The following parallels, which he instituted between Adam and Christ, have nothing of proof in them to the business in hand,— namely, that Christ was a public person, standing, in his obedience, in the room of all and every one that were concerned in the disobedience of Adam. There is, I say, nothing at all of proof in them, being a confused medley of some truths and divers unsavoury heresies. I shall only give the reader a taste of some of them, whereby he may judge of the rest, not troubling myself or others with the transcribing and reading of such empty vanities as no way relate to the business in hand.

First, then, In the second part of his parallel he affirms, "That when Christ finished his obedience, in dying and rising, and offering himself a sacrifice, and making satisfaction, it was, by virtue of the account of God in Christ, and for Christ with God (that is, accepted with God for Christ's sake), the death, resurrection, the sacrifice and satisfaction, and the redemption of all,—that is, all and every one;" and therein he compares Christ to Adam in the performance of the business by him undertaken. Now, but that I cannot but with trembling consider what the apostle affirms, 2 Thess. ii. 11, 12, I should be exceedingly amazed that any man in the world should be so far forsaken of sense, reason, faith, and all reverence of God and man, as to publish, maintain, and seek to propagate, such abominable, blasphemous, senseless, contradictious errors. That the death of Christ should be accepted of and accounted before God as the death of all, and yet the greatest part of these all be adjudged to eternal death in their own persons by the same righteous God; that all and every one should arise in and with Jesus Christ, and yet most of them continue dead in their sins, and die for sin eternally; that satisfaction should be made and accepted for them who are never spared, nor shall be, one farthing of their debt; that atonement should be made by sacrifice for such as ever lie undelivered under wrath; that all the reprobates, Cain, Pharaoh, Ahab, and the rest, who were actually damned in hell, and under death and torments, then when Christ died, suffered, made satisfaction, and rose again, should be esteemed with God to have died, suffered, made satisfaction, and risen again with Christ;—that, I say, such senseless contradictions, horrid errors, and abominable assertions, should be thus nakedly thrust upon Christians, without the least colour, pretence, or show of proof, but the naked authority of him who hath already embraced such things as these, were enough to make any man admire and be amazed, but that we know the judgments of God are ofttimes hid, and far above out of our sights.

Secondly, In the third of his parallels he goeth one step higher, comparing Christ with Adam in respect of the efficacy, effect, and fruit of his obedience. He affirms, "That as by the sin of Adam all his posterity were deprived of life, and fell under sin and death, whence judgment and condemnation passed upon all, though this be done secretly and invisibly, and in some sort inexpressibly" (what he means by *secretly and invisibly*, well I know not,—surely he doth not suppose that these things might possibly be made the objects of our senses; and for *inexpressibly*, how that is, let Rom. v. 12, with other places, where all this and more is clearly, plainly, and fully expressed, be judge whether it be so or no); " so," saith he, " by the efficacy of the obedience of Christ, all men without exception are redeemed, restored, made righteous, justified freely by the grace of Christ, through the redemption that is in Jesus Christ, the ' righteousness that is by the faith of Jesus Christ' being 'unto all,' Rom. iii. 22," (where the impostor wickedly corrupteth the word of God, like the devil, Matt. iv., by cutting off the following words, " and upon all that believe," both *alls* answering to believers). "What remains now but that all also should be saved? the Holy Ghost expressly affirming that those 'whom God justifieth, he also glorifieth,'" Rom. viii. 30. "Solvite mortales animas, curisque levate." Such assertions as these, without any colour of proof, doth this author labour to obtrude upon us. Now, that men should be restored, and yet continue lost; that they should be made righteous, and yet remain detestably wicked, and wholly abominable; that they should be justified freely by the grace of God, and yet always lie under the condemning sentence of the law of God; that the righteousness of God by the faith of Jesus Christ should be upon all unbelievers,—are not only things exceedingly opposite to the gospel of Jesus Christ, but so absolutely at variance and distance one with another, that the poor salve of Mr More's following cautions will not serve to heal their mutual wounds. I cannot but fear that it would be tedious and offensive to rake any longer in such a dunghill. Let them that have a mind to be captivated to error and falsehood by corruption of Scripture and denial of common sense and reason, because they cannot receive the truth in the love thereof, delight themselves with such husks as these. What weaker arguments we have had, to maintain that Christ, in his obedience to the death, was a public person in the room of all and every one, hath been already demonstrated. I shall now, by the reader's leave, a little transgress the rule of disputation, and, taking up the opposite part of the arguments, produce some few reasons and testimonies to demonstrate that our Saviour Christ, in his obedience unto death, in the *redemption* which he wrought, and *satisfaction* which he made, and *sacrifice* which he offered, was not a public person in the room of *all and every man* in the world, elect and reprobate, believers and infidels, or unbelievers ; which are briefly these :—

First, The *seed of the woman* was not to be a public person in the place, stead, and room of the *seed of the serpent*. Jesus Christ is the seed of the woman κατ᾽ ἐξοχήν᾽ all the reprobates, as was before proved, are the seed of the serpent: therefore, Jesus Christ was not, in his oblation and suffering, when he brake the head of the father of the seed, a public person in their room.

Secondly, Christ, as a public person, representeth only them for whose sake he set himself apart to that office and employment wherein he was such a *representative;* but upon his own testimony, which we have, John xvii. 19, he set himself apart to the service and employment wherein he was a public person for the sakes only of some that were given him out of the world, and not of all and every one: therefore, he was not a public person in the room of all.

Thirdly, Christ was a " surety," as he was a public person, Heb. vii. 22; but he was not a surety for all,—for, first, All are not taken into that covenant whereof he was a surety, whose conditions are effected in all the covenantees, as before; secondly, None can perish for whom Christ is a surety, unless he be not able to pay the debt:— therefore, he was not a public person in the room of all.

Fourthly, For whom he was a public person, in their rooms he suffered, and for them he made satisfaction, Isa. liii. 5, 6; but he suffered not in the stead of all, nor made satisfaction for all,—for, first, Some must suffer themselves, which makes it evident that Christ did not suffer for them, Rom. viii. 33, 34; and, secondly, The justice of God requireth satisfaction from themselves, to the payment of the utmost farthing.

Fifthly, Jesus Christ, as a public person, did nothing in vain in respect of any for whom he was a public person; but many things which Christ, as a public person, did perform were altogether in vain and fruitless, in respect of the greatest part of the sons of men being under an incapability of receiving any good by any thing he did,—to wit, all that then were actually damned, in respect of whom, redemption, reconciliation, satisfaction, and the like, could possibly be no other than empty names.

Sixthly, If God were well pleased with his Son in what he did, as a public person, in his representation of others (as he was, Eph. v. 2), then must he also be well pleased with them whom he did represent, either absolutely or conditionally; but with many of the sons of men God, in the representation of his Son, was not well pleased, neither absolutely nor conditionally,—to wit, with Cain, Pharaoh, Saul, Ahab, and others, dead and damned before: therefore, Christ did not, as a public person, represent all.

Seventhly, For testimonies, see John xvii. 9; Matt. xx. 28, xxvi. 26–28; Mark. x. 45; Heb. vi. 20; Isa. liii. 12; John x. 15; Heb. xiii. 20; Matt. i. 21; Heb. ii. 17; John xi. 51, 52; Acts xx. 28; Eph. v. 2, 23–25; Rom. viii. 33, 34.

CHAPTER V.

The last argument from Scripture answered.

III. I COME, in the next place, to the third and last argument, drawn from the Scripture, wherewith the Arminians and their successors (as to this point) do strive to maintain their figment of universal redemption; and it is taken from such texts of Scripture as seem to hold out the perishing of some of them for whom Christ died, and the fruitlessness of his blood in respect of divers for whom it was shed. And on this theme their wits are wonderfully luxuriant, and they are full of rhetorical strains to set out the unsuccessfulness and fruitlessness of the blood of Christ in respect of the most for whom it was shed, with the perishing of bought, purged, reconciled sinners. Who can but believe that this persuasion tends to the consolation of poor souls, whose strongest defence lieth in making vile the precious blood of the Lamb, yea, trampling upon it, and esteeming it as a common thing? But, friends, let me tell you, I am persuaded it was not so unvaluable in the eyes of his Father as to cause it to be poured out in vain, in respect of any one soul. But seeing we must be put to this defence,—wherein we cannot but rejoice, it tending so evidently to the honour of our blessed Saviour,—let us consider what can be said by Christians (at least in name) to enervate the efficacy of the blood-shedding, of the death of him after whose name they desire to be called. Thus, then, they argue:—

"If Christ died for reprobates and those that perish, then he died for all and every one, for confessedly he died for the elect and those that are saved; but he died for reprobates, and them that perish: therefore," etc.

Ans. For the *assumption*, or second proposition of this argument, we shall do what we conceive was fit for all the elect of God to do,—positively deny it (taking the death of Christ, here said to be for them, to be considered not in respect of its own internal worth and sufficiency, but, as it was intended by the Father and Son, in respect of them for whom he died). We deny, then, I say, that Christ, by the command of his Father, and with intention to make satisfaction for sins, did lay down his life for reprobates and them that perish.

This, then, they prove from Rom. xiv. 15; 1 Cor. viii. 11; 2 Pet. ii. 1; Heb. x. 29. Now, that no such thing as is pretended is proved from any of the places alleged, we shall show by the consideration of them in the order they are laid down in.

1. The first is Rom. xiv. 15, "But if thy brother be grieved with thy meat, now walkest thou not charitably. Destroy not him with thy meat for whom Christ died."

Ans. Had we not experience of the nimbleness of our adversaries in framing arguments for their cause, I should despair to find their conclusion pressed out of this place; for what coherence or dependence, I beseech you, is here to be discerned? "The apostle exhorteth strong and sound believers to such a moderate use of Christian liberty that they do not grieve the spirit of the weak ones, that were believers also (professors, all called 'saints, elect, believers, redeemed,' and so in charity esteemed), and so give them occasion of stumbling and falling off from the gospel: therefore, Jesus Christ died for all reprobates, even all those that never heard word nor syllable of him or the doctrine of the gospel." Must he not be very quick-sighted that can see the dependence of this inference on that exhortation of the apostle? But ye will say, "Is it not affirmed that he may perish for whom Christ died?" *Ans.* In this place there is no such thing at all once mentioned or intimated; only others are commanded not to do that which goeth in a direct way to destroy him, by grieving him with their uncharitable walking. "But why should the apostle exhort him not to do that which he could no way do, if he that Christ died for could not perish?" *Ans.* Though the one could not perish in respect of the event, the other might sinfully give occasion of perishing in respect of a procuring cause. May not a man be exhorted from attempting of that which yet if he should attempt he could not effect? No thanks to the soldier who ran a spear into the side of our dead Redeemer, that therewith he brake none of his bones. Besides, is every one damned that one attempts to destroy, by grieving him with uncharitable walking? Such arguments as these are poor men of straw. And yet, notwithstanding, we do not deny but that many may perish, and that utterly, whom we, in our walking towards them and converse with them, are bound to conceive redeemed by Christ; even all being to be thought so who are to be esteemed " saints and brethren," as the language of the Scripture is concerning the professors of the gospel. And this is most certain, that no one place makes mention of such to be bought or redeemed by our Saviour, but those which had the qualification of being members of this visible church; which come infinitely short of all and every one.

2. But let us see a second place, which is 1 Cor. viii. 11, "And through thy knowledge shall thy weak brother perish, for whom Christ died." This seemeth to have more colour, but really yieldeth no more strength to the persuasion for whose confirmation it is produced, than the former. A brother is said to *perish for whom Christ died.* That by *perishing* here is understood eternal destruction and damnation, I cannot apprehend. That which the apostle intimates whereby it is done, is eating of things offered to an idol, with conscience or regard of an idol, by the example of others who pretended to know that an idol was nothing, and so to eat freely of the things offered to them. That so doing was a sin in its own nature damnable, none can doubt. All sin is so; every time we sin, for any thing that lieth in us, we perish, we are destroyed. So did the eater of things offered to idols. But that God always revengeth sin with damnation on all in whom it is, we deny; he hath otherwise revealed himself in the blood of Jesus Christ. That every such a one did actually perish eternally, as well as meritoriously, cannot be proved. Besides, he that is said to perish is called a *brother,*—that is, a believer; we are brethren only by faith, whereby we come to have one Father. As he is said to be a *brother,* so Christ is said to *die for him.* That a true believer cannot finally perish may easily be proved; therefore, he who doth perish is manifestly declared never to have been any: "They went out from us, because they were not of us." If any perish, then, he was never a true believer. How, then, is he said to be a brother? Because he is so in profession, so in our judgment and persuasion; it being meet for us to think so of them all. As he is said to be a brother, so Christ is said to die for him, even in that judgment which the Scripture allows to us of men. We cannot count a man a brother, and not esteem that Christ died for him; we have no brotherhood with reprobates. Christ died for all believers, John xvii. So we esteem all men walking in the due

profession of the gospel, not manifesting the contrary; yet of these, that many may perish none ever denied. Farther; this, *so shall he perish*, referreth to the sin of him that layeth the offence; for aught that lieth in him, he ruins him irrecoverably. Hence see their argument:—"The apostle telleth persons walking offensively, that by this abusing 'their liberty, others will follow them, to the wounding of their conscience and ruin, who are brethren, acknowledged so by you, and such as for whom Christ died: therefore, Christ died for all the reprobates in the world. 'Is it just and equal,' saith the apostle, 'that ye should do such things as will be stumbling-blocks in the way of the weak brother, at which he might stumble and fall?' therefore, Christ died for all." We do not deny but that some may perish, and that eternally, concerning whom we ought to judge that Christ died for them, whilst they live and converse with us according to the rule of the gospel.

3. The next place is .much insisted on,—namely, 2 Pet. ii. 1, "There shall be false teachers, denying the Lord that bought them, and bringing upon themselves swift destruction." All things here, as to any proof of the business in hand, are exceedingly dark, uncertain, and doubtful. *Uncertain*, that by the *Lord* is meant *the Lord Christ*, the word in the original being Δεσπότης, seldom or never ascribed to him; *uncertain*, whether the purchase or buying of these false teachers refer to the eternal redemption by the blood of Christ, or a deliverance by God's goodness from the defilement of the world in idolatry, or the like, by the knowledge of the truth,—which last the text expressly affirms; *uncertain*, whether the apostle speaketh of this purchase according to the reality of the thing, or according to their apprehension and their profession.

On the other side, it is most *certain*,—First, That there are no spiritual distinguishing fruits of redemption ascribed to these false teachers, but only common gifts of light and knowledge, which Christ hath purchased for many for whom he did not make his soul a ransom. Secondly, That, according to our adversaries, the redemption of any by the blood of Christ cannot be a peculiar aggravation of the sins of any, because they say he died for all; and yet this buying of the false teachers is held out as an aggravation of their sin in particular.

Of the former *uncertainties*, whereon our adversaries build their inference of universal redemption (which yet can by no means be wire-drawn thence, were they most certain in their sense), I shall give a brief account, and then speak something as to the proper intendment of the place.

For the first, It is most *uncertain* whether Christ, as mediator, be here intended by *Lord* or no. There is not any thing in the text to enforce us so to conceive, nay, the contrary seems apparent,—

First, Because in the following verses, God only, as God, with his dealings towards such as these, is mentioned; of Christ not a word. *Secondly,* The name Δεσπότης, properly "Herus," attended by dominion and sovereignty, is not usually, if at all, given to our Saviour in the New Testament; he is everywhere called Κύριος, nowhere clearly Δεσπότης, as is the Father, Luke ii. 29, Acts iv. 24, and in divers other places. Besides, if it should appear that this name were given our Saviour in any one place, doth it therefore follow that it must be so here? nay, is the name proper for our Saviour, in the work of redemption? Δεσπότης is such a Lord or Master as refers to servants and subjection; the end of Christ's purchasing any by his blood being in the Scripture always and constantly expressed in other terms, of more endearment. It is, then, most uncertain that Christ should be here understood by the word *Lord.*

[Secondly], But suppose he should, it is most *uncertain* that by buying of these false teachers is meant his purchasing of them with the ransom of his blood; for,—*First,* The apostle insisteth on a comparison with the times of the Old Testament, and the false prophets that were then amongst the people, backing his assertion with divers examples out of the Old Testament in the whole chapter following. Now, the word ἀγοράζω, here used, signifieth primarily the buying of things; translatitiously, the redemption of persons;—and the word פָּדָה in the Old Testament, answering thereunto, signifieth any deliverance, as Deut. vii. 8, xv. 15, Jer. xv. 21, with innumerable other places: and, therefore, some such deliverance is here only intimated. *Secondly,* Because here is no mention of blood, death, price, or offering of Jesus Christ, as in other places, where proper redemption is treated on; especially, some such expression is added where the word ἀγοράζω is used to express it, as 1 Cor. vi. 20, Rev. v..9, which otherwise holds out of itself deliverance in common from any trouble. *Thirdly,* The apostle setting forth at large the deliverance they had had, and the means thereof, verse 20, affirms it to consist in the "escaping of the pollutions of the world," as idolatry, false worship, and the like, "through the knowledge of the Lord and Saviour Jesus Christ;" plainly declaring that their buying was only in respect of this separation from the world, in respect of the enjoyment of the knowledge of the truth; but of washing in the blood of the Lamb, he is wholly silent. Plainly, there is no purchase mentioned of these false teachers, but a deliverance, by God's dispensations towards them, from the blindness of Judaism or Paganism, by the knowledge of the gospel; whereby the Lord bought them to be servants to him, as their supreme head. So that our adversaries' argument from this place is this:—" God the Lord, by imparting the knowledge of the gospel, and working them to a professed acknowledgment of it and subjection unto it, separated and delivered from the world divers that were saints in show,—really wolves and hypocrites, of old ordained to condemnation: therefore, Jesus Christ shed his blood for the redemption and salvation of all reprobates and damned persons in the whole world." Who would not admire our adversaries' chemistry?

Thirdly, Neither is it more certain that the apostle speaketh of the purchase of the wolves and hypocrites, in respect of the reality of the purchase, and not rather in respect of that estimation which others had of them,—and, by reason of their outward seeming profession, ought to have had,—and of the profession that themselves made to be purchased by him whom they pretended to preach to others; as the Scripture saith [of Ahaz], "The gods of Damascus smote him," because he himself so imagined and professed, 2 Chron. xxviii. 23. The latter hath this also to render it probable,—namely, that it is the perpetual course of the Scripture, to ascribe all those things to every one that is in the fellowship of the church which are proper to them only who are true spiritual members of the same; as to be *saints, elect, redeemed,* etc. Now, the truth is, from this their profession, that they were bought by Christ, might the apostle justly, and that according to the opinion of our adversaries, press these false teachers, by the way of aggravating their sin. For the thing itself, their being bought, it could be no more urged to them than to heathens and infidels that never heard of the name of the Lord Jesus.

Now, after all this, if our adversaries can prove universal redemption from this text, let them never despair of success in any thing they undertake, be it never so absurd, fond, or foolish. But when they have wrought up the work already cut out for them, and proved,—*first,* That by the *Lord* is meant Christ as mediator; *secondly,* That by *buying* is meant spiritual redemption by the blood of the Lamb; *thirdly,* That these *false teachers were really and effectually so redeemed,* and not only so accounted because of the church; *fourthly,* That those who are so redeemed may perish, contrary to the express Scripture, Rev. xiv. 4; *fifthly,* Manifest the strength of this inference, "Some in the church who have acknowledged Christ to be their purchaser, fall away to blaspheme him, and perish for ever; therefore, Christ bought and redeemed all that ever did or shall perish;" *sixthly,* That that which is common to all is a peculiar aggravation to the sin of any one more than others;—I will assure them they shall have more work provided for them, which themselves know for a good part already where to find.

4. The last place produced for the confirmation of the argument in hand is Heb. x. 29, "Of how much sorer punishment, suppose ye, shall he be thought worthy, who hath trodden under foot the Son of God, and hath counted the blood of the covenant, wherewith he was sanctified, an unholy thing, and hath done despite unto the Spirit of

grace?"   " Nothing," say our adversaries, " could be affirmed of all
this concerning apostates,—namely, ' That they have trodden under
foot,' etc., unless the blood of Christ was in some sense shed for them."
Ans. The intention of the apostle in this place is the same with
the general aim and scope of the whole epistle,—to persuade and urge
the Jews, who had embraced the doctrine of the gospel, to perseverance and continuance therein.   This, as he doth perform in other
places, with divers and various arguments,—the most of them taken
from a comparison at large instituted between the gospel in its administration, and those legal shadows which, before their profession,
they lived under and were in bondage unto,—so here he urgeth a
strong argument to the same purpose " ab incommodo, seu effectu
pernicioso," from the miserable, dangerous effects and consequences of
the sin of backsliding, and wilful renunciation of the truth known
and professed, upon any motives and inducements whatsoever; which
he assureth [them] to be no less than a total casting off and depriving
themselves of all hopes and means of recovery, with dreadful horror of
conscience in expectation of judgment to come, verses 26, 27.   Now,
this he confirms, as his manner is in this epistle, from some *thing*,
way, and *practice* which was known to them, and wherewith they
were all acquainted by that administration of the covenant under
which they had before lived, in their Judaism; and so makes up his
inference from a comparison of the less; taking his example from
the punishment due, by God's own appointment, to all them who
transgressed Moses' law in such a manner as apostates sin against
the gospel,—that is, "with an high hand," or "presumptuously:" for
such a one was to die without mercy, Num. xv. 30, 31.   Whereupon,
having abundantly proved that the gospel, and the manifestation of
grace therein, is exceedingly preferred to and exalted above the old
ceremonies of the law, he concludes that certainly a much sorer punishment (which he leaves to their judgment to determine) awaits for
them who wilfully violate the holy gospel, and despise the declaration of grace therein contained and by it revealed; which farther
also to manifest, he sets forth the nature and quality of this sin in
all such as, professing redemption and deliverance by the blood of
Christ, shall wilfully cast themselves thereinto.   " It is," saith he,
" no less than to tread under foot or contemn the Son of God; to
esteem the blood of the covenant, by which he was set apart and
sanctified in the profession of the gospel, to be as the blood of a vile
man; and thereby to do despite to the Spirit of grace."   This being
(as is confessed) the plain meaning and aim of the apostle, we may
observe sundry things, for the vindication of this place from the abuse
of our adversaries; as,—

First, He speaketh here only of those that were professors of the faith
of the gospel, separated from the world, brought into a church state

and fellowship, professing themselves to be sanctified by the blood of Christ, receiving and owning Jesus Christ as the Son of God, and endued with the gifts of the Holy Spirit, as chap. vi. 4, 5. Now, it is most certain that these things are peculiar only to some, yea to a very few, in comparison of the universality of the sons of men; so that what is affirmed of such only can by no means be so extended as to be applied unto all. Now, if any one may be exempted, universal redemption falleth to the ground; from the condition of a very few, with such qualifications as the multitude have not, nothing can be concluded concerning all.

Secondly, The apostle doth neither declare what hath been nor assert what may be, but only adds a commination upon a supposition of a thing; his main aim being to deter from the thing rather than to signify that it may be, by showing the misery that must needs follow if it should so come to pass. When Paul told the soldiers, Acts xxvii. 31, that if the mariners fled away in the boat they could not be saved, he did not intend to signify to them that, in respect of the event, they should be drowned, for God had declared the contrary unto him the night before, and he to them; but only to exhort them to prevent that which of itself was a likely way for their ruin and perishing. Neither shall the Remonstrants, with all their rhetoric, ever persuade us that it is in vain and altogether fruitless to forewarn men of an evil, and to exhort them to take heed of those ways whereby it is naturally, and according to the order among the things themselves, to be incurred; although, in respect of the purpose of God, the thing itself have no futurition, nor shall ever come to pass. A commination of the judgment due to apostasy, being an appointed means for the preserving of the saints from that sin, may be held out to them, though it be impossible the elect should be seduced. Now, that Paul here deals only upon a supposition (not giving being to the thing, but only showing the connection between apostasy and condemnation, thereby to stir up all the saints to "take heed lest there should be in any of them an evil heart of unbelief in departing from the living God") is apparent from verse 26, where he makes an entrance upon this argument and motive to perseverance: "For *if* we sin wilfully." That *believers* may do so, he speaks not one word; but if they should do so, he shows what would be the event;—as, that the soldiers in the ship should perish, Paul told them not; but yet showed what must needs come to pass if the means of prevention were not used. Now, if this be the intention of the apostle, as it is most likely, by his speaking in the first person, "If *we* sin wilfully," then not any thing in the world can be hence concluded either for the universality of redemption or the apostasy of saints, to both which ends this place is usually urged; for "suppositio nil ponit in esse."

Thirdly, It is most certain that those of whom he speaks did make profession of all those things whereof here is mention,—namely, that Jesus Christ was the Son of God, that they were sanctified by the blood of the covenant, and enlightened by the Spirit of grace; yea, as is apparent from the parallel place, Heb. vi. 4, 5, had many gifts of illumination; besides their initiation by baptism, wherein open profession and demonstration was made of these things. So that a renunciation of all these, with open detestation of them, as was the manner of apostates, accursing the name of Christ, was a sin of so deep an abomination, attended with so many aggravations, as might well have annexed to it this remarkable commination, though the apostates never had themselves any true effectual interest in the blood of Jesus.

Fourthly, That it was the manner of the saints, and the apostles themselves, to esteem of all baptized, initiated persons, ingrafted into the church, as sanctified persons; so that, speaking of backsliders, he could not make mention of them any otherwise than as they were commonly esteemed to be, and at that time, in the judgment of charity, were to be considered. Whether they were true believers or no, but only temporary, to whom this argument against apostasy is proposed, according to the usual manner of speech used by the Holy Ghost, they could not be otherwise described.

Fifthly, If the text be interpreted positively, and according to the truth of the thing itself, in both parts thereof (namely, 1. That those of whom the apostle speaketh were truly sanctified; 2. That such may totally perish), then these two things will inevitably follow, —first, That faith and sanctification are not the fruit of election; secondly, That believers may fall finally from Christ;—neither of which I as yet find to be owned by our new Universalists, though both contended for by our old Arminians.

Sixthly, There is nothing in the text of force to persuade that the persons here spoken of must needs be truly justified and regenerated believers, much less that Christ died for them; which comes in only by strained consequences. One expression only seems to give any colour hereunto,—that they were said to be "sanctified by the blood of the covenant." Now, concerning this, if we do but consider,—first, The manner and custom of the apostles writing to the churches, calling them all "saints" that were called,—ascribing that to every one that belonged only to some; secondly, That these persons were baptized, (which ordinance among the ancients was sometimes called φωτισμός, "illumination," sometimes ἁγιασμός, "sanctification,") wherein, by a solemn aspersion of the symbol of the blood of Christ, they were externally sanctified, separated, and set apart, and were by all esteemed as saints and believers; thirdly, The various significations of the word ἁγιάζω (here used) in the Scripture, whereof one most frequent is, to consecrate and set apart to any holy use, as 2 Chron.

xxix. 33, Lev. xvi. 4;[1] *fourthly,* That Paul useth in this epistle many words and phrases in a temple sense, alluding, in the things and ways of the Christian church, unto the old legal observances; *fifthly,* That supposed and professed sanctity is often called so, and esteemed to be so indeed;—if, I say, we shall consider these things, it will be most apparent that here is indeed no true, real, internal, effectual sanctification, proper to God's elect, at all intimated, but only a common external setting apart (with repute and esteem of real holiness) from the ways of the world and customs of the old synagogue, to an enjoyment of the ordinance of Christ representing the blood of the covenant. So that this commination being made to all so externally and apparently sanctified, to them that were truly so it declared the certain connection between apostasy and condemnation; thereby warning them to avoid it, as Joseph [was] warned to flee into Egypt, lest Herod should slay the child; which yet, in respect of God's purpose, could not be effected. In respect of them that were only apparently so, it held out the odiousness of the sin, with their own certain inevitable destruction if they fell into it; which it was possible they might do.

And thus, by the Lord's assistance, have I given you, as I hope, a clear solution to all the arguments which heretofore the Arminians pretended to draw from the Scripture in the defence of their cause; some other sophisms shall hereafter be removed. But because of late we have had a multiplication of arguments on this subject, some whereof, at least in form, appear to be new, and may cause some trouble to the unskilful, I shall, in the next place, remove all those objections which Thomas More, in his book of the " Universality of Free Grace," hath gathered together against our main thesis, of Christ's dying only for the elect, which himself puts together in one bundle, chap. xxvi., and calleth them *reasons.*

CHAPTER VI.

An answer to the twentieth chapter of the book entitled, " The Universality of God's Free Grace," etc., being a collection of all the arguments used by the author throughout the whole book to prove the universality of redemption.

THE *title* pretends satisfaction to them who desire to have reason satisfied: which, that it is a great undertaking, I easily grant; but for the performance of it, " hic labor, hoc opus." That ever Christian reason, rightly informed by the word of God, should be satisfied with any doctrine *so discrepant* from the word, so full of contradiction in itself and to its own principles, as the doctrine of universal redemp-

In these passages the LXX. has ἡγιασμένοι μόσχοι, and χιτῶνα ἡγιασμίνον. — ED.

tion is, I should much marvel. Therefore, I am persuaded that the author of the arguments following (which, lest you should mistake them for others, he calleth *reasons*) will fail of his intention with all that have so much reason as to know how to make use of reason, and so much grace as not to love darkness more than light. The only reason, as far as I can conceive, why he calls this collection of all the arguments and texts of Scripture which he had before cited and produced at large so many *reasons*, being a supposal that he hath given them a logical, argumentative form in this place, I shall briefly consider them; and, by the way, take notice of his skill in a regular framing of arguments, to which here he evidently pretends. His first reason, then, is as followeth:—

I. "That which the Scripture oft and plainly affirmeth in plain words is certainly true and to be believed, Prov. xxii. 20, 21; Isa. viii. 20; 2 Pet. i. 19, 20;

"But that Jesus Christ gave himself a ransom, and by the grace of God tasted death for every man, is oft and plainly affirmed in Scripture, as is before shown, chap. vii. to xiii.:

"Therefore, the same is certainly a truth to be believed, John xx. 31, Acts xxvi. 27."

First, The proposition of this argument is clear, evident, and acknowledged by all professing the name of Christ; but yet universally with this caution and proviso, that by *the Scripture affirming any thing in plain words that is to be believed,* you understand the plain sense of those words, which is clear by rules of interpretation so to be. It is the thing signified that is to be believed, and not the words only, which are the sign thereof; and, therefore, the *plain sense and meaning* is that which we must inquire after, and is intended when we speak of believing plain words of the Scripture. But now if by *plain words* you understand the literal importance of the words, which may perhaps be *figurative,* or at least of *various signification,* and capable of extension or restriction in the interpretation, then there is nothing more false than this assertion; for how can you then avoid the blasphemous folly of the Anthropomorphites, assigning a body and human shape unto God, the *plain words of the Scripture* often mentioning his eyes, hands, ears, etc., it being apparent to every child that the true importance of those expressions answers not at all their gross carnal conception? Will not also transubstantiation, or its younger brother consubstantiation, be an article of our creed? With this limitation, then, we pass the proposition, with the places of Scripture brought to confirm it; only with this observation, that there is not one of them to the purpose in hand,—which, because they do not relate to the argument in consideration, we only leave to men's silent judgments.

Secondly, The assumption, or minor proposition, we absolutely deny as to some part of it; as that Christ should be said to give himself a ransom for every man, it being neither often, nor once, nor plainly, nor obscurely affirmed in the Scripture, nor at all proved in the place referred unto: so that this is but an empty flourishing. For the other expression, of "tasting death for every man," we grant that the words are found Heb. ii. 9; but we deny that *every man* doth always necessarily signify *all and every man in the world.* Νουθετοῦν-τες πάντα ἄνθρωπον, καὶ διδάσκοντες πάντα ἄνθρωπον, Col. i. 28,—" Warning every man, and teaching every man." *Every man* is not there every man in the world; neither are we to believe that Paul warned and taught every particular man, for it is false and impossible. So that *every man*, in the Scripture, is not universally collective of all of all sorts, but either distributive, for some of all sorts, or collective, with a restriction to all of some sort; as in that of Paul, *every man*, was only of those to whom he had preached the gospel. Secondly, In the original there is only ὑπὲρ παντός, *for every*, without the substantive *man*, which might be supplied by other words as well as *man*,—as elect, or believer.

Thirdly, That *every one* is there clearly restrained to all the members of Christ, and the children by him brought to glory, we have before declared. So that this place is no way useful for the confirmation of the assumption, which we deny in the sense intended; and are sure we shall never see a clear, or so much as a probable, testimony for the confirming of it.

To the conclusion of the syllogism, the author, to manifest his skill in disputing in such an argumentative way as he undertaketh, addeth some farther proofs. Conscious, it seems, he was to himself that it had little strength from the propositions from which it is enforced; and, therefore, thought to give some new supportments to it, although with very ill success, as will easily appear to any one that shall but consult the places quoted, and consider the business in hand. In the meantime, this new logic, of filing proofs to the conclusion which are suitable to neither proposition, and striving to give strength to that by new testimony which it hath not from the premises, deserves our notice in this age of learned writers. " Heu quantum est sapere." Such logic is fit to maintain such divinity. And so much for the first argument.

II. " Those whom Jesus Christ and his apostles, in plain terms, without any exception or restraint, affirm that Christ came to save, and to that end died, and gave himself a ransom for, and is a propitiation for their sin, he certainly did come to save, and gave himself a ransom for them, and is the propitiation for their sins, Matt. xxvi. 24; John vi. 38; 1 Cor. xv. 3, 4; Heb. x. 7; John viii. 38, 45; 2 Pet. i. 16; Heb. ii. 3, 4;

" But Jesus Christ and his apostles have, in plain terms, affirmed that 'Christ came to save sinners,' 1 Tim. i. 15; the 'world,' John iii. 17; that he died for the 'unjust,' 1 Pet. iii. 18; the 'ungodly,' Rom. v. 6;

for 'every man,' Heb. ii. 9; 'gave himself a ransom for all men,' 1 Tim. ii. 6; and is the 'propitiation for the sins of the whole world,' 1 John ii. 2; and every one of these affirmations without any exception or restraint, all being unjust, ungodly, sinners, and men, and of the world, Rom. iii. 10, 19, 20, 23; Eph. ii. 1–3; Tit. iii. 3; John iii. 4, 6:

"Therefore, Jesus Christ came to save, died, and gave himself a ransom for all men, and is the propitiation for their sins, John i. 29."

To the proposition of this argument I desire only to observe, that we do not affirm that the Scripture doth, in any place, lay an exception or restraint upon those persons for whom Christ is said to die, as though in one place it should be affirmed he died for all men, and in another some exception against it, as though some of those *all men* were excluded,—which were to feign a repugnancy and contradiction in the word of God; only, we say, one place of Scripture interprets another, and declares that sense which before in one place was ambiguous and doubtful. For instance: when the Scripture showeth that Christ died or gave himself a ransom for *all*, we believe it; and when, in another place, he declares that *all* to be his *church*, his *elect*, his *sheep*, all *believers*,—some of all sorts, *out of all kindreds, and nations, and tongues, under heaven;* this is not to lay an exception or restraint upon what was said of *all* before, but only to declare that the *all* for which he gave himself for a ransom were all his church, all his elect, all his sheep, some of all sorts: and so we believe that he died for all. With this observation we let pass the proposition, taking out its meaning as well as the phrase whereby it is expressed will afford it, together with the vain flourish and pompous show of many texts of Scripture brought to confirm it, whereof not one is any thing to the purpose; so that I am persuaded he put down names and figures at a venture, without once consulting the texts, having no small cause to be confident that none would trace him in his flourish, and yet that some eyes might dazzle at his supernumerary quotations. Let me desire the reader to turn to those places, and if any one of them be any thing to the purpose or business in hand, let the author's credit be of weight with him another time. O let us not be as many, who corrupt the word of God! But perhaps it is a mistake in the impression, and for Matt. xxvi. 24, he intends verse 28, where Christ is said to shed his blood for many. In John vi., he mistook verse 38 for 39, where our Saviour affirms that he came to save that which his Father gave him,—that none should be lost; which certainly are the elect. In 1 Cor. xv. 3, 4, he was not much amiss, the apostle conjoining in those verses the death and resurrection of Christ, which he saith was for us; and how far this advantageth his cause in hand, we have before declared. By Heb. x. 7, I suppose he meant verse 10 of the chapter, affirming that by the will of God, which Christ came to do, we are sanctified, even

through the offering of the body of Jesus,—ascribing our sanctification
to his death, which is not effected in all and every one; though perhaps he may suppose the last clause of the verse, "once for all," to
make for him. But some charitable man, I hope, will undeceive him,
by letting him know the meaning of the word ἐφάπαξ. The like may
be observed of the other places,—that in them is nothing at all to the
proposition in hand, and nigh them at least is enough to evert it.
And so his proposition in sum is:—"All those for whom the Scripture affirms that Christ did die, for them he died;" which is true,
and doubtless granted.

The assumption affirms that Christ and his apostles in the Scriptures say that he died to save *sinners, unjust, ungodly*, the *world*,
all; whereupon the conclusion ought barely to be, "Therefore Christ
died for sinners, unjust, ungodly, the world, and the like." To which
we say,—First, That this is the very same argument, for substance, with
that which went before, as also are some of those that follow; only
some words are varied, to change the outward appearance, and so to
make show of a number. Secondly, That the whole strength of
this argument lies in turning indefinite propositions into universals,
concluding that because Christ died for sinners, therefore he died
for all sinners; because he died for the unjust, ungodly, and the
world, that therefore he died for every one that is unjust, or ungodly,
and for every one in the world; because he died for all, therefore for
all and every one of all sorts of men. Now, if this be good arguing, I
will furnish you with some more such arguments against you have
occasion to use them:—*First*, God "justifieth the ungodly," Rom. iv. 5;
therefore, he justifieth every one that is ungodly. Now, "whom he justifieth, them he also glorifieth;" and therefore every ungodly person
shall be glorified. *Secondly*, When Christ came, "men loved darkness
rather than light," John iii. 19; therefore, all men did so, and so none
believed. *Thirdly*, "The world knew not Christ," John i. 10; therefore, no man in the world knew him. *Fourthly*, "The whole world
lieth in wickedness," 1 John v. 19; therefore, every one in the world
doth so. Such arguments as these, by turning indefinite propositions
into universals, I could easily furnish you withal, for any purpose that
you will use them to. Thirdly, If you extend the words in the conclusion no farther than the intention of them in the places of Scripture recited in the assumption, we may safely grant the whole,—
namely, that Christ died for sinners and the world, for sinful men
in their several generations living therein; but if you intend a universality collective of all in the conclusion, then the syllogism is
sophistical and false, no place of Scripture affirming so much that
is produced, the assignation of the object of the death of Christ in
them being in terms indefinite, receiving light and clearness for a
more restrained sense in those places where they are expounded to

be meant of all his own people, and the children of God scattered throughout the world. Fourthly, For particular places of Scripture urged, 1 Tim. i. 15; 1 Pet. iii. 18; Rom. v. 6, in the beginning of the assumption, are not at all to the purpose in hand. John iii. 17; Heb. ii. 9; 1 John ii. 2, have been already considered. Rom. iii. 10, 19, 20, 23; Eph. ii. 1–3; Tit. iii. 3; John iii. 4, 6, added in the close of the same proposition, prove that all are sinners and children of wrath; but of Christ's dying for all sinners, or for all those children of wrath, there is not the least intimation. And this may suffice in answer to the first two arguments, which might easily be retorted upon the author of them, the Scripture being full and plain to the confirmation of the position which he intends to oppose.

III. "That which the Scripture layeth forth as one end of the death of Christ, and one ground and cause of God's exalting Christ to be the Lord and Judge of all, and of the equity of his judging, that is certainly to be believed, Ps. xii. 6, xviii. 130, cxix. 4;

"But the Scripture layeth forth this for one end of the death and resurrection of Christ, that he might be the Lord of all, Rom. xiv. 9; 2 Cor. v. 14, 15. And for that cause (even his death and resurrection) hath God exalted him to be the Lord and Judge of all men, and his judgments shall be just, Rom. xiv. 9, 11, 12; 2 Cor. v. 10; Phil. ii. 7–11; Acts xvii. 31; Rom. ii. 16:

"Therefore, that Christ so died, and rose again for all, is a truth to be believed, 1 Tim. ii. 6."

First, The unlearned framing of this argument, the uncouth expressions of the thing intended, and failing in particulars, by the by, being to be ascribed to the person and not the cause, I shall not much trouble myself withal; as,—*First*, To his artificial regularity in bring his minor proposition, namely, Christ being made Lord and Judge of all, into the major; so continuing one term in all three propositions, and making the whole almost unintelligible. *Secondly*, His interpreting, "For this cause God exalted Christ," to be his death and resurrection, when his resurrection, wherein he was "declared to be the Son of God with power," Rom. i. 4, was a glorious part of his exaltation. To examine and lay open the weakness and folly of innumerable such things as these, which everywhere occur, were to be lavish of precious moments. Those that have the least taste of learning or the way of reasoning do easily see their vanity; and for the rest, especially the poor admirers of these foggy sophisms, I shall not say, "Quoniam hic populus vult decipi, decipiatur," but, "God give them understanding and repentance, to the acknowledgment of the truth."

Secondly, To this whole argument, as it lies before us, I have nothing to say but only to entreat Mr More, that if the misery of our times should be calling upon him to be writing again, he would cease expressing his mind by syllogisms, and speak in his own manner; which, by its confusion in innumerable tautologies, may a little puzzle his reader. For, truly, this kind of arguing here used,—for want of logic, whereby he is himself deceived, and delight in sophistry, whereby he deceiveth others,—is exceedingly ridiculous; for none can be so blind but that, at first reading of the argument, he will see that he asserts and infers that in the conclusion, strengthening it with a new testimony, which was not once dreamed of in either of the premises; they speaking of the exaltation of Christ to be judge of all, which refers to his own glory; the conclusion, of his dying for all, which necessarily aims at and intends their good. Were it not a noble design to banish all human learning, and to establish such a way of arguing in the room thereof? "Hoc Ithacus velit et magno mercentur Atridæ."

Thirdly, The force and sum of the argument is this:—"Christ died and rose again that he might be Lord and Judge of all; therefore, Christ died for all." Now, ask what he means by dying for all, and the whole treatise answers that it is a paying a ransom for them all, that they might be saved. Now, how this can be extorted out of Christ's dominion over all, with his power of judging all committed to him, which also is extended to the angels for whom he died not; let them that can understand it rejoice in their quick apprehension; I confess it flies my thoughts.

Fourthly, The manner of arguing being so vain, let us see a little whether there be any more weight in the matter of the argument. Many texts of Scripture are heaped up and distributed to the several propositions. In those out of Ps. xii. 6, xviii. 30 (as I suppose it should be, not 130, as it is printed), cxix. 4, there is some mention of the precepts of God, with the purity of his word and perfection of his word; which that they are any thing to the business in hand I cannot perceive. That of 2 Tim. ii. 6, added to the conclusion, is one of those places which are brought forth upon every occasion, as being the supposed foundation of the whole assertion, but causelessly, as hath been showed oft. [Among] those which are annexed to the minor proposition, [is] 2 Cor. v. 14, 15: as I have already cleared the mind of the Holy Ghost in it, and made it manifest that no such thing as universal redemption can be wrested from it, so unto this present argument it hath no reference at all, not containing any one syllable concerning the judging of Christ and his power over all, which was the medium insisted on. Phil. ii. 7–11; Acts. xvii. 31; Rom. ii. 16, mention, indeed, Christ's exaltation, and his judging all at the last day; but because he shall judge all at the last day, therefore he died for all, will ask more pains to prove than our adversary intends to take in this cause.

The weight, on the whole, must depend on Rom. xiv. 9, 11, 12; which being the only place that gives any colour to this kind of arguing, shall a little be considered. It is the lordship and dominion of Christ over all which the apostle, in that place, at large insists on and evidenceth to believers, that they might thereby be provoked to walk blameless, and without offence one towards another, knowing the terror of the Lord, and how that all men, even themselves and others, must come to appear before his judgment-seat, when it will be but a sad ˄thing to have an account to make of scandals and offences. Farther to ingraft and fasten this upon them, he declares unto them the way whereby the Lord Christ attained and came to this dominion and power of judging, all things being put under his feet, together with what design he had, as to this particular, in undertaking the office of mediation, there expressed by "dying, rising, and reviving,"—to wit, that he might have the execution of judging over all committed to him, that being part of the " glory set before him," which caused him to " endure the cross and despise the shame," Heb. xii. 2.

So that all which here is intimated concerning the death of Christ is about the end, effects, and issue that it had towards himself, not any thing of what was his intention towards them for whom he died. To die for others does at least denote to die for their good, and in the Scripture always to die in their stead. Now, that any such thing can be hence deducted as that Christ died for all, because by his death himself made way for the enjoyment of that power whereby he is Lord over all, and will judge them all, casting the greatest part of men into hell by the sentence of his righteous judgment, I profess sincerely that I am no way able to perceive. If men will contend and have it so, that Christ must be said to die for all, because by his death and resurrection he attained the power of judging all, then I shall only leave with them these three things:—*First*, That innumerable souls shall be judged by him for not walking according to the light of nature left unto them, directing them to seek after the eternal power and Godhead of their Creator, without the least rumour of the gospel to direct them to a Redeemer once arriving at their ears, Rom. ii. 12; and what good will it be for such that Christ so died for them? *Secondly*, That he also died for the devils, because he hath, by his death and resurrection, attained a power of judging them also. *Thirdly*, That the whole assertion is nothing to the business in hand; our inquiry being about them whom our Saviour intended to redeem and save by his blood; this return, about those he will one day judge: " quæstio est de alliis, responsio de cepis."

IV. " That which the Scripture so sets forth in general for the world of mankind, as a truth for them all, that whosoever of the particulars so believe as to come to Christ and receive the same shall not perish, but have everlasting life, is certainly a truth to be believed, Acts v. 20;

"But that God sent forth his Son to be the Saviour of the world is in Scripture so set forth in general for all men, that whosoever of the particulars so believe as they come to Christ and receive the same, they shall not perish, but have everlasting life, John iii. 16–18, 36, i. 4, 11, 12:

"Therefore, that God sent his Son to be the Saviour of the world is a certain truth, 1 John iv. 14."

I hope no ingenuous man, that knows any thing of the controversy in hand, and to what head it is driven between us and our adversary, or is in any measure acquainted with the way of arguing, will expect that we should spend many words about such poor flourishes, vain repetitions, confused expressions, and illogical deductions and argumentations, as this pretended new argument (indeed the same with the first two, and with almost all that follow), will expect that I should cast away much time or pains about them. For my own part, I were no way able to undergo the tediousness of the review of such things as these, but that "eundum est quo trahunt fata ecclesiæ." Not, then, any more to trouble the reader with a declaration of that in particulars which he cannot but be sufficiently convinced of by a bare overlooking of these reasons,—namely, that this author is utterly ignorant of the way of reasoning, and knows not how tolerably to express his own conceptions, nor to infer one thing from another in any regular way, I answer,—First, That whatsoever the Scripture holds forth as a truth to be believed is certainly so, and to be embraced. Secondly, That the Scripture sets forth the death of Christ, to all whom the gospel is preached [unto], as an all-sufficient means for the bringing of sinners unto God, so as that whosoever believe it and come in unto him shall certainly be saved. Thirdly, What can be concluded hence, but that the death of Christ is of such infinite value as that it is able to save to the utmost every one to whom it is made known, if by true faith they obtain an interest therein and a right thereunto, we cannot perceive. This truth we have formerly confirmed by many testimonies of Scripture, and do conceive that this innate sufficiency of the death of Christ is the foundation of its promiscuous proposal to elect and reprobate. Fourthly, That the conclusion, if he would have the reason to have any colour or show of an argument, should at least include and express the whole and entire assertion contained in the proposition,— namely, "That Christ is so set forth to be the Saviour of the world, that whosoever of the particulars believe," etc. And then it is by us fully granted, as making nothing at all for the universality of redemption, but only for the fulness and sufficiency of his satisfaction. Of the word *world* enough hath been said before.

V. "That which God will one day cause every man confess to the glory of God is certainly a truth, for God will own no lie for his glory, John iii. 33; Rom. iii. 3, 4;

"But God will one day cause every man to confess Jesus (by virtue of his death and ransom given) to be the Lord, even to the glory of God, Phil. ii. 7–11; Isa. xlv. 22, 23; Rom. xiv. 9, 11, 12; Ps. lxxxvi. 9:

"Therefore, it is certainly a truth that Jesus Christ hath given himself a ransom for all men, and hath thereby the right of lordship over them; and if any will not believe and come into this government, yet he abideth faithful, and cannot deny himself, but will one day bring them before him, and cause them to confess him Lord, to the glory of God; when they shall be denied by him, for denying him in the days of his patience, 2 Tim. ii. 12–14; Matt. x. 32, 33; 2 Cor. v. 10."

Ans. The conclusion of this argument ought to be thus, and no otherwise, if you intend it should receive any strength from the premises: "Therefore, that Jesus Christ is the Lord, and to be confessed to the glory of God, is certainly a truth." This, I say, is all the conclusion that this argument ought to have had, unless, instead of a syllogism, you intend three independent propositions, every one standing upon its own strength. That which is inserted concerning his giving himself a ransom for all, and that which follows of the conviction and condemnation of them who believe not nor obey the gospel, confirmed from 2 Cor. v. 10, 2 Tim. ii. 12–14, is altogether heterogeneous to the business in hand. Now, this being the conclusion intended, if our author suppose that the deniers of universal redemption do question the truth of it, I wonder not at all why he left all other employment to fall a-writing controversies, having such apparent advantages against his adversaries as such small mistakes as this are able to furnish his conceit withal. But it may be an act of charity to part him and his own shadow,—so terribly at variance as here and in other places; wherefore, I beseech him to hear a word in his heat, and to take notice,—[First,] That though we do not ascribe a fruitless, ineffectual redemption to Jesus Christ, nor say that he loved any with that entire love which moved him to lay down his life, but his own church, and that all his elect are effectually redeemed by him, yet we deny not but that he shall also judge the reprobates,—namely, even all them that know not, that deny, that disobey and corrupt the truth of his gospel,—and that all shall be convinced that he is Lord of all at the last day: so that he may spare his pains of proving such unquestionable things. Something else is extremely desirous to follow, but indignation must be bridled. Secondly, For that cause in the second proposition, "By virtue of his death and ransom given," we deny that it is anywhere in the Scripture once intimated that the ransom paid by Christ in his death for us was the cause of his exaltation to be Lord of all: it was his obedience to his Father in his death, and not his satisfaction for us, that is proposed as the antecedent of this exaltation; as is apparent, Phil. ii. 7–11.

VI. " That which may be proved in and by the Scripture, both by plain sentences therein and necessary consequences imported thereby, without wresting, wrangling, adding to, taking from, or altering the sentences and words of Scripture, is a truth to be believed, Matt. xxii. 29, 32; Rom. xi. 2, 5, 6;

" But that Jesus Christ gave himself a ransom for all men, and by the grace of God tasted death for every man, may be proved in and by the Scripture, both by plain sentences therein and necessary consequences imported thereby, without wresting, wrangling, adding, or taking away, or altering the words and sentences, as is already showed, chap. vii., xiii., which will be now ordered into several proofs:

" Therefore, that Jesus Christ gave himself for all men, and by the grace of God tasted death for every man, is a truth to be believed, Mark i. 15, xvi. 15, 18; 1 John iv. 14."

Ans. First, The meaning of this argument is, that universal redemption may be proved by the Scripture; which, being the very thing in question, and the thesis undertaken to be proved, there is no reason why itself should make an argument, but only to make up a number: and, for my part, they should pass without any other answer, namely, that they are a number, but that those *who are the number* are to be considered.

Secondly, Concerning the argument itself (seeing it must go for one), we say,—*First*, To the first proposition, that laying aside the unnecessary expressions, the meaning of it I take to be this: "That which is affirmed in the Scripture, or may be deduced from thence by just consequence, following such ways of interpretation, of affirmation, and consequences, as by which the Spirit of God leadeth us into the knowledge of the truth, is certainly to be believed;" which is granted of all, though not proved by the places he quoteth, Matt. xxii. 29, 32, Rom. xi. 2, 5, 6, and is the only foundation of that article of faith which you seek to oppose. *Secondly*, To the second, that Christ gave himself a ransom ὑπὲρ πάντων, for all, and tasted death ὑπὲρ παντός, for all, is the very word of Scripture, and was never denied by any. The making of *all* to be all men and every man, in both the places aimed at, is your addition, and not the Scripture's assertion. If you intend, then, to prove that Christ gave himself a ransom for all, and tasted death for all, you may save your labours; it is confessed on all hands, none ever denied it. But if you intend to prove those *all* to be all and every man, of all ages and kinds, elect and reprobate, and not all his children, all his elect, all his sheep, all his people, all the children given him of God,—some of all sorts, nations, tongues, and languages only, I will, by the Lord's assistance, willingly join issue with you, or any man breathing, to search out the meaning of the word and mind of God in it; holding ourselves to the proportion of faith, essentiality of the doctrine of redemption, scope of the places where such assertions are, comparing them with other places, and the like ways,—labouring in all humility to find the mind of the Lord, according to his own appointment. And of the success of such a trial, laying aside such failings as will adhere to my personal weakness, I am, by the grace of God, exceedingly confident; having, by his goodness, received some strength and opportunity to search into and seriously to weigh whatever the most famous assertors of universal redemption, whether Lutherans or Arminians, have been able to say in this cause. For the present, I address myself to what is before me; only desiring the reader to observe, that the assertion to be proved is, "That Jesus Christ, according to the counsel and will of his Father, suitable to his purpose of salvation in his own mind and intention, did, by his death and oblation, pay a ransom for all and every man, elect and reprobate,—both those that are saved and those that perish,—to redeem them from sin, death, and hell, [and] to recover salvation, life, and immortality for them; and not only for his elect, or church, chosen to an inheritance before the foundation of the world." To confirm this we have divers places produced; which, by the Lord's assistance, we shall consider in order.

Proof 1 *of argument* 6. " God so loved the world, that he gave his Son to be the Saviour of the world, 1 John iv. 14; and sends his servant to bear witness of his Son, that all men through him might believe, John i. 4, 7; that whosoever believes on him might have everlasting life, John iii. 16, 17. And he is willing that all should come to the knowledge of the truth, 1 Tim. ii. 4, and be saved, 1 Tim. i. 15. Nor will he be wanting in the sufficiency of helpfulness to them, if, as light comes, they will suffer themselves to be wrought on and to receive it, Prov. i. 23, viii. 4, 5. And is not this plain in Scripture?"

Ans. First, The main, yea, indeed, only thing to be proved, as we before observed, is, that those indefinite propositions which we find in the Scripture concerning the death of Christ are to be understood universally,—that the terms *all* and *world* do signify in this business, when they denote the object of the death of Christ, all and every man in the world. Unless this be done, all other labour is altogether useless and fruitless. Now, to this there is nothing at all urged in this pretended proof, but only a few ambiguous places barely recited, with a false collection from them or observation upon them, which they give no colour to.

Secondly, 1 John iv 14, God's sending his Son to be the "Saviour of the world," and his servant to testify it, is nothing but to be the Saviour of men living in the world; which his elect are. A

hundred such places as these, so clearly interpreted as they are in
other places, would make nought at all to the purpose. The next
thing is from John i. 4, 7. Verse 4 is, that Christ was the "life of
men;" which is most true, no life being to be had for any man but only
in and through him. This not being at all to the question, the next
words of verse 7 [are], "That all men through him might believe;"
which words being thrust in, to piece-up a sense with another fraction
of Scripture, seem to have some weight, as though Christ were sent
that all men through him might believe. A goodly show! seeming
no less to make for universal redemption than the Scripture cited by
the devil, after he had cut off part of it, did for our Saviour's casting
himself from the pinnacle of the temple. But if you cast aside the
sophistry of the old serpent, the expression of this place is not a little
available to invalidate the thesis sought to be maintained by it. The
words are, "There was a man sent from God, whose name was John.
The same came for a witness, to bear witness of the light, that all
men through him might believe." Now, who do you think is there
meant by δι' αὐτοῦ, "through him?" Is it Christ, think you, the
light? or John, the witness of the light? Certainly John, as almost all expositors do agree, except certain among the Papists, and
Grotius,—that Ishmael. So the Syriac interpreter, reading, "By his
hand or ministry." So the word infers; for we are not said to believe
διὰ Χριστοῦ, "by Christ," or, as it should be here, διὰ τοῦ φωτός, "by the
light;" but εἰς τὸ φῶς, John xii. 36, "in the light," not by it. And
ἐπὶ τὸν Κύριον, Acts ix. 42, "believed in the Lord;" so also, Rom. ix. 33,
Καὶ πᾶς ὁ πιστεύων ἐπ' αὐτῷ, "Every one that believeth on him."
So ἐν Χριστῷ, in divers places, in him; but no mention of believing by
him, which rather denotes the instrument of believing, as is the
ministry of the word, than the object of faith, as Christ is. This
being apparent, let us see what is affirmed of John, why he was sent
"that all through him might believe." Now, this word all here hath
all the qualifications which our author requireth for it, to be always
esteemed a certain expression of a collective universality, that it is
spoken of God, etc. And who, I pray you, were these all, that were
intended to be brought to the faith by the ministry of John? 'Were
they not only all those that lived throughout the world in his days,
who preached (a few years) in Judea only, but also all those that
were dead before his nativity, and that were born after his death,
and shall be to the end of the world in any place under heaven?
Let them that can believe it enjoy their persuasion, with this assurance that I will never be their rival; being fully persuaded that by all
men here is meant only some of all sorts, to whom his word did come.
So that the necessary sense of the word all here is wholly destructive
to the proposition.

For what, thirdly, is urged from John iii. 16, 17, that God so sent his Son, that "whosoever believeth on him might have ever-lasting life," as far as I know is not under debate, as to the sense of it, among Christians.

Fourthly, For God's willingness that all should be saved, from 1 Tim. ii. 4 (to which a word is needlessly added to make a show, the text being quite to another purpose, from 1 Tim. i. 15), taking *all men* there for the universality of individuals, then I ask,—*First,* What act it is of God wherein this his willingness doth consist? Is it in the eternal purpose of his will that all should be saved? Why is it not accomplished? "Who hath resisted his will?" Is it in an antecedent desire that it should be so, though he fail in the end? Then is the blessed God most miserable, it being not in him to accomplish his just and holy desires. Is it some temporary act of his, whereby he hath declared himself unto them? Then, I say, Grant that salvation is only to be had in a Redeemer, in Jesus Christ, and give me an instance how God, in any act whatsoever, hath declared his mind and revealed himself to all men, of all times and places, concerning his willingness of their salvation by Jesus Christ, a Redeemer, and I will never more trouble you in this cause. *Secondly,* Doth this will equally respect the *all* intended, or doth it not? If it doth, why hath it not equal effects towards all? what reason can be assigned? If it doth not, whence shall that appear? There is nothing in the text to intimate any such diversity. For our parts, by *all men* we understand some of all sorts throughout the world, not doubting but that, to the equal reader, we have made it so appear from the context and circumstances of the place, the will of God there being that mentioned by our Saviour, John vi. 40. That which follows in the close of this proof, of God's " not being wanting in the sufficiency of helpfulness to them who, as light comes, suffer themselves to be wrought upon and receive it," is a poisonous sting in the tail of the serpent, wherein is couched the whole Pelagian poison of free-will and Popish merit of congruity, with Arminian sufficient grace, in its whole extent and universality; to neither of which there is the least witness given in the place produced.

The sum and meaning of the whole assertion is, that there is a universality of sufficient grace granted to all, even of grace subjective, enabling them to obedience, which receives addition, increase, degrees, and augmentation, according as they who have it do make use of what they presently enjoy; which is a position so contradictory to innumerable places of Scripture, so derogatory to the free grace of God, so destructive to the efficacy of it, such a clear exaltation of the old idol free-will into the throne of God, as any thing that the decaying estate of Christianity hath invented and broached. So far is it from being "plain and clear in Scripture," that it is universally repugnant to the whole dispensation of the new covenant revealed

to us therein; which, if ever the Lord call me to, I hope very clearly
to demonstrate: for the present, it belongs not immediately to the
business in hand, and therefore I leave it, coming to—

Proof 2. " Jesus Christ, the Son of God, came into the world to
save the world, John xii. 47; to save sinners, 1 Tim. i. 15; to take
away our sins, and destroy the works of the devil, 1 John iii. 5, 8;
to take away the sins of the world, John i. 29: and therefore died
for all, 2 Cor. v. 14, 15; and gave himself a ransom for all, 1 Tim.
ii. 6; to save that which was lost, Matt. xviii. 11. And so his propitiation was made for the world, 2 Cor. v. 19; the whole world,
1 John ii. 2. And all this is full and plain in Scripture."

Ans. Those places of this proof where there is mention of *all* or
world, as John xii. 47, i. 29; 2 Cor. v. 14, 15; 1 Tim. ii. 6; 2 Cor.
v. 19; 1 John ii. 2, have been all already considered, and I am unwilling to trouble the reader with repetitions. See the places, and
I doubt not but you will find that they are so far from giving any
strength to the thing intended to be proved by him, that they much
rather evert it. For the rest, 1 Tim. i. 15; Matt. xviii. 11; 1 John
iii. 5, 8, how any thing can be extracted from them to give colour
to the universality of redemption I cannot see; what they make
against it hath been declared. Pass we then to—

Proof 3. " God in Christ doth, in some means or other of his appointment, give some witness to all men of his mercy and goodness
procured by Christ, Ps. xix. 4; Rom. x. 18; Acts xiv. 17; and there-
through, at one time or other, sendeth forth some stirrings of his
Spirit, to move in and knock at the hearts of men, to invite them to
repentance and seeking God, and so to lay hold on the grace and salvation offered: and this not in a show or pretence, but in truth and
good-will, ready to bestow it on them. And this is all fully testified
in Scripture, Gen. vi. 3; Isa. xlv. 22; Acts xvii. 30, 31; John i. 19."

Ans. First, "Parvas habet spes Troja, si tales habet." If the universality of redemption have need of such proofs as these, it hath indeed
great need and little hope of supportment. *Universal vocation* is here
asserted, to maintain *universal redemption.* "Manus manum fricat,"
or rather, "Muli se mutuo scabiunt;" this being called in oftentimes
to support the other; and they are both the two legs of that idol
free-will, which is set up for men to worship, and when one stumbles
the other steps forward to uphold the Babel. Of *universal vocation*
(a gross figment) I shall not now treat; but only say, for the present,
that it is true that God at all times, ever since the creation, hath
called men to the knowledge of himself as the great Creator, in
those things which of him, by the means of the visible creation,
might be known, "even his eternal power and Godhead," Rom. i. 19,
20; Ps. xix. 1, 2; Acts xiv. 17. Secondly, That after the death of
Christ, he did, by preaching of the gospel extended far and wide,

call home to himself the children of God, scattered abroad in the world, whereas his elect were before confined almost to one nation; giving a right to the gopsel to be preached to "every creature," Mark xvi. 15; Rom. x. 18; Isa. xlv. 22; Acts xvii. 30, 31. But, thirdly, That God should at all times, in all places, in all ages, grant means of grace or call to Christ as a redeemer, or to a participation of his mercy and goodness in him manifested, with strivings and motions of his Spirit for men to close with those invitations, is so gross and groundless an imagination, so opposite to God's distinguishing mercy, so contradictory to express places of Scripture and the experience of all ages, as I wonder how any man hath the boldness to assert it, much more to produce it as a proof of an untruth more gross than itself.   Were I not resolved to tie myself to the present controversy, I should not hold from producing some reasons to evert this fancy; something may be done hereafter, if· the Lord prevent not.   In the meantime, let the reader consult Ps. cxlvii. 19, 20; Matt. xi. 25, xxii. 14; Acts xiv. 16, xvi. 7; Rom. x. 14, 15.   We pass to—

Proof 4. "The Holy Ghost, that cometh from the Father and the Son, shall reprove the world of sin (even that part of the world that refuseth now to believe that they are under sin), because they believe not on Christ, and that it is their sin that they have not believed on him. And how could it be their sin not to believe in Christ, and they for that cause under sin, if there were neither enough in the atonement made by Christ for them, nor truth in God's offer of mercy to them, nor will nor power in the Spirit's moving in any sort sufficient to have brought them to believe, at one time or other?   And yet is this evident in Scripture, and shall be by the Holy Spirit, to be their great sin, that fastens all other sins on them, John iii. 18, 19, viii. 24, xii. 48, xv. 22, 24, xvi. 7–11."

Ans. The intention of this proof is, to show that men shall be condemned for their unbelief, for not believing in Christ; which, saith the author, cannot be unless three things be granted,—First, That there be enough in the atonement made by Christ for them.   Secondly, That there be truth in God's offer of mercy to them.   Thirdly, That there be sufficient will and power given them by the Spirit, at some time or other, to believe.   Now, though I believe no man can perceive what may be concluded hence for the universality of redemption, yet I shall observe some few things: and to the first thing required do say, That if, by "Enough in the atonement for them," you understand that the atonement, which was made for them, hath enough in it, we deny it; not because the atonement hath not enough in it for them, but because the atonement was not for them.   If you mean that there is a sufficiency in the merit of Christ to· save them if they should believe, we grant it, and affirm that this sufficiency is the chief ground of the proposing it unto them (understanding those to whom it is proposed, that is those to whom the gospel is preached). To the second, That there is truth, as in all the ways and words of God, so in his offer of mercy to whomsoever it is offered. If we take the command to believe, with the promise of life upon so doing, for an offer of mercy, there is an eternal truth in it; which is, that God will assuredly bestow life and salvation upon all believers, the proffers being immediately declarative of our duty; secondly, of the concatenation of faith and life, and not at all of God's intention towards the particular soul to whom the proffer is made: "For who hath known the mind of the Lord, and who hath been his counsellor?" To the third, the Spirit's giving will or power, I say,—*First*, That ye set the cart before the horse, placing will before power. *Secondly*, I deny that any internal assistance is required to render a man inexcusable for not believing, if he have the object of faith propounded to him, though of himself he have neither power nor will so to do, having lost both in Adam. *Thirdly*, How a man may have given him a will to believe, and yet not believe, I pray, declare the next controversy ye undertake. This being observed, I shall take leave to put this proof into such form as alone it is capable of, that the strength thereof may appear, and it is this: "If the Spirit shall convince all those of sin to whom the gospel is preached, that do not believe, then Christ died for all men, both those that have the gospel preached unto them and those that have not; but the first is true, for their unbelief is their great sin: ergo, Jesus Christ died for all." Which, if any, is an argument " a baculo ad angulum, " from the beam to the shuttle." The places of Scripture, John iii. 18, 19, viii. 24, xii. 48, xv. 22, 24, prove that unbelief is a soul-condemning sin, and that for which they shall be condemned in whom it is privative, by their having the gospel preached to them. But *quid ad nos?*

One place is more urged, and consequently more abused, than the rest, and therefore must be a little cleared; it is John xvi. 7-11. The words are, "I will send the Comforter to you. And when he is come, he will reprove the world of sin, and of righteousness, and of judgment: of sin, because they believe not in me; of righteousness, because I go to my Father, and ye see me no more; of judgment, because the prince of this world is judged." First, It is uncertain whether our author understands the words of the Spirit in and with Christ at the last day, or in and with the ministry of the word now in the days of the gospel. If the first, he is foully mistaken; if the latter, then the conviction here meant intends only those to whom the gospel is preached,—and what that will advantage universal redemption, which compriseth all as well before as after the death of Christ, I know not. But, secondly, It is uncertain whether he supposeth this conviction of the Spirit to attend the preaching of the gospel only, or else to consist in strivings and motions even in them who never hear the word of the gospel; if he mean the latter, we wait for a proof.   Thirdly, It is uncertain whether he supposeth those thus convinced to be converted and brought to the faith by that conviction and that attending effectualness of grace, or no.

But omitting those things, that text being brought forth and insisted on, farther to manifest how little reason there was for its producing, I shall briefly open the meaning of the words.   Our Saviour Christ intending, in this his last sermon, to comfort his apostles in their present sad condition, whereto they were brought by his telling them that he must leave them and go to his Father,—which sorrow and sadness he knew full well would be much increased when they should behold the vile, ignominious way whereby their Lord and Master should be taken from them, with all those reproaches and persecutions which would attend them so deprived of him,—bids them not be troubled, nor filled with sorrow and fear, for all this; assuring them that all this loss, shame, and reproach should be abundantly made up by what he would do for them and bestow upon them when his bodily presence should be removed from them.   And as to that particular, which was the head of all, that he should be so vilely rejected and taken out of the world as a false teacher and seducer, he telleth them he will send them ἄλλον παράκλητον, John xiv. 16, " another Comforter," one that shall " vicariam navare operam," as Tertul.,— be unto them in his stead, to fill them with all that consolation whereof by his absence they might be deprived; and not only so, but also to be present with them in other greater things than any he had as yet employed them about.   This again he puts them in mind of, chap. xvi. 7.   Now, ὁ παράκλητος, who is there promised, is properly " an advocate,"—that is, one that pleadeth the cause of a person that is guilty or accused before any tribunal,—and is opposed τῷ κατηγόρῳ, Rev. xii. 10; and so is this word by us translated, 1 John ii. 1.   Christ, then, here telleth them, that as he will be their advocate with the Father, so he will send them an advocate to plead his cause, which they professed, with the world; that is, those men in the world, which had so vilely traduced and condemned him as a seducer, laying it as a reproach upon all his followers.   This, doubtless, though in some respect it be continued to all ages in the ministry of the word, yet it principally intended the plentiful effusion of the Spirit upon the apostles at Pentecost, after the ascension of our Saviour; which also is made more apparent by the consideration of what he affirmeth that the advocate so sent shall do, namely,—1. "He shall reprove," or rather, evidently, " convince, the world of sin, because they believed not on him;" which, surely, he abundantly did in that sermon of Peter, Acts ii., when the enemies themselves and haters of Christ were so reproved and convinced of their sin, that, upon the pressing urgency of that conviction, they cried out, "Men and brethren, what shall we do to be saved?" Then was the world brought to a voluntary confession of the sin of murdering Jesus Christ. 2. He shall do the same of "righteousness, because he went to his Father;"—not of its own righteousness, to reprove it for that, because it is not; but he shall convince the men of the world, who condemned Christ as a seducer, of his righteousness,—that he was not a blasphemer, as they pretended, but the Son of God, as himself witnessed: which they shall be forced to acknowledge when, by the effusion and pouring out of the Spirit upon his apostles, it shall be made evident that he is gone to and received of his Father, and owned by him, as the centurion did presently upon his death. 3. He shall "convince the world of judgment, because the prince of this world is judged;" manifesting to all those of whom he speaketh, that he whom they despised as the carpenter's son, and bade come down from the cross if he could, is exalted to the right hand of God, having all judgment committed to him, having beforehand, in his death, judged, sentenced, and overcome Satan, the prince of this world, the chief instigator of his crucifiers, who had the power of death. And this I take to be the clear, genuine meaning of this place, not excluding the efficacy of the Spirit, working in the same manner, though not to the same degree, for the same end, in the majesty of the word, to the end of the world. But what this is to universal redemption, let them that can understand it keep it to themselves, for I am confident they will never.be able to make it out to others.

Proof 5. "God hath testified, both by his word and his oath, that he would that his Son should so far save as to work a redemption for all men, and likewise that he should bring all to the knowledge of the truth, that there-through redemption might be wrought in and upon them, 1 Tim. ii. 4, with John iii. 17. So he willeth not, nor hath any pleasure in, the death of him (even the wicked) that dieth, but rather that he turn and live, Ezek. xviii. 23, 32, xxxiii. 11. And dare any of us say, the God of truth saith and sweareth that of which he hath no inward and serious meaning? O far be such blasphemy from us!"

Ans. First, This assertion, "That God testifieth, by his word and oath, that he would that Christ should so far save us," etc., is a bold calling of God to witness that which he never affirmed, nor did it ever enter into his heart; for he hath revealed his will that Christ should save to the utmost them that come to him, and not save so far or so far, as is boldly, ignorantly, and falsely intimated. Let men beware of provoking God to their own confusion; he will not be a witness to the lie of false hearts. Secondly, "That Christ should so bring all to the knowledge of the truth, that there-through redemption might be wrought in and upon them," is another bold corruption of the word, and false-witness-bearing in the name of God. Is it a small thing for you to weary and seduce men? will you weary our God also? Thirdly, For places of Scripture corrupted to the sense imposed: In John iii. 17, God is said to "send his Son, that the world through him might be saved;" not be saved so far or so far, but saved "from their sins," Matt. i. 21, and "to the uttermost," Heb. vii. 25: so that the world of God's elect, who only are so saved, is only there to be understood, as hath been proved. In 1 Tim. ii. 4, there is something of the will of God for the saving of all sorts of men, as hath been declared; nothing conducing to the bold assertion used in this place. Fourthly, To those are added that of Ezek. xviii. 23, that God hath no "pleasure at all that the wicked should die;" and, verse 32, "no pleasure in the death of him that dieth." Now, though these texts are exceeding useless to the business in hand, and might probably have some colour of universal vocation, but none possibly of universal redemption, there being no mention of Christ or his death in the place from whence they are cited; yet because our adversaries are frequently knitting knots from this place to inveigle and hamper the simple, I shall add some few observations upon it to clear the meaning of the text, and demonstrate how it belongs nothing at all to the business in hand.

First, then, let us consider to whom and of whom these words are spoken. Is it to and of all men, or only to the house of Israel? Doubtless these last; they are only intended, they only are spoken to: "Hear now, O house of Israel," verse 25. Now, will it follow that because God saith he delights not in the death of the house of Israel, to whom he revealed his mind, and required their repentance and conversion, that therefore he saith so of all, even those to whom he never revealed his will by such ways as to them, nor called to repentance, Ps. cxlvii. 19, 20? So that the very ground-work of the whole conclusion is removed by this first observation. Secondly, "God willeth not the death of a sinner," is either, "God purposeth and determineth he shall not die," or, "God commandeth that he shall do those things wherein he may live." If the first, why are they not all saved? why do sinners die? for there is an immutability in the counsel of God, Heb. vi. 17; "His counsel shall stand, and he will do all his pleasure," Isa. xlvi. 10. If the latter way, by commanding, then the sense is, that the Lord commandeth that those whom he calleth should do their duty, that they may not die (although he knows that this they cannot do without his assistance); now, what this makes to general redemption, I know not. Thirdly, To add no more, this whole place, with the scope, aim, and intention of the prophet in it, is miserably mistaken by our adversaries, and wrested to that whereof there is not the least thought in the text. The words are a part of the answer which the Lord gives to the repining Jews, concerning their proverb, "The fathers have eaten sour grapes, and the children's teeth are set on edge." Now, about what did they use this proverb? Why, "concerning the land of Israel," verse 2, the land of their habitation, which was laid waste by the sword (as they affirmed) for the sins of their fathers, themselves being innocent. So that it is about God's temporal judgments in overturning their land and nation that this dispute is; wherein the Lord justifieth himself by declaring the equity of these judgments by reason of their sins, even those sins for which the land devoured them and spewed them out; telling them that his justice is, that for such things they should surely die, their blood should be upon them, verse 13,—they shall be slain with the sword, and cut off by those judgments which they had deserved: not that the shedding of their blood and casting out of their carcases was a thing in itself so pleasurable or desirable to him as that he did it only for his own will, for let them leave their abominations, and try whether their lives were not prolonged in peace. This being the plain, genuine scope and meaning of this place, at the first view presenting itself to every unprejudiced man, I have often admired how so many strange conclusions for a general purpose of showing mercy to all, universal vocation and redemption, have been wrested from it; as also, how it came to be produced to give colour to that heap of blasphemy which our author calleth his fifth proof.

Proof 6. "The very words and phrases used by the Holy Ghost in Scripture, speaking of the death of Christ, and the ransom and propitiation, to whom it belongs, and who may seek it, and in believing find life, implies no less than all men. As to instance: "All nations," Matt. xxviii. 19, 20; "the ends of the earth," Isa. xlv. 22, xlix. 6; "every creature," Mark xvi. 15; "all," 2 Cor. v. 14, 15, 1 Tim. ii. 6; "every man," Heb. ii. 9; "the world," John iii. 16, 17, 2 Cor. v. 19; "the whole world," 1 John ii. 2; "that which was lost," Luke xix. 10; "sinners," Matt. ix. 13; "unjust," 1 Pet. iii. 18; "ungodly," Rom. v. 6; and that whosoever of these repent and believe in Christ shall receive his grace, John iii. 16, 18, Acts x. 43. Now, all these so often and indifferently used, were it not pride and error to devise glosses to restrain the sense the Scripture holdeth forth, so full and large for all men?"

Ans. First, This argument, taken from the words and phrases whereby the object of the death of Christ is in the Scripture expressed, is that which filleth up both pages of this book, being repeated, and most of the places here cited urged, a hundred times over; and yet it is so far from being any pressing argument, as that indeed it is nothing but a bare naked repetition of the thing in debate, concluding according to his own persuasion; for the main *quære* between us is, whether the words *all* and *the world* be to be taken universally? He saith so, and he saith so; which is all the proof we have, repeating over the thing to be proved instead of a proof. Secondly, For those places which affirm Christ to die for "sinners," "ungodly," "that which was lost," etc.,—as Luke xix. 10; Matt. ix. 13; 1 Pet. iii. 18; Rom. v. 6,—I have before declared how exceedingly unserviceable they are to universal redemption. Thirdly, For those places where the words " all," " every man," " the world," " the whole world," are used, we have had them over and over; and they likewise have been considered. Fourthly, For those expressions of " all nations," Matt. xxviii. 19, 20, " every creature," Mark xvi. 15, used concerning them to whom the gospel is preached, I say,—*First,* That they do not comprise all individuals, nay, not all nations at all times, much less all singular persons of all nations if we look upon the accomplishment and fulfilling of that command; neither, *de facto,* was the gospel ever so preached to all, although there be a fitness and a suitableness in the dispensation thereof to be so preached to all, as was declared. *Secondly,* The command of preaching the gospel to all doth not in the least manner prove that Christ died with an intention to redeem all; but it hath other grounds and other ends, as hath been manifested. *Thirdly,* That the ransom belongs to all to whom it is proposed we deny; there be other ends of that proposal; and Christ will say to some of them that he never knew them: therefore, certainly, he did not lay down his life for them. *Fourthly,* " The ends of the earth," Isa. xlv. 22, are those that look up to God from all parts, and are saved; which surely are not all and every one. And Christ being given to be a "salvation unto the end of the earth," chap. xlix. 6, is to do no more among the Gentiles than God promiseth in the same place that he shall do for his own people,— even " gather the preserved of Israel;" so shall he bear forth the salvation of God, and gather the preserved remnant of his elect to the ends of the earth.

And now, I hope, I need not mind the intelligent reader that the author of these collections could not have invented a more ready way for the ruin of the thesis which he seeks to maintain than by producing those places of Scripture last recounted for the confirmation of it, granting that *all* and *the world* are no more than " all the ends of the earth," mentioned in Isa. xlv. 22, xlix. 6; it being evident beyond denial that by these expressions, in both these places, only the elect of God and believers are clearly intimated: so that, interpreting the one by the other, in those places where *all* and *the world* are spoken of, those only are intended. "If pride and error" had not taken full possession of the minds of men, they could not so far deny their own sense and reason as to contradict themselves and the plain texts of Scripture for the maintenance of their false and corrupt opinions.

Proof 7. "That whereas there are certain high and peculiar privileges of the Spirit contained in the New Testament, sealed by the
blood of Christ, which belong not to all men, but only to the saints,
the called and chosen of the Lord, and when they are alone distinctly
mentioned, they are even so spoken of as belonging to them only,
Matt. xiii. 11; John xiv. 17, 21–23, xvi. 13–15, xvii. 19, 20; Acts
ii. 38, 39; 1 Cor. ii. 9, 14; Heb. ix. 15, viii.; 1 Pet. ii. 3, 9;
yet many of these peculiar privileges are so spoken of as joined together with the ransom and propitiation, which belongs to all. Then
are they not spoken of in such a restraining and exclusive manner,
or with such appropriating words, but so, and with such words, as
room is left to apply the ransom to all men, in speech; and withal,
so hold out the privileges to them that believe that are proper to
them, that they may both have their comfort and especial hope, and
also hold forth the ransom and keep open the door for others, in
belief and receipt of the propitiation, to come in and partake with
them. And so it is said for his "sheep," and for "many;" but nowhere
but only for his sheep, or but only for many: which is a strong proof
of the ransom for all men, as is shown, chap. iii. x."

Ans. The strength of this proof, as to the business in hand, is
wholly hid from me; neither do I perceive how it may receive any
such tolerable application as to deserve the name of a proof, as to
the main thesis intended to be maintained. The force which it hath
is in an observation which, if it hath any sense, is neither true nor
once attempted to be made good; for,—First, That there are peculiar high privileges belonging to the saints and called of God is a
thing which needs no proof. Amongst these is the death of Christ for
them, not as saints, but as elect, which, by the benefit of that death and
blood-shedding, are to be made saints, and accounted to be the holy
ones of God: for " he redeemed his church with his own blood,"
Acts xx. 28; he "loved and gave himself for it," Eph. v. 25; even
"us," Tit. ii. 14;—even as divers of those [privileges] here intimated
are expressly assigned unto them, as elect, such as those, John xvii. 19,
20; amongst which also, as in the same rank with them, is reckoned
Jesus' "sanctifying himself for their sakes," that is to be an oblation,
verse 19. In a word, all peculiar saving privileges belong only to
God's elect, purchased for them, and them alone, by the blood of
Jesus Christ, Eph. i. 3, 4. Secondly, For the other part of the
observation, that where mention is made of these together with
the ransom, there is room left to extend the ransom to all, I
answer,—*First*, This is said, indeed, but not once attempted to be
proved. We have but small cause to believe the author, in any thing
of this importance, upon his bare word. *Secondly*, For the "leaving
of room for the application," I perceive that if it be not left, ye will
make it, though ye justle the true sense of the Scripture quite out

of its place. *Thirdly*, I have already showed that where "many" are mentioned, the ransom only (as ye use to speak) is expressed, as also where "sheep" are spoken of; the like is said where the word "all" is used;—so that there is not the least difference. *Fourthly*, In divers places the ransom of Christ and those other peculiar privileges (which indeed are fruits of it) are so united together, as it is impossible to apply the latter to *some* and the other to *all*, being all of them restrained to his saved ones only, Rev. v. 9, 10. The redemption of his people by the ransom of his blood, and their making kings and priests, are united, and no room left for the extending of the ransom to all, it being punctually assigned to those saved crowned ones, distinguished from the rest of the nations and languages from among whom they were taken, who were passed by in the payment of the ransom; which is directly opposite to all the sense which I can observe in this observation. *Fifthly*, Of "sheep, and sheep only," enough before.

Proof 8. "The restoration wrought by Christ in his own body for mankind is set forth in Scripture to be as large and full for all men, and of as much force, as the fall of the first Adam, by and in himself, for all men; in which respect the first Adam is said to have been a figure of Christ, the second Adam, Rom. iii. 22–25, v. 12, 14, 18; 1 Cor. xv. 21, 22, 45–47: as is before shown, chap. viii."

Ans. First, It is most true that Christ and Adam are compared together (in respect of the righteousness of the one, communicated to them that are his, and the disobedience and transgression of the other, in like manner communicated to all them that are of him) in some of the places here mentioned, as Rom. v. 12, 18. But evidently the comparison is not instituted between the righteousness of Christ and the disobedience of Adam *extensively*, in respect of the *object*, but *intensively*, in respect of the *efficacy* of the one and the other; the apostle asserting the effectualness of the righteousness of Christ unto justification, to answer the prevalency of the sin of Adam unto condemnation,—that even as the transgression of Adam brought a guilt of condemnation upon all them that are his natural seed, so the righteousness of Christ procured the free gift of grace unto justification towards all them that are his, his spiritual seed, that were the children given unto him of his Father.

Secondly, 1 Cor. xv. 21, 22, speaketh of the resurrection from the dead, and that only of believers; for though he mentions them all, verse 22, "In Christ shall all be made alive," yet, verse 23, he plainly interprets those *all* to be all that are "Christ's:" not but that the other dead shall rise also, but that it is a resurrection to glory, by virtue of the resurrection of Christ, which the apostle here treats of; which certainly all shall not have.

Thirdly, The comparison between Christ and Adam, verse 45 (to

speak nothing of the various reading of that place), is only in respect
of the principles which they had, and were intrusted withal to communicate to others: "Adam a living soul," or a "living creature;"
there was in him a principle of life natural, to be communicated to his
posterity;—"Christ a quickening Spirit," giving life, grace, and spirit
to his. And here I would desire that it may be observed, that all the
comparison that is anywhere instituted between Christ and Adam still
comes to one head, and aims at one thing,—namely, that they were as
two common stocks or roots, communicating to them that are ingrafted
into them (that is, into Adam *naturally*, by generation; into Christ
spiritually, by regeneration) that wherewith they were replenished;—
Adam, sin, guilt, and disobedience; Christ, righteousness, peace, and
justification. [As] for the number of those that do thus receive these
things from one and the other, the consideration of it is exceedingly
alien from the scope, aim, and end of the apostle in the places where
the comparison is instituted.

Fourthly, It is true, Rom. iii. 23, it is said, "All have sinned, and
come short of the glory of God," which the apostle had at large proved
before, thereby to manifest that there was no salvation to be attained
but only by Jesus Christ; but if ye will ask to whom this righteousness
of Christ is extended, and that redemption which is in his blood, he
telleth you plainly, it is "unto all and upon all them that believe,"
verse 22, whether they be Jews or Gentiles, "for there is no difference."

Proof 9. "The Lord Jesus Christ hath sent and commanded his
servants to preach the gospel to all nations, to every creature, and to
tell them withal that whoever believeth and is baptized shall be
saved, Matt. xxviii. 19, 20; Mark xvi. 15, 16: and his servants have
so preached to all, 2 Cor. v. 19; Rom. x. 13, 18. And our Lord
Jesus Christ will make it to appear one day that he hath not sent
his servants upon a false errand, nor put a lie in their mouths, nor
wished them to dissemble, in offering that to all which they knew
belonged but to some, even to fewest of all, but to speak truth, Isa.
xliv. 26, lxi. 8; 1 Tim. i. 12."

Ans. The strength of this proof is not easily apparent, nor manifest wherein it lieth, in what part or words of it: for,—First, It is
true, Christ commanded his apostles to "preach the gospel to all
nations and every creature,"—to tell them "that whosoever believeth
shall be saved," Matt. xxviii. 19, 20, Mark xvi. 15, 16; that is, without distinction of persons or nations, to call all men to whom the providence of God should direct them, and from whom the Spirit of God
should not withhold them (as from them, Acts xvi. 6, 7), warning them
to repent and believe the gospel. Secondly, It is also true, that, in
obedience unto this command, his servants did beseech men so to do,
and to be reconciled unto God, even all over the nations, without
distinction of any, but where they were forbidden, as above, labour-

ing to spread the gospel to the ends of the earth, and not to tie it up to the confines of Jewry, 2 Cor. v. 19, 20; Rom. x. 18.   Most certain also it is, that the Lord Jesus Christ sent not his servants with a lie, to offer that to all which belonged only to some, but to speak the truth; of which there needs no proof.   But now, what can be concluded from hence for universal redemption is not easily discernible.

Perhaps some will say it is in this, that if Christ did not die for all to whom the word is preached, then how can they that preach it offer Christ to all?   A poor proof, God wot!   For,—First, The gospel was never preached to all and every one, nor is there any such thing affirmed in the places cited; and ye are to prove that Christ died for all, as well those that never hear of the gospel as those that do.   Secondly, What do the preachers of the gospel offer to them to whom the word is preached?   Is it not life and salvation through Christ, upon the condition of faith and repentance?   And doth not the truth of this offer consist in this, that every one that believeth shall be saved?   And doth not that truth stand firm and inviolable, so long as there is an all-sufficiency in Christ to save all that come unto him?   Hath God intrusted the ministers of the gospel with his intentions, purposes, and counsels, or with his commands and promises?   Is it a lie, to tell men that he that believeth shall be saved, though Christ did not die for some of them?   Such proofs as these had need be well proved themselves, or they will conclude the thing intended very weakly.

Proof 10.   " The Lord willeth believers to pray even for the unjust and their persecutors, Matt. v. 44, 48; Luke vi. 28; yea, even 'for all men;' yea, even 'for kings and all in authority,' when few in authority loved Christianity.   Yet he said not, some of that sort, but, 'For all in authority;' and that on this ground,—it is good in the sight of God, 'who will have all men saved, and come to the knowledge of the truth,' Luke x. 5; 1 Tim. ii. 1–4.   Surely there is a door of life opened for all men, 2 Tim. i. 10; for God hath not said to the seed of Israel, 'Seek ye me in vain,' Isa. xliv. 19.   He will not have his children pray for vain things."

Ans. The strength of this proof lieth in supposing,—First, That *indefinite* assertions are to be interpreted as equivalent to *universal;* which is false, Rom. iv., v.   Secondly, That by " all," 1 Tim. ii. 1, is not meant all sorts of men, and the word *all* is not to be taken distributively, when the apostle, by an enumeration of divers sorts, gives an evident demonstration of the distribution intended.   Thirdly, That we are bound to pray for every singular man that he may be saved; which,—1. We have no warrant, rule, precept, or example for; 2. It is contrary to the apostolical precept, 1 John v. 16; 3. To our Saviour's example, John xvii. 9; 4. To the counsel and purpose of God, in the general made known to us, Rom. ix. 11, 12, 15, xi. 7, where evidently our praying for all is but for all sorts of men, excluding none, and that those may believe who are ordained to eternal life. Fourthly, It supposeth that there is nothing else that we are to pray for men but that they may be saved by Christ; which is apparently false, Jer. xxix. 7.   Fifthly, That our ground of praying for any is an assurance that Christ died for them in particular; which is not true, Acts viii. 22, 24.   Sixthly, It most splendidly takes for granted that our duty is to be conformed to God's secret mind, his purpose and counsel.   Until every one of these supposals be made good, (which never a one of them will be very suddenly), there is no help in this proof nor strength in this argument, "We must pray for all; therefore God intends by the death of Christ to save all and every one," its sophistry and weakness being apparent. From our duty to God's purpose is no good conclusion, though from his command to our duty be most certain.

Proof 11. "The Lord hath given forth his word and promise to be with his servants so preaching the gospel to all, and with his people so praying for all where they come, that they may go on with confidence in both, Matt. xxviii. 20; 1 Tim. ii. 3, 8; Luke x. 5; Isa. liv. 17.

Ans. That God will be with his people, whether preaching or praying, according to his will and their own duty, is as apparent as it is that this makes nothing for universal redemption; than which what can be more evident.

Proof 12. "The Lord hath already performed and made good his word to his servants and people, upon some of all sorts of men and all sorts of sinners, showing them mercy to the very end, that none might exclude themselves, but all be encouraged to repent, believe, and hope thereby, Acts ii., iii., viii.–xi., xvi., xix., xxviii.; 1 Cor. vi. 10, 11; 1 Tim. i. 13–16."

Ans. If ye had told us that God had already made good his word to his servants, in saving all and every man, and proved it clearly, ye had evidently and undeniably confirmed the main opinion; but now, affirming only that he hath showed mercy to some of all sorts, and all sorts of sinners, that others of the like sort (as are the remainder of his elect, yet uncalled) might be induced to believe, ye have evidently betrayed your own cause, and established that of your adversaries, showing how the Lord in the event declareth on their side, saving in the blood of Jesus only some of all sorts, as they affirm, not all and every one, which your tenet leads you to.

Proof 13. "The blessing of life hath streamed in this doctrine of the love of God to mankind; yea, in the tender and spiritual discovery of the grace of God to mankind (in the ransom given and atonement made by Christ for all men, with the fruits thereof) hath God, in the first place, overcome his chosen ones to believe and turn to God, Acts xiii. 48; Titus ii. 11, 13, iii. 4, 5."

Ans. First, That the freedom of God's grace, and the transcendency of his eternal love towards men, with the sending of his Son to die for them, to recover them to himself from sin and Satan, is a most effectual motive, and (when set on by the Spirit of grace) a most certain operative principle of the conversion of God's elect, we most willingly acknowledge. It is that wherein our hearts rejoice, whereby they were endeared, and for which we desire to return thankful obedience every moment. But that ever this was effectual, extending this love to all, or at least that any effectualness is in that aggravation of it, we utterly deny; and that,—1. Because it is false, and a corrupting of the word of God, as hath been showed; and of a lie there can be no good consequence. 2. It quite enervates and plucks out the efficacy of this heavenly motive, by turning the most intense and incomparable love of God towards his elect into a common desire, wishing, and affection of his nature (which, indeed, is opposite to his nature), failing of its end and purpose; which might consist with the eternal destruction of all mankind, as I shall abundantly demonstrate, if Providence call me to the other part of this controversy, concerning the cause of sending Jesus Christ. Secondly, There is nothing of this common love to all in the places urged; for,—1. The "grace" mentioned, Tit. ii. 11, 13, is the grace that certainly brings salvation, which that common love doth not, and was the cause of sending Christ, "that he might redeem us from all iniquity, and purify to himself a peculiar people, zealous of good works;" where our redemption and sanctification are asserted to be the immediate end of the oblation of Jesus Christ; which how destructive it is to universal redemption hath been formerly declared. 2. So also is that "love and kindness" mentioned, chap. iii. 4, 5, such as by which we receive the "washing of regeneration and renewing of the Holy Ghost," verse 5; and justification, and adoption to heirship of eternal life, verse 7;—which, whether it be a common or a peculiar love, let all men judge. 3. Acts xiii. 47 (for verse 48, there cited, contains as clear a restriction of this love of God to his elect, as can be desired) sets out the extent of the mercy of God in Christ, through the preaching of the gospel to the Gentiles also, and not only to the Jews, as was foretold by Isaiah, chap. xlix. 6; which is far enough from giving any colour to the universality of grace, it being nothing but the same affirmation which ye have John xi. 52, of "gathering together in one the children of God that were scattered abroad."

Proof 14. "Those that, when the gospel comes, and any spiritual light therein, to them, when they refuse to believe, and suffer themselves to be withdrawn by other things, they are affirmed to love or choose "darkness rather than light," John iii. 19, (which how could it

be, if no light in truth were for them?) in following lying vanities; to
forsake their own mercies, Jonah ii. 8; to harden their own hearts,
Rom. ii. 5; to lose their souls, Matt. xvi. 26; and to destroy themselves, Hos. xiii. 9. And they being from Adam fallen into darkness,
hardness, and their souls [lost], and death passed on them, how could
these things be if by Jesus Christ no life had been attained, no atonement made, no restoration of their souls, nor means procured and
used, that they might be saved? God is no hard master, to gather
where he hath not strown."

Ans. The sum of this argument is, That those who do not believe
upon the preaching of the gospel are the cause of their own ruin
and destruction; therefore, Jesus Christ died for all and every man
in the world. Now, though it cannot but be apprehended that it is
time cast away and labour lost, to answer such consequences as these,
yet I must add a few observations, lest any scruple should remain
with the weakest reader; as,—First, All have not the gospel preached
to them, nay, from the beginning of the world, the greatest part of men
have been passed by in the dispensation of the means of grace, Rom.
ii. 14; Acts xiv. 16, xvii. 30,—" winked at." All these, then, must be
left out in this conclusion, which renders it altogether useless to the
business in hand; for the universality of redemption falls to the
ground if any one soul be not intended in the payment of the ransom.
Secondly, It is not the disbelieving the death of Christ for every individual soul that ever was or shall be (which to believe is nowhere
in Scripture required) that is the cause of man's destruction, but a
not-believing in the all-sufficiency of the passion and oblation of
Jesus Christ for sinners, so as to accept of the mercy procured thereby,
upon those terms and conditions that it is held forth in the gospel;
which doth not attend the purpose and intention of God for whom
Christ should die, but the sufficiency and efficacy of his death for all
that receive him in a due manner, he being the only true way, life,
and light, no other name being given under heaven whereby men
may be saved. It is a " loving darkness rather than light," as in
John iii. 19, the place urged in the proof; which word μᾶλλον, "rather,"
there, doth not institute a comparison between their love of darkness
and light, as though they loved both, but darkness chiefly; but plainly
intimates an opposition unto the love of light by a full love of darkness. And this "men" are said to do; which being spoken indefinitely,
according to the rules of interpreting Scripture followed by this
author, should be taken universally, for all men: but we are contented
that it be the most of those men to whom Christ preached; for some
also of them " received him," to whom he " gave this privilege, that
they should become the sons of God," John i. 12.

Why ye should interpret " love" here by " choose," as though either
the words were equivalent, or the word in the original would signify

either, I can see no reason, for both these are exceeding false. There is a difference between loving and choosing; and as for ἠγάπησαν, he would be as bad a translator as ye are an interpreter that should render it " they choose." Now, what is this loving of darkness more than light, but a following and cleaving in affection and practice to the ways wherein they were, being alienated from the life of God, labouring in the unfruitful works of darkness, and refusing to embrace the heavenly doctrine of the gospel, holding forth peace and reconciliation with God through Christ, with life and immortality thereby. To conclude from hence, [that] therefore Christ died for all and every man in the world, because the greatest part of them to whom he preached the gospel did not believe, is a wild kind of reasoning; much better may we infer, that therefore he died not for all men, because it is not " given unto them, for his sake, to believe on him," Phil. i. 29.

Neither will that parenthesis—"Which how could it be, if no light in truth were for them?"—give any light to the former inference; for if the word " for" should denote the intention and purpose of God, the truth is, we dare not say that God intends and purposeth that they should receive light who do not, lest by so saying we should make the Strength of Israel to be like to ourselves, and contradict him who hath said, " My counsel shall stand, and I will do all my pleasure," Isa. xlvi. 10. " The counsel of the LORD standeth for ever," Ps. xxxiii. 11; he being " the LORD, and changing not," Mal. iii. 6; James i. 17; 2 Tim. ii. 19; Rom. ix. 11. If by " for them," ye mean such a stock and fulness of light and grace as there is of light in the sun for all the men in the world, though some be blind and cannot see it, then we say that such a light there is for all in the gospel to whom it is preached, and their own blindness is the sole cause of their not receiving it: so that this hath not got the stone a step forward, which still rolls back upon him.

Thirdly, The other scriptures urged have not so much as any colour that should give advantage to consider them, as with any reference to the business in hand. That of Jonah ii. 8 is concerning such as forsake the true God to follow idols, so forfeiting the mercies, temporal and spiritual, which from the true God they had before received. Rom. ii. 5 speaks of the Gentiles who had the works of God to teach them, and the patience of God to wait upon them, yet made no other use of them both than, by vile rebellions, to add new degrees of farther hardness upon their own hearts. That of men's losing their souls, Matt. xvi. 26, and destroying themselves (Hos. xiii. 9) by sin, is of equal force with what went before.

But, fourthly, The close of this reason seems to intimate a farther view of the author, which at the first view doth not appear,—namely, that all men are in a restored condition by Christ; not a door of mercy opened for them all, but that they are all actually restored into grace and favour, from which if they do not fall, they shall surely be saved. And the argument whereby he proves this is, because, being lost in Adam, they could not be said to lose themselves unless they were restored by Christ; being darkness and hardness in him, unless all were enlightened and mollified by Christ, they could not be said to love darkness nor to harden themselves. Now, if this be his intention (as it is too apparent that so it is), I must say something,—first, To the argument; secondly, To the thing itself. And,—

First, For the argument, it is this:—Because by original sin men are guilty of death and damnation, therefore they cannot by actual sins make sure of and aggravate that condemnation, and so bring upon themselves a death unto death: or, Because there is a native, inbred hardness of heart in man, therefore, none can add farther degrees of contracted hardness and induration by actual rebellions; that because men are blind, therefore they cannot undervalue light (when indeed the reason why they do so is because they are blind); that men who have time, and opportunity, and means, to save their souls, cannot be said to lose them, that is, to be condemned, unless their souls were in a saved condition before. Now, this is one of the proofs which, in the close, is called "plain, and according to Scripture;" when, indeed, nothing can be more contrary to reason, Scripture, and the principles of the oracles of God, than this and some other of them are. I shall add no more, knowing that no reader can be so weak as to conceive that the refusing of a proposed remedy, accompanied with infinite other despites done to the Lord, is not sufficient to make men guilty of their own condemnation. I speak of those that enjoy the preaching of the gospel.

Secondly, For the thing itself, or an actual restoration of all men by Christ into such a state (as is intimated) as they had at the first in Adam (I mean in respect of covenant, not innocency), which I take to be the meaning of the author, and that because in another place he positively affirms that it is so, and that all are justified by Christ, though how it should be so he is not able to declare. To this, then, I say,—1. That there is nothing in the Scripture that should give the least colour to this gross error, nor can any thing be produced so much as probably sounding that way. 2. It is contrary,—(1.) To very many places, affirming that we are "dead in trespasses and sins," Eph. ii. 1; that "except we be born again, we cannot see the kingdom of God," John iii. 3; that until we come by faith to Christ, "the wrath of God abideth on us," chap. iii. 36; with those innumerable places which discover the universal alienation of all men from God, until actual peace and reconciliation be made through Christ. (2.) To the very nature and essence of the new covenant of grace, proceeding from the free mercy of God to his elect, carried along with distinguishing promises from the first to the last of them, putting a difference between the seed of the woman and the seed of the serpent, as well in the members as in the Head; being effective and really working every good thing it promised in and towards all to whom it doth belong (which certainly it doth not in all), and being everywhere said to be made with the people of God, or those whom he will own, in opposition to the world;—of all which, and divers other things, so plentifully affirmed of it in the Scripture, not one can be true if all men receive a restoration by Christ into covenant. (3.) To the eternal purpose of God in election and reprobation; of which the latter is a resolution to leave men in their fallen condition, without any reparation by Christ. (4.) It is attended with very many strange, absurd, groundless consequences; as,—

[1.] That all infants dying before they come to the use of reason and the committing of actual sin must necessarily be saved (although our Saviour hath said, that "except a man be born again, he cannot see the kingdom of God," John iii. 3; and Paul from him, that the children of infidels are "unclean," 1 Cor. vii. 14;—now no unclean thing shall enter the new Jerusalem, Rev. xxi. 27), whereby the infants of Turks, Pagans, infidels, persecutors, are placed in a far more happy condition than the apostles of Christ, if they depart in their infancy,—than the best of believers, who are not, according to the authors of this doctrine, out of danger of eternal perishing.   [2.] That there is no more required of any to be saved than a continuance in the estate wherein he was born (that is, in covenant, actually restored by Christ thereunto). when the whole word of God crieth out that all such as so abide shall certainly perish everlastingly.   [3.] That every one that perisheth in the whole world falls away from the grace of the new covenant, though the promises thereof are, that there shall never be any total falling away of them that are in covenant.   [4.] That none can come unto Christ but such as have in their own persons fallen from him, for all others abide in him.

Innumerable other such consequences as these do necessarily attend this false, heretical assertion, that is so absolutely destructive to the free grace of God.   I doubt not but that such proofs as these will make considering men farther search into the matter intended to be proved, and yield them good advantages to discover the wretched lie of the whole.

Fifthly, To the last words of the proof I answer, that God sowed that seed in Adam, and watered it with innumerable temporal blessings towards all, and spiritual in some, whose fruit he will come to require from the world of unbelievers, and not in the blood of Jesus

Christ, any farther than as it hath been certainly proposed to some of them and despised.

Proof 15. "God's earnest expostulations, contendings, charges, and protestations, even to such as whereof many perished, Rom. ix. 27; Isa. x. 22. As, to instance :—'O that there were such an heart in them, that they would fear me,' etc., 'that it might be well with them!' Deut. v. 29. 'What could have been done more to my vine-yard, that I have not done in it?' etc., Isa. v. 4, 5. 'What iniquity have your fathers found in me, that they are gone far from me?' ᵀer. ii. 5. 'Have I been a wilderness unto Israel? a land of darkness? wherefore say my peoₗle, We are lords; we will come no more unto thee?' verse 31. 'O my people, what have I done unto thee? wherein have I wearied thee? testify against me,' Mic. vi. 3. 'How often would I have gathered,' etc., 'and ye would not!' Matt. xxiii. 37. 'O that my people had hearkened unto me!' etc., 'I should soon have subdued their enemies,' etc., Ps. lxxxi. 13, 14. 'Because I have called, and ye refused; I have stretched out my hand, and no man regarded,' etc., Prov. i. 24–31. 'Because, when they knew God, they glorified him not as God,' etc., Rom. i. 21, 28. 'Therefore thou art inexcusable, O man,' etc. 'Thou, after thy hardness and impenitent heart, treasurest up unto thyself wrath,' etc., Rom. ii. 1, 5. No Christian, I hope, will reply against God, and say, 'Thou never meantest us good; there was no ransom given for us, no atonement made for us, no good done us, no mercy shown us,—nothing, in truth, whereby we might have been saved, nothing but an empty show, a bare pretence.' But if any should reason so evilly, yet shall not such answers stand."

Ans. To this collection of expostulations I shall very briefly answer with some few observations, manifesting of how little use it is to the business in hand; as,—First, That in all these expostula-tions there is no mention of any ransom given or atonement made for them that perish (which is the thing pretended in the close), but they are all about temporal mercies, with the outward means of grace. To which [add] what we observed in the argument last foregoing,—namely, that as God doth not expostulate with them about it, no more shall they with God about it at the last day. Not that I deny that there is sufficient matter of expostulation with sinners about the blood of Christ and the ransom paid thereby, that so the elect may be drawn and wrought upon to faith and repentance, and be-lievers more and more endeared to forsake all ungodliness and worldly lusts, to live unto him who died for them, and that others may be left more inexcusable; only for the present there are no such expostu-lations here expressed, nor can any be found holding out the purpose and intention of God in Christ towards them that perish. Secondly, That all these places urged (excepting only those of Rom. i. 28, ii. 5, which apparently and evidently lay the inexcusableness of sin upon that knowledge which they might have had, by the works of creation and providence, of God, as eternal, almighty, and powerful, without the least intimation of any ransom, atonement, and redemption),— that all the rest, I say, are spoken to and of those that enjoyed the means of grace, who, in the days wherein those expostulations were used towards them, were a very small portion of all men; so that from what is said to them nothing can be concluded of the mind and purpose of God towards all others, Ps. cxlvii. 19, 20,—which is destructive to the general ransom. Thirdly, That there are no men, especially none of those that enjoy the means of grace, but do receive so many mercies from God, as that he may justly plead with them about their unthankfulness and not returning of obedience proportionable to the mercies and light which they received. Fourthly, It is confessed, I hope by all, that there are none of those things for the want whereof God expostulateth with the sons of men, but that he could, if it so seemed good before him, effectually work them in their hearts, at least, by the exceeding greatness of his power: so that these things cannot be declarative of his purpose, which he might, if he pleased, fulfil; "for who hath resisted his will," Rom. ix. 19. Fifthly, That desires and wishings should properly be ascribed unto God is exceedingly opposite to his all-sufficiency and the perfection of his nature; they are no more in him than he hath eyes, ears, and hands. These things are to be understood Θεοπρεπῶς. Sixthly, It is evident that all these are nothing but pathetical declarations of our duty in the enjoyment of the means of grace, strong convictions of the stubborn and disobedient, with a full justification of the excellency of God's ways to draw us to the performance of our duties; *ergo*, Christ died for all men, ὅπερ ἔδει δεῖξαι. Seventhly, Some particular places, that seem to be of more weight than the rest, have been already examined.

Proof 16. "The Scripture's manner of setting forth the sin of such as despise and refuse this grace, and their estate, and the persons perishing; as to say they 'turn the grace of God into wantonness,' Jude 4; 'tread under foot the Son of God, profane the blood of the covenant, with which they were sanctified, offer despite to the Spirit of grace,' Heb. x. 29; 'deny the Lord that bought them,' 2 Pet. ii. 1; 'they perish for whom Christ died,' 1 Cor. viii. 11; 'trees twice dead, plucked up by the roots,' Jude 12, 13; 'and bring upon themselves swift destruction,' 2 Pet. ii. 1. And how could all this be if God had given his Son in no sort for them? if Christ had shed no blood to procure remission for them? if he had not bought them, nor had any grace or life by his Spirit to bestow on them?"

Ans. First, There are in this proof three places of Scripture which are frequently urged in this cause,—namely, Heb. x. 29; 2 Pet. ii. 1; 1 Cor. viii. 11: and, therefore, they have been considered already apart at large; where it was evidenced that they no way incline to the assertion of that whereunto they are violently wrested, and their sense for that end perverted. Secondly, For those other places out of Jude 4, 12, 13, I cannot perceive how they can be hooked into the business in hand. Some are said, verse 4, to "turn the grace of God into wantonness,"—that is, to abuse the doctrine of the gospel and the mercy of God revealed thereby, to encourage themselves in sin; whence to conclude that therefore Jesus Christ died for all men is an uncouth inference, especially the apostle intimating that he died not for these abusers of his grace, affirming that they were "before of old ordained to condemnation;" which ordination standeth in direct opposition to that love which moved the Lord to send his Son Christ to procure the salvation of any. The strength of the proof lieth in the other places, which have been already considered.

Proof 17. "Jesus Christ, by virtue of his death, shall be their judge, and by the gospel, in which they might have been saved, will he judge them to a second death; and how can that be, if he never died the first death for them, and if there were not truth in his gospel preached to them? Rom. xiv. 9–12; Phil. ii. 7–11; Rom. ii. 16; John xii. 47, 48, 50."

Ans. First, That Jesus Christ shall be judge of all, and that all judgment is already committed to him, is confessed: that it doth not hence follow that he died for all hath been already declared, unless ye will affirm that he died for the devils also, because they also must be judged by him. Secondly, That all shall be judged by the gospel, even such as never heard word of it, is directly contrary to the gospel: "For as many as have sinned without law shall also perish without law: and as many as have sinned in the law shall be judged by the law," Rom. ii. 12. Every man, doubtless, shall be judged according to the light and rule which he did or might have enjoyed, and not according to that whereof he was invincibly deprived. Thirdly, That Christ should be said to die only the first death is neither an expression of the word, nor can be collected from thence; he died the death which was in the curse of the law: but of this only by the way. Fourthly, Ye intimate as though there were no truth in the gospel preached unless Christ died for all, when indeed there is no assertion more opposite to the truth of the gospel. The places urged mention Christ being Lord of all, exalted above all, being Judge of all, judging men according to the gospel,—that is, those men who enjoy it; but how they may be wrested to the end proposed I know not.

Proof 18. "Believers are exhorted to contend for the faith of this common salvation, which was once delivered to the saints; which some having heard oppose, and others turn the offers of it into wantonness, and, through not heeding and not walking in the faith of this salvation, already wrought by Christ for men, they deprive themselves of, and wind out themselves from, that salvation, which Christ by his Spirit, in application of the former, hath wrought in them, and so deprive themselves of the salvation to come, Jude 3–5.

"And every [one] of these proofs be plain and according to Scripture, and each of force, how much more altogether!—still justifying the sense that 1 Tim. ii. 6 and Heb. ii. 9 importeth, and the truth of the proposition in the beginning."

Ans. I can see nothing in this proof, but only that the salvation purchased by Christ is called "common salvation;" which if ye conclude from thence to be common to all, ye may as well conclude so of faith that it belongs to all, because it is called the "common faith," Tit. i. 4, though termed the "faith of God's elect," verse 1. Doubtless there is a community of believers, and that is common amongst them which is extended to the whole church of God; there is *totus mundus ex toto mundo;* and that common salvation is that whereby they are all saved, without any colour of that strange common salvation whereby no one is saved, maintained by this disputer. The remainder of this proof is a fulness of words, suitable to the persuasion of the author, but in no small part of them exceedingly unsuitable to the word of God and derogatory to the merits of Christ, making the salvation purchased by him to be in itself of no effect, but left to the will of sinful, corrupted, accursed men, to make available or to reject.

And these are the proofs which this author calls "*plain* and according to Scripture," being a recapitulation of almost all that he hath said in his whole book; at least, for the argumentative part thereof, there is not any thing of weight omitted: and therefore this chapter I fixed on to return a full and punctual answer unto. Now, whether the thing intended to be proved, namely, *The paying of a ransom by Christ for all and every man, be plainly, clearly, and evidently* from the Scripture *confirmed,* as he would bear us in hand; or whether all this heap of words, called arguments, reasons, and proofs, be not, for their manner of expression, obscure, uncouth, and ofttimes unintelligible,—for their way of inference, childish, weak, and ridiculous,—in their allegations and interpretations of Scripture, perverse, violent, mistaken, through ignorance, heedlessness, and corruption of judgment, in direct opposition to the mind and will of God revealed therein,—is left to the judgment of the Christian reader that shall peruse them, with the answers annexed.

CHAPTER VII.

The removal of other remaining objections.

THE removal of some usual sophisms and captious arguments of the Arminians, of late made common and vulgar, shall be the close of our treatise, and wind up the whole controversy, which hath drawn us with violence thus far. And in this performance I shall labour to be as brief as possible; partly because these things have been handled at large by others; partly because all colour of opposition to the truth by us maintained from the Scriptures being removed, all other objections will indeed naturally sink of themselves. Yet, because great boastings and swelling words of vanity have been used concerning some that follow, it is necessary that something be said to show the emptiness of such flourishes, that the weakest may not be entangled by them.

OBJECTION I. That which we shall begin withal is an argument of as great fame and as little merit as any that, in this cause, or indeed in any other controversy, hath been used of late days; and it is this:—"That which every one is bound to believe is true; but every one is bound to believe that Jesus Christ died for him: therefore it is true, namely, that Jesus Christ died for every one."

This is an argument which, to discover their conviction of the weakness of the rest of their arguments, the Arminians and their friends never use, but withal they add some notable encomium of it, with some terms of affront and threatening to their adversaries; insomuch as, by consent on both sides, it hath obtained the name of the Remonstrants' Achilles. Now, truly, for my part, as I shall not transcribe any thing hither out of the many full answers given to it by our divines, by which this Achilles, or rather Goliath, hath been often cast to the ground, so I heartily wish that the many operose, prolix answers which the boasting of our adversaries hath drawn forth had not got, [for] this poor nothing, more repute a thousand times than its own strength, or any addition of force from the managers of it could have procured unto it. Supposing then, first, That the term " believe," be used in the same sense in both propositions (for if otherwise the syllogism is false in the form of it); secondly, That by *believing* is understood *a saving application of Christ to the soul, as held out in the promise,* for to believe that Christ died for me in particular, as is asserted to be the duty of every one, can be nothing else but such a saving application; thirdly, That believing that Christ died for any, according to the business in question, must be with reference to the purpose of the Father and intention of Jesus Christ himself, for that is it which, with regard to any *universality,* is by us opposed; fourthly, For the term "every one," it must relate unto all men as considered in an *alike condition*, for several respects and conditions of the same persons may cause them to come under several obligations unto duties: now, there is no one condition common unto all but only the state of wrath and death, Eph. ii. 3, and therefore every man must be considered as in that condition; so that, in sum, the sense of the minor proposition is, " All men in the world, as considered in a state of wrath and unregeneracy, are bound to believe, as before described, that it was the intention of God that Christ should die for every one of them in particular."

Now, not to say any thing to the major proposition, which yet is false, that which men are bound to believe in this sense being, as hath been observed by many, neither *true* nor *false*, but *good*, the assumption is absolutely false, and hath not the least colour of rea· son or Scripture to support it; and (taking "every one" for every individual in the world) when our adversaries prove it, I engage myself to be their proselyte: for,—First, Then must some be bound to believe that which is false; which cannot be, every obligation to believe being from the God of truth. Now, it is false that Christ died for all and every individual of human kind, as hath been before proved at large. Secondly, Then should men be bound immediately to believe that which is not revealed, though *divine revelation* be the object of all faith; for the Scriptures do not hold out anywhere that Christ died for this or that particular man as *such*, but only for sinners indefinitely, specified ofttimes antecedently by God's purpose, and *consequently* by their own purchased obedience. Thirdly, Neither, indeed, is the *intention* and *purpose* of God, concerning which we now inquire, proposed as the object of the faith of any; but only his commands, promises, and threatenings,—the other being left to be collected and assured to the soul by an experience and sense of some sweet infallible issue and effect thereof in the heart actually enjoyed. Nor, fourthly, can any command in the Scripture to believe be interpreted by the purpose and intention of God, as though the meaning of it should be, " God intended that Christ should die for thee in particular;" nor doth any promise contain that sense. Besides, fifthly, which of itself is enough to break the neck of this argument, all have not any such object of faith as Christ's death at all proposed to them. How can they believe unless they hear? Can they be bound to believe that of which they never heard the least rumour? How many millions of infants and others, in barbarous nations, go to their "own place" without hearing the least report of Jesus Christ, or his sufferings for them or others, even in these days of the gospel! how much more, then, before the coming of Christ in the flesh, when the means of grace were restrained to one small nation, with some few proselytes! Were all these, are they that remain, all and every one, bound to believe that Christ died for them, all and every one in particular? Those that think so are, doubtless, bound to go tell all of them so; I mean those that are yet in the land of the living. Is not *unbelief* the great damning sin, where faith is required? John iii. 36? and yet doth not Paul prove that many shall be condemned for sinning against the light of nature, Rom. ii. 12? an evident demonstration that faith is not required of all,—all are not bound to believe.

But perhaps our adversaries will except, as they must except if they intend to have any colour or show of strength left unto this argument, that they mean it only in respect of them who are called by the word, and so it is of force; to which end let it be thus proposed:—

" That which every one called by the word, to whom the gospel is preached, is bound to believe, is true; but that Christ died for him in particular, every one so called is bound to believe: *ergo*," etc.

Ans. 1. Only the last exception foregoing is taken off by this *reformed argument;* all the rest stand in their full force, which are sufficient to evert it. 2. Who seeth not that this very reforming of the argument hath made it altogether useless to the cause in whose defence it was produced? for if any one, much more the greatest part of men, be excepted, which are now excluded from the verge of this argument, the *general ransom* falls to the ground. From the *innumerable multitudes of all*, we are come to the *many that are called*, and doubt not but that we shall instantly descend to the *few that are chosen.* Unto the exception, that that which is true in respect of them to whom it is proposed would also be true in respect of all if it should be proposed to them, I answer, by the way,—First, That the argument is to be taken from the scriptural obligation to believe, and can be extended no farther than it is actually extended. Secondly, That it is no safe disputing of what would be or should be, if things were not as God hath appointed and ordained them. We see the will of God for the present; neither are we to suppose so as to make our supposal a bottom for any argument that they could have been otherwise disposed. Thirdly, That if the gospel should be preached to all the world, or all in the world, this is all the mind and will of God that would or can in general be signified to them by it, " He that believeth and is baptized shall be saved, but he that believeth not shall be damned;" or, that God hath concatenated and knit these two things together, *faith* and *salvation*, so that whosoever will enjoy the latter must perform the former. If the gospel should now be preached to the Turks and the Indians, and they should reject it, certainly they should be damned for not believing that which they were, upon the preaching of it, bound to believe. Now, what is this? that Christ died for every one of them in particular? No, doubtless; but this, "There is none other name under heaven given among men, whereby we must be saved," but only by the name of Christ, made known to us in the gospel, Acts iv. 12. [They would be damned] for rejecting the counsel and wisdom of God to save sinners by the blood of Jesus; for not believing the necessity of a Redeemer, and that Jesus of Nazareth was that Redeemer,—according to his own word to the Jews, "If ye believe not that I am he, ye shall die in your sins;" as, indeed, the peculiar infidelity of that people was their not believing him to be their Messiah, whom they saw to be declared to be the Son of God with power. The not believing these things would be the soul-damning infidelity of such obstinate refusers to come in upon the call of the gospel, and not a refusing to believe that Christ died for every one of them in particular; which could not, by the rule of the gospel, be proposed unto them, and which they never come so far as to question or esteem.

Still, then, we deny the minor proposition of the reduced syllogism; and that partly for the reasons before produced, partly for these subjoined:—

1. They to whom the gospel is preached are bound to believe with that faith which is required to justification only. Now, this is not a full persuasion that Christ died for any one in particular, in the intention and purpose of God, which revealeth not the object of justification, nor the way whereby a sinner may be justified.[1]

2. Because there is an order, natural in itself, and established by God's appointment, in the things that are to be believed; so that until some of them are believed the rest are not required (a man is not commanded, nor can he reasonably, to get to the top of a ladder by skipping all the lower rounds),—namely, (1.) Repent, and believe the gospel to be the word of God, to contain his will, and that Jesus Christ, therein revealed, is the wisdom and power of God unto salvation. (2.) That there is an inseparable connection, by God's appointment, between faith and salvation, gospel faith carrying a sinner quite out of himself and from off his own righteousness. (3.) That there be a particular conviction, by the Spirit, of the necessity of a Redeemer to their souls in particular; whereby they become weary, heavy laden, and burdened. (4.) A serious full recumbency and rolling of the soul upon Christ in the promise of the gospel, as an all-sufficient Saviour, able to deliver and save to the utmost them that come to God by him; ready, able, and willing, through the preciousness of his blood and sufficiency of his ransom, to save every soul that shall

---

[1] The last clauses of this sentence are obscure. In the edition by the Rev. Adam Gib, 1755, it is proposed to render them,—"which is not revealed to the object of justification, or in the way whereby a sinner may be justified." If we were at liberty to change the "nor" into "but," a meaning sufficiently intelligible would be obtained, without any violent alteration of the text, and quite in harmony with the scope of the reasoning.—ED.

freely give up themselves unto him for that end, amongst whom he is resolved to be. And in doing of all this, there is none called on by the gospel once to inquire after the purpose and intention of God concerning the particular object of the death of Christ, every one being fully assured that his death shall be profitable to them that believe in him and obey him.

Now, fourthly, after all this, and not before, it lies upon a believer to assure his soul, according as he finds the fruit of the death of Christ in him and towards him, of the good-will and eternal love of God to him in sending his Son to die for him in particular. What a preposterous course, and how opposite to the rule of the gospel, were it, to call upon a man to believe that it was the intention and purpose of God that Christ should die for him in particular, and desire him to assure his soul thereof, before he be convinced either,— 1. Of the truth of the gospel in general; or, 2. That faith is the only way of salvation; or, 3. That himself standeth in need of a Saviour; or, 4. That there is enough in Christ to save and recover him if he give up himself unto him in his own way! Now, it is most apparent that it is only such as these that are bound to believe that whereof we discourse.

The argument, then, must be once again reformed, and thus proposed:—

"That which every one, convinced of the necessity of a Saviour, and of the right way of salvation, hungering, thirsting, and panting after Jesus Christ, as able alone to give him refreshment, is bound to believe, is true; but every such a one is bound to believe that Christ died for him in particular: *ergo*, it is true." And some grant the whole without any prejudice to the cause we have undertaken to defend. It is most apparent, then,—1. That all that are called by the word are not, in what state or condition soever they continue, bound to believe that Christ died for them; but only such as are so qualified as before described. 2. That the precept of believing, with fiduciary confidence, that Christ died for any in particular is not proposed nor is obligatory to all that are called; nor is the non-performance of it any otherwise a sin, but as it is in the root and habit of unbelief, or not turning to God in Christ for mercy. 3. That no reprobate, for whom Christ died not, shall be condemned for not believing that Christ died for him in particular, which is not true; but for not believing those things whereunto he was called, before related, which are all most true, and that in reference to him. 4. That the command of believing in Christ, which is especially urged as given unto all, is not, in that particular contended about, obligatory unto any but upon fulfilling of the conditions thereto required. 5. To "believe on the name of Jesus Christ," which is the command, 1 John iii. 23, is not to believe that it was the intention

of God that Christ should die for us in particular, but to rest upon
him for salvation, as Isa. l. 11.   Neither,—6. Is the testimony
of God, to which we ought to set our seal that it is true, any other
but this, "He that hath the Son hath life, but he that hath not the
Son of God hath not life," 1 John v. 12; which reprobates disbelieving, do what in them lies to make God a liar, and are justly
condemned for it.   He that desireth to see more of this argument,
let him consult, if he please, Piscator, Perkins, Twisse, Synod of Dort,
Du Moulin, Baronius, Rutherford, Spanheim, Amesius, others, etc.

OBJ. II. "That doctrine which fills the minds and souls of poor
miserable sinners with doubts and scruples whether they ought to
believe or no, when God calls them thereunto, cannot be agreeable
to the gospel.   But this doth the doctrine of the particularity of
redemption.   It fills the minds of sinners with scruples and fears
whether they may believe or no, and that because they are uncertain whether it was the intention of God that Christ should die for
them in particular or no, seeing it is supposed that he died not for
all, but only for his elect; whereupon the soul, when it is called upon
to believe, may justly fall a-questioning whether it will be available
or no for him so to do, and whether it be his duty or no, seeing he
knoweth not whether Christ died for him or no."

Ans. 1. That scruples, doubts, and fears, the proper issue of uncon-
quered remaining unbelief, will often arise in the hearts of sinners,
sometimes against, sometimes taking occasion from, the truth of the
gospel, is too evident upon experience.   All the question is, whether the
doctrine itself scrupled or stumbled at do of itself, in its own nature,
give cause thereto unto those who rightly perform their duty? or whether all those fears and scruples be the natural product and issue of
corruption and unbelief, setting up themselves against the truth as
it is in Jesus?   The first we deny, concerning the doctrine of the particularity of effectual redemption; the latter God alone can remedy.

2. This objection supposeth that a man is bound to know and be
persuaded (that is, to believe) that Jesus Christ died by the appointment of God for him in particular, before he believe in Jesus Christ.
Nay, this they make the bottom of their argument, that men, according to our persuasion, may scruple whether they ought to believe or
no, because they are not assured before that Christ died for them in
particular, by the designation and appointment of God.   Now, if this be
not to involve themselves in a plain contradiction, I know not what is;
for what, I pray, is it, according to Scripture, for a man to be assured
that Christ died for him in particular?   Is it not the very highest improvement of faith? doth it not include a sense of the spiritual love of
God shed abroad in our hearts?   Is it not the top of the apostle's consolation, Rom. viii. 34, and the bottom of all his joyful assurance, Gal.
ii. 20?   So that they evidently require that a man must believe before

he do believe,—that he cannot believe, and shall exceedingly fear whether he ought to do so or no, unless he believe before he believe! Methinks such removing of scruples were the ready way to entangle doubting consciences in farther inextricable perplexities.

3. We deny that a persuasion that it was the will of God that Christ should die for him in particular either is or can be any way necessary that a sinner be drawn to believe. For, considering sinners as such whose duty it is to believe the call of Christ, Matt. xi. 28, Isa. lv. 1; that command of God, 1 John iii. 23; that promise of life upon believing, John iii. 36; that threat of unbelief, *ibid;* the all-sufficiency of the blood of Christ to save all believers, Acts xx. 21, Eph. v. 2; the assured salvation of all believers without exception, Mark xvi. 16, and the like, are enough to remove all doubts and fears, and are all that the Scripture holds out for that purpose.

4. That persuasion which (1.) asserts the certainty of salvation by the death of Christ unto all believers whatsoever; (2.) that affirms the command of God and the call of Christ to be infallibly declarative of that duty which is required of the person commanded and called,—which, if it be performed, will be assuredly acceptable to God; (3.) that holds out purchased free grace to all distressed, burdened, consciences in general; (4.) that discovers a fountain of blood, all-sufficient to purge all the sin of every one in the world that will use the appointed means for coming unto it;—that doctrine, I say, cannot possibly be the cause of any doubt or scruple in the minds of convinced, burdened sinners, whether they ought to believe or no. Now, all this is held forth by the doctrine of particular effectual redemption, in the dispensation of the gospel suitable thereto.

I shall, then, let go this objection without farther pursuit, only attended with this query, What it is that, according to the authors of universal redemption, men are bound to believe, when they know beforehand that Christ died for them in particular? A persuasion of the love of God and good-will of Christ it cannot be; that they have beforehand, John iii. 16; Rom. v. 8: nor a coming to God by Christ for an enjoyment of the fruits of his death; for what is that, I pray? No fruits of the death of Christ, according to them, but what are common to all; which may be damnation as well as salvation, for more are damned than saved,—infidelity as well as faith, for the most are unbelievers. The immediate fruits of the death of Christ can be nothing but that which is common to them with those that perish. Plainly, their faith in Christ will at length appear to be Socinian obedience.

There be two[1] things that remain, about which there is no small contention, both things in themselves excelling and valuable, both laid claim to by the several persuasions concerning which we treat;

---

[1] From the particulars enumerated in the following sentence, and the three objections that are considered, "two" seems to have been written, by an oversight, for "three."—ED.

but with such an unequal plea, that an easy judgment might serve to decide the controversy. Now, these are, first, the exaltation of God's free grace, the merit of Christ, and the consolation of our souls. Let us consider them in order, and let each persuasion take its due.

OBJ. III. For the first, or the *exaltation of God's free grace.* I know not how it comes to pass, but so it is, men have entertained a persuasion that the opinion of *universal redemption* serveth exceedingly to set forth the *love and free grace of God,* yea, they make free grace, that glorious expression, to be nothing but that which is held forth in this their opinion,—namely, that God loveth *all,* and gave Christ to die for *all,* and is ready to save *all,* if *they will come to him.* "Herein," say they, "is *free grace* and love magnified indeed; this is the universality of free grace,"—and such other flourishing expressions; "whereas the contrary opinion chains up the love and grace of God to a few."

But stay a little. What, I pray, is this your grace, free grace, that is universal? Is it the grace of election? Truly no; God hath not chosen all to salvation, Rom. ix. 11, 12; Eph. i. 4; Rom. viii. 28. Is it the grace of effectual vocation? No, neither. Doubtless that it cannot be; for "whom God calls he also justifies," and "glorifies," Rom. viii. 30, xi. 25, 26, 29. Nay, all have not been, are not, outwardly called, chap. x. 14. Is it the grace of cleansing and sanctification? Why, are all purged? are all washed in the blood of Jesus? Or is it the church only, Eph. v. 25–27. Some, sure, are also defiled still, Tit. i. 15. Faith is the principle of the heart's purification, and "all men have not faith." Is it the grace of justification, —the free love and mercy of God in pardoning and accepting sinners? But, friends, is this universal? Are all pardoned? are all accepted? see Rom i. 17, iii. 22, v. 1. Is it the grace of redemption in the blood of Christ? see, I pray, Rev. v. 9. What then, I pray, is this your universal free grace? Is it not universally a figment of your own brains? or is it not a new name for that old idol free-will? Is it not destructive to free grace in every branch of it? Doth it not tend to the eversion of the whole covenant of distinguishing grace, evidently denying that the conditions thereof are wrought in any of the federates by virtue of the promise of the covenant? Are not the two great aims of their free grace to mock God and exalt themselves? Do not they propose the Lord as making a pretence of love, good-will, free grace, and pardon unto all, yet never once acquainting incomparably the greatest number of them with any such love or good-will at all, although he know that without his effecting of it they can never come to any such knowledge? For those that are outwardly called to the knowledge of these things, do they not, by their universal grace, feign the Lord to pretend that he loves them all, has sent his Son to die for them all, and to desire that they all may be saved, yet upon such a condition as, without him, they can no more effect than to climb to heaven by a ladder, which yet he will not do? Do not they openly make God to say, "Such is this my love, my universal grace, that by it I will freely love them, I dare joyfully embrace them, in all things but only that which will do them good?" Would not they affirm him to be a grossly counterfeiting hypocrite that should go to a poor blind man, and tell him, "Alas, poor man, I pity thy case, I see thy want, I love thee exceedingly; open thine eyes, and I will give thee a hundred pounds?" And dare they assign such a deportment to the most holy God of truth? Is their universal grace any thing but a mock? Did that ever do good to any, as to salvation, which is common to all? Are they not the two properties of the grace of God in the Scripture, that it is discriminating and effectual? And is not their grace any thing else but these? Let it be granted that all is true which they say concerning the extent of grace; is it such grace as that ever any soul was saved by? Why, I pray, then, are not all? "Why," they will say, "because they do not believe." So, then, the bestowing of faith is no part of this free grace. See your second aim, even to exalt yourselves and your free-will into the room of grace; or, at least, leaving it room to come in, to have the best share in the work of salvation,— namely, believing itself, that makes all the rest profitable. See, now, what your universality of free grace leads and tends to. Are not the very terms opposite to one another? In a word, to bring in reprobates to be objects of free grace, you deny the free grace of God to the elect; and to make it universal, you deny it to be effectual. That all may have a share of it, they deny any to be saved by it; for saving grace must be restrained.

On the other side; in what one tittle, I pray you, doth the doctrine of the effectual redemption of God's elect only, in the blood of Jesus, impair the free grace of God? Is it in its *freedom?* Why, we say it is so free, that if it be not altogether free it is no grace at all. Is it in its *efficacy?* Why, we say that by grace we are saved, ascribing the whole work of our recovery and bringing to God, in "solidum," thereto. Is it in its *extent?* We affirm it to be extended to every one that is, was, or ever shall be delivered from the pit. It is true, we do not call grace that goeth into hell free grace, in a gospel notion; for we deem the free grace of God so powerful, that wherever it hath designed and chosen out itself a subject, that it brings God, and Christ, and salvation with it, to eternity.

"But you do not extend it unto all; you tie it up to a few." *De te largitor, puer.* Is the extending of the love and favour of God in our power? Hath he not mercy on whom he will have mercy, and doth he not harden whom he will? Yet, do not we affirm that it is extended to the universality of the saved ones? Should we throw the children's bread to dogs? Friends, we believe that the grace of God in Christ worketh faith in every one to whom it is extended; that the conditions of that covenant which is ratified in his blood are all effectually wrought in the heart of every covenantee; that there is no love of God that is not effectual; that the blood of Christ was not shed in vain; that of ourselves we are dead in trespasses and sins, and can do nothing but what the free grace of God worketh in us: and, therefore, we cannot conceive that it can be extended to all. [As] for you, who affirm that millions of those that are taken into a new covenant of grace do perish eternally, that it is left to men to believe that the will of God may be frustrate and his love ineffectual, that we distinguish ourselves one from another,—you may extend it whither you please, for it is indifferent to you whether the objects of it go to heaven or to hell.

But in the meanwhile, I beseech you, friends, give me leave to question whether this you talk of be God's free grace, or your fond figment? his love, or your wills? for truly, for the present, it seems to me the latter only. But yet our prayers shall be that God would give you infinitely more of his love than is contained in that ineffectual universal grace wherewith you so flourish. Only, we shall labour that poor souls be not seduced by you with the specious pretences of free grace to all,—not knowing that this your free grace is a mere painted cloth, that will give them no assistance at all to deliver them from that condition wherein they are, but only give them leave to be saved if they can; whereas they are ready, by the name you have given to the brat of your own brain, to suppose you intend an effectual, almighty, saving grace, that will certainly bring all to God to whom it is extended, of which they have heard in the Scripture; whilst you laugh in your sleeves, to think how simply these poor souls are deluded with that empty show, the substance whereof is this, " Go your ways; be saved if you can, in the way revealed; God will not hinder you."

OBJ. IV. Each party contests about the *exaltation of the merit of Christ;* for so are their mutual pretences. Something hath been said to this before, so that now I shall be brief. Take, then, only a short view of the difference that is between them, where each pretends to exalt the merit of Christ in that which is by the other denied, and this plea will suddenly be at an end.

There is but one only thing that concerns the death of Christ in which the authors of the *general ransom* are upon the affirmative, and whereby they pretend to set forth the excellency of his death and oblation, namely, that the benefits thereof are extended unto all and every one, whereas their adversaries straiten it unto a few, a very few,—none but the elect; which, they say, is derogatory to the honour of the Lord Jesus Christ. And this is that wherein they pretend so exceedingly to advance his name and merit above the pitch that they aim at who assert the effectual redemption of the elect only. The truth is, the measure of the honour of Jesus Christ is not to be assigned by us, poor worms of the dust; that he takes to be honour which he gives and ascribes unto himself, and nothing else. He hath no need of our lie for his glory: so that if *this* did, in our eyes, seem for the exaltation of the glory of Christ, yet, arising from a lie of our own hearts, it would be an abomination unto him. Secondly, We deny that this doth any way serve to set out the nature and dignity of the death of Christ; because the extent of its efficacy to all (if any such thing should be) doth not arise from its own innate sufficiency, but from the free pleasure and determination of God: which how it is enervated by a pretended universality was before declared. Thirdly, The value of a thing ariseth from its own native sufficiency and worth unto any purpose whereunto it is to be employed; which the maintainers of effectual redemption do assert, in the death of Christ, to be much above what any of their adversaries ascribe unto it.

Should I now go about to declare in how many things the honour of Christ, and the excellency of his death and passion, with the fruits of it, is held forth in that doctrine which we have sought to open from the Scriptures, above all that can be assigned to it agreeable to their own principal maxims who maintain universal redemption (and that according to truth itself), I should be forced to repeat much that hath already been spoken, so that it shall suffice me to present the reader with this following antithesis:—

Universalists.

1. Christ died for all and every one, elect and reprobate.

2. Most of them for whom Christ died are damned.

3 Christ, by his death, purchased not any saving grace for them for whom he died.

4. Christ took no care for the greatest part of them for whom he died, that ever they should hear one word of his death.

5. Christ, in his death, did not ratify nor confirm a covenant of grace with any federates, but only procured by his death that God might, if he would, enter into a new covenant with whom he would, and upon what condition he pleased.

Scriptural Redemption.

1. Christ died for the elect only.

2. All those for whom Christ died are certainly saved.

3. Christ by his death purchased all saving grace for them for whom he died.

4. Christ sends the means and reveals the way of life to all them for whom he died.

5. The new covenant of grace was confirmed to all the elect in the blood of Jesus.

Universalists.	Scriptural Redemption.
6. Christ might have died, and yet no one be saved.	6. Christ, by his death, purchased, upon covenant and compact, an assured peculiar people, the pleasure of the Lord prospering to the end in his hand.
7. Christ had no intention to redeem his church, any more than the wicked seed of the serpent.	7. Christ loved his church, and gave himself for it.
8. Christ died not for the infidelity of any.	8. Christ died for the infidelity of the elect.

Divers other instances of the like nature might be easily collected, upon the first view whereof the present difference in hand would quickly be determined. These few, I doubt not, are sufficient, in the eyes of all experienced Christians, to evince how little the *general ransom* conduceth to the honour and glory of Jesus Christ, or to the setting forth of the worth and dignity of his death and passion.

OBJ. V. The next and last thing which comes under debate in this contest is *gospel consolation,* which God in Christ is abundantly willing we should receive. A short disquisition whether of the two opinions treated on doth give the firmest basis and soundest foundation hereunto, will, by the Lord's assistance, lead us to an end of this long debate. THE GOD OF TRUTH AND COMFORT GRANT THAT ALL OUR UNDERTAKINGS, OR RATHER HIS WORKINGS IN US, FOR TRUTH, MAY END IN PEACE AND CONSOLATION!

To clear this, some things are to be premised ; as,—

1. All true evangelical consolation belongeth only to believers, Heb. vi. 17, 18,—God's people, Isa. xl. 1, 2; upon unbelievers the "wrath of God abideth," John iii. 36.

2. To make out consolation unto them to whom it is not due is no less a crime than to hide it from them to whom it doth belong, Isa. v. 20; Jer. xxiii. 14; Ezek. xiii. 10.

3. T. M[ore]'s attempt to set forth the death of Christ so that all might be comforted, meaning all and every one in the world, as appeareth, is a proud attempt to make that straight which God hath made crooked, and most opposite to the gospel.

4. That doctrine which holds out consolation from the death of Christ to unbelievers, cries, "Peace, peace," when God says, "There is no peace."

These things being premised, I shall briefly demonstrate these four following positions:—1. That the extending of the death of Christ unto a universality, in respect of the object, cannot give the least ground of consolation to them whom God would have to be comforted by the gospel. 2. That the denying of the efficacy of the death of Christ towards them for whom he died cuts the nerves and sinews of all strong consolation, even such as is proper to believers to receive, and peculiar to the gospel to give. 3. That there is nothing in the doctrine of redemption of the elect only that is yet in the least measure to debar them from consolation to whom comfort is due. 4. That the doctrine of the effectual redemption of the sheep of Christ, by the blood of the covenant, is the true solid foundation of all durable consolation.

1. Begin we with the first,—that the extending of the death of Christ unto a *universality*, in respect of the object, hath nothing in it, as peculiar unto it, that can give the least ground of consolation unto them whom God would have to be comforted. That gospel consolation, properly so called, being a fruit of actual reconciliation with God, is proper and peculiar only to believers, I laid down before, and suppose it to be a truth out of all question and debate. Now, that no consolation can be made out to them as such, from any thing which is peculiar to the persuasion of a general ransom, is easily proved by these following reasons:—

(1.) No consolation can arise unto believers from that which is nowhere in the Scripture proposed as a ground, cause, or matter of consolation, as the general ransom is not: for,—first, That which hath no being can have no affection nor operation; secondly, All the foundations and materials of consolation are things particular, and peculiar only to some, as shall be declared.

(2.) No consolation can accrue unto believers from that which is common unto them with those whom,—first, God would not have comforted; secondly, that shall assuredly perish to eternity; thirdly, that stand in open rebellion against Christ; fourthly, that never hear one word of gospel or consolation.   Now, to all these, and such as these, doth the foundation of *consolation*, as proposed with and arising from the *general ransom*, equally appertain with the choicest of believers.

(3.) Let a man try in the time, not of disputation, but of desertion and temptation, what consolation or peace to his soul he can obtain from such a collection as this, " Christ died for all men; I am a man: therefore, Christ died for me." Will not his own heart tell him, that notwithstanding all that he is assured of in that conclusion, the wrath of God may abide on him for evermore? Doth he not see that, notwithstanding this, the Lord showeth so little love unto millions of millions of the sons of men, of whom the former collection (according to the present opinion) is true as well as of himself, as that he doth not once reveal himself or his Son unto them? What good will it do me to know that Christ died for me, if notwithstanding that I may perish for ever? If you intend me any consolation from that which is common unto all, you must tell me what it is which all enjoy which will satisfy my desires, which are carried out after assurance of the love of God in Christ. If you give me no more to comfort me than what you give, or might have given, to Judas, can you expect I should receive settlement and consolation? Truly, miserable comforters are ye all, physicians of no value, Job's visitors,—skilful only to add affliction unto the afflicted.

"But be of good comfort," will Arminians say; "Christ is a propitiation for all sinners, and now thou knowest thyself so to be." *Ans.* True; but is Christ a propitiation for all the sins of those sinners? If so, how can any of them perish? If not, what good will this do me, whose sins perhaps (as unbelief) are such as for which Christ was not a propitiation? "But exclude not thyself; God excludeth none; the love which caused him to send his Son was general towards all." Tell not me of God's excluding; I have sufficiently excluded myself. Will he powerfully take me in? Hath Christ not only purchased that I shall be admitted, but procured me ability to enter into his Father s arms? "Why, he hath opened a door of salvation to all." Alas! is it not a vain endeavour, to open a grave for a dead man to come out? Who lights a candle for a blind man to see by? To open a door for him to come out of prison who is blind, and lame, and bound, yea dead, is rather to deride his misery than to procure him liberty. Never tell me that will yield me strong consolation, under the enjoyment whereof the greatest portion of men perish everlastingly.

2. The opinion concerning a general ransom is so far from yielding firm consolation unto believers from the death of Christ, that it quite overthrows all the choice ingredients of strong consolation which flow therehence; and that,—first, By strange divisions and divulsions of one thing from another, which ought to be conjoined to make up one certain foundation of confidence; secondly, By denying the efficacy of his death towards them for whom he died: both which are necessary attendants of that persuasion.

First, They so divide the *impetration* of redemption and the *application* thereof,—the first being in their judgments the only proper immediate fruit and effect of the death of Christ,—that the one may belong to millions who have no share in the other; yea, that redemption may be obtained for all, and yet no one have it so applied unto them as to be saved thereby. Now, the first of these, such as it is, is an ineffectual possible redemption, notwithstanding which all the sons of men might perish everlastingly, being the whole object of the death of Christ (as is asserted), separated and divided from all such application of redemption unto any as might make it profitable and useful in the least measure (for they deny this application to be a fruit of the death of Christ; if it were, why is it not common to all for whom he died?) What comfort this can in the least degree afford to any poor soul will not dive into my apprehension. " What shall I do?" saith the sinner; "the iniquity of my heels compasseth me about. I have no rest in my bones by reason of my sin: and now, whither shall I cause my sorrow to go?" Be of good cheer; Christ died for sinners. " Yea, but shall the fruits of his death be certainly applied unto all them for whom he died? If not, I may perish for ever." Here let them that can, answer him, according to the principles of Universalists, without sending him to his own strength in believing, or that which, in the close, will be resolved into it, " et erit mihi magnus Apollo:" and if they send him thither, they acknowledge the consolation concerning which they boast properly to proceed from ourselves, and not from the death of Christ.

Secondly, Their separating between the oblation and intercession of Jesus Christ makes little for the consolation of believers, yea, indeed, quite everts it.

There are, amongst others, two eminent places of Scripture wherein the Holy Ghost holdeth forth consolation to believers, against these two general causes of all their troubles and sorrows,—namely, their afflictions and their sins. The first is Rom. viii. 32–34, the other 1 John ii. 1, 2; in both which places the apostles make the bottom of the consolation which they hold out to believers in their afflictions and failings to be that strait bond and inseparable connection that is between these two, with the identity of their objects, —namely, the oblation and intercession of Jesus Christ. Let the reader consult both the texts, and he shall find that on this lies the stress, and herein consists the strength, of the several proposals for the consolation of believers; which, in both places, is principally intended. A more direct undertaking for this end and purpose cannot be produced. Now, the authors of universal redemption do all of them divide and separate these two; they allow of no connection between them, nor dependence of one upon another, farther than is effected by the will of man. His oblation they stretch to all; his intercession to a few only. Now, the death of Christ, separated from his resurrection and intercession, being nowhere proposed as a ground of consolation, yea, positively declared to be unsuitable to any such purpose, 1 Cor. xv. 14, certainly they who hold it out as so done are no friends to Christian consolation.

Thirdly, Their denial of the procurement of faith, grace, holiness, —the whole intendment of the new covenant,—and perseverance therein, by the death and blood-shedding of Jesus Christ, unto all them, or any of them, for whom he died, doth not appear to be so suitable an assertion for to raise consolation from his cross as is vainly pretended. I pray, what solid consolation can be drawn from such dry breasts as from whence none of these things do flow? That they have not immediate dependence on the death of Christ, according to the persuasion of the assertors of universal grace, hath been before declared, and is by themselves not only confessed, but undertaken to be proved. Now, where should a soul look for these things, but in the purchase of Christ? Whence should they flow, but from his side? Or is there any consolation to be had without them? Is not the strongest plea for these things, at the throne of grace, the procurement of the Lord Jesus? What promise is there of any thing without him? Are not all the promises of God yea and amen in him? Is there any attainment of these things in our own strength? Is this the consolation you afford us, to send us from free grace to free will? Whither, I pray, according to this persuasion, should a poor soul go that finds himself in want of these things? "To God, who gives all freely." But doth God bless us with any spiritual blessings but only in Jesus Christ? Doth he bless us with any thing in him but what he hath procured for us? Is not all grace as well procured by as dispensed in a Mediator? Is this a way to comfort a soul, and that from the death of Christ, to let him know that Christ did not procure those things for him without which he cannot be comforted? "Credat Apella."

It is, then, most apparent, that the general ransom (which is pretended) is so far from being the bottom of any solid consolation unto them whose due it is, that it is directly destructive of, and diametrically opposed unto, all those ways whereby the Lord hath declared himself willing that we should receive comfort from the death of his Son, drying up the breast from whence, and poisoning the streams whereby, it should be conveyed unto our souls.

3. The next thing we have to do is, to manifest that the doctrine of the effectual redemption of the elect only by the blood of Jesus is not liable to any just exception as to this particular, nor doth any way abridge believers of any part or portion of that consolation which God is willing they should receive. That alone which, by the opposers of it, with any colour of reason, is objected (for as for the exclamation of shutting out innumerable souls from any share in the blood of Christ, seeing confessedly they are reprobate unbelievers and persons finally impenitent, we are not at all moved at it), comes to this head:—"That there is nothing in the Scripture whereby any man can assure himself that Christ died for him in particular, unless we grant that he died for all."

First, That this is notoriously false, the experience of all believers who, by the grace of God, have assured their hearts of their share and interest in Christ as held out unto them in the promise, without the least thought of universal redemption, is a sufficient testimony. Secondly, That the assurance arising from a practical syllogism, whereof one proposition is true in the word, and the second by the witness of the Spirit in the heart, is infallible, hath hitherto been acknowledged

by all. Now, such assurance may all believers have that Christ died
for them, with an intention and purpose to save their souls. For
instance: all believers may draw out the truth of the word and the
faith created in their hearts into this conclusion:—[*First*,] " Christ
died for all believers,"—that is, all who choose him and rest upon
him as an all-sufficient Saviour; not that he died for them as such,
but that all such are of those for whom he died. He died not for
believers as believers, though he died for all believers; but for all the
elect as elect, who, by the benefit of his death, do become believers,
and so obtain assurance that he died for them. [As] for such of those
that are elected who are not yet believers, though Christ died for them,
yet we deny that they can have any assurance of it whilst they continue such. You suppose it a foul contradiction, if a man should be
said to have assurance that Christ died for him in particular, and yet
continue an unbeliever. This first proposition, as in the beginning
laid down, is true in the word, in innumerable places. *Secondly*,
The heart of a believer, in the witness of the Spirit, assumes, " But I
believe in Christ;" that is, " I choose him for my Saviour, cast and
roll myself on him alone for salvation, and give up myself unto
him, to be disposed of unto mercy in his own way." Of the truth
of this proposition in the heart of a believer, and the infallibility
of it, there are also many testimonies in the word, as is known
to all; from whence the conclusion is, " Therefore the Lord Jesus
Christ died for me in particular, with an intention and purpose to
save me."

This is such a collection as all believers, and none but believers,
can justly make, so that it is peculiar to them alone; and unto
those only is this treasure of consolation to be imparted. The sufficiency of the death of Christ for the saving of every one, without
exception, that comes unto him, is enough to fill all the invitations
and entreaties of the gospel unto sinners, to induce them to believe;
which when, by the grace of Christ, they do, closing with the promise, the fore-mentioned infallible assurance of the intention and
purpose of Christ to redeem them by his death, Matt. i. 21, is made
known unto them. Now, whether this be not a better bottom and
foundation for a man to assure his soul unto rest and peace upon,
than that reasoning which our opposers in this business must, suitably
to their own principles, lay as a common stone,—namely, " Christ
died for all men; I am a man: therefore Christ died for me,"—let
any man judge; especially considering that indeed the first proposition is absolutely false, and the conclusion, if it could be true, yet,
according to their persuasion, can be no more ground of consolation
than Adam's fall. All this is spoken not as though either one opinion or other were able of itself to give consolation, which God alone,
in the sovereignty of his free grace, can and doth create; but only to

show what principles are suitable to the means whereby he worketh on and towards his elect.

4. The drawing of gospel consolation from the death of Christ, as held out to be effectual towards the elect only, for whom alone he died, should close up our discourse; but considering, first, how abundantly this hath been done by divers eminent and faithful labourers in the vineyard of the Lord already; secondly, how it is the daily task of the preachers of the gospel to make it out to the people of God; thirdly, how it would carry me out, besides my purpose, to speak of things in a *practical,* so *atheological* way, having designed this discourse to be purely *polemical;* and, fourthly, that such things are no more expected nor welcome to wise and learned men, in controversies of this nature, than knotty, crabbed, scholastic objections in popular sermons and doctrinal discourses, intended merely for edification,—I shall not proceed therein. Only, for a close, I desire the reader to peruse that one place, Rom. viii. 32–34; and I make no doubt but that he will, if not infected with the leaven of the error opposed, conclude with me, that if there be any comfort, any consolation, any assurance, any rest, any peace, any joy, any refreshment, any exultation of spirit, to be obtained here below, it is all to be had in the blood of Jesus long since shed, and his intercession still continued; as both are united and appropriated to the elect of God, by the precious effects and fruits of them both drawn to believe and preserved in believing, to the obtaining of an immortal crown of glory, that shall not fade away.

Μόνῳ σοφῷ Θεῷ, διὰ Ἰησοῦ Χριστοῦ ἡ δόξα εἰς τοὺς αἰῶνας. Ἀμήν.

SOME FEW TESTIMONIES OF THE ANCIENTS.

I. The confession of the holy Church of Smyrna, a little after the commendation given it by the Holy Ghost, Rev. ii. 9, upon the martyrdom of Polycarpus:—
Ὅτι οὔτε τὸν Χριστόν ποτε καταλείπειν δυνησόμεθα τὸν ὑπὲρ τῆς τοῦ κόσμου τῶν σωζωμένων σωτηρίας παθόντα, οὔτε ἕτερον τιμῇ σέβειν.—Euseb. Hist. Eccles., lib. iv. cap. 15.—
"Neither can we ever forsake Christ, him who suffered for the salvation of *the world of them that are saved*, nor worship any other."
[It is an extract from a letter of the church of Smyrna to the churches of Pontus, giving an account of the martyrdom of Polycarp.]

II. The witness of holy Ignatius, as he was carrying to Rome from Antioch, to be cast to beasts for the testimony of Jesus, Epist. ad Philad. [cap. ix., A.D. 107]:—Οὗτός ἐστιν ἡ πρὸς τὸν Πατέρα ἄγουσα ὁδός, ἡ πέτρα, ὁ φραγμός, ἡ κλείς, ὁ ποιμήν, τὸ ἱερεῖον, ἡ θύρα τῆς γνώσεως δι᾽ ἧς εἰσῆλθον Ἀβραὰμ καὶ Ἰσαὰκ καὶ Ἰακώβ, Μωσῆς, καὶ ὁ σύμπας τῶν προφητῶν χορός, καὶ οἱ στύλοι τοῦ κόσμου οἱ ἀπόστολοι καὶ ἡ νύμφη τοῦ Χριστοῦ, ὑπὲρ ἧς, φερνῆς λόγῳ, ἐξέχεε τὸ οἰκεῖον αἷμα ἵνα αὐτὴν ἐξαγοράσῃ.—"This is the way leading to the Father, this the rock, the fold, the key; he is the shepherd, the sacrifice; the door of knowledge, by which entered Abraham, Isaac, Jacob, Moses, and the whole company of prophets, and the pillars of the world, the apostles, and the spouse of Christ; for whom, instead of a dowry, he poured out his own blood, that he might redeem her."
Surely Jesus Christ gives not a dowry for any but his own spouse.

III. Clemens, "whose name is in the book of life," Phil. iv. 3, with the whole church at Rome in his days, in the epistle to the church of Corinth:—Διὰ τὴν ἀγάπην ἣν ἔσχεν πρὸς ἡμᾶς τὸ αἷμα αὐτοῦ ἔδωκεν ὑπὲρ ἡμῶν ἐν θελήματι αὐτοῦ καὶ τὴν σάρκα ὑπὲρ τῆς σαρκὸς ἡμῶν καὶ τὴν ψυχὴν ὑπὲρ ψυχῶν ἡμῶν.—"For the love which he had unto us, he gave his blood for us, according to his purpose, and his flesh for our flesh, and his life for our lives."
Where you have assigned, 1. The cause of Christ's death,—his love to us; 2. The object of it,—us, or believers; 3. The manner how he redeemed us, even by commutation.
This triple testimony is taken from the very prime of undoubted antiquity.

IV. Cyprian, Epist. lxii. to Cæcilius, a holy, learned, and famous martyr, A.D. 250:—"Nos omnes portabat Christus, qui et peccata nostra portabat."—"He bare all us, who bare our sins;" that is, he sustained their persons on the cross for whom he died.
The same to Demetrian :—"Hanc gratiam Christus impertit, subigendo mortem trophæo crucis, redimendo *credentem* pretio sanguinis sui."—"This grace hath Christ communicated, subduing death in the trophy of his cross, redeeming believers with the price of his blood."
The same, or some other ancient and pious writer of the cardinal works of Christ, Serm. 7, secund. Rivet. Crit. Sac. in Cyp. [lib. ii. cap. 15] Scultet. Medul. Pat. Erasm. præfat. ad lib.[1]

1 These seven sermons on the cardinal works of Christ are the production of Arnoldus Carnotensis, abbot of the Benedictine monastery of Bonneval, in the diocese of Chartres. He flourished about the middle of the twelfth century. Several of his practical treatises were for a time ascribed to Cyprian.—Ed.

The same author also, in express terms, mentions the sufficiency of the ransom paid by Christ, arising from the dignity of his person :—" Tantæ dignitatis illa una Redemptoris nostri fuit oblatio, ut una ad tollenda mundi peccatum sufficeret."— " Of so great dignity was the oblation of our Redeemer, that it alone was sufficient to take away the sins of the world."

V. CYRIL of Jerusalem, Cataches. xiii. [A.D. 350]:—Καὶ μὴ θαυμάσῃς εἰ κόσμος ὅλος ἐλυτρώθη, οὐ γὰρ ἦν ἄνθρωπος ψιλὸς ἀλλὰ υἱὸς Θεοῦ μονογενὴς ὁ ὑπεραποθνήσκων— καὶ εἰ τότε διὰ τὸ ξύλον τῆς βρώσεως ἐξεβλήθησαν ἐκ παραδείσου, ἆρα διὰ τὸ ξύλον Ἰησοῦ νῦν εὐκοπώτερον οἱ πιστεύοντες εἰς παράδεισον οὐκ εἰσελεύσονται;—" Wonder not if the whole world be redeemed ; for he was not a mere man, but the only-begotten Son of God that died. If, then, through the eating of the tree" (forbidden) "they were cast out of paradise, certainly now by the tree" (or cross) " of Jesus shall not believers more easily enter into paradise?"

So also doth another of them make it manifest in what sense they use the word *all*.

VI. ATHANASIUS, of the incarnation of the Word of God [A.D. 350]:—Οὗτός ἐστιν ἡ πάντων ζωή, καὶ ὡς πρόβατον ὑπὲρ τῆς πάντων σωτηρίας ἀντίψυχον τὸ ἑαυτοῦ σῶμα εἰς θάνατον παραδούς.—" He is the life of *all*, and as a sheep he delivered his body a price for the souls of *all*, that they might be saved."

All in both places can be none but the *elect;* as,—

VII. AMBROSE de Vocat. Gen., lib. i. cap. 3; or rather, PROSPER, lib. i. cap. 9, edit. Olivar. [A.D. 370]:—" Si non credis, non descendit tibi Christus, non tibi passus est."—" If thou believe not, Christ did not descend for thee, he did not suffer for thee."

Ambr. de Fide ad Gratianum:—" Habet populus Dei plenitudinem suam. In electis enim et præscitis, atque ab omnium generalitate discretis, specialis quædam censetur universitas, ut de toto mundo totus mundus liberatus, et de 'omnibus hominibus omnes homines videantur assumpti."—"The people of God hath its own fulness. In the elect and foreknown, distinguished from the *generality of all*, there is accounted a certain *special universality;* so that the whole world seems to be delivered from the whole world, and all men to be taken out of all men."

In which place he proceedeth at large to declare the reasons why, in this business, " all" and " the world" are so often used for " some of all sorts."

These that follow wrote after the rising of the Pelagian heresy, which gave occasion to more diligence of search and wariness of expression than had formerly been used by some.

VIII. AUGUSTINE, de Cor. et Grat. cap. xi. [A.D. 420]:—" Per hunc Mediatorem Deus ostendit eos, quos ejus sanguine redemit, facere se ex malis in æternum bonos."—" By him the Mediator, the Lord declareth himself to make those whom he hath redeemed with his blood, of evil, good to eternity." "Vult possidere Christus quod emit; tanti emit ut possideat."—" Christ will possess what he bought; he bought it with such a price that he might possess it."

Idem, Serm. xliv. de Verbis Apost. :—" Qui nos tanto pretio emit non vult perire quos emit."—" He that bought us with such a price will have none perish whom he hath bought."

Idem, Tract. lxxxvii. in Johan. :—" Ecclesiam plerumque etiam ipsam mundi nomine appellat ; sicut est illud, ' Deus erat in Christo mundum reconcilians sibi ; ' itemque illud, 'Non venit Filius hominis ut judicet mundum, sed ut salvetur mundus per ipsum;' et in epistola sua Johannes ait, 'Advocatum habemus ad Patrem, Jesum

Christum justum, et ipse propitiator est peccatorum nostrorum, non tantum nostrorum sed etiam totius mundi.' Totus ergo mundus est ecc.esia, et totus mundus odit ecclesiam. Mundus igitur odit mundum; inimicus reconciliatum, damnatus salvatum, inquinatus mundatum. Sed iste mundus quem Deus in Christo reconciliat sibi, et qui per Christum salvatur, de mundo electus est inimico, damnato, contaminato."—"He often calleth the *church* itself by the name of *the world*; as in that, 'God was in Christ reconciling the world unto himself;' and that, 'The Son of man came not to condemn the world, but that the world through him might be saved.' And John in his epistle saith, 'We have an Advocate, and he is the propitiation for [our sins, and not for ours only, but also for] the sins of the whole world.' The whole world, therefore, is the church, and the world hateth the church. The world, then, hateth the world; that which is at enmity, the reconciled; the condemned, the saved; the polluted, the cleansed world. And that world which God in Christ reconcileth to himself, and which is saved by Christ, is chosen out of the opposite, condemned, defiled world."

Much more to this purpose might be easily cited out of Augustine, but his judgment in these things is known to all.

IX. PROSPER [A.D. 440], Respon. ad Capit. Gall. cap. ix.:—"Non est crucifixus in Christo qui non est membrum corporis Christi. Cum itaque dicatur Salvator pro totius mundi redemptione crucifixus, propter veram humanæ naturæ susceptionem, potest tamen dici pro his tantum crucifixus quibus mors ipsius profuit. Diversa ab istis sors eorum est qui inter illos censentur de quibus dicitur, 'Mundus enim non cognovit.'"—"He is not crucified with Christ who is not a member of the body of Christ. When, therefore, our Saviour is said to be crucified for the redemption of the whole world, because of his true assumption of the human nature, yet may he be said to be crucified only for them unto whom his death was profitable. Diverse from these is their lot who are reckoned amongst them of whom it is said, 'The world knew him not.'"

Idem, Resp. Object. Vincen. Res. i.:—"Redemptionis proprietas, haud dubie penes illos est, de quibus princeps mundi missus est foras. Mors Christi non ita impensa est humano generi, ut ad redemptionem ejus etiam qui regenerandi non erant pertinerent."—"Doubtless the propriety of redemption is theirs from whom the prince of this world is cast out. The death of Christ is not to be so laid out for human-kind, that they also should belong unto his redemption who were not to be regenerated."

Idem, de Ingrat., cap. ix.:—

> " Sed tamen hæc aliqua sivis ratione tueri
> Et credi tam stulta cupis; jam pande quid hoc sit,
> Quod bonus omnipotensque Deus, non omnia subdit
> Corda sibi, pariterque omnes jubet esse fideles?
> Nam si nemo usquam est quem non velit esse redemptum,
> Haud dubie impletur quicquid vult summa potestas.
> Non omnes autem salvantur" ——

" If there be none whom God would not have redeemed, why are not all saved?"

X. CONCIL. VALEN.,[1] can. iv.—"Pretium mortis Christi datum est pro illis tantum quibus Dominus ipse dixit, 'Sicut Moses exaltavit serpentem in deserto, ita exaltari oportet Filius hominis, ut omnis qui credit in ipso non pereat, sed habeat vitam eternam.'"—"The price of the death of Christ is given for them alone of whom the Lord himself said, 'As Moses lifted up the serpent in the wilderness, so must the Son of man be lifted up, that whosoever believeth on him should not perish.'"

---

[1] This was a council held at Valence in A D. 855, and convened from the three provinces of Lyons, Vienne, and Arles. Remigius presided, five canons by a council in A.D. 853, at Chiersey, were condemned, and the cause of Godeschalcus, who had raised the controversy, was warmly supported. The canon quoted above is designed to contradict the fourth canon of the council at Chiersey, according to which "there never was, is, or will be a man for whom Christ has not died."—ED.